What They Didn't Teach at the Academy

Topics, Stories, and Reality
beyond the Classroom

What They Didn't Teach at the Academy

Topics, Stories, and Reality beyond the Classroom

Edited by
Dale L. June

CRC Press
Taylor & Francis Group
Boca Raton London New York

CRC Press is an imprint of the
Taylor & Francis Group, an **informa** business

CRC Press
Taylor & Francis Group
6000 Broken Sound Parkway NW, Suite 300
Boca Raton, FL 33487-2742

© 2014 by Taylor & Francis Group, LLC
CRC Press is an imprint of Taylor & Francis Group, an Informa business

No claim to original U.S. Government works

Printed on acid-free paper
Version Date: 20130806

International Standard Book Number-13: 978-1-4398-6919-2 (Paperback)

Library of Congress Cataloging-in-Publication Data

What they didn't teach at the academy : topics, stories, and reality beyond the classroom / editor, Dale L. June.
    pages cm
Includes bibliographical references and index.
ISBN 978-1-4398-6919-2 (pbk. : alk. paper) 1. Police training. I. June, Dale L.

HV7923.W483 2014
363.2'2--dc23
          2013027683

Visit the Taylor & Francis Web site at
http://www.taylorandfrancis.com

and the CRC Press Web site at
http://www.crcpress.com

To Nicole, a camp counselor I met in Catalina, California in 2003. Unfortunately, I didn't get your last name but you saved me from a very horrible death. I told you if I ever wrote this book, it would be dedicated to you. (See my story about PTSD, Chapter 12.)

God will not look you over for medals, degrees or diplomas, but for scars.

—**Elbert Hubbard**

Contents

Section II

GENERAL LIFE LESSONS

Section III
HUMOROUS LESSONS

About the Cover

Self-knowledge is a requirement for self-correction.

—**Kevin Starr, Professor of History, University of Southern California**

Cover photo by Katherine D. June, November 24, 2012.

The Tree of Life

The Tree of Life symbolizes many things, including wisdom, protection, strength, bounty, beauty, and redemption … the tree is seen as a powerful symbol of growth, as the tree is the only living thing that continues to grow throughout its lifetime. The tree is also a symbol for the true self and serves as a positive, healthy model for the unfolding development of both psyche and spirit. As we grow and develop, a larger and more mature personality emerges and begins to flower and fruit, providing its gifts and bounties to the wider world.[*]

TREES[†]

I THINK that I shall never see
A poem lovely as a tree.
A tree whose hungry mouth is prest
Against the earth's sweet flowing breast;
A tree that looks at God all day,
And lifts her leafy arms to pray;
A tree that may in Summer wear
A nest of robins in her hair;
Upon whose bosom snow has lain;
Who intimately lives with rain.
Poems are made by fools like me
But only God can make a tree.

—JOYCE KILMER (1886–1918)

---

[*] "Tree of Life," *Tree of Life Teachings*, http://www.treeoflifeteachings.com/tree-of-life/, retrieved November 25, 2012.
[†] Poetry Archive, http://www.poetry-archive.com/k/trees.html, retrieved November 26, 2012.

Photo courtesy of Kara June Baker.

Trees can be seen as metaphors for man. They continue to flourish in spite of the ravages of the sea, wind, seasons, and hard-learned lessons: lessons that can't be taught in any school or academy.

In Special Remembrance

Born December 29, 1984 in Sioux City, Iowa. Graduate of South Sioux City Senior High, Class of 2003.

Enlisted in the United States Navy, 2003.

Awards:

Purple Heart, The Defense Meritorious Service Medal
Bronze Star with "V" Device
Joint Service Commendation Medal with "V" Device
Army Commendation Medal, Presidential Unit Citation (2)
Good Conduct Medal (2)

National Defense Service Medal
Afghanistan Campaign Medal (3)
Iraq Campaign Medal, Global War on Terrorism Medal
Sea Service Deployment Ribbon (3)
Overseas Service Deployment Ribbon (3)
Rifle Marksmanship Medal and Pistol Marksmanship Medal

Killed in Action August 6, 2011, in the Wardak Province, Afghanistan, alongside Bart, a military work dog, and 29 fellow soldiers.

A WARRIOR'S PRAYER

Lord, make me fast and accurate. Let my aim be true and my hands be faster than those who would seek to destroy me. Grant me victory over my foes and those that would wish to do harm to me and my brothers. Let not my last thought be, "if only I had my gun." And Lord, if today is truly the day that you choose to call me home, let me die in a pile of brass and grenade pins.*

---

* http://therealrevo.com/blog/wp-content/uploads/2012/07/a-free-mans-prayer.jpg, original source unknown, revised and submitted by David Marris, a warrior in Afghanistan.

Preface

It is with a great deal of pride that the following prayer-poem by my youngest son (Mohammed Ali-Mehdi June, age 20) is presented. It is a sample of the thinking of a new generation, giving us hope for the future and reminding us that violence is not the best alternative.

Dale L. June, Editor

JUSTICE©

Today we are challenged in many ways,
Nonviolence is key to keeping our peaceful days.
If we believe like Doctor MLK
Living out principle six, justice˙ will stay.
The universe dwells on justice and I stand today
With my deep faith that justice will never stray.
It separates good from evil but we are all victims,
The nonviolence resister cleans out all our evil symptoms,
I am challenged but given wisdom,
Doctor MLK has shown me how to live them.
For the ones that fall victim of violence we pray,
But leading by example is the best way,
I will bring peace and love
But the fight is not easy.
Creating resistance by bringing justice daily,
Choosing right from wrong.

˙ King's notion of nonviolence had six key principles. First, one can resist evil without resorting to violence. Second, nonviolence seeks to win the "friendship and understanding" of the opponent, not to humiliate him. Third, evil itself, not the people committing evil acts, should be opposed. Fourth, those committed to nonviolence must be willing to suffer without retaliation as suffering itself can be redemptive. Fifth, nonviolent resistance avoids "external physical violence" and "internal violence of spirit" as well: "The nonviolent resister not only refuses to shoot his opponent but he also refuses to hate him." The resister should be motivated by love in the sense of the Greek word *agape*, which means "understanding," or "redeeming good will for all men." The sixth principle is that the nonviolent resister must have a "deep faith in the future," stemming from the conviction that "the universe is on the side of justice." (Martin Luther King, Jr., Research and Education Institute, http://mlk-kpp01.stanford.edu/index.php/encyclopedia/encyclopedia/enc_nonviolent_resistance/.)

Is how to become strong.
Doing the right thing shall never fail,
At the end righteousness will prevail.
As I stand beside it with the universe in my hand,
Leading an army with God I stand.

—MOHAMMED JUNE

Acknowledgments

Like all books, the author wouldn't have been able to accomplish the task without the help and understanding of many people. This book and its author-editor are no different. I thank every contributor to this book for taking the time out of their busy lives to write essays and stories that are intended to help and guide others. Everyone has a story of lessons not taught at any type of school or academy. Often, those lessons are learned through hard (and perhaps sad or tragic) circumstances. We can learn from the mistakes and experiences of others, as well our own. ("We learn from our mistakes, only a fool fails to learn from the mistakes of others."—Anonymous) If readers of this book take away even one idea, thought, or lesson they wouldn't have received by other means, then we who have brought this book to life have been successful in our endeavors.

Of course first recognition must go to Carolyn Spence of CRC Press/Taylor & Francis for her acceptance of the idea for the book. She extended my deadlines again, and again, and …

Jennifer Ahringer, also of Taylor & Francis helped me withstand my frustration about the lengthy and time-consuming process of making sure "every brick was in place" for bringing this book into what I had envisioned and worked way beyond the call of duty with her kind words and patience.

Dr. Bernadette Kutcher, whose story is so powerful, and the lessons of life she learned and teaches is the lead story in this book. She wrote and rewrote her contribution many times to get it just right. She truly writes from her heart and soul. Her spirit gives us lessons in life that most assuredly will never be taught in any place except in life and by those who experience life-altering diseases. Her chosen path in life was to become a doctor of medicine to help others mend their broken and sick bodies, never nightmarishly thinking that her own life would be wracked with pain and suffering. Though she followed her long-held dream and became a practicing physician, that was not her true calling. Her mission in life was (and is) to teach others how to live, even if every dream is shattered and destroyed, as was hers. Her story is one of courage and inspiration that we all must hope we never have to be tested. Other aspects of her story can be read in *Protection, Security, and Safeguards: Practical Approaches and Perspectives* (CRC Press, 2012).

I give a special acknowledgment and a father's pride to my youngest daughter, Katherine (Katy) June, whose adventurous courage, spiritual convictions, and confidence led her to undertake journeys that most would shudder to consider. She passed through lands that an average tourist will never see or experience. What makes her story so unique is that as a twenty-year-old college student, she traveled to Southeast Asia alone and inexperienced, mingling with the indigenous people and tramping through jungles. Her preparations and precautions were very complex, yet complete and are excellent advice for anyone who travels away from the comfort and security of their homeland. I have been in the security-related field all my adult life (beginning with the military police at the age of eighteen), yet this young woman provided me with many security learning opportunities, lessons, preparations, and techniques I never could have imagined.

The most dangerous time in a person's life is when they travel, especially if ill-prepared. She assured me she was prepared for nearly any emergency. As her father, I told her, at the airport in Los Angeles as she was about to depart to Bangkok, Thailand, on the initial leg of her first really big adventure to a foreign land, "I'll worry every minute you are gone, but IF you return, I'll be the proudest dad in the country." Obviously, she did return, and you can read her story in this book. Her contribution to this book is her first attempt, and hopefully not the last, at professional writing. I'm sure she has many stories to tell of her many trips as a "traveler."

Thanks go to Leslie Martinez and Gloria Padron (policewomen of the future) for traveling back to 2013 to contribute their photos from the year 2020.

Then I want to thank and acknowledge all of the contributors who so generously took the time and made the effort to provide stories, thoughts, and ideas that are not only informative but entertaining with their contributions of lessons learned from no academy, but from life. They are (in alphabetical order):

Rommel R. Aclan
Azadeh Afsahi
Joel P. Altman
Keila Alvarenga
Jared Axen
Charles Berry
Murray Cox
Kyle Day
Michael De Montaigne
Janine Francovich
Edgar A. Guest
Veda Hall

Tiffany Harrison
H.C.S. (name withheld for
    security purposes)
Cheyenne Hill
Carly Jennings
Jason Johnson and Others
Katherine Denise June
Mohammed Ali Mehdi June
Mohamad Khatabloo
Bernadette A. Kutcher
Larry Mayberry
E. Alan Normandy

Dan Mott Perez
Jes Poppelvig
Richard Repasky
Jennifer J. Schneider
Ruth Stortroen
Charles Swindoll

Nicole Tye
Yesenia Vega
J. Branch Walton
Craig Weller
Stefanie Winkler

Introduction

Life is a Journey ... There are many Roads to Choose from; Each Road goes two ways and we always have a choice which way to travel ...

—Katy June

Two roads diverged in a wood, and I—
I took the one less traveled by,
And that has made all the difference

—Robert Frost (1874–1963), "The Road Not Taken," 1920

We receive three educations, one from our parents, one from our schoolmasters, and one from the world. The third contradicts all that the first two teach us.

—Charles Louis de Secondat, Baron de Montesquieu

It is anticipated that the majority of the readers of this book will be criminal justice practitioners, but it has been developed to include anyone interested in social thinking and living. When the idea for the book was conceived, the intent was to collect stories of police officers who have been exposed to every imaginable (or perhaps unimaginable) scenario of the state of affairs called "humanity." It was thought that the stories could be an inspiration to our men and women in blue, from the beginner to the gray-bearded veteran. The stories were to be real incidents of humor, tragedy, heartbreak, or other lessons of life learned not from an academy or school of learning but from the hard way by experience of life in the "thin blue line" on the streets of America.

As the saying by the Scottish poet Robert Burns goes, "The best laid schemes o' mice an' men/Gang aft a-gley" (The best laid plans of mice and men oft go astray), and stray I did. This series of stories reflects more than police stories, but they remain true to the theme of lessons learned not in school. As it came to pass and as time went by and stories were collected, not only from police officers or criminal justice people, something happened. Stories came from many sources, especially "older" university students who have been in the real world of work for a few years and have experienced lessons not taught in school. Every story is a lesson, every lesson is a story. Whatever the source of the story, regardless of its theme, a critically thinking reader can easily convert it into his own professional or personal life. The original intent of making it a police-story book had to be altered to embrace a diverse plurality of people including the medical profession and students, all having one thing in common—the lessons of life are not taught in colleges, universities, and academies but through hard experience, supposing that man is made from iron, wood, or a water balloon.

There are three reasons for writing: (1) to inform, (2) to entertain, and (3) to persuade. If we have accomplished any of these tasks, we can feel our mission accomplished.

This volume you hold in your hand is neither a how-to book, nor is it anything more than what it is: a book of thoughts, philosophies, and shared experiences. But the end result will be (hopefully) an experience of life lessons learned by others that will entertain, inform, and maybe reinforce or change your attitudes about many things in this land of America.

To this point in your life you have been living a prelude to what is to come. The people in your life, your spouse, your parents, friends, peers, cohorts, and teachers have been preparing you for your pathway of life—the road you chose to take and the direction you travel. Teachers and instructors can give you guidance and the tools for success and help you with your decisions, but in the end, it is up to you to work hard and make your dreams come true. That is your responsibility. Pick up the challenge and carry it forward. Don't enter a career just to make a great amount of money and to reap the benefits. Your rewards and self-actualization will come from job satisfaction and doing what you enjoy. If it helps your fellow man, even better.

"Do what you do, do well"* and "You gotta get a little dirt on your hands"†—two lines from two different old country-western songs meaning, "If you are going to do a job, do it to the very best of your ability and beyond what is minimally required and don't be afraid to get your hands dirty." Volunteer even if it is a dirty job. Someone has to do it. Why not you?

"Live your life so you have no regrets when you die." This is advice I have been freely giving for several years. What I mean is, if there is a career path you would like to pursue, do it! Don't accept a job just to make your parents or others in your life happy, or for what you think others want you to do. Do it for yourself. If you are in a career only for the money and benefits, or what others want you to do, you are on the wrong career path.

Yes you can! In this land, everyone has the opportunity to experience life success: become president, a Supreme Court justice, a senator, a loving and respected parent, a humanitarian, and friend. Treating everyone who comes into your life with dignity and respect will earn rewards, opportunities, and success. Life is a matter of decision making, and we all get to where we are and what we want to be by taking the paths and trails we follow. It is a matter of decision and choice. Decide and choose well. What we do, or fail to do, will

---

* Sonny James, http://www.youtube.com/watch?v=t-d2HewfKKQ, retrieved June 8, 2012.
† David Allen Coe, http://www.youtube.com/watch?v=-goUr84ip1I, retrieved June 8, 2012.

have consequences. Those consequences are the lessons of life, be they bitter or sweet. ("Every action of our lives touches on some chord that will vibrate in eternity."—Edwin Hubbel Chapin[*])

Schools, universities, and academies are important centers of learning in our lives. From preschool and through our college years we learn things that prepare us with the necessities that will carry us through our lives regardless of what it is we choose to do. The best teacher, though, doesn't necessarily come from the world of academe. The life lessons taught at the school of hard knocks are the tutorials that shape us and our character. Some life lessons of life come to us by serendipity, whereas others are earned by hard experience and heartache. One question remains open as we earn our life lesson degrees from experience: Do we take something from the school of hard knocks and use it to enrich our world, or do we hope the scale is graded on a curve and slough off occurrences of opportunity to learn? No scholarships are given in the real world.

Happiness is a process, not an end goal. It is found in living an ethical and honorable life, doing the right things for all the right reasons. That is the lesson hardest to teach in academies or institutions of higher learning. As you settle or continue on your professional career path, ask yourself, "Is this the right thing for me, and are my reasons for doing it clear, honorable, and for all the right reasons?" If your answers are an easy yes, then don't hold back. Go for it. "Do what you do, do well" even if you have to get your hands in the dirt. If your intent is honorable, the mud will wash off and success with happiness will come. Happiness and success are never found with wrongful intent. If your intent is not honest and you do things for the wrong reasons, you will feel dirty and that mud will never wash off. In the words of Shakespeare's Lady Macbeth wringing her hands in a hand-washing motion: "Out, damned spot! ... Here's the smell of the blood still; all the perfumes of Arabia will not sweeten this little hand. Oh, oh, oh! ... What's done cannot be undone."[†]

The way is open. Do you have the will to make the effort to learn from life, no matter the expense? We are never too old to learn lessons of life … or death. People say they will learn until the day they die. I say I will learn one more lesson of life when I die: I'll learn what it is like to die; I have never died before.

The more you learn, the more you don't know. It's because every known fact opens a door to a universe of unknown facts. —Unknown

---

[*] "Quotations about karma," *The Quote Garden*, http://www.quotegarden.com/karma. html.
[†] William Shakespeare, "*Macbeth*, Act V, Scene 1," Bartleby.com, http://www.bartleby. com/46/4/51.html, retrieved August 12, 2012.

About the Editor

Dale L. June is a former U.S. Secret Service Agent, Presidential Protective Division at the White House for four presidents. He also served in the Sacramento, California and San Diego, California field offices. He is a former military policeman and member of a military Honor Guard (110th MP Platoon, Stuttgart, Germany), deputy sheriff (Shasta County, California); city police officer (Redding, and Sacramento, California); a U.S. Customs Intelligence Specialist, specializing in organized crime and terrorism; a private investigator and executive protection specialist; and author. He has worked directly with executives of multinational corporations, VIPs, political figures, royalty, and celebrities and liaised and interacted with law enforcement, fire department and medical personnel, as well as international law enforcement agency personnel.

June has an MA in criminal justice from George Washington University; a BA in public administration, Sacramento State University; is co-founder of Henley-Putnam University and the writer of approximately forty university courses; and a developer of homeland security, terrorism, and emergency management courses for Career Education Corporation. Currently he teaches part-time at National and Argosy Universities in Los Angeles. He has nearly three decades of experience teaching at the college and university levels as an instructor of criminal justice, psychology, sociology, history, and drug- and addiction-related courses. He is also an avid reader of psychology-related material to gain insight into the psychological, sociological, and biological causes and remedies of dysfunction, depression, and personality profiles.

June is the author of *Introduction to Executive Protection, Second Edition* (CRC Press, 2008), and is a contributing author and editor of *Protection, Security, and Safeguards: Practical Approaches and Perspectives, Second Edition* (CRC Press, 2012), He has written security-related articles for international security magazines in Canada, the United Kingdom, Mexico, New Zealand, and Germany, and is a contributing author and editor of *Homeland Security and Terrorism: Perspective, Thoughts and Opinions* (CRC Press, 2010).

June is a former member of the National Black Belt Association, Tae Kwon Do; and was named as the U.S. Martial Artist's Hall of Fame Martial Artist of the Year (2005). He has trained in judo, boxing, free fighting, traditional Wing Chun and dim mak kung fu, tae kwon do, police hybrid self-defense and combatives (the quick method of self-defense), and combat bayonet fighting.

His favorite sayings are (1) "Treat all persons with dignity and respect"; (2) "Temper justice with compassion and heart"; and (3) "Do one spontaneous good thing for someone every day, expecting nothing in return, and you will be rewarded ten times over."

His favorite police motto and credo: "We Are Here To Help!"

Hard-Knock Lessons

I

The Final Educational Degree: Life

1

BERNADETTE A. KUTCHER

Contents

Introduction

I graduated with a medical degree to be a physician, but every day since I have been earning the ultimate educational degree: life.

Most believe the soul is what gives life to the human body. However, during all my training and studying to become a physician, including dissecting human cadavers, assisting in various surgeries, and participating in autopsies, never once did any of my professors or physician mentors point out a body part called the soul. I held in my hands both living and deceased livers, lungs, brains, veins, nerves, and hearts, but I never touched the part of the human body that has been, for centuries, the focus of scientific research and theological controversy as to its actual existence. I don't remember any class or faculty physician ever teaching about a soul, so how do I know, how do any of us know, it exists, let alone possesses the ability to instill lung-breathing, heart-beating life into a human body?

I know, I know, and I accept the existence and power of a soul, not from what I was taught in medical classes or training and not even from what I was taught in religious education classes. I know from living the soul-giving life my human body has so far survived. And it has been survival.

Hours upon hours and years upon years I studied medicine, but after all the classes, the training, and the time in practice, it was by way of years upon years of my own human suffering that I learned the forever-more-important revelations of human existence.

If only every person could be so blessed as to learn these same revelations. How much different—better—the world would be!

*   *   *

At the older age of thirty-one, I entered my medical education emboldened by aspects of life I had learned beginning as a young child from my parents. I also carried with me general life attitudes garnered from my adult years working out in the world prior to beginning the road to becoming a doctor.

After completing intense medical education programs, it seemed like all was learned, well, about everything. Wrong! Medical school did teach valuable life lessons but it mainly taught the science involved in the working of the machine called the human body. Sadly, fortunately, painfully, and excitingly, the majority of my education, that is, life's most profound lessons, came *after* receiving my physician license.

During my time in medical practice while taking care of many patients with varying needs and diagnoses, a deeper understanding of life began to develop for me. But the deepest discoveries presented when I was forced to live out the answer to the question: *How does a physician survive life and near-death when she is the patient?*

Nothing in medical school prepared me for what was to come upon my body and the resultant effects to all areas of my life. Nothing prepared me for the death battles waged against me by a disease few had heard of and few were able to pronounce: sarcoidosis ("sarcoid" for short). The life my soul had bestowed upon me was quickly being challenged with a war it was losing. *Medical school never taught me how to live to die ... or how to die to live.*

The Very Long and Curvy Turning Point in My Life

I believe at some point, every person experiences a turning point in his or her life. Still, the question is whether or not the person recognizes and accepts the insight that comes with it. Is his or her heart changed? Is the person's soul affected, and if yes, is it affected for good? Or is it affected for very bad?

To understand the depth of good to which my soul was transformed, I believe it is necessary to explain the impetus to the turning point that was thrust upon me and the curves that led to it.

The First Long, Slow, Ascending Curve

Medical school taught a few brief details about the disease called sarcoidosis, which most members of the medical profession believed to not be a very troublesome illness. The agreed-upon theory was that sarcoid rarely caused a patient to exhibit more than a few relatively short-lived symptoms mainly involving the skin and lungs. Usually, treatment was limited to a brief course of steroids, namely prednisone. There is no known cause of sarcoidosis, and no cure exists. The disease occurs in the United States but at a much lower incidence than in other countries, with Sweden having the highest statistical number of cases. Because of its perceived low morbidity and mortality rates, research on sarcoidosis is very limited.

During my third year of medical school, mounting symptoms became too much for me to handle, forcing me to drop out for a full semester. But during this time away from crucial classes and lab training, my eventual diagnosis of sarcoidosis did not come easily. Sarcoidosis is called "the masquerader" because it often presents with symptoms similar to other diseases including cancer. Until I underwent chest surgery called a mediastinoscopy, which confirmed sarcoidosis as the diagnosis, my physicians believed I had cancer and advised me I would not graduate, and most likely I would die. I lived through three weeks of emotional grieving as I came to terms with my doctors' words. I felt I was living in a foreboding bubble away from my fellow students, instructors, and my family back home, all the while thinking my time on Earth was coming to an end. I was going through the motions of living but I didn't feel alive. Then when the diagnosis of sarcoid came back, all feelings and thoughts of death disintegrated as celebration rose up within me. Unfortunately (I use this word a lot simply because it seems to be the most appropriate word when I use it), my physician didn't know all that would transpire in the years to come as a result of this correct, and supposedly nonconsequential, diagnosis.

One of the initial complications came two months before I was to graduate from medical school. A more uncommon symptom presented involving my heart, this time necessitating a one-month leave of absence. I got through the hospitalization, but the emotional roller coaster was made worse by the fact my father was back home dying from heart disease. One month later, and one month before graduation to become a physician, my dad died. My mom came to my graduation but, sadly, she was shrouded in grief and shock. My life-long dream had become a reality but death reigned over it.

Six weeks after graduation, death tried to overpower my body once again. The sarcoid relapsed. A bone marrow biopsy revealed the disease had shut down my immune system, which required me to remain in a hospital isolation room for over a week until the doctors were able to stabilize my system.

When recovered, I began my internship, although the start date was six weeks postponed. The disease wasn't kind with its waxing and waning, and it prompted yet another short leave of absence during this training period.

Three months after completing that internship—finally—I began my family medicine residency but it, too, began on a delayed schedule from the other residents in my program. Nevertheless, I entered into this family physician training believing with everything in me that illness would no longer interfere. I was going to forge ahead and excel during my residency!

Unfortunately, sarcoidosis had its own agenda. It became a monstrous living menace, cunningly maneuvering and advancing its way throughout my body. The course of the disease turned out to be nothing like what the medical profession considered to be true of sarcoid. I surpassed the generally believed time limit for remission, and I experienced complications that few physicians knew to be part of the illness. The living menace had no intention of retreating. It was on the move!

Ongoing flare-ups and new symptoms continually hit my body, making my training even more exhaustive than residency was normally with its usual twelve- to fourteen-hour workdays and on-call schedules filled with thirty-six hour shifts every few days. But the curve of the turning point of my life began to arch when sarcoid infiltrated my brain. At first, it caused a dramatic eighty-pound weight gain over a period of about five to six months. However, it was the second symptom and the most terrifying—that made an extended leave of absence absolutely unavoidable.

During the leave that stretched into five months, I underwent extensive and sophisticated brain tests, some of which utilized machines that appeared to be more suitable for use in a horror movie. Various treatments were tried with little to no change in my symptoms. Eventually, the doctors diagnosed neurosarcoidosis (sarcoid of the brain and nervous system) as the cause of the striking weight gain followed by the devastating complication of violent, repetitive seizures.

Most often, when people hear the word "seizure," the image that comes to their minds is that of a grand mal (tonic-clonic) seizure during which a person loses consciousness, falls to the ground, and shakes all over. Although this is one of the top types of seizures, my type was not under this category. I was diagnosed with complex partial seizures manifesting with loss of awareness of what I was doing or saying and loss of awareness of what was happening around me. I did not lose consciousness but, most definitely, I lost awareness. The seizure also manifested with intense and hostile argumentativeness and sometimes violent changes, including kicking, spitting, or hitting. However, one aspect was the same as grand mal seizures. When the seizures were over, as in grand mal and most all seizures, I had no memory of what had taken place, and I was disoriented and totally exhausted. This disorientation and exhaustion after a seizure is referred to as a postictal state. Ranging from minutes to several hours, how long this state may last is variable from person to person and from seizure to seizure, but rest and sleep most always are needed for it.

If it wasn't for my strong faith in God, I'm not sure how I would have gotten through this awful period made worse by what I had to endure from my colleagues. I came face-to-ugly-face with the mindset of associates who were not about to be understanding of a fellow colleague in trouble. Their mindset was not to ask questions to find out the truth behind my physical and psychological changes. Instead, they demonstrated their proficiency in offering up condemnation and rejection. After months of criticism and rebuffs, I was cornered into a head-on confrontation with all the residents, most of the faculty physicians, and the program director. The ordeal they subjected me to was nothing less than an act of total selfishness and vile disregard. But I stood against my accusers, making clear the facts that brought to light those of true guilt.

An affirmation of my vindication came the next day after that horrific encounter. The day was also my last day of work before starting my extended leave of absence. When I came into work, one of the faculty physicians who had defended me during the "ambush" met me in the hallway asking permission to hug me as he voiced, "Bernadette, I am so proud of you. You stood up and voiced facts that many of us have wanted to say but never had the courage to say." Following behind this physician were outstretched hands of others offering their apologies saying, "We never knew what you were going through." All they had to do was ask.

In the end, truth prevailed over those colleagues who lobbed unconscionable attacks against my honor and integrity. And as a result of their actions and words, a lesson came forth that impacted my life as no other experience ever had before.

Lesson learned: Don't assume the worst about any person in any situation. Go to the person, and learn the truth. Follow up with a sincere offer of empathy and assistance.

When I returned from my leave of absence to finish my remaining one and one-half years of residency, I was in remission from the neurosarcoidosis. My soul-life had been restored and my spirit energized. I was alive, and I was happy.

Over the remainder of my training, I was appointed chief of recruitment for the residency program. I dramatically upped my scores on all proficiency tests, and I even planned and orchestrated several office parties for the holidays and other special occasions.

On the final day of my residency program as the afternoon clinic hours came to a close, I finished with my last patient and completed all the associated paperwork including signing my signature, Dr. Bernadette A. Kutcher, D.O., to the very last patient chart of my residency. I gathered up my belongings, and I walked out of the family practice center with my head held high knowing I had fought both disease and colleague abuse, and I had won. All these were significant without a doubt, but as I walked out the door for the last time, the most important fact was that in six weeks from that day, I would be starting my family medicine office practice.

I was forty-one years of age. If I had any doubt whether patience, especially long term, was part of my character, becoming a physician definitely proved it was a major component. I was a full-fledged doctor ready to begin my medical practice, and it had taken me only forty-one years!

Straight Road Interspersed with Curves

Life certainly has its times of great irony, doesn't it? Since the time I was a three-year-old toddler, I dreamed of becoming a doctor. My dad brought home leftover parts of butchered animals from the meat market for me to dissect. My mom would turn green while watching television medical shows with me. A fear of studying dead bodies kept me away from medical school until I overcame that fear when God "arranged" for me to date a mortician/funeral director. (I'm pretty sure this shows God has a sense of humor, even a little bit warped at times.) I was thirty-one years of age when I began medical school, and after delays and leaves of absences; I finally started practice at age forty-one. Then what happened? True irony.

Opening a new medical practice, excitement abounded interspersed with moments of anxiety as I started my new life and career. The usual stressors of a new business presented; however, several sad occurrences marred my first year. Three months after my first day of practice, my closest brother-in-law, Ray, died of cancer. Four months later, my closest sister Mary Ellen, wife of Ray, died from complications of pneumonia. And three months after my sister's death, one of my best friends passed away from a complication of a medical illness she had long endured. It seemed like a string of bombs had been strategically placed to encircle me, and the explosives were rigged to go off about every three months. What should have been the most exciting time of my life was invaded by death.

After all the challenges of the initial ten months of practice, I settled into my career. I thoroughly loved being a doctor, and I experienced a joy in helping my patients I never thought possible. But two years later, a transformation occurred in me that convincingly appeared to be permanent. I became one of those thousands of people I was supposed to care for over the course of my career, which was just beginning and would extend, I trusted, a good thirty years. I became one of those people whom I was supposed to examine, diagnose, treat, encourage, offer hope, console, and handhold as he or she died out of this life and passed into eternal life. *I became a patient, but medical school never taught a class as to how a physician adapts to patienthood.*

Lesson learned: Never assume—or trust—life will proceed according to plans made or to a desired timeline.

Dead Man's Curve Up Ahead!

Changes to our healthcare system were jammed upon all physicians, hospitals, and patients. My practice was no different. After only two years, I was readying to move into another office setup; however, the start date had to be delayed a few months to complete the construction of the office building. I never made it into that office. I never made it into that medical practice. The neurosarcoidosis relapsed with a vengeance. My prognosis was poor.

As the saying goes, to make a really long story short, the complex partial seizures, secondary to the neurosarcoidosis, kept coming and coming. At my worst, I was experiencing up to five seizures a day. My doctors considered several life-threatening treatments, including a bone marrow transplant; brain surgery, which the doctor explained would kill me, cure me, or make me a vegetable; and finally the treatment of last resort, chemotherapy. I did not meet the criteria for either of the first two treatments. That left me with the IV chemotherapy drug Cytoxan. I received the treatment every two weeks for over three years. The length of treatment was necessary for the drug to pass through the blood–brain barrier, which prohibits the passage of many medications into the brain.

For over three years (I repeat this time frame because it seemed more like three hundred years), I suffered all the side effects known to occur with chemotherapy drugs, including hospitalization for dehydration, incredible fatigue, mouth ulcers, and so on. The nausea was just a joy. Not! And the vomiting kept on coming to the point, I swear, I saw a piece of my stomach being swirled around as it flushed down the toilet bowl! I didn't lose my hair, but it changed texture, curliness, and color, which proved troublesome because hair styling was not a skill I possessed. There was one particular and very "lovely" side effect I did experience, however. Menopause! At age forty-four, one month after I started the treatment, my menstrual cycles ceased as if they stopped cold turkey, and hot flashes took off like a racehorse in the Kentucky Derby. Those explosions of internal combustion superseded by arctic chill blasts inflicted their own brand of havoc onto my everyday life, including sleep disruptions, aggravation to the seizures, and more fatigue secondary to the sleep depriva-tion and the increased use of my body's energy reserves as the need arose for more laundry days and laundry loads because of daily repeated changing of clothes and bed sheets from the unrelenting sweating during the explosions of internal combustion. Unfortunately (there's that word again) after the chemo-therapy was halted, long-term side effects began to present one after another, each requiring its own set of medical tests, treatments, and, at times, hospi-talizations. One additional warning from my doctors, as the saying goes, took the prize. The threat of more long-term side effects would never be gone.

As bad as all the treatment effects and other disease symptoms were, the seizures were a living torture no person should ever have to go through. The anticonvulsant medications' trials were extremely unpleasant, with none of them bringing relief to the seizures. But what made things worse was what I had to do to protect against the danger of the seizures. I told my doctor the seizures were so severe I felt like I needed a bodyguard to protect me and those around me. I thought he would laugh, but instead he agreed this was a good idea. We began contacting home health care services and other medical agencies to supply this type of necessary medical care. Not one agency would accept me; too much concern about liability. I was so dejected. I had provided any help I was able to provide as a physician, but no one would help me.

As strange as it sounds—and I certainly have been victimized by endless ridicule—I was forced to hire bodyguards. The ordeals that came from this medical necessity etched deep ditches in my memory. The men who professed their abilities to protect me both from the seizures and from the actions of misunderstanding bystanders, failed me terribly. Instead, my life was put in more danger because of their incompetence and lack of professionalism.

My life was finally made safe when God "hired" two of our country's most elite protection specialists to protect me: Bazzel Baz, a former CIA officer, and Ron Franklin, a former Army Delta Force soldier. Not only did they have the skills to protect, but these two angel-men offered me unwav-ering compassion and support. Very quickly we recognized a shared belief and trust in God. Their obvious devotion bolstered my confidence in their abilities and commitment to keep me out of harm's way. They kept me alive, and we believed God had purposefully brought us together.

'The money I had inherited from my sister and brother-in-law was used to cover all the protection costs, but it didn't take long for the funds to be drained. My physicians, the two protection specialists, my attorney, and I fought hard with the insurance companies to cover the costs of the very necessary care of protectors, but I ran out of money to pay the attorney to take the battle any further. Therefore, I was forced into living as a recluse to ensure if I did have a seizure, no one, including me, would be hurt.

During these years, death never left my side. Because of repeated episodes of life-threatening complications, over and over I brought out my funeral directions and end-of-life documents to be followed by my appointed representative. I made arrangements to donate my body to science, but with all the destruction sarcoidosis had rendered, I wondered if there would be anything left to study.

Truth known: There would be one part of my body remaining, my soul, and it would continue to provide life to me. Only this time, it would be eternal life with God in Heaven.

So Many Curves ... Traveling in Circles

Eventually, the chemo came to an end although the sarcoidosis specialist wanted me to continue at a weaning dose for another year. I refused because I was unable to withstand any more side effects. Enough was enough.

The seizures stabilized from both the chemotherapy and the anticonvulsant medication called gabapentin, which worked the best of all the anticonvulsant medications tried. The doctors said I would be on the gabapentin indefinitely with the hope I would continue to tolerate a couple of its side effects. The frequency and the intensity of the seizures greatly decreased, but they still occurred often enough, thus necessitating a continuation of my reclusive life. Ironically, something I had lived with as a child and young adult enabled me to live this pronounced life of disease-imposed seclusion.

Lesson learned: Never discount the usefulness of anything experienced throughout life, whether during youth age, middle age, or old age.

Recluse in Training

Up until the age of about twenty-five, I was excruciatingly shy. As a child and young adult, I was afraid of my own shadow. I didn't make a lot of friends, and the only thing that kept me going was baton twirling lessons my parents had provided to enable me to be around other children. My shyness didn't improve, but I did become one darn good baton twirler! In high school, my passion for baton twirling continued as a majorette during my sophomore, junior, and senior years. It was amazing how I was able to perform in front of large audiences but remained afraid to interact with friends or adults.

When I entered college, the shyness continued. Limiting myself to only a couple friends, I lived at home to avoid most all college campus interactions. I received my degree in elementary education, but I didn't move forward much in extroversion character development.

It wasn't until about age twenty-five that I decided I had to either overcome the shyness or live in a cave the rest of my life as a hermit. I'm afraid of bats and rats, so I opted for conquering shyness. I set out into life and challenged myself constantly in ways that would take me beyond shyness into friendship with many diverse individuals, new experiences including performing in theatre productions, and reaching out to strangers or to anyone I felt my smile and "hello" would bring a bright moment. With hard work, prayer, and—trust me—lots of courage, I overcame the bondage of introversion.

My soul-life blossomed. It was all good until neurosarcoidosis and its seizures threw me into a life of aloneness and loneliness. After several years of reclusiveness, I remembered back to my shyness, and a profound revelation came to light. After all the years of hard work to overcome my intense, painful introversion, and after years of enjoying the fruits of my labors that manifested in many, many friendships and adventures, the seizures forced me to revert back to the skills I had developed as a shy, little girl to survive childhood, adolescence, and make a way into adulthood.

Lesson learned: Who knew? Shyness has benefits. It teaches observation skills and survival skills that might just help save a life.

Observation Skills

When a person essentially spends the first twenty-five years of life, both literally and figuratively, shaking in the background, one develops great observation skills. I watched people behave in all sorts of ways in all sorts of situations. I formulated a basic understanding of body language and eye language, and I learned many do's and don'ts about human behavior from most anyone I came in contact.

Developing observation skills during my years of shyness served me well, but they proved especially beneficial when I entered medicine. Observation is absolutely paramount when dealing with patients, and as I begrudgingly discovered, observation skills are quite needed also when the physician becomes the patient.

We all must learn to observe our own bodies for signs and symptoms that either point to potential health problems or signal the need for immediate care. And, as I pointed out earlier, we human beings would do well to make a conscious effort to observe those around us for any indication that one of those individuals may need our help or need our praise.

Regarding the seizures themselves, I learned to "observe" my brain on pretty much a constant basis for signs of impending trouble. One blessing did come with my seizures. They started with an aura, which is a warning system for looming seizure activity. I became very good at recognizing the aura, which helped me tremendously handle the seizures over the years.

I also became very good at watching for all the other effects the sarcoidosis wreaked upon my body. This was extremely important during and after chemotherapy, when hypervigilance was necessary for any forthcoming long-term effects from either the disease or the therapy.

Where I failed to use the observation skills optimally was with people, because I never thought I needed to use them in particular circumstances or with certain individuals. It turned out, to my detriment, those circumstances and individuals proved to be exactly when I needed to put those observation skills on high alert.

I endured many horrifying situations involving the bodyguards I had initially utilized. When the truth of my observation skills prevailed, I knew I had to fire each one of those men.

Besides the "nightmares" with the bodyguards, I dealt with many bad encounters from strangers, store clerks, church members, and others unfamiliar with my history. It took me a long time to understand I had no choice but to always be on alert for people who might retaliate against me because of something said or done during a seizure. I went through situations when clerks threw me out of their stores. When I tried to explain afterward, people argued with me because they thought I was lying about the seizures. I was subjected to four-letter words I never knew existed. I faced unfeeling church members who knew me to be a kind and friendly person. They also knew I had a serious illness that involved seizures. Nonetheless, more than once after seizure activity, they chose to ignore me and walk away. They displayed total disregard during my time of need. They failed to seek the truth.

During these examples, and several other times, I did not apply my observation skills, and I ended up suffering greatly. I failed to use them to ensure I was hiring fully trained, professional bodyguards. In businesses I patronized, I verified they provided the services I sought, but I failed to observe if the employees were kind and friendly with a willingness to help those in distress. And painfully in the church I had chosen to be my spiritual home, I failed to observe it included members not sincere in following the example of the Bible's Good Samaritan.

Lesson learned: Do the mandatory homework of checking out references, credentials, and services of professionals, businesses, or churches; but don't overlook observing their employees and members to ensure they have the skills at being caring and considerate human beings.

I went through so many bad experiences with people as a result of an unrelenting disease but the worst had to do with those closest to me, including friends and a fiancé. If I ever failed to use my observation skills, it was certainly with these. How was I ever so wrong about the love I believed I had observed in their hearts and actions for me?

Here again, I use the saying "to make a very long story short." The number of individuals is too many, and the stories of all are too wounding. The life lesson I learned from these I don't wish on anyone—false accusations, unfair disdain, and, finally, callous abandonment.

For each person involved, it didn't matter the kind of relationship we shared or the length of that relationship. Once the seizures began, I was seen to be only one way: a mean, obnoxious b----.

Those individuals chose not to do their homework to understand the full extent of my disease and the complete nature of the complex partial seizures. They, like the majority of people, thought seizures cause loss of consciousness while falling to the ground. Across society, there has been an increased acceptance of this type, but seizures that cause loss of awareness miss out on much of the understanding offered to those with the grand mal (tonic-clonic) type. Sadly though, there are still too many people who attach a stigma and misconception to grand mal seizures as well as to most every kind of seizures.

The bottom line, I was unable to provide enough explaining, pleading, or medical articles to gain understanding by those people who had claimed to love me or who had declared continued friendship. To this day, I don't understand how they ignored the years of sharing our lives with full knowledge and acceptance of my heart, and instead persisted in their thinking the worst of me. To this day, I don't understand how they witnessed the dramatic changes in my appearance and behavior and not accept something had to be desperately wrong. To this day, I don't understand how they failed to seek help for me. To this day, I don't understand how they took back their support and love after so many years. I guess I do understand; everything had been a lie.

It didn't take many observation skills for me to recognize those individuals' soon-to-be final actions. Some ended their relationships with me by a gradual decrease in phone calls or visits. Literally overnight, two different friends cut me off. Flat out, they both stated they didn't want to deal with my problems. But the worst losses: the man who had professed perpetual love for me and a marriage never to be. I was damaged goods. I was no longer lovable.

Lesson learned: Our society seems to have formulated a fifteen-minutes-of-compassion rule. If a person has a long-term, exhaustive challenge to deal with, be warned. The person may witness slowly but surely "the troops' of support dwindle to the point of almost nonexistence or, most heartbreaking, total nonexistence.

For me, in spite of the disappointment, hurt, and loneliness that replaced the presence of friends, a future husband, family, and colleagues, I never gave up on one firm belief, which, to this day, I embrace dearly ...

Lesson learned: Use observation skills so as not to become a doormat to anyone, but don't be afraid to both offer and seek love and friendship. Hurt may come, but there is nothing to be cherished more than the deep love of a mate or the love of a true friend. The risk is always worth taking.

Survival Skills

I didn't always apply fully or correctly the observation skills I developed during my shyness years, but fully and correctly I did make use of the survival skills I mastered my first two and one-half decades of life. The proof? I'm still alive.

The skills I employed were not those necessary to find food or shelter while stranded for days or weeks in the wilderness. The survival abilities I adhered to are comparable to the mental, emotional, and spiritual skills a soldier or kidnap victim hangs on to while being held prisoner or hostage locked away alone in a confined environment for long periods of time. In order to endure unbearable situations of forced isolation and the threat of death, such a person survives through basic primal instincts that include *mental acuity, emotional fortitude,* and for most *spiritual faith and hope.*

Mental acuity may include thought games in order to stay focused, to make time go faster, and to avoid the torment of the captor. Emotional fortitude is reaching down to the depths of one's being to harness the courage to do whatever is necessary to stay alive. And spiritual faith and hope is trusting in one's God even at the moment of death.

Having lived through years of shyness-induced isolation, these same instincts and skills had become a part of me long before I fell ill. Thank God. Through mental acuity, emotional fortitude, and spiritual faith and hope in God fused with my primal instincts, I survived all the years of living the isolated life "ordered" by neurosarcoidosis.

I perfected observation and survival skills through years of being an introvert. Ironically, these youth-acquired gifts were the force behind my continued existence through the life-debilitating, progressive effects of a rare brain disease that many others might have failed to survive.

Lesson learned: Never underestimate a person's will to survive or, put another way, will to live.

An Unexpected Curve

Sooner or later, a decision must be made by anyone up against *the* turning point in his/her life. Ignore it? Reject it? Deny it? Go around it? Or accept it?

For me, well, let's see. First, I ignored the initial symptoms that beset my body. Second, I rejected the possibility of anything being seriously wrong. Third, I denied the diagnosis and came up with many creative alternative explanations. Fourth, I went round and round about the disease and its consequences with doctors, colleagues, friends, family, strangers, protection specialists, business people, God; and even me, myself, and I. Alas, this step never ended, that is, until recently.

A few years ago, my neurologist found a new tumor in my brain. After a period of watchful waiting followed by multiple sets of tests, my physicians only recently made the final determination that the tumor is neurosarcoidosis. It has far-reaching consequences that I am only beginning to fully grasp. I'm faced with major decisions on whether or not to treat the tumor and the effects of the tumor. The recommended treatments may provide potential help but they also carry their own dangers. In addition, the treatments pose a serious risk to the seizures with the chance of increased activity far surpassing the seizures I suffered at any time in the past. Basically, I'm between the proverbial rock and a hard place.

I might want to ignore making a decision, or I might want to deny I have to make a decision. Maybe a total rejection of the new findings is the best way to go. Then again, it's pretty hard to reject them when my body is suffering in so many ways as a result. One effect that is impossible to reject is my ever-increasing jumbo body size, which contributes to other increased health issues. My weight has become such an issue; I'm beginning to think a jumbo jet flying internationally will soon be the only way to make a complete circle around me.

I jest as I work through the decisions I must make. Humor: It's definitely another great tool for survival.

Lesson learned: Always look for a bit of humor, no matter how dire the situation.

Lesson learned: Don't automatically assume an obese person is that way because of eating hot fudge sundaes every night. There are true medical reasons for weight gain, and usually these carry other damaging effects.

Cures, Treatments, and Death

Throughout my years of disease, every time I faced a new crisis, I'd remember back to my childhood dream of becoming a doctor. Starting with my first inclination, I believed in medicine. As time went on, whether medicine was designated traditional Western, Eastern, integrative, or complementary, I continued to believe. And I trusted medicine. I trusted new advancements would be continual, thus making come true my childhood vision of medicine in which no disease or infirmity would be left untreatable or incurable.

In witnessing life personally and during my training and medical practice, I came to understand the folly in my childhood vision. I participated in the care of many patients with diagnoses, injuries, or genetic disorders for which there was no cure, and for many, no treatments even existed. Suffering worsened, and death came when nothing else was left to try. I faced this truth with the illnesses and deaths of my father, mother, sister, and brother-in-law. I experienced the pain of feeling helpless when I was unable to offer further help to any of those family members. Helplessness is such a powerful force, but eventually for me, I had to accept it especially when death overpowered it.

Death is a mysterious thing. We fear it but we ferociously fight against it. And yet, death is capable of great beauty and joy. I have seen peace come upon the facial countenance of a person as death approaches. I have seen a person take on an almost angelic appearance when near death. It's true; we don't want to answer its knock at the door anytime sooner than necessary but I don't think death is where our fear lies. I believe we fear how death will take us. We ask questions such as: Will I die from murder, torture, an accident, or a devastating illness? Will I die by inhuman means accompanied by agonizing suffering? Will I have been maimed and left to die a slow, miserable death? Will I die after having been unable to care for myself, even to go to the bathroom on my own? Will I die in my sleep? And the ultimate question reveals the biggest fear of all: Will I die alone?

Personally, I no longer see death as an enemy. When each person's time of death comes, I believe it has not been set by any man or circumstance. My faith in God assures me the last steps to this passing have been designated only by Him. Does He cause the exact way we each die? Does He allow particular circumstances that then contribute to our deaths? I don't have the answer to either of these questions. I do know, however, whatever the manner in which we die or whenever the time, we each have a choice in how we experience our dying. I've seen some who welcomed it. I've seen some who cursed it. I've seen some who denied it would ever come. When death comes, my personal faith promises whoever dies believing in the Son of God will share eternal life with Him in Heaven. There is no greater blessing than this.

When the person who died is our loving spouse, dear parent, or our love-consuming child, we don't see death as a blessing. Clichés are rampant at funeral homes trying to offer consolation to those left behind. Most times, they don't help. Grieving is a harsh emotion. Its pain is inexpressible. For me, tears were, and are, my best form of consolation. When love is abiding for another person, memories and tears seem to be the only true way to reach acceptance of the person's passing. Thus the beauty and the blessing of death.

I've heard people say, "If only I could have my loved one for one more day." After my father died, and then my brother-in-law, sister, and mother, I realized my last gift to each of them would be *not* wanting him or her back for one more day or even one more minute. The person is free. Finally and completely free. Do we really want our loved one forced to experience life on Earth, yet again, however short?

Lesson learned: For those who are God-believing, usually one cliché does provide some comfort for a loved one's death: He or she really is in a better place.

While my next statement may be fraught with controversy, I believe for all of us, we will receive our ultimate "cure" when we pass from this Earthly soul-life to our eternal soul-life in Heaven with Jesus as our Way. I don't believe in assisted-death, euthanasia, abortion, or suicide, but I do accept as truth that God will supply help for every step of life—good or bad—and this includes death. Belief in God and an afterlife is a very personal choice I know, and I'm only able to speak for myself, but I have a difficult time comprehending how anyone survives anything in life without faith in God. I pray for everyone to accept God as their helper but I fully acknowledge that it is each person's decision to make.

Negotiating the Final Curve

Earlier I stated that sooner or later, a decision will need to be made by anyone up against the turning point in his or her life. For my decision, I explained my personal ways to ignore it, reject it, deny it, and go around it. But what about my acceptance of it?

In the past, I had times when I really thought I was going to achieve either a permanent remission or a cure. I prepared for the new life I had longed for, but each time my hope was dashed. At this time, I have a chance for new hope once again if I agree to the treatments for the latest brain complication, but I regret to admit, I'm scared.

The risks are so high for the two treatments my doctors are recommending, and the cost of those risks may be my death. Sarcoidosis, *the monstrous living menace*, never lets up.

I must make a decision, but medical school never taught me how to make this kind of decision *about me*!

Medical school also never taught me how to *accept* I will have no cure and that no cure means dramatic effects to my soul-giving life.

Lesson learned: I hate being a patient!

My Turning Point

Disease became the turning point in my life. For a lot of people, turning points take place over a short span of time, sometimes immediate. Mine took years, and it cost me my career, a marriage, children, family, friends, colleagues, finances, health—almost everything that makes life, life.

So much *bad* contributed to my turning point, but out of the bad *amazing good* came forth. So far, I have shared some important lessons learned. Still to come are more lessons learned. I want them to offer guidance to the doubting. I hope they inspire the indifferent to reach beyond mediocrity. I desire the lessons to be passed on to another. And most of all, I pray they uplift a downward-turning soul-life, while also providing an extra little boost to keep all upward-turning soul-lives, upward turning.

Still More Things Learned while Making the Turn in My Turning Point

Open the "Window" a Crack

As most people, when things take a turn toward the not-so-good I, too, go through periods of questioning, doubt, and fear. However, somewhere along the line I came to realize every situation, whether fantastic or awful, has a message to make better our soul-giving lives. Therefore, I try to always keep an open mind even if only a narrow "crack" to any *secrets* the experience may reveal to me. Ironically, as sarcoidosis has weakened my body, inversely my spirit has gained insight, purpose, knowledge, and contentment.

Where Help May Come From

Earlier I wrote that God led me to a former CIA officer and a former Army Delta Force soldier to protect me during the seizures. When I first hired Mr. Baz and Mr. Franklin, with their particular backgrounds, I accepted they knew how to keep me safe. I did not expect them to become a source of great compassion, understanding, and God enlightenment. From these two men I learned one never knows where help may come from. Those we expect it from may fail us. Those we barely know may save our lives. Since those two men, I always keep my mind and heart open to the possibility that help may show up in the most unexpected ways, at the most unexpected times, and from the most unexpected people.

The Interruption to Plans and Timeline

What's the saying? "The best laid plans ..."

As I look back over my life, I'm amazed how the seemingly most inappropriate and mistimed interruptions usually led to a much better outcome than I would have ever planned. Never underestimate the good that is possible from a worst-ever interruption.

Aloneness versus Loneliness

There's a big difference between aloneness and loneliness. I was taught that a sign of true, inner, psychological health is the ability to spend one hour alone feeling peaceful and content and not becoming lonely. I think this should be expanded to one day and then one week. If a person keeps an open mind, aloneness is able to produce great self-discoveries. Making the honest assessments "I like myself" and "I enjoy being with me" is representative of character maturity. Going off alone and doing something adventuresome enhances the character even more. These things uplift the spirit. It is healthy to find happiness and joy within oneself that does not depend on anyone or anything. Finding *joy of the soul* enables survival when all seems lost. I have experienced the paralyzing effects of loneliness. It has the potential to create a death of a whole different kind. Yes, I surmise most all think life is much better experienced with others who share mutual interests, respect, and love, but if accepted and not fought against, aloneness offers unimaginable rewards.

And if nothing else, aloneness allows for preferential toppings on a pizza or the personal choice of which mountain to climb to victory!

The Person "Hidden"

Speaking of pizza ... it doesn't have to be a bad food, but mostly, this is how it is perceived. This is similar to what I've experienced since gaining weight from the brain disease. It seems society equates being fat to not as good.

When I was physically fit at my normal weight, I heard stories of discrimination against overweight people, but I never believed them until I became one of the stories. Clothing store clerks try to be nonchalant as they walk in the opposite direction to avoid having to assist any customer over a size six. Drop something on the sidewalk, and no one reaches to help pick it up out of courtesy. Those unchallenged by weight issues chat up great sales and bargain finds, but they don't understand those finds are usually found only in smaller sizes. And, if a good-looking item of clothing in a larger size is discovered, usually the price is higher, even if it is on sale. Approach a seat in the movie theater, and the persons closest to that seat cringe. I myself cringe when I hear on the news about some new rule put in place by a company whereby the obese must pay extra for whatever, pay a penalty for whatever, or face refusal altogether because of being obese. Having studied medicine for a good part of my life, I know obesity is not a healthy state for anyone. The risks to almost all aspects of life beckon a truly critical need for action against obesity. But since I gained weight, I'm appalled at the way fat is equated with being a lesser-quality person. Fortunately, not everyone presents this way of thinking but I've experienced enough of this attitude to question many times my self-worth.

Hopefully, I would have remained fit and a normal weight had I not gotten sick, and hopefully one day I will again be fit and a normal weight, but gaining all the extra weight has surely taught me a lot, with one revelation topping the list: Disappointingly, society seems to have accepted as truth that fat on a body chews up and swallows the quality person hidden underneath.

Besides Obesity

By the way, besides the torment dished out to overweight individuals, as I'm getting older I've noticed the higher numbers of age aren't well accepted by society's open arms either. This is a real shame because with age comes wisdom, experience, and reflection. It's deserving of respect. It's exhausting listening and attempting to sort out what new concoction, body treatment, or piece of equipment will knock years off your; well, pick a body part, any part. There's something out there for every inch of an antiager's body. But remember, no amount of fibbing about one's age will ever scientifically alter the true age "hiding" in every person's DNA. A man or woman may fail in recollecting vacations or special occasions from each year of his or her years of life, but trust me, the years will always "remember" the person.

And while I'm at it, let me say this: All my wrinkles, I'm keepin' 'em! I've paid dearly for every single one. They stay!

Less Is More

Losing the pounds that lead to obesity is a great accomplishment and has lasting positive effects. Another accomplishment that has positive effects is losing the pounds of unnecessary stuff we believe essential to everyday life.

I explained earlier that the insurance companies refused to insure me. This included physician disability companies; therefore, when I had to give up my career, my income disappeared with it. For me as for many Americans, Social Security Disability became a great blessing. But at times, bills outnumbered the ability to pay. I sold off belongings that I saw as indispensable when I originally purchased them. Little by little, I was forced to downsize, whether I wanted to or not. I cried after certain items were carried out my front door by those believing they had snagged a great deal. It broke my heart. But an amazing thing began to happen. I realized I didn't actually *need* those things, and in time, having less stuff was a great relief. I had less to clean. I had less to move, and less storage space was needed. Let's face it; we buy things, use them maybe once or, at most, a few times, and they get relegated to closet shelves, basements, attics, or garages. People have garage sales or yard sales after clearing out all the stuff in those same closets, basements, and attics. And if anyone thinks a garage or yard sale will recoup a reasonable amount of the original prices of all items up for sale, well, don't think it because it won't be happening!

My best advice for everyone is to follow the same process I had to learn to better deal with my financial difficulties. When shopping, every time an item is picked up to be purchased, get into the new habit (if not already in it) of asking the following series of questions.

- For what purpose am I buying this item?
- Is the purpose achievable through an alternative source that will make buying this product avoidable?
- Is it something I may be able to borrow from someone for a short time instead of buying new?
- If I do buy it, do I have the cash to pay for it, or do I have to put it on a credit card with potential interest charges attached?
- Holding this item in my hand right at this minute, do I provide myself with a self-personal guarantee that it will be used long term and many times over? If no guarantee, it becomes a put-back-on-the-store-shelf item.

Then an uplifting statement gets to be said:

- The money I save by not buying this, I'm able to put to better use, such as depositing into savings, paying an electric bill, paying off debt, or better yet, helping another person in need.

When all these questions get answered, and hopefully the end result is money saved—and less stuff to clean, store, or later toss—one or two rewards await: (1) feeling great about the decision made, and (2) if the extra money was used to help someone in need, a sincere thank you with a bear hug awaits from the person to whom assistance was given.

Yep, less is definitely more!

Laughter as Medicine

I don't know if I agree with the common statement that laughter is the *best* medicine, but I do know it is an absolute necessity in surviving the basics of everyday life as well as the calamities that come with it. When all else fails, read a funny book, watch a funny movie, think of a funny joke. Laugh and then laugh some more until the tears come and the tummy hurts. This one moment of reprieve from the toughest of struggles may be all that's needed to muster up the last bit of strength and courage to overcome the last hurdle to success, whatever it may be.

Validation Brings Consolation

Don't we all love to have a parking garage ticket validated for either free parking or at least a lower parking fee? We get an adrenaline rush knowing we saved a few bucks. Or don't we feel special when a hostess leads us to the hot-spot table in a restaurant because she believes we are someone with clout? Of course is the answer to both of these questions. If a person gets an emotional bump from having a parking ticket validated or snagging a good table at a restaurant, how much greater of a bump will a person experience if a co-worker, friend, family member, minister, or stranger offers validation during a time of need? But what is true, honest-to-goodness validation?

Many people think offering a few words—usually in the form of a cliché—does the trick. In our new world of tweets and text messages, these few words are narrowed down further to a set number of characters on a teeny-tiny keyboard. Live-person-to-live-person communication is pretty scarce today, but following are some of the comments I have been offered when I was fortunate to find myself in a live-person encounter.

- Sorry to hear about your illness, loved one's death, etc.
- These things happen.
- Everyone has problems.
- Don't sit at home thinking about it.
- You've got to move on.
- We've been thinking about you.
- Having a pity party won't help.
- We've been praying for you.
- We'd offer to help, but ...
- Take care of yourself.
- Well, hang in there.

I have no doubt most everyone means well. Many times, people don't know what to say for fear their words will make a person sadder or more upset. Some believe it's better to say nothing. For unknown reasons, people seem to get a little freaked out when it comes to giving another person empathy, encouragement, support—*validation*. So many times, there is a dramatic failure in doing this good deed, and in my opinion, new technology has served up a great cover-up for this failure. Being faceless behind a screen is more tolerable than being face-to-face with the one in need.

So what makes for good validation? Some would protest that communication by such modern media as tweeting, texting, or Facebook enables superior validation since these afford the opportunity for many more to "speak" their support. I guess the accepted thought here is quantity automatically means quality. I'm not convinced. Social media might be a great way to comfort a person who lives a great distance away or when it is a physical impossibility to get to the place of the person in need, but I truly hope live-person-to-live-person support is never lost. I fear social media is becoming the accepted way of validation, but I simply won't accept that a limited number of characters on a handheld screen will ever be enough to truly offer heartfelt empathy to another person.

And how will anyone become a good listener or find a good listener when the chances for people to hear the human voice have drastically decreased? Words or the letters forming abbreviations on a phone or computer screen greatly limit the development of or the advancing of observation skills, such as looking at and then admiring his or her beautiful eyes, listening to and then comforting a hurting soul, or smelling and then remembering the scent of his or her cologne or perfume. What is better than these in-person experiences?

We are human beings. We're not machines with only thumbs and bent-over necks with eyes. Human beings need touch. A hug, a kiss on the cheek, a hand placed on top of another person's hand. We need to feel each of these, but instead we're becoming capable of only feeling whether a cell phone is in a pocket or in its holster on a belt. We need a real face with a real human-affirming smile, not a screen with an emoticon or a colon typed before a parenthesis. We need to hear the voice of another human being. We must not allow a screen filled with symbols or abbreviations to be the "voice" of comfort. Computers are being programmed for voice recognition, but will people recognize, or even remember, the voice of a friend or family member? Will it soon be that only pets receive a touch from a human being? Will pets be the only living creatures to recognize a human voice? Will pets only receive the validation of a human smile?

I have lived through times of unbearable despair. I have spent hours and days in the grips of loneliness when I desperately needed someone sitting beside me to offer consolation and encouragement. I acknowledge it's not the easiest thing to know how to validate a person with an ongoing difficult set of circumstances, especially if the one in need has fallen into the trap of thinking that he or she is no longer a viable, worthwhile, lovable human being. It's our human nature to rely on *avoidance* when we don't know how to be what another needs. One of the most difficult situations to assist in involves someone who has lost the ability—and freedom—to be independent.

This often leads to depression and a total lack of self-worth. Helping the person follow the steps of mourning a loss (see the section "Grieving the Loss of Me") may lead to resolution and peace, but loss of independence may be as traumatic as losing a loved one to death. And for many who have suffered the loss of independence, it may be perceived most definitely as death.

Prayers are extremely important avenues of assistance. With few exceptions, anyone is appreciative for prayers, but sometimes, prayer is not enough when a hurting person is overwhelmed by deep confusion and anguish. I personally have had times when prayer became an irritation because I fell into the trap of thinking maybe even God wanted to avoid me or leave me altogether as many others had done in the past.

Observation skills come in handy when working out ways to offer validation to anyone in need. Keep watch for clues. They will be there.

On the flip side, I know firsthand it's not the easiest thing to tell others what is needed. Thoughts start creeping in, such as the following:

- I don't want to bother her.
- They think I'm always strong, so I must be strong this time, too.
- They have a family so I can't ask for help.
- I try to work around their schedule, but I can't control when a crisis hits.
- Why do I have to tell anybody what I need? Surely he or she is smart enough to figure it out.
- Are they blind!?
- I've explained before; what more can I say?
- I've been specific in the past about what I needed, and I heard back all the "reasons" why they couldn't do those things.
- They just don't get it, and I'm too exhausted to explain it one more time.

My best advice to the "supporter": Ask the person-in-need to be specific of his or her needs each time a contact is made. One day may bring one need, but a week or a month later a whole different need may be in play. Supply a list of things the supporter is able to actually offer to the person. If payment is required, be upfront with the costs. Above all, take time—*make time*—to listen and truly hear. And understand tears and sobs may be the only way a person in need is able to communicate during the most stressful of moments.

My best advice to the "supportee": Be specific in voicing needs. Following are some guidelines:

- If wanting emotional support, suggest praying together, phone calls, visits, cards, or a tweet if there is absolutely no way for a live-person-to-live-person encounter.

- If errands must be done, ask for a ride outlining beforehand the details of the when, where, and how long. Offer to pay for the person's time or fuel for the vehicle used. These suggestions also apply if asking for rides to church services, doctors' appointments, a day of window shopping, or other business affairs.
- If needed, outline household chores being requested.
- If companionship is desired, suggest things such as putting up the Christmas tree and later taking it down, going for a walk, or watching a movie together.
- To enhance a feeling of being respected, ask for the specifics of what a supporter is willing or able to provide. Does he or she have a time limit, or must a time frame be adjusted? Inquire if payment is required, and if yes, make an agreement regarding the specifics.

Three important "rules" must be remembered by any person seeking assistance. First, don't be embarrassed to ask for help; second, don't be afraid to ask for help; and third, above all, don't forget to offer empathy in return because the supporter also may be having a not-so-good day and is in need of a little TLC.

And for both parties of the "support organization": Find something to laugh about with each other.

Grieving the Loss of Me

Dr. Elisabeth Kubler-Ross wrote books on the grieving process. She outlined the stages, which consist of anger, denial, bargaining, depression, and finally acceptance—not necessarily in this order. We mostly associate these steps as being applicable when one loses a spouse, child, parent, friend, or other significant loved one to death. But grieving is needed when dealing with other losses also, such as loss of a job, loss of a home from a natural disaster, loss of a special relationship, or "loss" of oneself.

I personally suffered losses of loved ones by death, including my parents, sister, brother-in-law, friends, and relatives. If a patient died, this, too, was a loss for me, which I tried to convey to family members. And I, as most people, tear up even at the loss of a highly respected, high-profile individual.

Beyond the losses resulting from death, the losses of friends and other loved ones through abandonment caused me great heartache. But the most difficult loss without question was the loss of *me*.

In a way, how I lost me doesn't really matter. How I've dealt with the loss is what does matter. For a long time, I never knew my circumstances were considered a loss, per se. And I never thought anything about needing to grieve. But one evening, I attended a sarcoidosis support group meeting organized by my sarcoid specialist. The speaker for the gathering spoke about the applicability of the grieving process when one is diagnosed with a chronic, debilitating illness. My eyes exploded with tears. I was hardly able to control my sobbing, but yet I felt such a relief. I finally knew how to deal with the pain consuming me. In time, I too went through the stages of anger, denial, bargaining, depression, and acceptance; although I have found, from time to time, a repeat of one of the stages may be needed.

A lot of people don't grasp the idea that my situation or similar ones require grieving, but trust me, grieving is most indeed needed. Our culture binds self-identity to job, income, home, friends, spouse, or what not. It's bad enough to lose one, but when loss comes to most every category, one right after the other, a person wonders if there is any hope that his or her *me* will be resurrected.

There was a particular phrase I used to tell my patients, and I have used it often to help validate others in need: "Your reactions and feelings are normal for a very abnormal situation."

Losing oneself is definitely a very abnormal situation, and grieving is undeniably a normal reaction.

Two Last Things for Me to Teach

Doctors Also Get Sick

I receive calls from all over the world from individuals seeking advice and support regarding sarcoidosis. Sometimes, the individual has been diagnosed with the disease. Other times, the person is calling on behalf of someone they know who has sarcoid. Some callers know I have the disease myself, and some find out for the first time when speaking with me. I cherish these calls because I'm still being a physician but in a different capacity. The calls offer me a great deal of satisfaction when I'm able to give hope when all hope seemed lost for the person calling me. But there are a few calls I don't cherish. I have been verbally attacked with statements, including, "It's good you're sick! It's about time a doctor gets sick," and "How do you like going through what you doctors put us through?" There have been others not quite so nice, but I won't bother with those.

In spite of those harboring "ill" feelings toward physicians, the truth of my message is that doctors do get sick, and we, too, have our lives torn apart, our finances drained, insurance problems, family disruptions, and death shows up at our doors, too, when least expected.

Most definitely, doctors' pain and suffering are as real as anyone's.

Bedside Manner

Patients desire their doctors to have great bedside manners. I think my own was pretty good before I got sick, but I'm fairly sure it's gotten better considering all the bedside manners I've observed in my own physicians.

When I was receiving the chemotherapy, the physician who was administering it to me had been one of my mentors. One day he made a profound statement, "Bernadette, if we ever get you back to practicing medicine, you will be great with patients because you've experienced almost everything a patient can go through." My response was, "Yep, the only thing I haven't experienced is prostate problems, and it won't surprise me if one of these days God spouts me one of those, too." That doctor had a great bedside manner, and I believe I did, too. Both of us incorporated humor whenever appropriate. And if the situation warranted, neither of us hesitated to offer a supportive hug.

I bring up bedside manners as a sort-of addendum to the section titled "Validation Brings Consolation." The very nature of a bedside manner is to deliver explanation and validation of a patient's problems. Consolation is the other main component meant to ease the fears and sorrows of a patient. In a sense, every person has a bedside manner, and it's used in some way in every person-to-person interaction. How it will transfer over into the cyber world of interactions, I don't have the answer to this. For now, I watch and wait, but for anyone interested, one has only to ask this question: How good is *my* bedside manner?

In the End, Have I Touched a Soul?

At the beginning of this writing, I wrote that I never had touched a soul, or specifically, the part of a human body that supposedly is the source of its life. That statement is not accurate.

In a brief but concise essay of my life, I have opened and shared moments of my greatest heartache as well as moments of my attempts to be humorous. It has not been an easy task to write of my life, but it will be fulfilling if the messages I deliver are taken to heart and followed to lessen the life-load of another.

My life has been strange and wonderful. It has been terrifying and boring. It has been mystifying, and it has been jubilant. But most of all, it has been *mine*. I would never give it back, and I would never trade it for another.

The lessons learned from my soul-giving life have been many. Some have been harsh, while others have been very tender and sweet. But the basis of all is one thing—my faith. And it is through this same faith that I will strive harder to complete my true mission.

Earlier I wrote I never touched the part of a human body that supposedly is the source of its life, but that is not accurate. For it is through my own soul-giving life that I have been given the opportunity to touch—and love—the souls of many. And upon my soul, those patients, friends, family, and strangers have left behind impressions of their own.

So to answer the question above, have I touched a soul? Yes. Many, many.

I close with a new question: Have you touched a soul?

Watch Out for Bees: They Can Ruin Your Career

2

J. BRANCH WALTON

Contents

Bees can hurt you. Their stings can cause anything from minor irritations to immobilizing injury or even death. Knowledge of bees and how to deal with them is the key to avoiding these personal problems.

This chapter deals with bees. You'll get a brief understanding of them and how they can ruin your career. However, unlike the aforementioned insects of the superfamily Apoidea in the order Hymenoptera, we'll be discussing those irrational, stupid, incomprehensible, criminal, devious, and juvenile decisions law enforcement officers sometimes make that end up harming or ruining a career. Those acts will be identified in categories beginning with a *B*. Thus, we can call them the "Killer B's."

Law enforcement is an honorable career. By far, the greatest portion of federal, state, and local law enforcement officers in this country are honest and dedicated, and have a sincere desire to make the country safer and more secure. Their daily lives revolve around their families and jobs.

When enforcing laws, you as a law enforcement officer are entrusted with a considerable amount of latitude. As this chapter will show you, many law enforcement officials abuse this power. Many of the acts of these officers may be based upon the officer's sincere (and frequently understandable) desire to give offenders what they deserve. Some activity raises important ethical questions about permissible activity. Other acts are committed by the officers solely for personal gain in one form or another, and where the offending officer clearly knows the activity is illegal or unethical. This chapter assays those unethical or criminal acts done intentionally.

It identifies many incidents where a career was ended because of bad decisions or bad judgment made by a law enforcement officer, corrections officer, or security officer. The subject matter of those decisions could probably fall into a category identified in this chapter as starting with a B, such as an incident involving drugs (barbiturates) or misuse of an official vehicle (Buick). Hopefully, an understanding of these potential problems will make you more aware of how important it is to avoid making regrettable personal decisions as you progress in your career.

Make no mistake about it, you will face many temptations in your job. You will be challenged on many occasions to make decisions where the best choice is not necessarily easy to make. Every occupation has moments like this, and you can only hope your decision turns out to be the best under the circumstances. There will be other situations where the choices are clearly either right or wrong. There can be heavy temptations to make a decision or choice that is knowingly wrong or even a violation of law. A violation of your agency's or department's policies or procedures may seem less serious to you and therefore more tempting to knowingly violate. Think again!

Some popular questions frequently used in ethics classes are, "Would you feel comfortable telling your family what you just did?" or "Would you feel comfortable if the press released information about what you did?" Most decisions made by employees involving the B's were decisions made with the knowledge that they were wrong decisions.

So, you want to have a little fun at the expense of a demotion, suspension, or even possibly losing your job? Choose a B and go for it while you examine what happened to others who have made similar choices. Employees who work in your internal affairs office, inspector general's office or office of inspection love to see violations like this. It's called job security for them.

Read the following real-life examples under the respective B category. The examples range from small infractions to serious felonies. There is no shortage of examples out there.

You will see many similar incidents during your law enforcement career. You'll wonder why someone making a very good salary, with good promotional possibilities, within a year of retirement, or with a great family might knowingly make a decision that could cause them to lose everything. Don't let that bad decision maker be you.

Finally, read and absorb the quote on attitude by writer and clergyman Charles Swindoll in Chapter 7.

Barbiturates (Involvement with Illicit Drugs)

This B focuses on the use of these drugs, while "Bucks" (see next section) might involve drug trafficking where the motive is money. Sometimes the violations involve both dealing and use.

In an incident in the southwest United States, three employees of a well-known sheriff's department were arrested in a drug and human trafficking case. A deputy and two female detention officers at the sheriff's largest jail facility were among twelve people taken into custody and accused of being in a metro-area-based international drug smuggling ring.

Bucks (Money)

Money can be a temptation. Following are three examples of law enforcement personnel giving in to this temptation.

A South Florida department's Officer of the Year was indicted for conspiring to possess and traffic 500 grams of methamphetamine. The five-year veteran, a twenty-eight-year-old officer, was accused of drug dealing from June 2009 until March 4, 2011. He faced a potential life sentence if convicted. The department chief released a statement saying, "The Police Department vigorously polices itself, and this case is an example of how law enforcement roots out corruption from within its own ranks."

In 2010, this officer worked eleven burglaries resulting in nineteen arrests and eighteen narcotic cases leading to twenty-five arrests. He was caught in a Drug Enforcement Administration (DEA)-led Organized Crime Drug Enforcement Task Force investigation. "The decision to deal drugs while carrying a badge is not only a breach of the law enforcement oath, but a community tragedy as well," the DEA Special Agent in Charge said in a statement.

The police chief said, "We realize that when an officer stands accused of a violation of the public trust, all of law enforcement pays the price in eroded citizen confidence and the perception of diminished integrity."

In another example, in a case of abuse of public trust, a sheriff suddenly resigned just after his trial began. The indictment alleged that the sheriff diverted close to $50,000 for personal use from a drug asset forfeiture account. The prosecutor said the sheriff used the funds "like a personal checking account."

In yet another example of money becoming the motive for questionable behavior, six police officers in a major city were arraigned on charges of using drug forfeiture money to pay for prostitutes, alcohol, and marijuana. The officers included four detectives and a former chief. The wife of the former chief was also charged. Prosecutors said all six had operated a criminal enterprise for over five years.

Buicks (Misuse of Official Vehicles)

There are exceptions but department vehicles are normally issued to be used strictly for official use. The temptation to use them for personal reasons is always there. Taking short personal trips, having friends or family drive the vehicle, and taking the vehicle on vacations all are examples of misuse. Departments have strict policies on vehicular use. Officers should thoroughly understand these policies and abide by them. Misuse of vehicles is a topic the media loves to release to the public. The release of such information can be a big embarrassment to the department. Other incidents that the media would love to release to the public are speeding and the violation of other traffic laws when not responding to an emergency.

Bullets (Misuse of Duty Weapons)

Many serious cases of misuse of a duty weapon are on the records books. Some incidents involved homicide charges against the officer. Some are embarrassing. Most are not that serious yet are worthy of note if only to remind law enforcement officers of the need to be alert to the potential problems in this category.

A police officer in a northeastern state was sentenced to probation after being involved in a road rage incident. He was accused of breaking a motorist's windshield, choking him, and pointing a gun at him. This occurred after a minor fender bender incident.

In another incident, a deputy, while off duty, was arrested on a charge of drunk driving and a related weapons charge.

Badges (Misuse of Official Identification)

There are many examples out there to reinforce the potential problem of misuse of official identification. Here's a slight variation on the "I have a badge. You can't tell me what to do or not do" attitude.

A sheriff's deputy, relatively new on the job, and his mother were charged with disorderly conduct after the deputy vomited on people at a concert and refused to leave when asked. The deputy's mother was accused of pulling and pushing officers, screaming profanities, and trying to prevent an officer from escorting her son out of the concert. An assumption is made here was that alcohol may have been involved.

Seemingly small incidents can also be the cause of dismissal, suspension, or criminal charges. Although a police officer was not involved in the following incident, there have been similar situations involving law enforcement personnel A former Department of Revenue employee of a Southeastern state used state funds to put gas in his personal vehicle. He used a co-worker's state-issued gas card personal identification number without authorization. He was sentenced to thirty days in jail and fined $1,000. As of this writing, charges were pending against four co-defendants.

Bravado or Bragging

Talking too much can also get you in trouble. "Don't worry. I can take care of it for you." A major Northeastern police department was under investigation over allegations of widespread ticket fixing. It was a "professional courtesy" that extended to officers as well as their families and friends. The investigations involved hundreds of police officers in multiple precincts.

A deputy police chief was under investigation for allegedly lying under oath when he testified he had permission to testify in his uniform while on the stand in a civil case. This may seem like a small violation yet the fact that he lied would be a huge smack in the face for the police department and its reputation within the community.

Bodies and Beauties (Sexual Misconduct)

Sexual misconduct can involve extramarital activity, sexual exploitation of children, rape, molestation, abuse of animals, or several other sexually related activities. A law enforcement officer's job provides many opportunities to get in trouble here.

A city in a Southeastern state settled a lawsuit with a female police officer, paying her $48,000. The officer claimed her supervisor sent her sexually explicit and racist text messages. Maybe another B category should be added to this chapter to include misuse of battery-operated communications devices.

A police officer in a large Western city was suspended recently without pay while he faced charges that he sexually exploited children. He was charged with ten counts of sexual exploitation of a child, a Class 4 felony. The city's code stated that police department employees can be suspended without pay for any of a laundry list of offenses, ranging from workplace violence to immoral conduct to "any other reasonable and just cause." The officer was arrested after police were notified by military investigators looking into Internet crimes against children that the officer may have bought child porn online. Child pornography DVDs were found in the officer's bedroom, along with a laptop that had pornographic images of children on it.

An officer in another city gave in to temptation when a local prostitute he was interviewing offered him a free service. He unfortunately gave in to the offer but was even more unfortunate when a local bystander took a picture of the event. He was sitting in his patrol car with the door open as she leaned into his lap. The experienced officer lost his job.

Here's another example. The case against two Midwestern police officers was centered on the word "no" and that the woman accusing them of sexual assault said it. Attorneys for the two officers said that the sex was consensual and that the officers were only guilty of "bad judgment." One officer allegedly had sex in the squad car with the victim, while the other went to a liquor store to buy booze. When they reached the victim's apartment, they played strip poker and both officers sexually assaulted her, according to prosecutors. A witness in the case said she heard the victim pounding on the walls and screaming for help. Parts of one officer's uniform were recovered in her apartment. One of the officers is also suspected of committing another sexual assault of a woman he and his partner picked up at a bus stop. He's alleged to have forced himself upon this woman. The woman did not report the incident at the time because she lives in the police district the two officers were assigned to and feared intimidation.

At the federal level, a high-ranking, twenty-seven-year career law enforcement officer in a large Southeastern state was arrested on charges of possessing, receiving, and transferring child pornography. In his job, he was responsible for investigating child pornography trafficking. He faces up to fifty years in prison. His criminal activity was traced back to at least two years prior to his arrest.

In an infamous and embarrassing incident to the United States, twelve U.S Secret Service agents while temporarily assigned as supplemental support to a presidential visit to Colombia became embroiled in a scandal involving Colombian prostitutes, resulting in the loss of their jobs and a smear on the entire agency.

> As a few lines from the 1960s song "Secret Agent Man" says,
> Beware of pretty faces that you find
> A pretty face can hide an evil mind
> Oh, be careful what you say, you'll give yourself away.
> Secret Agent Man, Secret Agent Man.

Booze

Alcohol has probably been the primary cause of many off-duty incidents involving law enforcement officers. It has also been the cause of incidents while on duty. Two officers on duty and in uniform visited a popular "cop bar" in a coastal bench town. It sounds like the beginning of a joke but that isn't the case here. The two officers had several drinks each, then invited a young lady to ride with them on their department-issued four-wheel beach ATV. After a short reckless ride up and down the beach, they ran over a woman who was lying on the beach. Bystanders took pictures of the vehicle and the victim with their cell phones just after the incident. She received serious injuries and had an extended hospital stay due to the severity of her injuries. The officers were fired. Both the police department and the two officers are targets of lawsuits and more than likely will have to pay a large sum of money to settle.

Bullying

Bullying is the use of official status to intimidate, harass, or coerce others. The internal files of law enforcement officers will show the volume of investigations that cover this type of unacceptable activity by police officers. Many of these cases involve personal domestic issues where the officer uses his or her official capacity to intimate their divorced or separated spouse or their new friends. In the defense of many officers, there are many cases filed by citizens that have no basis and are soon dismissed after appropriate investigation of the facts. Still, this is an area where many officers get in trouble because of bad decisions.

Blowing Smoke (a.k.a. Lying)

False statements on official reports or lying on the witness stand are, of course, serious offenses. Here is another example of how telling lies can get you in trouble. A fifteen-year veteran county school district police officer was arrested and charged with filing a false report about the theft of his weapon. The fifty-three-year-old deputy told supervisors his home had been broken into and that his police-issued duty belt was among the items stolen. The belt contained a department-issued Glock handgun, handcuffs, a police radio, and pepper spray, according to the report. An investigation revealed that the missing weapon was recovered during a robbery attempt and held as evidence by police, four days before the police officer reported it stolen. When confronted with these facts, the officer changed his story to say the weapon, belt, and other equipment were actually stolen on a different date and that he had tried to recover them on his own by putting word out on the street. With no success, the officer decided to add the missing gun and duty belt to the list of other items stolen from his home. He has been reassigned to a nonschool, nonpolice position within the school system police department pending the outcome of the criminal case and the just-launched personnel investigation.

Conclusion

Law enforcement is a great profession, and has very professional and ethical personnel. There will always be a few who discredit the others. Don't be one of those few. Think about your decisions and actions. Will your mother or spouse be happy when they see or read about you in the news? How would you explain to your spouse that you lost your job, perhaps your entire career and reputation, for a few minutes of pleasure or indulgence in poor judgment?

Torch of Intuition, Flames of Preparation: Safely Lighting Your Way through Traveling's Uncertainties

3

KATHERINE DENISE JUNE

Contents

Introduction

After years of traveling abroad alone as a twenty- and now thirty-something-year-old woman, there is one thing I've come to understand: I can only be as cautious of my safety as fate allows. By this I mean that while it has greatly benefitted me to take all the right precautions to keep myself alert and vigilant in practicing strategic rules of safety, I also recognize that if I were to end up in the wrong place at the wrong time, well, there isn't much I can do about that.

During my time abroad, I observed two sorts of travelers. There are those who could be more persistent in keeping their safety a priority, but because they don't, they end up having to deal with major headaches. And then there are those who take just as many precautions as I do, yet still, somehow, end up having to contend with a nightmarish bout of being in the wrong place at the wrong time—an acute syndrome far more devastating than any traveler's diarrhea you've ever had! (Think time spent in a foreign jail after being arrested for something you didn't even know was illegal, or needing stitches where there wasn't a hospital, etc.) This just goes to show that no matter how prepared a person is, horrible things can still happen.

Yet, when you know some of the ways to sidestep the possibilities of bad things happening by going the extra mile to look after yourself and your travel companions, your trip instantly ups its chances at having more of the fun kind of adventure and less of the not-so-fun kind. Learning difficult life lessons is hard enough in your own country where you speak the same verbal and cultural language as the people *outside* of the courts *and* where you have legal rights as a citizen *within* the courts. But learning these lessons in an international domain can be exponentially more challenging. Not only will you find yourself desperately trying to navigate a murky communication barrier, but you'll also be flailing in a cultural soup of ambiguous mannerisms and body language (not to mention your complete lack of rights as a noncitizen, that is, if you're in a country that even grants its citizens any rights).

For example, did you know that in Thailand it's considered disrespectful to make eye contact with a man who is speaking to you and that it's best to keep your eyes low in a submissive manner? No? Well, you probably just landed yourself in deeper water by making eye contact—something that we do in the United States to show respect—with the police officer who has wrongly accused you of trying to sneak away without paying your hotel bill. My point is that the more you know *before* you go, the more comfortable you'll be, because however hard your hotel bed might be in Thailand, a stay in their deplorable jails will always be much, much harder.

In an attempt to lessen possible hardships in the lives of fellow travelers, in the next several pages I will walk you through some of the precautionary safety strategies that I've implemented over the past thirteen years. They are all tried-and-true methods and have worked well enough for me to not be dead right now in a ditch somewhere in a small coastal village in Costa Rica or for sale on the human market anywhere in Southeast Asia. In fact, these strategies have worked so well that my executive-protection-teaching father has asked me to write this chapter. And if a man who has spent his adult life professionally looking after the safety of domestic politicians and executives, foreign monarchists and clergy, the general public, and five of his own—now grown—children thinks that what I've done to keep myself safe is noteworthy, then there must be something to that. As a child, when any one of my siblings or I would return home from anywhere outside of our house—whether it was from a weekend trip with friends or just a run to the store for milk—our Dad would always greet us with, "Ah! You made it home: Safe, sound, sane, and sober!"

And so I have.

After all these years and all the many miles, his catchphrase still remains true. I've made it back (mostly) unscathed from my adventures, and I can confidently say that I did it by weaving myself a strong safety net using only the sturdiest threads of common sense, pretrip planning, and intuition. Following are the details of how I wove my protective blanket and guidelines as to how you might weave your own.

Decisions, Decisions

Whether or not you have the luxury of deciding where it is you're going to be traveling, or if it's been mandated through work, family, or other obligations, one of the first places to begin your journey is actually not online booking your ticket. A smart first thing to do is to visit your local library to check out some books on the country/countries you might be visiting. I recommend checking out books that were published both long ago and recently, so that you can get a clear idea of where this country has been and where it is today, culturally and politically speaking. Doing your initial research is the first step to deciding if you want to go there in the first place. You will find out if it is safe to travel there, what to expect, what some of the religious and political viewpoints are, how women are treated, what will be expected of you, and what you might be able to expect from a world that most likely will be vastly different from the one you currently live in.

At the age of twenty, when I decided to go on a solo trip abroad for the very first time, I was torn between Southeast Asia and Central America. I'd just finished reading the book *I, Rigoberta Menchu* and had become very interested in the struggle of the indigenous people of Guatemala and Southern Mexico. A trip to Central America seemed like an appropriate destination so that I could see firsthand the rich jungle slopes, high-elevation lakes, and the quickly disappearing world of the indigenous people of this region. However, I had also been speaking with friends who had just returned from Thailand where, they said, two dollars a night would get me a beachside bungalow—with breakfast included! This information definitely piqued the interest of my student-size bank account.

To the library I went. I checked out several books on each of these countries; books that included histories, maps, discussions on cultural practices, and so on. I also picked up books on traveling alone as a woman, how to stay healthy abroad, and, just for good measure, an action novel that took place in Thailand to get an artist's perspective on a country I was seriously thinking about visiting. As I read through these books, I also researched the Web sites of local papers and government warnings (for both continents) and got myself up to date on local current events. I spent a good month reading a seemingly million different perspectives on these places and here's what I uncovered.

Guatemala has had an extremely violent ancient and recent history, but was currently (in 1999) undergoing a peaceful renaissance and a certain quiet had fallen over its battlefields. Its indigenous people were rebuilding their lives and were relying heavily on tourist dollars for their livelihoods. Foreign women had reported being able to travel there safely on their own and (similar to Thailand) I would easily be able to find two-dollar-a-night accommodations both beachside and in monkey-laden jungles.

I assessed the facts about traveling in Guatemala and Belize: Countries currently void of bloody Armageddon, check. Using my American dollars to help the local people rebuild their cultural heritage by selling their weavings and indigenous crafts, check. Generally safe for women traveling alone, check. Inexpensive places to stay that would enable me to stretch my shoestring budget to its max, check. This didn't sound so bad.

I then looked over the notes I'd taken about Southeast Asia, particularly Indonesia, Thailand, and Laos. I'd discovered that Indonesia was about to hold an election that sought to vote in Indonesia's first female president, Megawati Sukarnoputri, daughter of Indonesia's first president, Sukarno. I found that not only were there frequent riots on Java (the island-nation's political capital) to protest the intentions of Megawati's political party, but there were also religious riots in Aceh off the northern tip of Sumatra, as well as a volcano of violent eruptions in East Timor, where the tiny island was striving for its independence from the rest of Indonesia. However Bali, the only Hindu island in this predominantly Islamic country, sounded serene in its rice paddy growing ways, where the women were viewed on par with the men, and the biggest thing to look out for (as reported by a woman in her book about her solo journey there) were the monkeys who might steal your water bottle and hold it hostage until you feed it a banana. I decided this was mild in comparison to the rest of Indonesia's troubles.

My research on Thailand found essays on the underground trade of white women as sex slaves, on foreigners going to jail for life on small drug charges, and a book written about a colony of Western-culture dropouts who had established an idyllic isle on one of Thailand's remote islands but who had succumbed to a sort of "Lord of the Flies" mentality of trying to figure out who rules when there are no rules, leading to this garden of Eden's corruption and inevitable downfall. I admit that this part of my research came from a fictional action-novel written by Alex Garland, but it detailed some Thai specifics as far as cultural and geographical landscapes, so I took note of it as fact.

And as far as Laos as a possible destination, my research showed me that it too was a land of paradox. It's not-too-distant past was painful and bloody, and the Vietnam war still impacted it in the present moment as parts of the country were (are) still teeming with land mines. However, the Laotian government, in an attempt to bring financial recovery to this small and unstable corner of Southeast Asia, had just recently opened its borders to tourists and this country of Buddhists and hill tribes were welcoming foreign dollars, even though there wasn't (yet) any real infrastructure to support the needs of the tourists they beckoned. The guide books I'd read, published only a year before, promised peaceful walks through vibrantly green rice fields, home stays with Hmong families, raft rides down the Mekong, and sumptuous feasts of pineapple curry and chicken skewers for less than a dollar. Hmmm, such trade-offs.

Similar to how I concluded my research on Central America by looking over my notes and formulating an assessment, I looked over my research on Southeast Asia. In Indonesia: political unrest, check. Religious violence, check. Collapsing economy, a new world order, and the first female president to be elected in the world's most populace Muslim country, check, check, and check. In Thailand: underground cults and gangs, check. Infinite amounts of lonely islands surrounded by heavenly turquoise-colored seas, check. And finally, my research on Laos concluded: undetonated land mines but deliciously spicy curry for the price of a pack of gum, check.

So there I had it. I had rigorously slogged through books, newspapers, and Web sites to decide on where to spend my summer vacation between my sophomore and junior years of college, and I had produced a small notebook full of pros and cons for all of the countries I had researched. The rational-logical side of my brain had taken its inventory and was now trying to endorse its stance.

"Just go to Central America. Politically it's mostly settled; the indigenous people want you there; and it's been a tourist destination for at least twenty years, so it will be easier to get around. Southeast Asia just seems like disaster waiting to happen. And hey! Both places have monkeys so I might as well choose the statistically safer destination!"

It was then I heard a booming voice declare, "The Great and Powerful Wizard of Logic HAS SPOKEN!"

And as the thunderbolts, lightening, and puffs of smoke cleared, it seemed as though the decision had been made. Yet, after coming to this conclusion on one level, I knew I still had one more very important process ahead of me. I needed to weigh the realities of each of these places with one more important tool of assessment: a weightless tool that comes from within, that of personal intuition. This tool has nothing to do with the so-called realities typed in permanent ink in all the books I'd read on the subject. It has nothing to do with government websites, other tourists' opinions, or the first-person perceptions of a couple of already-been-there novelists. Instead, this tool has everything to do with gut instinct. It's what ultimately keeps one out of harm's way, when all other "rational" signs are pointing to safety but something just below the surface tells you to go the other way, away from where the rational mind is pointing.

I knew I needed to get quiet within and feel into the possibilities rather than think about them. I put everything I had just learned aside for the moment and took several deep breaths. As I sank into the place of my own inner knowing, I was still bombarded by trap after well-meaning trap of the rational mind trying to plant its agenda in the front yard of my awareness. Now, while one definitely needs the input of one's rational mind, it is only one of two very important perspectives. Understanding that this is how this side of the mind functions, I continued to breathe and let the thoughts go and let the feelings in. As I did so, a sort of alchemical response began to unfold. I followed the sensations of my body. When I sat with the feelings brought up by the words "Central America," I felt edgy. There was tightness in my belly. An internal blindness unfolded; I could literally not see myself there. I took note of this, and for the time being put those feelings on the back burner.

Then I quietly said to myself "Southeast Asia." I breathed. I relaxed. I let any logically prescribed anxiety drop away. Doubt and hesitation melted. A warm sense of well-being fanned through each cell of my body. Something about it just felt like I'd be going home. There was a sense of warmth, of safety, and, strangely, of determination. Something in my gut knew that Southeast Asia was the right destination, even though the stats said otherwise. Through my logic-led research I had learned the locations of some of the more politically unstable parts of Indonesia, of undetonated bomb-laden areas of Laos, and about some of the more shady parts of Thailand—all to avoid. But I'd been given the intuitive green light, and because Southeast Asia is an enormous area, rationally I knew there had to be areas that I could travel to safely. By integrating logic with intuition, cold-hard research with the warmth of gut feelings, I had made my decision.

The next day I picked up the phone and called the travel agent to book a logistically complicated ticket that would take me to and through Indonesia, Laos, and Thailand.

And sure enough, one month later, after a two-day stopover in Bangkok, I stepped off the plane to exit down the stairs onto the open tarmac of Bali's international airport, and as soon as the moisture-rich tropical air touched my skin, I felt just like I had a month before when I had decided to travel to Southeast Asia. I felt as though I was arriving home after an extremely long stay elsewhere, and instinctually I knew that my decision had been correct and that I was where I was meant to be.

(As a quick side note, it turned out that I ended up taking that well-researched trip to Guatemala five years later instead, and that trip ended up occurring at just the right time too. I met a handful of people that added to my life's experiences in profound ways, who wouldn't have been there had I gone in 1999. A poignant truth I took note of—and thanked my intuition for—when I returned from Guatemala in the late summer of 2004.)

Preparing, Departing, and Arriving

There is a lot that occurs between deciding on where to go and actually arriving there. Before my first time traveling abroad (on the aforementioned trip to Southeast Asia), I put countless hours into researching the safest way to do it. When going to a developing country, one needs to be prepared, as it can be overwhelming for many reasons. But when going to a developing country for your first time, alone, as a young woman, one needs to be extra, extra ready for all the possible twists and turns that an adventure like this can present.

To begin with, I read books about and by women who had been there before and what their experiences had been. I devoured cultural, religious, and political histories. I practiced basic phrases in all of the languages I'd be speaking. I studied customs; holidays; body language; social norms and mores; federal laws; art; music; places to go and when; how to get around domestically; exchange rates; bartering systems; places to safely swim, surf, hike, and sleep; and just about any other topic under the sun that I felt I needed to be aware of *in order to be aware of* what I was getting myself into. I basically turned myself into a P.I.T. of information—yes, a P.I.T., Privately Investigating Traveler. I wanted the goods and I wanted the dirt on all the people and places before I got there so that I wouldn't become one of those ridiculous tourists you see fudging up all over the place. Like the woman who wears short-shorts in an Islamic country, or the man who speaks too loudly and with force in a bartering situation, and like the couple that doesn't know to take their shoes off when entering someone's home or a sacred site.

If there is any difference between a traveler and a tourist, it is this: The traveler takes her time in acquainting herself with the social protocols of the country she is traveling to before she gets there, whereas the tourist waits to learn these things until she's in the country, and then does so through much blundering and offense. Of the two, who do you think has a better chance of sticking out like a sore thumb, attracting attention to herself, and thus becoming a possible target for an unpleasant experience? Yes, definitely not the traveler.

While going through this initial process of preparation for Southeast Asia back in 1999, I imagined myself as a toddler, waking up in a world where I didn't speak or understand the social cues, nor did I know how to perceive the subtleties of culturally specific body language. It feels a lot like being a small child when stepping into a developing country (or into a developed country whose language you don't speak and whose customs you don't practice). In our rapidly globalizing world, you might expect that *someone* would be around who is able to speak English and would be able to guide you, but you'd be setting yourself up, because what if there isn't anyone to rely on? Or what if there was but you felt you couldn't trust him or her? How would you get your needs met? How would you know what to do, or how to get to where you needed to go? The really big question when traveling into foreign territory is, *How will you look after yourself if and when there is no one else to look after you?*

This is exactly where all those hours of reading and of doing your homework come in handy. In school when you didn't do your homework, maybe your teacher marked you down a few points. In this sort of situation, if you don't do your homework, the consequences may prove to be more dire, and it will be nobody's fault but your own.

Thus, the moral of the story is to READ! Study. Practice the language. Get a grasp on exchange rates. Know the customs (as much as possible). And try, to the best of your ability, to leave your own cultural beliefs at home. If you are able to step out of what you've always believed, the world will open itself to you, and locals will open their doors. The term "Ugly American" exists for good reason. It describes those who travel all the way to a small village in central Laos to demand a hamburger and fries, and then get angry when told that it's not on the menu. Be a good traveler, and prepare yourself as much as possible for what's in store. The point of traveling is to not feel like you are at home in the States. Taking yourself out of your comfort zone will prove to be both a daunting challenge and an exciting adventure, but you'll have more fun if you are prepared.

That said, let me explain some of the ways I decided to chameleonize myself in order to slip through the watchful gaze of those who might prey on me for being a solo female traveler overseas. For that first trip to Asia (after doing my pretrip research!), I decided that I didn't need to be blonde. I had read that Bangkok had a slimy tentacle in the underground trade of white women and that street vermin often targeted non-brown-haired women. Why tempt the fates? I took myself down to the drug store a week before my departure and bought a bottle of chestnut brown hair dye. Though I didn't go as far as getting colored contact lenses, and while my green eyes probably still sifted me apart from the other women on the streets of Bangkok who almost all had brown hair and brown eyes, I felt more confident walking down those roads knowing that I wasn't a beaming lighthouse of blonde hair, which gave me the courage to go to more of the places that I wanted to go. Plus, it was kind of fun sporting a new identity in a new country. It helped me to further—temporarily—leave my life back home by becoming someone else. I kind of felt like Cat Woman sneaking through the city streets, blending into buildings, and disappearing when I felt like it. Talk about feeling empowered!

Another tactic that was and continues to be helpful is to the best of my ability plan my trip so that my plane arrives in daylight hours, so that I can get a taxi to my hotel and get settled before the shadows of night descend. One of the best pieces of advice that I was given before my first trip abroad that I've followed for every one of my trips where I'd be landing in a place where English wasn't spoken, was to write down, clearly and simply, the name and address of my accommodation translated into the local language, so that all I had to do was hand the card with this information to my taxi driver at the airport. This ensured there weren't any communication breakdowns and I arrived where I intended to arrive. Doing this has been especially helpful when I've been dazed after a long flight, like on that first trip to Asia, which landed me in Bangkok at two in the morning. (Ironically I was unable to arrange to get a daylight arrival time my very first time abroad.) But that little piece of paper was like gold, and it got me to where I needed to go in a city bigger than Los Angeles, where not many of the taxi drivers speak even a lick of English.

Something else I did on that trip to more smoothly integrate myself into my new surroundings was upon arrival to each new country I entered was to go to the local market and buy local-looking clothes. In Thailand I bought long-sleeve shirts made of a thin material that kept me cool by keeping the sun off me yet keeping me demurely covered in the style of Thai women. When entering Indonesia, I purchased multiple sarongs and wore them in a multitude of ways: as a long skirt, as a shawl, and, when journeying to more conservative Islamic areas, as a head covering. In Laos, I bought an embroidered sash (as these sashes needed to be worn by women into all of the temples and sacred caves) as well as a pair of shin-high super baggy shorts made from a local fiber that all of the rice farmers and other locals wore to beat the incredibly humid air and scorching sun. Not only did I camouflage myself and stay cooler in a respectful, "non-standoutish" sort of way, but I created all sorts of opportunities for myself to meet and have tea with many different locals who were impressed—quite tickled actually!—that a woman from the United States would go to such great lengths to blend in and experience life the way they did. I was invited to have meals,

Figure 3.1 In this photo, I'm not sure who had more fun: me being outfitted by this kindly shop owner or the shop owner who thought it was quite interesting to see a Westerner taking her fashion cue from a small Laotian village. (Luang Prubang, Laos, July 1999.) Photo courtesy of Katherine June.

Figure 3.2 I feel honored to be the guest of honor, after being invited to an all-night shadow puppet performance by a Javanese girl who I met on the bus going to the local market. (Java, August 2000.)

hold babies, meet grandparents, walk and talk in rice fields, attend a wedding, and in Java I was even invited to be the guest of honor at one village's annual shadow puppet performance (Figure 3.2), all because of my attempts at getting to know the local people by being more like them. Danger never even had the chance to sniff in my direction as local people took me under their protective wings.

Those are a few examples of how I planned ahead on the *physical* level in order to keep my experiences favorable while abroad. Following are a couple of other things that I've done and that you might want to consider doing on a *bureaucratic* level before leaving home. These steps may seem tedious and you may feel like a circus poodle jumping through flaming hoops, but by doing so, you are building yourself a safety net that may come in handy once you're overseas and all your money, contacts, and connections are back home.

First things first: Make at least three copies of your passport, itinerary, insurance card(s), and any other important documents that you have and leave them with at least three different people whom you can trust to be there for you should you need them. Be sure they won't be gone on their own vacations during the entire length of your trip. If you need this information given to you over the phone, you must be sure that someone will first be there *to* answer the phone. I know this sounds obvious, but I'm spelling it out because it can be critical.

Here's a great example, or two or three, of what not to do: A friend of mine had gone to Thailand a year before my own departure and had gotten caught up in a scam where the local cafe owner was selling marijuana to international travelers, and then the oblivious travelers would get on their scooters to drive the sandy trail through the jungle back to their beach bungalows only to be pulled over into a police roadblock set up a mile or so from the cafe. The police and the cafe owners were working together to make money for the town by arresting travelers by busting them for possession of marijuana, and then charging them ludicrous amounts of their national currency in exchange for their freedom. In cases where the travelers didn't have enough money in their wallets to pay the fine upon their arrest, they were immediately transported (first) to the nearby port town, and then were shipped off to Bangkok where more officials waited to be paid off.

Well, my friend was one of those unlucky few who, although he had money in his bank account, didn't have the cash he needed on hand and thus was placed on the next police boat off this small island town. Terrified of what his not-so-distant future held, he racked his brain about who to call for help. But then he wasn't even sure about how his friends or family might help him, as he had not left copies of his credit cards or bank account information with any of them. A very long story made short, my friend unfortunately sat in the jail on Koh Samui for almost a week and was then transferred to Bangkok. Fortunately (very fortunately), an English friend of his who he'd been traveling with showed up with a Thai lawyer and together they worked to contact people back home who could help arrange a money transfer from my friend's account to the proper Thai authorities. If the Englishman hadn't shown up, my friend might still be enduring the filth and stink of a Thai jail cell, and none of us would have known where he'd disappeared to.

How could my friend have better ensured his safety? Well, besides not partaking in an illicit drug in a country with a zero-tolerance drug policy (duh), he could've had a copy of his bank account information safely tucked into his passport and placed into a security box back at his bungalow. This would've enabled him access right then and there to the funds he needed to be set free (or at least from the port town, rather than spending time in a jail in Bangkok as well). He was given a few phone calls, two of which were wasted on people who didn't pick up, but even if they did, they did not have copies of all of the important documents that I listed earlier and so helping him out would have proven to be even more challenging. The fact that the English guy took it upon himself to go get a Thai lawyer to get my friend out of jail was an act of divine grace or at least an act of a very, very good friend. The point is that there should be a few people back home who have a general idea of your time frame and whereabouts by leaving them an itinerary, and who can start arranging help for you should they not hear from you for an extended period of time. (I e-mailed my dad once a week or not more than every ten days and informed him of where I was, where I was going next, and if anyone was traveling with me.) Trusted people should also have access to your money by way of copies of your credit cards and bank account information. And should you lose your passport, it will be light-years easier to get it replaced if you (1) have a copy with you, and (2) if you don't have a copy with you, someone back home does and can fax it to whatever embassy you need it to be sent to.

Which leads me to the next precautionary step.

If at all possible, find a contact or two who live in the country where you will be traveling. In-country help will prove to be much more, well, helpful than out-of-country assistance if and when a time arrives when you find yourself needing some financial, medical, or bureaucratic support. When I told my dad that I was heading to Southeast Asia in the late spring of 1999, he did this homework for me because I had zero connections in that part of the world. He researched friends and friends of friends who lived in the countries where I'd be traveling to and proceeded to contact them all to ask if they'd be willing to assist me should I require assistance while I was abroad. He then printed out a page worth's of names and phone numbers (and even some addresses) so that I had a copy in hand to place with my other important documents. He also e-mailed me their information so that I had access to each contact in two separate places. I never had to use any of their numbers, but it still gave me a little peace of mind knowing that I would have someone to call should I find myself in some crazy, unforeseen situation.

If you have no way of creating in-country contacts, don't worry. You can still create a very worthy support network by creating a list of important numbers that can be easily accessed. Again, be sure to e-mail yourself a copy of all the following information as well as having a hard copy tucked into your other important travel papers (as Internet access might not be an option). You will need a phone list of the following helpful resources: domestic and international calling card phone and PIN numbers, your country's embassy (both domestic and international offices), your international travel insurance company, friends and family back home, and contact information for the domestic and international offices of the airlines on which you travel. Finding this information abroad seems like it would be easy, and it is if you can find an available Internet connection. But again, nothing is guaranteed when you're traveling, especially in developing countries.

In a pinch, it'll save you time and frustration if you've already created this list of helpful numbers. I lovingly refer to it as the "Shovel List," as it has the capability of digging you out when you're in over your head. Next is a little story to illustrate how the Shovel List helped me out while I was abroad in Central America.

I went on my third surf trip to Costa Rica in the summer of 2009. I was two weeks into my trip at Dominical, and, along with a heavy haze that had settled itself like an elephant resting on the sea, the waves had been fickle and mostly nonexistent. I was starting to think that all the hype about Costa Rica being a fun surf destination was all lies until one morning I finally woke to clear skies and head-high swell. Without hesitation I paddled out into the early morning light and got several fun rides for the first hour. However, I then began to notice that dark clouds were gathering on the horizon, a strong wind was picking up, and the waves were starting to become much bigger and super warbly. I felt like an aquatic cowgirl trying to wrangle an enormous bucking ocean-cow into a faraway pen; not at all an easy thing to do, and very, very tiring. I decided to catch a wave in because I knew the conditions were rapidly exceeding my experience level. I had a difficult time getting in though because the wave I had caught only took me half-way in, and I then had to navigate a very turbulent inside section. The water in the space between me and the shore began to create huge overhead closeouts (imagine the Great Wall of China rising up high over your head, turning itself into water and then slamming itself down with powerful force, and then doing it again and again). Along with these closeouts, a heavy suction sought to draw me back out to sea each and every time a wave broke. After quite a fight, I finally made it to the beach and proceeded to sit there for a long time, just grateful to be on solid ground again. I caught my breath, then went back to my bungalow to rinse off. Once I had showered, I quickly headed back to the village to get my daily fix of huevos rancheros and cafe con leche. I was starving after my victory at sea.

About twenty minutes later, I was back on the dirt track walking past the spot I had just been surfing. I looked out and saw a whitish lump lying on the dune not far from where the ocean pounded the beach. There were several people around this mysterious lump and as I picked my way around the people, I saw a young woman, about my age, pale in the face and slightly blue in the lips. I froze. I caught my breath in my throat. This woman had just been swimming where I'd been surfing and now she was dead on the beach, having drowned in the time it took me to drop off my board and grab my breakfast money.

To say that I was traumatized would be an understatement. Suddenly my solo surf trip seemed like a ridiculously foolish idea and a fear entered my bones that I couldn't shake for days to come. I no longer wanted to surf in that town and I no longer wanted to be alone. The realization hit me hard that it could've been me, dead and alone on the beach. The degree of sadness I felt for this woman—and for her family, as I put myself in their shoes— dropped me into such a deep level of despair that it made it difficult for me to function for the rest of the day. I wanted to go home right then and there, and by nighttime I was hatching a spontaneous trip northward.

On my previous trips to Costa Rica, it had been my personal experience that the Costa Rican phone operators had been less than helpful, and because I'm not completely fluent in Spanish, I'd had a difficult time making phone calls. But on this trip, I'd come prepared. I had my Shovel List tucked into my safe deposit box back at the office of the bungalows where I was staying, and in the midst of my intense emotional upset, all I had to do was get the phone contact list and dial. There was no need to have to walk around in my distraught state trying to find a shop that sold international calling cards; the number was on top of the list. I didn't have to dial myself in circles trying to find the number for Continental Airlines, it was fourth on the list. And it only took me a second to reach out to a friend back home, as his number was second on the list. Under normal circumstances I would've dialed him from memory, but because I was such an emotional wreck in that moment, even his number had gone missing from my memory. Within an hour, I had changed my flight, had found the emotional support that I desperately needed, and had found rides to and from the airport.

I can't stress enough how important it is to have all these phone number ducks sitting in a row before you go abroad. You will save yourself from a serious headache by just taking care of this simple step. Things can change rapidly. Repeat: *so rapidly*! You can be your own superhero if you've got the backup you need already in place and ready to go should you need to initiate a plan B (or C, D, or E).

And here's another note on being your own superhero. Should some sort of disturbing upheaval find its way into your itinerary, there are a couple of quick-fix, on-the-fly techniques you can use. Now, before I disclose what these techniques are, I'm going to ask that you take a deep breath and as you exhale, try and let go of any judgments you may have about these words: *alternative approaches to keeping yourself safe*. Did you manage it? Are you feeling open-minded? If not, take another breath and try again. Continue until you feel ready and then read on.

Stepping Outside the Box

The following are what I'd consider "alternative approaches to safety" because they're not exactly what you'd read about in a mainstream how-to travel book, which is some of what I included earlier. No, the following are strategies that I've learned along the way from various sources, including martial artist friends, books written by Native American and Guatemalan shamans, through my yoga practice, and from my Reiki teacher. (Note: Reiki is a form of energy healing that is more profound, in my experience, than just about any other healing modality. It creates in the practitioner a keen sensitivity to the flow of positive and negative energy in oneself and in the environment around them. It sharpens one's ability to read what's behind someone's words and hones one's intuition to detect the intentions of others that come from below face value... in other words, to be able to pick up on undercurrents and to deal with them appropriately. More on this later.)

If you're already having an adverse reaction to this last paragraph and are feeling skeptical, take a break and go rent the movie *Men Who Stare at Goats*. Or read the article at the website posted next, and it will provide you with ways that the U.S. Government has employed alternative practices, such as those that I'm about to describe, based on yogic, shamanic, and other traditional methods: http://www.wired.com/dangerroom/2009/11/psychic-spies-acid-guinea-pigs-new-age-gis-the-true-men-who-stare-at-goats/. (Although I'm kind of being tongue in cheek about mentioning the movie and the article connected to it, there is, actually, some poignant relevancy to them.) Following is an illustration of some of my own experiences of a couple of interesting out-of-the-ordinary safety tactics.

Technique one is learning how to *energetically* camouflage yourself. Now this may sound silly, but it is an ancient technique that has been used cross-culturally from samurais and ninjas to shamans and witches. Don't worry: There is no eye of newt and tongue of bat powder needed. It is simply a way of blending into the background by calming your breath, quieting your inner dialogue, and using the power of visualization to energetically blend yourself into your surroundings.

Now, to skeptics this may sound extremely far-fetched. But before you vomit pessimistic judgments all over this technique, let me clarify an important point: This strategy is much more Jedi mind trick than an actual David-Copperfield-type of disappearance. Don't expect that you will just vanish into thin air. (Though, who knows? Maybe you will!) A simple way of thinking about this is to think of a situation that you've experienced where someone was *really* making themselves noticed. What was that person doing? How did he or she sound? What were their body movements like? Now imagine what the opposite of this behavior might evoke. When a person is able to take on an air of calm awareness yet remains energetically distant and removed, that person will fare well in walking through a scene unnoticed; or perhaps *physically* noticed, but because their energy is so downplayed, they make it impossible for others to engage them.

Just for fun, try practicing this technique at a party if you don't want to be seen (or bothered) by someone. That way you'll have some practice under your belt and will be more ready to use it when you really need it to work for you. Here's what to do:

Become very still inside by taking deep breaths. Imagine that there is a dial within you that you can mentally turn down to *energetically* dim the light that you naturally emanate. (This dial can also be turned up when you want to be seen.) As you snuff out your light, also imagine that you are dissipating into the colors that are in the environment around you. It's like watching your hand as someone in the room slowly turns the light down until it has completely gone out. Your hand goes from being visible to being completely *enmeshed with* the darkness. As you visualize yourself dimming and vaporizing into particles, you successfully begin to energetically merge into the environment in which you are standing. Like a chameleon changes its color to fit its surroundings, you enable yourself to change your energetic configuration in order to make yourself unseen.

I have used this tactic in a wide spectrum of situations. One as harmless as being at a party and not wanting to be seen by an annoying acquaintance, to having to walk to my hotel alone at night in a bustling Indonesian city and feeling the need to blend myself into my surroundings in order to go unseen by eyes that may have wanted to rob me or worse.

Technique two can be used before, during, or after technique one. It is the practice of imagining a bright light *around* your entire being that acts as a kind of shelter in which any negative energy that seeks to harm you will be repelled by the force of your white-light shield. I have this kind of inside joke with myself that I say in my mind to turn on this light. A friend and I started saying it during our college years when we would go out dancing. She and I were both very much into yoga and chi gong, and so had an awareness about "chi" (energy) and how to draw it in or repel it. When we would get unwanted attention from whatever drunken loser happened to be around us on the dance floor, we would look at each other and say, "Chi shield up!"

It was kind of like that cartoon from the 1980s where those superhero twins would touch one another, then say, "Wonder Twin powers activate!" and suddenly they'd find themselves surrounded by an invisible force that kept the bad guys out and kept their vibrant life force in.

We'd activate our chi shields by imagining a huge white light around us, would draw our energy into ourselves, and would refrain from engaging any part of the imposing force fields around us. And I can tell you, it *always* worked. It's like putting up an invisible protective wall in the subtlest of ways. The space invaders got the picture to stay away from us, and we were freed up to dance.

On that first trip to Southeast Asia, I happened to discover that this works in international dance club situations too. Energy, it turns out, is a universal language.

Of course, technique two also works outside dance clubs. You can use it while walking down streets; in the middle of heated or emotional discussions with friends, family, or strangers (to keep their negativity from affecting you); in situations with scary animals (animals are *very* sensitive to energy and you can let them know energetically that you are off-limits as a meal or as an attackee); and in any other of a number of possibly threatening situations.

I'd also recommend a combination of techniques one and two, where you first create a protective energy shield around you *and then* visualize yourself camouflaging into your surroundings. In conjunction with your intuition, you'll enable yourself to sense an iffy situation coming your way and be able to employ your defenses *before* the situation has you entangled.

This brings me to the third technique: that of using your intuition, which I touched on at the beginning of this article but want to expand on briefly. Part of being a good traveler is knowing how and when to escape certain situations. You can do this by developing your intuition, and the way you do this is by listening to it, and then by following its guidance. *There is a fine line between keeping yourself safe and being paranoid,* and your intuition can act as the gauge between these two frames of mind. How many times have you heard an inner voice telling you something and then proceeded to ignore it? And down the road, found that your intuition had been correct and you chastised yourself for not listening to it? I think it happens to all of us at some point, since from a very early age, most of us are socialized to follow an authority outside of ourselves. We ask parents, friends, doctors, bankers, teachers—even strangers!—and many other people outside of ourselves for their advice on our personal matters. And while gaining the opinions of others can be helpful, ultimately it is the quiet voice within each of us that will tell us exactly what it is that we need to know in order to take the next step in our lives. Our intuition exists for the sole purpose of keeping us safe and happy. It has the ability to direct us toward being at the right place at the right time, while pulling us away from being at the wrong place at the wrong time. As important as the other techniques are in dealing with danger, there is nothing as important as listening to your intuition to help you avoid danger altogether.

I have been in many situations that upon first glance would seem like I wasn't using common sense and was putting myself in harm's way. But a gut instinct told me that I could trust the situation and that the person or place in question would turn out fine for me. The exact opposite of that is true, too. People and places that seemed trustworthy on a superficial level actually sent out an undercurrent of distrust, and (again) it was that inner voice that told me to leave the situation as soon as possible. Following this instinct, I have kept myself out of who-knows-what sort of catastrophes. And by not following it, I've ended up kicking myself when the situation ended up exploding, like I knew—intuitively—that it would.

Take the time and get to know your inner voice before, during, and after your travels. It is a lifelong learning curve. And like any muscle, the more you exercise it, the stronger it becomes. Exercise your inner knowing by listening to it when it speaks to you, and then by following what it says. *Begin to discern between the voice of fear and the voice of truth,* and know that the only way to make the distinction between the two is to first practice hearing both of them and then to follow the sensations in your body that each of the voices brings up for you.

For me personally, the voice of fear tends to ignite all my muscles into a tight, pretzel-like anxious feeling; my stomach starts feeling acidic, my mouth gets dry, and my bones start to feel heavy as though my body is slowing its pace. Meanwhile, the voice of my intuition fills my body with a certain lightness; there's s deep resonance of knowing, often felt through sensations of warmth, relaxation, inner peace, and a sense of courage and perseverance. Take note, however, that everybody is different, and every individual will experience their intuition uniquely. That is why it is so important for you to begin working with your own, so that you know the various signals, sensations, feelings, and signs that your personal intuition uses to guide you toward all things joyful and wholesome, and away from third-world kidnappings and other such unpleasantries.

The final topic that I'd like to cover before closing this chapter is that which many of us learned at a very young age: That of *always* treating others how you, yourself, would like to be treated, especially if and when you are abroad. Following the Golden Rule is just as important as any of the physical precautionary tactics you can take while traveling to ensure your safety. Worldwide, nobody likes dealing with a jerk. And while negative experiences still happen to good people, the positive energy you put out certainly helps by acting like a magnet to attract positive experiences to you. In a confusing transaction in a small local textiles shop, who do you think gets the fair outcome he is looking for: The belligerent man screaming at the shopkeeper to meet his demands or the respectful man who calmly works with the shopkeeper to figure out where the discrepancy occurred? In being arrogant, arrogance is often returned.

Your positive attitude and respect for others also has the ability to attract needed help and support from trustworthy strangers, while keeping

Figure 3.3 Even though we spoke two very different languages, we managed to understand each other perfectly when it came to sing-a-longs and clapping games. (Volunteer work in Phattalung, Thailand, August 1999.)

Figure 3.4 The beauty of open-air dining: good food and great company. Here, Laotian children were serving up barbecued bananas with a huge side of laughter. (Phongsali, Laos, 1999.)

away those that might want to take advantage of you. Over my several years of traveling abroad, perfect strangers have come out of the woodwork to assist me along the way. I firmly believe that I attracted these people into my life because when the shoe was on the other foot—when I've seen someone with a need that I knew I could assist with—I've stepped up to be of service.

I'm not giving you the following list as a way to pat myself on the back for the good deeds I've done or to boast my respectful diligence toward helping out strangers. I'm sure many of us have a similar list. My point is that whether or not we believe in karma, what we put out returns to us in some form. Think of your energy as a boomerang. You throw assistance out there; assistance returns. Throw disrespect and arrogance; see what you get!

I never travel without a first-aid kit (and to my great shock, most people don't travel with them) and so I've found myself on most my surf trips with sterilized tweezers in hand, picking pieces of coral reef out of many a surfer's shoulder; washing them, bandaging them, and sending them away with clean bandages for later. I've administered grapefruit seed extract (GSE) to those with intestinal issues, given packets of Emergen-C® to the dehydrated, and I've been a shoulder to cry on for younger women who were traveling abroad for the first time and were awash in homesickness. I've played with local children as if they were my own, have watched over storekeeper's wares while they've run out to grab tea. I've helped carry the bags of women who were overburdened with children, chickens, and bags of rice, bananas, and beans. There was even a time when I stepped up to save the life of a street cat that was about to be mauled by a hungry dog.

In return, like I said, perfect strangers have shown up for me, like angels in human form. There was the time I got on the wrong bus in the heart of Bangkok, only to realize very quickly that I was extremely lost. The young man next to me noticed my stress as I clumsily unfolded and refolded my map several times, desperately trying to glean any words on it and out on the street, not written in Thai characters. He introduced himself with very broken English and asked if I needed help. In the end, we were able to play charades long enough for me to convey where I was needing to go and he readily helped me off that bus, walked me several blocks to a church where he asked a young woman to take me with her (whom he—randomly and serendipitously—knew would soon be heading in the direction that I needed to go), and two hours and five bus transfers later had gotten me safely to my enigmatic destination, only to stay with me while I ran the errand I needed to, and then escorted me safely all the way back to my hotel. I don't know if anyone in the United States would even go that far out of their way for me, the way these Thai people did. I was beside myself at their generosity!

Then there was the time I picked up Bali Belly, a horrible consequence for absentmindedly rinsing my toothbrush with the tap water in Kuta, and was in the middle of an eighteen-hour bus and ferry ride from Bali to Java when it kicked in, full force. I was vomiting into a wastebasket that ended up having a small hole in the bottom of it—you do the math—while trying to balance myself over the bus's toilet, while the bus itself was screaming around the jungle-like corners of Java's interior. After several hours of this, I was beyond exhausted. With nothing left in me (literally) and my final destination rapidly approaching, I was scared and confused about where I was going to go and how I was going to get myself and my heavy backpack there. Another traveler, this time a middle-aged man from Florida, asked me if I needed assistance. At his kindness and at my sudden relief that I was not alone to deal with this, I burst into tears. When I finally calmed down, we got off that god-awful bus, and he carried my bags to a taxi, which he hailed and paid for, and then assisted me to a hotel. Unlike me, he had already worked out where he was heading. He checked me into a room upstairs that had a bath and hot water (a real luxury in that part of the world), and he checked himself into a room downstairs. For the week that followed, he checked in on me a few times daily, bringing water, ginger tea, soup, and rice. He even asked me if there was anyone back home that I would like for him to contact to let them know that I was so sick. By the next week, with this stranger's help, I was feeling myself again—and without him, I have no idea the miserable fate I might've suffered. (I don't even want to imagine what it would've been like for me had that man not appeared.)

These two experiences illustrate the more dramatic situations I've lived through that strangers have helped me out of, but there are countless others that, although smaller in impact, have still been of consequential importance. It's never bad advice to treat others how you want to be treated but (as mentioned) when you are abroad, you are in a world where things don't always function how they do back home, and so you are placed in a position where it can only benefit you to be hypervigilant in your respect and helpfulness toward others. In this way, you're setting yourself up to receive the assistance you need, when you need it. It's a win–win situation, and believe me, it's so much more fun being the one who people want to help out than the one people want to knock over.

Putting It All Together

In closing, I'll be the first to admit that bad things happen all over this planet, every second of the day. I can't get over the irony that I am writing this conclusion on the night that my truck got broken into. I parked it on the side of the highway across the street from the beach, then went for a fun two-hour hike up into the hills with my boyfriend. As we were silently jogging the remainder of the way back, the sun was setting and a gorgeous full moon was rising over a powdery blue horizon. During our run, I had mentally worked out all sorts of challenges I've been having lately, including how to wrap up this chapter, and was coming down the hill feeling victorious. The moon as my witness, I had won the battle of my internal conflicts, and I was going to get in my truck to drive home feeling clear and at peace. I felt happy and was looking forward to our evening plans of going downtown to have dinner. Over pad thai and fresh spring rolls, we were going to daydream about the possibility of taking a winter surf trip to Nicaragua. And that's the thing about plans; they often change without even a whiff of warning.

When we reached my truck, I dug out the spare key from its hiding place and opened the passenger side door to a sight that caused instant confusion. I just stood there staring at the ransacked vehicle that was blankly staring back at me. The entire front seat was filled with debris that had been pulled out from under the seats, from inside the glove box, and from the truck's cabinets inside the covered bed. My heart sank. Did a raccoon do this? An enormous rat, maybe? (I had been smelling a weird, mildewy, woodlike scent in the cab recently. Had the rat rebelled while we'd been running?) But then I heard my boyfriend say, in what sounded like a slow, faraway voice, "Oh no, they got you."

His words took an immeasurable amount of time to float through the ether land in my ears and settle into the part of my brain that detects certain input as something of significance.

"Who got me? Why? Wait ... what?" I asked, as I stood there numb, trying to piece together what he was talking about. Then the weight of his words plowed over me and I suddenly felt how the Swedish Chef on the Muppets must've felt when he got plunked over the head with that dead, silvery fish; it hurt and it stunk. Ouch.

This wasn't the work of any beach or forest creature. This was a human-made mess, and things from my truck had been stolen. We'd locked the doors and had hidden our valuables out of sight; I'd even hid the hide-a-key before we left the house so as not to let anyone in the parking lot see me do it.

I'm a conscientious truck-parker. I've jogged and surfed this spot for several years, and though there is a consistent flow of sparkling glass on the ground, where other people's cars have been broken into, I just always thought that it was some tourist's fault who didn't take the right precautions (like I do) and therefore became easy prey for these coastal perusers whose day job it is to burglarize cars. But now, here I was looking at my own truck disheveled by violating hands, even after I put all my safety strategies in place. Damn them! As I rummaged through the scattered remains in my truck, the list of missing objects grew rapidly, including my work and house keys, my phone (with all my contact numbers), a few pieces of clothing, three books filled with CDs, a bag, and at this point, I'm still not sure what else. We cleared enough space on the seats to be able to sit, got in, and used the spare key to drive ourselves home.

With our dinner plans fizzled, I made us salad and tamales at home, while my boyfriend got on the computer and helped me sort out my phone, make a police report, and contact my car insurance company. I've got at least an hour of cleanup to do inside the truck the next morning, which also happens to be my last day of summer vacation. I've spent the last two weeks in the serenity of Colorado's high country, only to return to my hometown to have to contend with this random violation.

Yet, it's an absolutely perfect opportunity to highlight the idea that I started this chapter with: We can only protect ourselves as much as fate allows, and that sometimes, for whatever reason, bad things happen to good people. However, there is a very important caveat to this statement. Statistically, if people take precautions and are diligent in looking out for themselves, their belongings, and other people, the probability that they will be victimized is much, much less than someone who constantly throws care to the wind and mindlessly stumbles through their day. Danger is patient and thorough. Predators will find the cracks and trails that sloppy prey leaves. Yet, as I'm seeing tonight, predators sometimes have the ability to strike invisibly even when measures have been taken to keep them at bay. There are often bigger lessons to learn when things like this happen.

That night I felt like my lesson was to let go of the past. My phone was filled with contacts and pictures of old friends whose friendships have melted away. The CDs that were stolen were filled with music that held me to years past, memories that I don't necessarily need to reminisce. And the funny part of this that really highlights this idea for me is that one of the articles of clothing that was stolen was an old pair of board shorts that once belonged to a former boyfriend of mine whom I'd really like to see disappear completely out of my life. And so in a way, these creepers have helped me out. In a way, they hit the restart button for me. I am now liberated from yet another chunk of the past, and am now able to enter my current life with more awareness and vitality, as those chains are now gone.

With all this in mind, I think: Well, what were the bigger lessons for my friend to learn when he ended up in that Thai jail cell? Answer: He became aware of how many people are rotting in Thai prisons because they cannot afford the few hundred dollars it takes to get them out, and therefore it became his mission to get money to them once he was free and back home in the States. He did this by giving me a check for $1,000 when he found out I was going to Thailand that following year after his arrest, so that I could give it to a Jesuit priest whom he had met while he (my friend) was in jail, who assiduously dispensed all financial donations equally into the files of the (mostly) African men that were in the jails for very minor violations, such as overstaying their visas in order to work.

When trouble happens in our lives, there is sometimes a mysteriously benevolent reason for it. When I became lost in Bangkok, I was on my way to find that Jesuit priest to give him the money, and when I explained this to a perfect stranger (whom I intuitively knew I could trust), who went out of his way to make sure that my friend's donation made it to where it was intended to go. In a way, I think I got lost so that I could meet him, as well as his friend named Maam, who ended up inviting me to stay with her for three days before I returned to the States so that we could share our life's experiences, simply to better understand the humanness of our connection.

That young man on the bus, my Thai friend Maam, the Jesuit priest, a handful of African men sitting in a Bangkok cell, and me were all touched in some way by my friend's arrest. Something that seemed so horribly unfair at the time turned out to be a positive event in the lives of many people.

To say that we are completely powerless as to what happens in our lives would be a lie. In fact, I think we are very powerful creators with the ability to manifest happy, healthy, and safe lives. But life is life. It has unforeseen chapters of many kinds, including illness, theft, and income tax. This puts us in the position of having to choose *how* we perceive the various challenges that come our way, so that our challenges can teach us different ways to float when they threaten to sink our boat. Hopefully this chapter has given you some practical ways to plan the safest route to and from your different destinations in life. I also hope that you'll practice some of the other methods given, when the unplannable comes swaggering down your side of the street.

Remember: Although anything can happen, we can empower ourselves by taking a proactive role by adopting strategies that will serve to keep us safe in daily life at home and while traveling. We can research foreign places before going to them in order to minimize our surprise and to lessen our culture shock, so that we know how to behave appropriately. We can find ways to chameleonize ourselves so that we blend in better, lessening our chances of sticking out and becoming an easy target. We can create safety nets by making a list of contacts to call (both domestically and internationally) to more easily reach help if and when we need it. We can leave copies of important documents behind with loved ones, so that when we need help, they already have the needed paperwork in hand to better serve us.

And then there are the "alternative" techniques in keeping safe. As empowered humans, we can call up a protective force field of light to protect ourselves, others, and our belongings. (This is something I actually do on a regular basis when I park my truck in sketchy places; but that night my car was broken into, I was enmeshed in a conversation while parking and completely forgot to do it. An interesting thing for me to pay attention to, I think!) We can also turn down our inner light that draws others to us, and can energetically blend into our surroundings by doing so.

Then there is the enormous power of intuition. Culturally, our sixth sense has been degraded to a figment of our imaginations, something we are taught to ignore. But when we strengthen this sense by paying attention to it, it has the capability of leading us toward happiness as well as safety. When perceived as a survival tool, we begin to recognize our intuition as an ally whose sole purpose is to keep watch over our best interests. In combination with our intellect, we create a decision-making team that will absolutely lead us toward the happier outcome of any given situation. Why not develop this sense and see what begins to happen?

And while we're at it, why not throw out a boomerang of loving kindness and compassion by treating others as we would like to be treated. We never know what the future holds, but if we build a net of respect for others by being helpful and trustworthy, when a time comes that we need support, others will surely rise up to care for those needs.

I've traveled to over a dozen countries as a woman on her own, and here I am writing about how I've survived it all, only to come home to be victimized four miles from my house. But what a beautiful way to wrap up this chapter, by saying that I *know* that I've done what I *can* do to keep myself out of harm's way, and though a shadow or two occasionally falls on my path, I can learn important lessons from them and can carry on without delay.

In closing, life can sometimes get dark, and we need both the rational mind *and* our gut instincts to create safe passage. We each enter this world with a Torch of Intuition—the instinctual, internal compass that has the ability to lead us through the fog when our human eyes cannot find the

Figure 3.5 When in Rome (or Bali, as it were). Here I am trying to walk my talk, by doing as the Balinese do, (Ubud, Bali, June 1999.)

way. However, the torch without its fire is only half-way helpful. To harness its full power, we must be sure to *ignite* it on the Flames of Preparation, which signify the logical and physical *actions* we can take to help ensure our safety.

Together, the Torch and the Flames burn brightly, lighting the path ahead.

Don't Outrun Your Headlights ... or Your Guardian Angel

4

DALE L. JUNE

Contents

At 85 miles per hour, you're not driving a car; you're aiming it!

—Unk

A car traveling at 65 miles per hour takes the entire length of a football field to come to a stop ... unless it is stopped by some obstacle like another car, a tree, or a pole ...

If all the cars in the world were lined up end to end, some fool would pull out and try to pass them all.

—Unk

Don't Outrun Your Headlights

It's approximately 355 miles from Jacksonville to Key Biscayne, straight down Interstate 95, from the northern part of Florida to nearly its southernmost tip. You drive to Miami and take a left turn across the causeway and there are the beautiful Keys. Home to many rich and famous people, including, in the 1970s, President Nixon.

I was on a protective detail in Jacksonville, working the three-to-eleven shift. One particular night, I and another agent were relieved early and told to drive two of the detail cars to Key Biscayne and exchange them for two others "and be back in time for your shift tomorrow." It was nearly ten at night, after fully filling the gas tanks and going to a local Jacksonville restaurant famous for its barbeque and "Southern-style, home-cooked chicken dinners," that we were ready for the quick journey south.

My fellow agent took the lead, with me following. His "lead" meant he drove in one lane and I in another with the front bumper of my car even with the rear bumper of his car. In the 1970s there was a movie called *Smokey and the Bandit*. The theme song (by co-star Jerry Reed) featured two lines that went "East bound and down/We have a long way to go and a short time to get there." This was the thought in my mind as we "hammered down and put the pedal to the metal" (in other words, we put the gas pedal to the floor and let the car roll). I found a great country-western radio station and turned the volume up to hear it better over the sound of the wind and the roar of the engine as I tapped out the rhythms with my right hand and drove with my left.

Not to say we weren't wasting time but to paraphrase another country song, "Wolfcreek Pass," the white lines looked like dots and the utility poles looked like a picket fence. At one point, I looked down at my speedometer to see how fast we were going. I assumed we were going about ninety. In those days, the speedometer in cars was marked by a red line (similar to a thermometer) that moved in a horizontal position across the numbered line. When I looked down, there was no red line! It had gone completely out of sight past the 120 miles per hour mark!

By this time, I had long turned off the radio for 100 percent concentration and focus on the road ahead, using the taillights of the cars in front and the headlights of oncoming traffic on the other side of the divided highway as guidelines to "map" the road ahead as to curves and obstacles that might cause problems or hazards, because I was outracing my headlight distances; both of my hands were gripping the steering wheel in eleven and four o'clock positions, and I tapped the brake slightly when entering a curve and accelerated halfway through.

Before long, the city of Miami came into view and as we entered the city limits, I saw a blinking red light behind. The Dade County patrol officer stopped both of us and said, "Men, I have you going seventy-five in a fifty-mile zone."

"Seventy-five?" I said to myself. "We must have been going at least ninety-five!"

After a quick explanation of our mission, the officer extended a professional courtesy and allowed us to continue on our way. A quick check-in at the hotel and a short sleep, a change of car, and we were on our way again back to Jacksonville in time for lunch and our next shift.

"Drive 55; Drive to Arrive Alive"

Average speed going to Miami: 104 miles per hour (which included "pit stops" for gas). Average speed returning to Jacksonville: 110 miles per hour. We were lucky. We certainly outran our headlights that quick night, but not our guardian angel.

... Don't Outrun Your Guardian Angel

Ahhh ... The joy of rush hour. We are all like millions of displaced ants, singlemindedly trying to find our way, no one caring about the other, only the speed with which we arrive at our destinations. Heartless souls having no true direction ... only predestined mundane routines.

—Waukita Ray

What Does One-Tenth of a Second Mean to You?

Buckle Your Seatbelts

*Lucille Groat**

Do you know what happens in the first fatal seconds after a car going 55 miles per hour hits a solid object?

In the first tenth of a second, the front bumper and grill collapse.

In the second tenth of a second, the hood crumbles, rising from the ground striking the windshield as the spinning rear wheels lift off the ground. Simultaneously, fenders begin wrapping themselves around the solid object. Although the car's frame has been halted, the rest of the car is still going 55 mph. Instinct causes the driver to stiffen his legs against the crash, and they snap at the joints.

During the third tenth of a second, the steering wheel starts to disintegrate and the steering column aims for the driver's chest. The fourth tenth of a second finds two feet of the car's front end traveling at 55 mph.

In the fifth tenth of a second, the driver is impaled on the steering column and blood rushes into the lungs. The sixth tenth of a second, the impact has built up to the point that the driver's feet are ripped out of tightly laced shoes, the brake pedal breaks off, the car frame buckles in the middle, and the driver's head smashes into the windshield as the rear wheels, still spinning, fall back to earth.

The seventh tenth of a second, hinges break loose, doors fly open and the seat breaks free striking the driver from behind. The seat striking the driver from behind does not bother the driver however. The last three tenths of a second, 8, 9, and 10, mean nothing to the driver because he is already dead.

* As quoted by Cindy Genau, "One Tenth of a Second Is All You Have," University of Delaware Cooperative Extension, http://ag.udel.edu/ncc/cg-onetenthofasecond.html, retrieved June 8, 2012. Originally published in "Newark Outlook," *The Newark Post.*

One tenth of a second or seven tenths of a second means that death plucks a driver as quickly as it takes to blink an eye one time. No time for prayer or to ask God for anything. The clock has run and time is gone. There is no more waiting. You have outrun your guardian angel.

Suicide

5

AZADEH AFSAHI

Contents

Thirty years with the department, most of them spent in a patrol car chasing whores, pimps, and scumbags populating the seamy side of society. There were one or two gunfights that he survived, but the memories haunted him like a bad case of heartburn. He was always downing antacid pills just to quiet the flame that seemed to burn him up. Day after day; weeks and months turned into years. He knew everyone in the department and on the streets of his regular beat. Though the bitterness of knowing he really hadn't made a difference ached inside him, he managed to keep it well hidden. When that time of retirement finally came, he looked forward to it with split vision.

On one side he was anxious to put all those things in the past: the guts, hair, and severed legs and arms scattered on the highway after some drunk driver ran a traffic signal; the homeless man whose skull was smashed by another homeless person who claimed the large city dumpster as his own private reclamation project; the little baby whose mother hadn't put him in a car seat and whose head was decapitated as he went through the windshield. Plus all the other crap he had had to put up with: a stiff bureaucratic administration, and young sergeants and lieutenants with their college-degree experience but who didn't know what good police work really was; working overtime and night shifts in all kinds of weather; telling a mother and father that their son wouldn't be coming home because he was the victim of a drive-by shooting.

He looked forward to retirement, spending time with the family (though now split by a divorce and seeing them now even less than when he was working); no more inspections and rotating shifts. He could do with his time as he wished; maybe go fishing, play golf, watch a high-school baseball game, or just sit on the front porch and soak up the warming sun.

On the other side of the coin, he missed the old times of having a beer after work with his partner; telling stories of past events, burglars he had chased over backyard fences, and the young punks who had no respect for the law. The police culture was his life. The thrill of a "code three" chase, the adrenaline high from confronting and collaring the kid who knocked down the old lady and grabbed her purse, or the dopeheaded schizo who said his friends from Altagora ("A small planet just 139 degrees and a left turn from Mars") were coming to the city and living undetected by earthlings, was always good for a laugh with the retelling.

Now that the retirement ceremony, where eighteen months ago, they gave him an honorary detective's gold badge and a handshake was a thing of the past, he wondered what his life had really meant. He knew there were lots of good memories but now nobody wanted to hear them. As time away from the department grew longer, his frequent visits to his old cronies became fewer and fewer. Times had changed and the officers were now younger, brasher, and more disrespectful. He hadn't made friends outside the department and now he sat alone in his small house that had lost all laughter and happiness after his wife left him and the children moved away.

This night, the only light in the house was in the kitchen, casting just enough light into the living room where he sat in his old favorite chair and the lights of the flashing television made the welcome semidarkness his hideaway. A bottle of ninety-proof whiskey was his only companion besides the police show on television. As he drank more and more, his depression took him deeper and deeper into despair. There was about a fourth of the bottle left when he put it down for the last time and picked up his service weapon that had been on his side for all those years. With one slow motion, he placed the gun in his mouth, closed his eyes, and pulled the trigger.

"Suicide is a permanent solution to a temporary problem."[*]

Suicide is a sudden self-inflicted death occurring without forewarning, though there may be indicators of the pending action. Suicide is unanticipated by the survivors. A traumatic death, in addition to being sudden, suicide can be preventable. A sudden, accidental, unexpected, or traumatic death shatters the world of loved ones, leaving the survivors feeling shaken, unsure, and vulnerable. In the next few pages, suicide, suicide prevention, and suicide within the law enforcement community will be explored.

---

[*] Franklin Cook and others have argued that this statement is wrong and may be very misleading with tragic consequences. See Franklin Cook, "Please stop saying, 'Suicide is a permanent solution ....'" March 5, 2010, http://suicidepreventioncommunity.wordpress.com/2010/03/05/please-stop-saying-suicide-is-a-permanent-solution/, retrieved January 10, 2012.

History and Data of Suicide

Among the historically famous who have taken their own lives are Mark Antony, Cleopatra VII of Egypt, Hannibal, Sigmund Freud, Adolf Hitler, Kurt Cobain, Marilyn Monroe, Vincent Van Gogh, Socrates, Yukio Mishima, Ernest Hemmingway, and many more. According to the American Foundation for Suicide Prevention (AFSP), over 34,000 people die each year by suicide. In 2007, according to the latest available data released by the Centers for Disease Control and Prevention, there were 34,598 reported suicide deaths in United States and one million in the world. Suicide is the fourth leading cause of death for adults between the ages of 18 and 65 years in the United States.[*] Every 15 minutes a person commits suicide in the United States and every 40 seconds in the world. According to the Badge of Life Organization, there were 143 police suicides in 2009 compared to 127 deaths in the line of duty.[†]

Officer suicide rates are rising in numbers compared to the general population. The 2009 (most recent study) Badge also provided additional information in regard to the demographics. Ages 40 to 44 are the highest risk of suicide, representing 27 percent of all suicides. Officers with less than ten years on the job had a suicide rate of 17 percent and officers with 20-plus years of service time were at the highest risk. Last but not least 64 percent of all the suicides were a surprise.

Ninety percent of all the people who die by suicide have a diagnosable psychiatric disorder such as major depression (especially when combined with alcohol or drug abuse), bipolar depression, alcohol and drug dependence, schizophrenia, posttraumatic stress disorder, eating disorders, or personality disorder at the time of their death. There are four male suicides for every female suicide, but three times as many females as males attempt suicide. Firearms are the number-one cause of suicide.[‡] Firearms account for 60 percent of all suicides, and death by firearm is the fastest-growing method. Same statistics are true about firearms among police officers: 90 percent of all suicides within the law enforcement community are by firearm. Additionally, 90 percent of the time, an officer is heavily under the influence of alcohol when they decide to end their lives.

Statistics reflect that police have a significantly higher rate of suicide than the national average. According to LaPointe, the most common pathology associated with law enforcement is clinical depression. According to Nancy Gibbs, a *Time* magazine writer, a three-year study by the New York

---

[*] "FactandFigures," American Foundation for Suicide Prevention, http://www.afsp.org/index.cfm?fuseaction=home.viewPage&page_id=04EA1254-BD31-1FA3-C549D77E6CA6AA37
[†] The Badge of Life, http://badgeoflife.com/.
[‡] American Foundation for Suicide Prevention (AFSP), http://www.afsp.org/.

City Police Department found that "police officers were more than twice as likely to kill themselves as were members of the general population."[*]

Statistically, most officers who commit suicides are white males, working patrol, and are entering middle age. Most shoot themselves while off duty and don't have any record of misconduct. There are other methods being used by people who commit suicide such as hanging, jumping off tall buildings, slitting wrists, overdosing on prescribed or over-the-counter medication or sleeping pills, or jumping in front of fast-moving vehicles.

Although women are three times more likely to attempt suicide than men, men are more successful at it, according to the American Foundation for Suicide Prevention. In 2009, 79 percent of all suicides were men. Suicide rates for men spike after age 65; seven times more men over 65 commit suicide than their female peers.

More than 60 percent of all those who die by suicide have major depression. If you include alcoholics, that number rises to 75 percent. In older adults, social isolation is another key contributing factor, which is why older suicide committers are often widowers. (Men often equate depression with "sadness" or other emotions, and fail to realize that common warning signs of depression include fatigue or excessive sleep, agitation and restlessness, trouble concentrating, irritability, and changes in appetite or sleep. Depression is treatable at any age, and most cases are responsive to treatment, according to the National Institute of Mental Health.[†])

In Europe during the sixteenth century, when one took his own life, the state's penalty was to drag the body through the streets, face down, and then be hanged by the feet as a public example. The person was not given a proper burial and his family was forced to leave their hometown. The family was often ridiculed, blamed, and shunned by the rest of the community.[‡]

Sometimes suicide has been used as a form of execution. Perhaps the most famous of Greek suicides was the philosopher Socrates, who was required to drink hemlock to end his life in 399 B.C., after being found guilty of corrupting the youth of Athens. He was against suicide, reasoning that humans belonged to God, so suicide was destruction of God's property.[§] In some societies, suicide has had social ties. In Japan, for example, popularly known as *seppuku* (hara-kiri), which means "self-disembowelment," has been viewed

---

[*] N. Gibbs, "Officers on the edge," *Time*, 144, 62. As cited by J.A. LaPointe, May 1, 1999. Personal communication with Ronald, W. Collins, "Psychological perspectives on security issues (with a 2012 update)," in *Protection, Security, and Safeguards; Practical Approaches and Perspectives*, edited by Dale L. June, CRC Press/Taylor & Francis, 2012.

[†] Paula Spencer Scott, "7 top health risks for men over 40," http://health.yahoo.net/articles/mens-health/photos/7-top-health-risks-men-over-40#6, July 2, 2012.

[‡] L. Lieberman, *Leaving You: The Cultural History of Suicide* (Chicago: Ivan R. Dee, 2003).

[§] N.L. Farberow, *Suicide in Different Cultures*. University Park Press, 1975.

as an honorable method of taking one's life. Warriors used it after losing a battle to avoid the dishonor of defeat. Three-time Nobel Prize nominee Yukio Mishima, Japanese author, poet, and playwright, committed suicide through seppuku. His work reflected and broke cultural boundaries, with a focus on sexuality, death, and political changes.[*]

In other cultures, suicide was not only tolerated, but also encouraged. The Goths and the Celts believed natural death was shameful. If Vikings didn't die in the battlefield, they would purposely kill themselves to enter Valhalla (the great hall of Odin for slain heroes in Norse mythology).[†] In some Eskimo tribes, it was believed that is better to kill oneself before becoming old. They would enter the next life in the same healthy condition they left this one. In several societies, it was demanded that the wives, servants, and ministers kill themselves so that they could continue to serve the needs of their master after he died. In some cases, it was competition among the widows to be the first to follow the husband in death because that privilege identified his favorite.[‡]

Survivors of Suicide

The "survivors," the ones whom suicide leaves behind, are overwhelmed with intense grief wrapped in guilt. Feeling a roller coaster of emotions and thoughts, such as shock, anger, shame, guilt, despair, loneliness, depression, abandonment, grief, confusion, and disorientation, is usual for survivors of suicide. Also, the survivors may lose trust, being afraid that others will commit suicide. Surviving the suicide of a loved one is one of the most difficult challenges one will ever face. This grief hurts desperately but must be borne. The grief that comes with suicide is unique. "Grief is like snowflakes or fingerprints,"[§] there are no two alike. As a result of fear and misunderstanding, survivors of suicide deaths are often left with a feeling of abandonment at a time when they desperately need unconditional support and understanding. Without a doubt, suicide survivors suffer in a variety of ways because they need to mourn the loss of someone who has died and because they are often shunned by a society unwilling to enter into the pain of their grief. Because of the social stigma surrounding suicide, survivors feel the pain of the loss, yet may not know how, or where, or if they should express it. Yet, the only way to heal is to mourn. Just like other bereaved persons grieving the loss of someone loved, suicide survivors need to talk, cry, and scream in order to heal. Often, families of suicide victims feel stigmatized or cast out by the rest of society.

[*] J.S. Piven, *Madness and Perversion of Yukio Mishima* (Westport, CT: Praeger, 2004).
[†] N.L. Farberow, n.d.
[‡] N.L. Farberow, n.d.
[§] Shane Koyczan, 2008. Atlantis; www.youtube.com/watch?v=Hung20npy.

Depression

"Depression kills." Oftentimes, the people who are suffering from depression or a similar mental illness do everything they can to hide their illness because of the social stigma associated with it. Only in the past two decades have depression and suicide been taken seriously.[*] Depression is an illness that involves the body, mood, and thoughts. Depression affects the way a person eats and sleeps, feels about themselves, and the way they think of the things around them. The signs that most directly warn of suicide include threatening to hurt or kill oneself; making plans or preparation for potentially serious attempts to kill oneself (weapons, pills, or other means); and talking or writing about death, dying, or suicide.[†] There are other warning signs that indicate suicide in addition to depression, including insomnia, intense anxiety, pain or internal tension, panic attacks, feeling desperate or trapped like there is no way out, feeling hopeless, feeling there is no reason or purpose to live, and rage or anger.[‡]

Certain behaviors can also serve as warning signs, particularly when they are not characteristic of the person's normal behavior. These include acting reckless or engaging in risky activities, engaging in violent or self-destructive behavior, increased alcohol or drug use, and withdrawing from friends or family.[§] Research shows that risk factors for suicide include depression and other mental disorders, prior suicide attempt, family history of mental disorder or substance abuse, family history of suicide, family violence including physical or sexual abuse, firearm in the home (the method used in more than half of suicides), incarceration, and exposure to suicidal behavior of others (e.g., family members, peers, or media figures).[¶]

It is said that most suicidal people are undecided about living or dying, meaning that one state doesn't appear to have any significant advantage over the other. Suicide can seem to be the only way out of problems, the ultimate solution and an exit. A person who commits suicide dies once, but the spouses, partners, and children grieve and weep every day for the rest of their lives.

Another indicator that a person "has found the final solution" is that he or she will suddenly become happy, excited, and more animated, especially if having been going through a period of depression, and will begin giving away personal belongings, sometimes saying, "I don't need or want this anymore. I have grown beyond it."

---

[*] AFSP, http://www.afsp.org/.
[†] Ibid.
[‡] Ibid.
[§] Ibid.
[¶] Ibid.

Suicide as a Tool

Suicide affects all socioeconomic groups, but mass suicides are typically thought of as rare and affecting only brainwashed people belonging to cults.* Mass suicides are more common than most people would think or believe. The basic requirement for a definition of mass suicide would be three or more people killing themselves together with a common element or interest, and all or most of the members going along with the suicide willingly at the same time. Mass suicide comes in multiple forms and it can be politically driven by dictators.

Not many people may think of it as suicide, but war is a form of mass suicide with hundreds of eager participants, thus making it the largest form of expressed group suicide.† Hundreds of examples of wartime battles abound where soldiers knowingly charged into the face of certain death. Most battles of the American Civil War were simply suicide charges of massed soldiers running and screaming toward the onslaught of deadly fire from the opposite side. Most major battles and invasions of the World War II required soldiers to run into deadly enemy fire. The "banzai" charges of the Japanese in that war and the charges of the North Koreans during the Korean War of the 1950s are further examples.

The three most well-known mass suicides in the United States are the Heaven's Gate group; David Koresh and his followers in Waco, Texas; and Jonestown. The Heaven's Gate mass suicide occurred in a mansion near San Diego, California, in 1997. It was a UFO-based religion believing the Earth was contaminated and an alien spaceship was hiding behind the Hale-Bopp comet. Followers killed themselves, hoping their souls would reach the spaceship. The victims were self-drugged and then suffocated by other members in a series of suicides over a period of three days. Thirty-nine died; most were in their forties and came from a wide range of backgrounds.‡

Vernon Howell, better known as David Koresh, claimed to be a reincarnation of Jesus. He had the Bible memorized and used it to mentally and physically hold control over his followers. He built the Branch Davidian ranch outside Waco, Texas. The buildings were burned in a controversial raid by federal authorities, killing fifty-four adults and twenty-one children.§

The suicide action in Jonestown, Guyana, was the largest event in modern history resulting in the largest single mass suicide loss of American

* Freydis, 2002. www.hology.com/suicide
† Freydis, 2002.
‡ Ibid.
§ Rick Ross, "The Waco Davidian standoff," Cult Education and Recovery, http://www.culteducation.com/waco.html, September 1999.

civilian life in a nonnatural disaster until the events of September 11, 2001.* Reverend Jim Jones was the leader of the Peoples Temple religious group and claimed he was God. He built Jonestown in Guyana, South America, and preached to his followers that Jonestown is the only place they could live in peace and harmony. In 1978 he ordered everyone to drink cyanide poison mixed with Kool-Aid® and ended up killing 909 people, including 270 children. Jim Jones' followers were composed of two groups: low-income blacks and idealistic affluent whites.

Suicide among Law Enforcement Officers

Several factors contribute to police officers being on the top-ranking suicide rate charts. Stress is the foremost factor in the life of an officer. The job as an officer lacks balance. Most professions experience more of a blend of the good with the bad. But officers tend to see people at their worst. They do not regularly interact with the majority of citizens who are good, hard working, and law abiding. Their daily job is to deal with the most horrible death scenes. An individual can prepare himself for any kind of profession but a police officer's job is unpredictable. Nothing can possibly prepare a police officer for what he or she might encounter during their career. Once an officer puts on the uniform and steps outside of his or her home, they never know what the day has to offer or what to expect. They are first on scene when a child dies, a woman is raped, a teenager commits suicide, a drug overdose, and domestic violence calls. They are there to help and be the mental and emotional support that the victims need and also serve as a hero. One thing that tends to be overseen is that officers are not being acknowledged for their job and the mounting daily stress being carried around. Rape, murder, suicide, overdose, and violence have an enormous effect on any individual, even on the most seasoned officers. And they should not be taken for granted.

For instance, studies show that within the medical field, neurosurgeons have the highest rate of immortality among their patients. To be able to save one's life is enough to keep them happily pursuing the field of medicine. That's what drives surgeons to excel and be able to cope with the daily stress they face. Unfortunately, the same conclusion cannot be made about law enforcement officers. They are faced with one heart-wrenching call after another. Additionally, officers' lives are in danger every day, and they can never let their guard down, never turn off the adrenaline pump. Once they walk outside their homes, no one knows if they will ever return because the job hinges on uncertainty. This being said, officers generally operate well under

---

* Richard Rapaport, "Jonestown and City Hall slayings eerily linked in time and memory," *San Francisco Chronicle*, November 2003.

stress but at the same time too much stress may have devastating outcomes. Officers have rotating shifts, work ten- to twelve-hour shifts. There is often disruption in their lives due to the rotating shifts, which tends to separate them from their family, friends, and other areas of socialization. Most often, their relationships are forced to take a backseat. They do everything and anything to protect their families from the horrors they have to deal with and witness routinely.

Officers tend to bottle up their emotions, fearing the stigma of appearing weak in a macho profession. In society they are perceived to be superheroes. In the officers' way of thinking, they are not supposed to be vulnerable and show affection and emotion. To them, this characteristic is a sign of weakness. This significantly hinders them from sharing and discussing their work with others, even with their family members. This makes the family members feel left out, confused, and neglected. Shortly, resentments build up, leading to divorce, split families, and loss of a firm support system, adding to the officer's burden. Consequently, the officer may turn to the use of alcohol or drugs to dull the pain, further dissolving into depression.

Another factor that society doesn't shed light on is the training that is being required by officers. The training academy is between twelve and fourteen weeks, heavily focused on elements of the job, physical, and firearms training. Very little, if any time, is spent on discussing job stress, burnout, family issues, and the potential price to be paid in emotional and mental anguish. Officers are not being fully prepared for the human cost and the stressors the position has to offer. They are not mentally prepared for the exposure they are about to face in their career. They are thrown into the field, having to deal with all the varied emotions associated with the job. Over time, idealistic and enthusiastic officers become cynical, adapting an us-versus-them attitude. The most vulnerable may go on to adopt an attitude of it's them against me, and feel he is carrying the burden of society on his shoulders while trying to balance a troubled family life.

Again going back to physicians and the medical field comparison, physicians have more than ten years of schooling and experience before they don the white coat and become independent. Officers are not even being exposed or even warned of the stress and heartbreaking issues they are about to encounter in their professional career. What is most important is the macho image and being strong and dealing with calamity and danger in a calm and safe matter. When an officer must kill someone in the line of duty, often he is congratulated and singled out by his peers as courageous, "making his bones," sometimes receiving a medal. But the individual officer who has killed may suffer guilt, posttraumatic stress, or other related individual emotions. Over time, the effect may lead him to contemplate or commit suicide.

It's been an expressed fact that suicide is an impulsive act. As mentioned earlier, over 60 percent of all suicides among the United States population is conducted by firearms. Among police officers, the rate is 90 percent. Many people can ride out the momentary impulses to kill themselves due to not having a gun available. The story ends up differently with officers, who have the ever-present availability of the firearm on their belt, and combined with the number-one cause of suicide—stress—this combination is deadly.

The stigma of mental illness remains rampant among many law enforcement officers. Officers with history of depression or anxiety are identified as weak. They are seen as the guy who can't handle pressure and is not good enough. They believe if they were to seek help, their careers would be ruined, they will not fit the job description, which is perceived to be strong, and not have any mental issues. Seeking help implies cowardice and inability to fulfill the role of an officer. Their gun will be confiscated and they will lose their dignity. Officers fear they will be terminated from their job if they mention their struggles and concerns. These obstacles will prevent an officer from seeking help for depression, anxiety, or suicidal thoughts. Imagine all the concerns an officer is being faced with in just wanting to solve a problem, which, results in quietly solving the issue by themselves and unfortunately oftentimes the result is disastrous.

Posttraumatic Stress Disorder

Posttraumatic stress disorder (PTSD) is a mental health condition that affects many law enforcement officers. PTSD is a type of anxiety disorder that occurs after a traumatic event that involves the threat of injury or death. Symptoms include reliving the event, which can disturb the day-to-day activity; flashbacks; nightmares of the event; avoidance; feeling detached; lacking interest in normal activities; avoiding places, people, or thoughts that are constant reminders of the event; difficulty concentrating; startling easily; and having trouble falling or staying asleep.

As one can imagine, PTSD can disrupt a life and shake a person's very belief system to the core. It can produce overwhelming, if not illogical, guilt feelings. It can make a police officer question whether the job has any meaning or value. It can make someone so paranoid that the person is unable to trust or let his guard down even in safe environments. It can lead to maladaptive coping skills, including suicidal thoughts and ideations. Most important, law enforcement officers are subject to repeated critical incidents that are stress producing, and any critical incident can trigger PTSD. The effects of PTSD may be evidenced by an officer's decreased job performance, divorce, alcohol and substance abuse, and eventually suicide. Statistics show that suicide rates multiply when alcohol and other chemicals are used in an attempt to relieve stress.

Real prevention is the key, not waiting until the person is in crisis. Prevention should prepare a person for trouble before it becomes a crisis. The law enforcement field is an emotional, toxic environment. Officers are exposed to horror and trauma continually for years and decades. Seeking professional help is crucial for law enforcement officers. People seek physicians for yearly checkups, not because something might be wrong with them but to prevent something from going wrong. Why not seek counseling when your mind is troubled or before even getting to that place. Seeking professional mental help can enhance and help a law enforcement officer who is experiencing emotional anguish and trouble. It will build strength, and the person can develop tools and recourses that can be useful when confronted by stress or a traumatic event.

The History of Suicide Prevention in the United States

Drs. N. Farberow, R. Litman, and E. Shneidman founded a suicide prevention center in California in 1959. The Didi Hirsch Suicide Prevention Center hosts a 24-hour suicide prevention crisis line. Ten years later, the American Association of Suicidology was founded by Edwin Shneidman. In 2004, the National Suicide Prevention Lifeline (1-800-273-TALK) was founded by the Substance Abuse and Mental Health Services Administration, U.S Department of Health and Human Services. The Suicide Prevention Center is now staffed with 150 trained volunteer and supervisors. The 24-hour Crisis Line receives over 22,000 calls each year and recently expanded to 1-877-7CRISIS and is a part of national suicide prevention line.*

Virtually all suicides are preventable with appropriate intervention. Police departments should acknowledge that many police officers are killing themselves due to the lack of appropriate help, and include suicide awareness and prevention programs as part of training. They should also have support groups for the survivors. Studies show that survivors of suicide are up to nine times more likely to commit suicide themselves in comparison with the average person.

Conclusion

Suicide leaves survivors shaken and in search of answers that may never be found. People who have lost a loved one to something as painful and awful as suicide, must not only deal with grief to deal but also anger, guilt, confusion, shock, remorse, horror. and trauma that go beyond the "normal" emotions

---

* Suicide Prevention Resource Center, http://www.sprc.org/index.asp.

of death. The survivors may be angry for being left behind, and they may also feel incapable for not being able to prevent it. They may not be aware of the struggles that were experienced by their loved ones. The victims of suicide are not just limited to the person who commits the act; suicide leaves a life-long mark on all those around it. The same type of feeling is seen across the board among law enforcement agencies.

Trying to help and support an individual who has been a victim of suicide can be difficult and confusing. As a suicide survivor myself, I believe the best way to help survivors is to listen to their pain instead of trying to justify the loss by sayings such as, "He is in a better place where he can be happy." Survivors don't want to be rushed into recovery. It takes time to accept that their loved ones have intentionally left them behind. Unfortunately, suicide has a degrading social stigma attached to it, and survivors don't feel comfortable publicly sharing their pain. The survivors have to deal with all the unanswered questions for the rest of their lives. Unfortunately, suicide is an act of desperation, carried out when less drastic solutions or answers of relief seem unavailable or inadequate. Family, friends, loved ones, and law enforcement agencies should ensure that other options are available in the time of need and also provide the much-needed help prior to the escalation of a problem. As discussed earlier, law enforcement officers are at a higher risk for taking their own lives and the number has grown as we speak. Since this is a known fact, law enforcement agencies should be at the forefront of developing and implementing suicide intervention programs.

It is very crucial to emphasize the awareness of mental health so people who are being affected by it can recognize their symptoms and reach out and receive the necessary help they need. Especially in law enforcement agencies where mental health is a taboo issue, it is important that help is available and easily accessible. As it is true with addressing any problem, the first and most important step is to recognize the existing problem. Additionally, law enforcement agencies should invest more time to train supervisors so they are savvy enough to recognize the warning signs of suicide and help officers before it is too late. Suicide among police officers occurs for the same reason that it occurs in anyone else. When the pain becomes unbearable, the only option to release this pain is to take their life. The only difference between an ordinary individual and a law enforcement officer is that the stress they experience is not situational; there is a constant and chronic stress. When individuals feel powerless and helpless, especially officers who are being defined by their power, they seek to reestablish that control and that power by suicide.

Finally, mental health issues account for ninety percent of all suicides. Prevention and awareness would decrease the incidence significantly. With regard to police suicide, this fact no longer can be ignored.

Suicide by Cop: Victims from Both Sides of the Badge

6

DALE L. JUNE

Jumping off a bridge or walking off a tall building, ingesting pills, in haling carbon monoxide from a car engine, cutting the wrists, hanging, and other more dramatic methods have been used to self-inflict death. A growing phenomenon, estimated to be approximately ten to eleven percent of suicides, is what has come to be termed "suicide by cop" (SBC).

The hotly pursued suspect on a freeway or some other type of person coming to the attention of the police suddenly emerges with a gun in his hand, then fires off a quick couple shots. Perhaps the rounds are only blanks or he intentionally shoots randomly, expecting to miss. Possibly the gun is only a toy. Maybe he is only holding a cell phone that in the darkness is mistaken for a gun. Whatever his actions, his real intent is to draw return fire from the police, knowing the police shoot to kill. His real intention is to commit suicide but he does not want to pull the trigger himself. "Going out in a blaze of glory," he fancies the nightly news telling about the "gunfight" police were engaged in, giving them no alternative but to kill him.

Upon further review and investigation, it is learned the dead person was depressed, was failing in business, or had some other motivation for taking his life but chose to be killed by the police.

A generally and widely accepted definition of SBC, created by Rebecca Stincelli[*]:

> Suicide-by-cop[†]—A colloquial term used to describe a suicidal incident whereby the suicidal subject engages in a consciously life-threatening behavior to the degree that it compels a police officer to respond with deadly force.

---

[*] Rebecca Stincelli is a recognized expert in the area of suicide by cop. She began researching suicide by cop in 1986 while working with the deputies of the Sacramento County (CA) Sheriff's Department as a crisis interventionist and posttrauma liaison for victims of violent crimes. During the next decade, Stincelli became a law enforcement instructor where she was given the opportunity to present the perspectives of both the loved ones of the decedent and the officers involved.

[†] Rebecca Stincelli, "Suicide by cop: Victims from BOTH sides of the badge," 2008–2012, http://www.suicidebycop.com/7601.html, retrieved August 14, 2012.

In this manner, the officer becomes the instrument the suicidal victim has selected as the means of taking his own life. There is no fault on the part of the officer as a "wrongful shooting," because the scenario was scripted by the suicidal person for the specific action that he expected, or wanted, the officer to take. If an officer believes his life is in imminent danger, he must take reasonable and necessary measures, meaning that he must/can use deadly force.

A Message to Officers

Do not be alarmed if you are feeling overwhelmed. A post shooting incident is a numbing event even for the most veteran of officers. [See previous section and Chapter 12 regarding posttraumatic stress disorder (PTSD). A police officer involved in any kind of action taking a human life is commonly vulnerable to PTSD.] You are about to embark on a personal struggle that is uniquely yours. Though singular in the circumstances surrounding the shooting, talking with others who have come through a similar event can be helpful. Seek out your peers. Consider that professional counseling does NOT diminish your character.

Yes, you are a cop, but you are human first, with frailties and strengths, all of which form your character. You did what you had to do—what you were trained to do. The moral excellence that is part of you still exists. Whether you decide to continue in a law enforcement career or seek another profession, remember … you went home alive.

Be safe, be well.*

* Stincelli, "Suicide by cop."

Time and Attitude

7

DALE L. JUNE

Contents

Karma plays strange games with our lives.

—Hindu proverb

There is a destiny that makes us brothers: none goes his way alone. All that we send into the lives of others comes back into our own.

—Edwin Markham*

Time

"Time: We can't see it. We can't touch it. We all wish we had more of it.

Time keeps track of what we are doing with our lives. Typically, people do something similar to the following: work a forty-hour week, take one-hour lunches, attend fifty-five-minute classes, go to work at nine, leave at five, have dinner at six, watch the eight o'clock news and the ten o'clock news. Time is one of our most valuable resources. Yet, time can't be bought or sold, replaced, or repeated."†

Once I overheard a friend tell someone, "If I knew I had only twenty-four hours to live, I would want to spend it with you." The person to whom he was speaking was flattered and replied, "Why would you want to spend your last twenty-four hours with me?" My friend, in all solemnity, deadpanned, "Because you are so boring, you make one minute feel like an hour."

That pretty much sums up our natural feelings. We want to stretch time for living. All of us have a certain allotted time. How much do we have?

Recently I read a book, *If Only It Were True* by Marc Levy.‡ The female protagonist had been in an accident and suffered brain damage. She was in

---

* http://www.quotegarden.com/karma.html, retrieved August 26, 2012.
† Leaders' legend; a statement of Career Education Corporation Corporate Human Resources policy, 2(3), September 2006.
‡ Marc Levy, *If Only It Were True* (New York: Simon & Schuster, 2000).

a stage four coma—brain dead—with no hope of recovery. For all purposes, she was dead, except her heart and other bodily functions continued to operate. Her "spirit" returned to her apartment where the male protagonist met her as a real person and in the course of time they fell in love. As time was running out on the woman's body before the doctors removed her from a respirator, the "spirit" asked her lover to play a game with her.

"Pretend that everyday a financial institution gave you $86,400 to spend anyway you pleased. The only conditions being that you had to spend it all before the next deposit or you would lose what remained. This would continue for an unspecified time, which you do not know when, but the institution can and will stop the payments any time. What you would you do? How would you spend all the money?"

The man was a little confused as to the "spirit's" reason for asking. "Let me explain," she told him. "To put it in other terms, the 'financial institution' is God and he gives you eighty-six thousand four hundred seconds every day, until one day he stops giving you the time. How you choose to spend that time is your own business. But when every second counts, I want to live every one of those seconds to the last tick of the clock."

Attitude

Time marches forward. Our attitude is a huge player in our lives. Life is how we choose to live it. A perfect example of attitude and its potential consequences is best described in the Charles Dickens novel *A Christmas Carol* as Ebenezer Scrooge finds joy and happiness in Christmas observation after he is visited by the ghosts of the past, present, and future. If we all had the opportunity to view our attitudes through the years, would it make a difference in our lives? The choice is ours.

In the words of former Vice President Agnew, we have "nabobs of negativism" who as pessimists are cynical and fail to see the good side of life or in their association with others. There is nothing as contagious and perhaps uplifting than a smile and friendly word toward others that will brighten and uplift our own life. Very often we see our attitude reflected back by the people we come in contact with. A smile and kindly word wrapped in good cheer will generate positive light, whereas a dour and unenthusiastic word brings further depressing emotions and attitudes in others.

Pastor and writer Charles Swindoll said:

The longer I live, the more I realize the impact of attitude on life. It is more important than the past, than education, than money, than circumstances, than failures, than successes, than what other people think or say or do. It is more important than appearance, giftedness or skill. It will make or break a company ... a church ... a home.

The remarkable thing is we have a choice every day regarding the attitude we will embrace for that day. We cannot change our past ... we cannot change the fact that people will act in a certain way. We cannot change the inevitable. The only thing we can do is play on the one string we have, and that is our attitude ... I am convinced that life is 10% what happens to me and 90% how I react to it. And so it is with you ... we are in charge of our Attitude.*

It's a Matter of Attitude†

We live in a world of words. No matter what happens, we have a word for it. Some words mean a great deal to us, such as love, happiness, success, achievement, joy, and ability. But one word controls them all: attitude!

If your attitude is good, you obtain good results; if it is excellent, you obtain excellent results. If bad, then bad results. If your attitude is so-so, your results are not bad, but not good. They are so-so. Now if you wish to test your own attitude, answer the question, "Do you feel the world is treating you well?" If the answer is a quick yes, your attitude is good. If it's no, your attitude is bad, and if you have trouble deciding, you need help.

The world is nothing more than a reflection, a mirror of our own attitude. One of the most pitiful aspects of society is the large percentage of people who become discontented because of what they think they don't have, while the truth is that they don't look at what they do have.

It would be impossible to estimate the number of jobs lost, promotions missed, sales not made, marriages ruined, all due to a poor attitude. All because people waited for others to change toward them instead of being big enough to realize that we only get back what we put out.

Sir Walter Scott said, "Success or failure in any undertaking is caused by the mental attitude even more than by mental capabilities." In thirty days you can change your little world by a simple method. For thirty days, treat every person you meet, without exception, as the most important person on Earth. You will find they will be treating you the same.

Live in a world for others ... not for yourself; and you will find that you come out ahead. A generous attitude with a keen sense of humor is far better medicine than a tranquilizer or psychiatric couch.

Twenty percent of what we do is knowledge; 80 percent of what we do is our attitude.

---

* "Charles R. Swindoll quotes," Thinkexist.com, http://thinkexist.com/quotes/charles_r._swindoll/, retrieved June 8, 2012.
† Source: Unknown.

Keep in mind, "You'll never have a second chance to make a good first impression."

The world is a matter of balance and circles. The mirror of our attitude is a recycling of the balance and circle of other's attitude toward us as we extend our attitude toward them.

(Not) One of the Guys

8

TIFFANY HARRISON

Never try to win someone over by changing your strategy in hopes of befriending them.

—**Sun Tzu**
The Art of War

As the first wave of tension tries to fatigue the muscles in my arms and core, I start silently counting the push-ups as I do them, my internal reference point overriding the agony of muscles still sore from the week's previous workouts.

Thirty. Thirty-one. Thirty-two …

Another local police department that I'd applied to is holding its physical fitness test at the end of the week. I've always been healthy and in great shape; it's not the test I'm concerned about. I need to be stronger. Stronger than the many men out there who are taller than me, bigger than me, faster than me. Stronger than even the smallest female driven insane by the influence of amphetamines. Stronger than those who would go through me if it meant their freedom. Stronger than the fatalities I might witness that could keep me up at night. Stronger than the strain of a job that is notorious for tearing families apart. Stronger than I was the last time I was a cop. Stronger than the supervisors who tormented me. Stronger than the self-pity, the isolation, the fear.

I can't afford to be weak. Weaknesses are exploited.

Forty. Forty-one. Forty-two …

Since I was very young, I was very much a tomboy. I grew up alongside boys, roughhousing and playing with mud and trucks. I began my martial arts career when I was nine years old, and my dad introduced me to weightlifting and conditioning when I was twelve. By the time I was in high school, I had given up wearing makeup and had perfected a very intimidating exterior. My strong, muscular physique led my volleyball teammates to wonder if I was using performance-enhancing drugs, and my combat boots and black clothing made everyone in a post-Columbine world a little nervous. My entire life, I can count on one hand the number of female friends I've had. The vast majority of girls I came across rejected me, even bullied me, and I came to despise females and their ways. Instead of assimilating into femininity, I chose to be more masculine. Eventually, I got what I wanted, and I had scared them all away.

It confuses people to discover that I've never been a feminist (or homosexual, for that matter). I find merit in various schools of philosophical thought regarding feminism, but I never rallied against menfolk as the oppressive evil that feminism makes them out to be. After all, females were the ones who ostracized me; I openly disliked women. Where there was disagreement between the two sexes, I usually sided with the guys. I trusted them and dismissed the cliché cries of "misogyny" or "sexual harassment" or "discrimination" as the typical female's attempt to get attention because she can't keep up with the boys. Not me, I told myself; I'm one of the guys.

Fifty-five. Fifty-six. Fifty-seven ...

I focus on my breathing, my brain convincing my muscles they can keep going despite the tiny tears I'm repeatedly subjecting them to. It hurts like hell, but pain is weakness leaving the body. And I can't give up on myself. Not now. Not ever.

Fifty-nine. Sixty ...

There is something wonderfully comforting about belonging to a group that accepts you without question. It's the glue that keeps a healthy family together. It's the allure of joining a gang. And it's what every rookie police officer dreams about. My entire life, it was what I always wanted.

I was so excited to begin a career in law enforcement that I acted like an officer before I was even in the academy, outwardly judging others' traffic violations, interjecting quotes from the criminal law manual into everyday conversations, and watching *Cops* as if it was the only thing on television besides the news.

My godfather is my teacher. He has given me his priceless knowledge from his service in the Army, in law enforcement, and as a federal air marshal. I can now shoot a pistol, fletch arrows, hunt with a longbow, and look someone in the eyes when I speak to them. My godfather has taught me many things. Unfortunately for him, he jokes, he wasn't the one who taught me to drive.

Though I forget our destination, I was driving my godfather somewhere in my car one day, and we were sharing a box of palm-sized cookies. I suppose the rides before had always been rough—quick turns that tossed about my passengers and cargo, abrupt stops when I paid more attention to conversation than to the road, and getting lost after not printing directions— but that particular day, my godfather had had enough. When we came to a red light, he took the last cookie and set it on the dashboard. "Your training begins now," he said with that former drill instructor glare. "Don't let the cookie leave the dashboard." That one, simple lesson required all I could muster from my prior driver's education and police training. If I was to be a professional, my godfather asserted, I had better learn to drive like one.

The police department, an extension of the state university that was my alma mater, hired me and one of the university's music instructors, a slightly older man with a great sense of humor. For me, the academy was a new adventure. No matter what subject matter we focused on or which instructor showed up for that day, my class spent just as much time swapping jokes as we did being studious.

Our class discussed issues like sexual harassment and discrimination because they were topics included in the academy curriculum, but we did so with almost a cavalier attitude, as if these things were arcane issues from decades past. I don't think anyone ever considered that such problems never really went away—they only became more subtle, under the radar, disguised as something else.

It was in the academy that the rumblings began, as the little things piled up. I'd be late, or I'd forget something, or my uniform wouldn't be pressed correctly (thanks to the cheap dry cleaners my department insisted we use). Even as others made similar mistakes, there was this unspoken assumption that I couldn't get my act together, not because I was a goofball then (which, admittedly, I was), but because I was a female. I dismissed it as paranoia; after all, no one in the class had said those words out loud.

That changed when we divided in half for our tactical training. I was assigned to one group, and the only other female in our class—an older, woman who claimed to be a former officer from pre-Katrina New Orleans (a claim that would later prove to be an utter lie)—was in the other. Maybe it was because she was older. Maybe it was because she (supposedly) had previous experience as an officer. Maybe it was because she claimed to have escaped the epic disaster that was Hurricane Katrina. Or maybe it was because she was black and some may have feared appearing racially biased and out of that same fear, were not openly critical of her. Whatever the reason, I never heard a negative thing uttered about the other female in our class. That harassment, it would seem, was being reserved just for me.

The first hint of it came during our driving training. As luck would have it, I picked the one, aging Crown Victoria in the parking lot that just didn't have any oomph; I couldn't get it to accelerate the way the course required it to, and my scores reflected its slow performance. Because I couldn't accelerate the vehicle through turns very well, I often flattened nearly every cone in my path, cones that represented fairly important things like pedestrians, buildings, curbs, or other vehicles. It was then that the annoying "typical female driver" comments surfaced, easily getting under my skin since I didn't consider myself a "typical female." I tried desperately to explain that it was the car's poor performance, not that of its driver. One instructor pushed my buttons repeatedly, and everyone in our group adopted his assumption that I just didn't know how to drive. I grew frustrated and took it very personally, losing all respect for the instructor and distancing myself from my group, my team, as my scores dropped to failing levels. Eventually one of the other, kinder instructors took notice. In an attempt to demonstrate what I needed to do, he ran one of the courses in my vehicle. When he had finished, he stepped out from behind the wheel and blurted, "This [expletive] car sucks!" It was then that I was finally vindicated, and with a new vehicle that did what it was supposed to do, my scores quickly blew everyone out of the water. After so many weeks of burning hot rubber on the blistering tarmac, we had all grown closer as a group. And I laughed harder than anyone else when the instructors presented me with a special award certificate for being the "Most Improved Driver," affectionately dubbing me Tiffany "Cone Killer" Harrison. Enjoying myself once again, I pushed the sexist name-calling episodes out of my mind, forgave my instructor, and moved on to the other phases of our academy training.

The peace of mind was short-lived. It seemed like there was always something I was doing wrong, and while the mistakes my male classmates made were quickly overlooked and forgotten, I became an easy target. When we practiced the active shooter diamond formation, everyone complained when my short legs either prevented me from keeping up as the rear or nearly getting me trampled as the point officer. One time, during a night shoot, I stepped up to the line after grabbing the wrong magazine—the empty one. Of course, the instructor who noticed was the same instructor who enjoyed publicly humiliating me during the driving course. He made sure everyone knew about my error, and the mistake earned my entire class a set of fifty push-ups on the gravel ground. I remember doing mine in bitter silence on my knuckles. It seemed so unfair; no one else was degraded like this. I began to wonder, was I being picked on because I was a woman or because they just didn't like me?

Then, one sweet day, the revelation hit me—they were jealous. My scores were among the highest in the class, both on paper and out in the exercises. Thanks to my martial arts background, no one else understood the defensive tactics (DT) as well as I did, and our DT instructor—a small but powerful man who reminded me of Yoda—was impressed by my skills. The Red Man we dueled was a brick-fisted cop they called "The Hammer," who hit me so hard that my classmates thought I should have been knocked unconscious. The Hammer was so amazed by the fierce determination in my eyes that he asked if I was a mom; he'd only seen such ferocity in the eyes of a parent protecting her child. It all made sense when I realized that the unintended consequence of being just as tough as all the guys is the fact that they eventually feel utterly emasculated.

The ultimate turning point was a moment I will never forget. One of my classmates had forgotten to bring a class T-shirt, a mistake I empathized with, so I loaned him one of mine. Though both shirts were wrinkled and unkempt, I let him have the cleaner shirt, and wore the more wrinkled one from the day before. The T-shirt of the shortest person in class stretched smoothly over the tallest person in class, and he was very grateful. The day was almost over when everything fell apart. I can't remember exactly how things escalated so quickly, but in the middle of a seemingly typical class conversation, the class leader, an older Native American man who was a straight-laced Army veteran, turned around in his chair and, completely unprovoked, proceeded to chew me out for my shirt being so wrinkled. Though he was still seated in his chair, he was wide-eyed and shaking, practically spitting at me, shouting about how "disgraceful" my attire was in front of the entire class and our instructor. The aggressive scolding was too reminiscent of the ones I'd received from my impatient and intolerant father for years of my life. After assuming I'd been accepted by everyone despite all the chaos we'd gone through as a class, it was all I could do to keep the tears in my eyes; I remember debating if I would be in trouble if I left the room. And when the one student in the class who I thought disliked me the most stood up for me and told the class leader to ease up among agreement from others that that was enough, the tears had to be wiped away before more of them flowed. I struggled to compose myself, and the class continued in awkward silence. It was only after graduation that I learned the entire class had taken the class leader aside and berated him for his behavior toward me, defending my choice to give my classmate the nicer shirt and take the heat for dressing improperly. The gesture warmed my heart—even a classmate who could have easily been my nemesis had defended me. Later on, I even received an e-mail at my department from the class leader, who offered a heartfelt apology for such an unnecessary outburst.

They might not have ever called themselves my friends, but my classmates had eventually accepted me, even protected me. When all was said and done, I had thoroughly enjoyed my time at the academy. I got paid to learn law, shoot guns, drive cars recklessly, pretend to find bad guys in dark buildings, get in great shape, practice martial arts, and fight a monster with concrete fists. As far as I was concerned, it was the best job in the world. Despite all the bumps in the road, I looked back fondly on those last four months, just one of the guys.

It would soon be apparent that I had been lulled into a false sense of security. I should have heeded the first red flag in front of me when our department didn't even bother to badge us at the graduation ceremony.

From day one, it was startling, almost disturbing, how quiet the department would get when I walked into a room, all eyes suddenly disdainfully upon me. That second red flag was the foreboding feeling that I was unwelcome, like a stray dog. Seeing my male academy counterpart laughing jovially with everyone else, I dismissed the fleeting assumption that they didn't want me there merely as leftover adolescent insecurity. I was just nervous, I assured myself. They'll warm up to me. I'm likable. I'm one of the guys.

My department seemed terribly disorganized about hiring us. My male counterpart and I were shuffled into several department continuing education classes on topics like Spanish (which he was fluent in anyway) and some sort of emergency management tabletop exercise before we ever began field training. It took them forever to order our gear, uniforms, and vests; something that should have been taken care of in the four months we were training at the academy. It was as if they hired us because they had to, not because they wanted to. As my training progressed, I would come to believe that about myself more than the male officer whom everyone instantly befriended. I quickly noticed that of fifty total sworn police officers, only three were female—one was the wife of a K9 officer, another was a painfully shy detective, and the third was a young lesbian who had been hired just before the two of us. All of them were so quiet that they seemed to disappear within the ranks. Fifty officers and only four of us were women? Had I been hired because I was a female, because the department didn't have enough? Was this some remnant of affirmative action?

On top of all of that, the female lieutenant who had hired us was transferring to another department. I am haunted by her stern warning that "this department is not friendly to women." She also echoed what many others outside of the department had said about being a female rookie: "Keep your head down and your mouth shut." How unfortunate that I dismissed her as just another female who didn't understand guys or didn't approve of my outspoken personality. I didn't realize it at the time, but her departure would leave me without any female supervisor, another red flag that I just didn't see coming.

During our field training, my male counterpart and I were separated, and we were often shuffled around from supervisor to supervisor, so I don't know much about his experiences save for what I heard from other officers. In their infinite wisdom, the department scheduled our first phase, the majority of which is devoted to familiarization of geography, during the night shift from 1800 to 0600 hrs (6 p.m. to 6 a.m.). My field training officer (FTO) was an older Hispanic man, a remnant of the university police department when it was much smaller and less official. My memory fails me now, but it was likely that they weren't even sworn police officers then, merely security guards. The FTO was a lighthearted man with plenty of stories and jokes. I appreciated my FTO's laid-back attitude. Unlike a lot of the other officers and supervisors, who often pushed people into confrontations, he preferred that even something as simple as a traffic violation be blatant and clear-cut. While observing a four-way intersection, for example, he mentioned that he preferred to stop drivers that "really run" the stop sign. For him, life wasn't complicated, so why should this job be any different? He assured me that the job was easy and that other officers or supervisors like to "make a big deal" out of things that are really minor. He also cautioned that "the place can be a rumor mill."

And then came the phrase that I would hear uttered to me from *every single person* in that police department: "Don't trust anyone here, not even me." That would be the biggest red flag of all—the most important one that I should have heeded and didn't.

It was obvious by phase two that I hadn't learned as much as I should have. My repeated mistakes, though minor, were glossed over when they should have been addressed and remedied. And apparently, I should have taken the opportunity to dabble in the requirements for phase two. Had I known how far behind I was then, I would have been more active about patching the leaks in my training. Everyone debated about whose fault it was. My first phase FTO was so frustrated by the suffocating bureaucracy of it all that he stepped down, choosing to be demoted from corporal back to a line officer. From that moment onward, my mistakes were then added to an ever-growing list, and my successes overlooked in search of my next shortcoming. And the other phrase I heard time and time again was, if even the minor mistakes continued, "I wasn't going to make it."

Just as phase one was doomed from the beginning, phase two, which included primarily nighttime lessons like the standardized field sobriety test and DWI arrests, was arranged during the day shift. A majority of phase two also fell within the Christmas and New Year holiday, when the university and campus were closed for an entire month. With only a handful of people on campus, especially during the day, it was nearly impossible to complete my requirements for the phase. My bored FTO, a young former drill instructor, entertained himself by routinely commenting on any attractive females we happened to pass. I understood that the corporal wanted to develop a rapport with me, but his obsession with gratuitous and sometimes graphic sexual innuendo grew tiresome and eventually made me uncomfortable. Still, I did as so many had told me, and I kept my mouth shut. It was clear that I didn't have any friends in the department; I didn't want to make anyone madder at me than they already were by "complaining" about anything. I shook off the discomfort and reminded myself that I was one of the guys.

I was told that my male counterpart "wasn't having any trouble," and had already scored his first DWI arrest. I knew it was only luck that helped him find an intoxicated driver during the day on a deserted college campus, but they were already starting to compare us. Maybe at that point, they had already made their decision. I never thought about it then, but maybe it was a competition all along.

The sergeant of that shift seemed almost sadistic. He was an unfriendly and bitter man, one of many military veterans in the police department. To escape the stress of his marriage and children, he would often leave the overnight shift early and drive nearly five hours south to go deer hunting. I always wilted under his piercing glare and soul-crushing demeanor. He would often stop me in the hallways and quiz me on bizarre scenarios in front of everyone. If I couldn't remember or didn't know the answer, no one around would help me. When I thought I knew the answers, he would always retort, almost with a disgusted snicker, "Are you sure?" Eventually, I started second-guessing myself, something the callous sergeant would capitalize upon. When he stood in as my FTO, he often belittled my performance with such animosity that tears eventually surfaced from somewhere so deep down inside that I couldn't hold them back despite my embarrassment. Trying to keep up with him on foot patrol one shift, he asked over his shoulder if I was a Muslim because I was always ten paces behind him.

The department was always so devoid of sympathy. At that point, I got the feeling from everyone who was there to teach me that doing so was a waste of their time. I always felt as if I wasn't learning anything; and when I corrected one mistake, I'd just trip over a new one. My supervisors pounced on every error and went to great lengths to find more. It was as if everything I had learned in the academy was wrong or somehow didn't apply to any situation I found myself in. Was I really doing that badly? Was I really that clueless *all* the time? And what hurt most of all was the fact that I never saw anyone else being treated that way.

To make everything worse, no one else in the department seemed to care that I was torn down on a daily basis. No one would even have a conversation with me. Some avoided eye contact or ignored me completely. Whenever I sat at a computer in the lab to type a report or study (while my supervisors spent time in their offices), anyone already there would finish, rise, and leave as soon as they could. It was as if the adult world was no different than high school. Young and so eager to belong, I took everything so personally. Why didn't they like me? Did they really not want me there? And why not? Aren't I a likable person? Where was the camaraderie, the second family I had hoped for? Aren't I one of the guys?

It didn't occur to me until much later that my male counterpart was being taught, but I was being *tested*, toyed with. And though I assumed then that it was all directed at me as a person, it could very well have been because I was a female. The harassment was so constant that I honestly couldn't tell.

They criticized my driving as well as my performance as an officer, and an old wound was reopened when my male counterpart joked about my experience in the academy's driving course, reigniting the "stereotypical female driver" comments like a wildfire. I knew I was a good driver, a skilled driver, and I was anything but a stereotypical female. Because the person in the passenger seat was always chastising me, I was so nervous behind the wheel of the department's cruisers that I didn't dare drive it as fast (or as recklessly) as many of my supervisors wanted me to. Frustrated, my second-phase FTO took me to the university's science research facility in a remote area of the city and instructed me to navigate to the parking lots at the highest speed I could, and he noted in my training log that doing so constituted "remedial training." Afterward, I realized he had done so in a childish attempt to irritate the sergeant who was in charge of the substation within the facility. I had become a pawn in the politics of the department, as if it was all a game to them.

Whatever brief, shining moments of glory and dignity I did have were quickly snuffed out. One day, my FTO and I had swiftly come to the rescue of a university maintenance worker who had suffered a stroke and lay unconscious, nearly choking on the banana he had been eating. My FTO and I cleared his airway and propped up his head before paramedics arrived, actions that the physicians at the hospital said had ultimately saved his life and cognitive functioning. The fact that I had navigated the one-way maze of the campus so efficiently that we had saved someone's life was a victorious leap forward in my progression as a police officer; I felt that it was what being a public servant was all about. My FTO was very pleased and thought we deserved some sort of recognition, maybe even a "life-saver" pin.

But the moment was short-lived. The cruel sergeant didn't seem fazed by our swift heroism. All he seemed to notice was my hair. After sleeping through my alarm and forgoing a morning shower in order to avoid being late, I had hastily thrown my hair into a small ponytail instead of the bun-clip it was used to; when dry, it was obvious that the last half of my brown hair had once been dyed black. The sergeant decided to counsel me on having a "punk" hairstyle; and when I explained that I was letting my hair grow out to its natural color, he retorted that the department's General Orders forbade "punk" hairstyles and insisted I "do something" about it.

There was one day shift where my FTO and I were dispatched to a report of a suspicious person in a locked and gated part of the college's astronomy research center, a collection of portable classrooms far-removed from civilization. When we arrived, there was a maintenance truck parked on the road but the gate was closed and locked. The cold sergeant arrived soon after we did. After notifying dispatch of our arrival and reporting the license plate of the truck, I unlocked the gate and entered the premises. We were met by an older man dressed in blue jeans and cowboy boots who appeared to be a maintenance worker. My FTO and the sergeant stood back and waited for me to glean an explanation from the man. He was stubborn about answering any questions, and it soon became obvious that he had a key to the padlock on the gate. Something was awry; instead of supporting me, my FTO and the sergeant merely stood by and watched. When I asked the man for his first name, he responded that it was "Oliver." While I wrote that down, I asked him what his last name was. The man replied, "Clothesoff"—"Oliver Clothesoff," that is, all of her clothes off. As my FTO snickered, I knew the whole thing had been a poorly crafted scenario, maybe even a practical joke. How was I supposed to take my training seriously if no one else took *me* seriously?

One day, I was up all night and early morning, sick and dehydrated with food poisoning; I couldn't imagine being of any use to anyone without any sleep. Begrudgingly, my FTO gave me the day off. But it would haunt me later when everyone's shift had to be rearranged so I could make up for the lost training hours—an inconvenience that everyone bemoaned and blamed me for even though I couldn't have anticipated or prevented my sickness.

The following morning, as I approached my car in my decrepit apartment parking lot, I saw that the driver's side window had been shattered, and some of my belongings had been stolen. I called my FTO, and he advised me to file a report with the city police department, even though we all knew it would be unlikely that my belongings would ever be recovered. When I arrived to work late (because I had to file the report), I was chastised for my tardiness by the sergeant.

The next day, my supervisors also couldn't help but notice a tiny scratch or blemish just under my eye, which was so minor that even I had forgotten it. When they questioned me about it, I explained that I probably received it during jiu jitsu class or by just being my clumsy self and bumping into something. For all I knew, it could have been a defeated pimple. To my utter surprise, no one believed me. Instead, they linked together my sick day, the broken car window, and the insignificant scratch on my cheek—otherwise isolated incidents—into the conclusion that I must be having "issues" with my boyfriend, suggesting that he and I had a problem with domestic violence. Because other females at that department had experienced violent arguments with their significant others, I obviously could have the same problem. After all, women *are* crazy. The twisted logic allowed them to assume that, like other female officers before me, I was emotionally unstable—and therefore a problem.

I'm not entirely sure what transpired behind closed doors, but at the end of my second phase, my FTO resigned and left the department entirely. To this day, I wonder about the missed call from my FTO that appeared on my cell phone without a message to explain. Did he suspect—maybe even *know*—right then and there that they had no intention of keeping me there? I considered calling him back to ask, but I was told not to speak to him anymore. Fearful and submissive, I obeyed.

I remember being counseled one day (by appointment) by the deputy chief regarding where I had parked one morning. Unable to find a parking spot on the street, I had hastily parked in the front parking lot, apparently in a visitor parking space. I explained that I was in such a hurry that morning that I hadn't seen any open parking spaces along the street where we were told to park. The deputy chief countered that, having reviewed the security camera footage, he knew that there were parking spaces, and he accused me not only of being lazy in parking where I did but also of lying about it. I couldn't convince him otherwise, and it took all I had to subdue tears of frustration. Why on earth would they bother investigating something so petty? Didn't they have better things to do? The deputy chief continued, explaining that he'd been informed I was in a rock band. Despite the fact that I had only performed once with my band while I was in the academy, a very half-hearted endeavor on a weekend, the deputy chief insisted that I refrain from doing anything of the sort until I was free from field training. I returned home to sleep before my shift that night, frustrated and hopeless. I felt more and more trapped, suffocated. If I lashed out in anger, they would terminate me. They were trying to get me to crack, trying to make me quit. Stubborn as I am, I knew quitting was never an option, though it should have been. Quitting was the one thing that could have saved both my sanity and my career.

Within the same week, both my male counterpart and I had caused some damage to our vehicles. The other officer had apparently tried to drive his cruiser over the parking block at the head of a parking spot, the ones that are taller than a curb and are certainly not meant to be driven over. The damage to the vehicle was so great that it couldn't be driven until it was repaired. In my case, I had difficulty making the tight U-turn in the crowded city jail garage, and as I cautiously exited one night, the side of the cruiser briefly and lightly scraped the doorway. Even though my male counterpart had caused far more damage to his vehicle, everyone laughed off his mistake, while I was severely scolded.

At a fundamental level, I was never given an opportunity to get comfortable in my own uniform. At least once every training phase, an FTO or supervisor had me completely restructure my duty belt during my shift. I never could tell if it stemmed from an effort to help me experiment with the limited real estate around my waist, or if it was just a hazing ritual repeated a few times a month for their own amusement. Whatever their reason, it was exhausting to crunch every piece of equipment off and back onto the stiff, new leather. And I was never afforded the chance to decide for myself what should go where and why, a cornerstone to both professionalism and officer survival.

Contrary to what others in the department might have assumed, I was not afraid of the civilians I encountered, no matter how many had warrants for charges like "evading arrest" and "assault on police." In fact, there were several instances in which I flaunted my cop plumage, puffed out my chest, and put the bad guys in their place. I deescalated several encounters that could have gone from bad to ugly thanks to the short tempers of my supervisors. As early as phase one, I remember transporting a foul-mouthed drunk that another officer had arrested for assaulting another patron at a bar. The tall young man bragged that his handcuffs were loose enough for him to take off, so when the officer pulled him out of the vehicle to secure them, I circled the drunk like a shark, reminding him with a steady glare that he'd only get one good shot at my FTO before it would be my turn. In my second phase, my FTO and I briefly chased and caught a female who bolted after not paying her taxi fare. I also remember joining my third phase FTO in a struggle with a drunken arrestee who wouldn't sit up in the back of the cruiser. Positioning himself as if he were about to kick my FTO in the head, I leaned in close and put my game face on, barking, "You kick my corporal, and I'll make you eat those cowboy boots!" The distraction allowed us to wrangle the large man into the seat and properly secure the seatbelt around him.

Back on the night shift, my phase three FTO, a kind but firm Army veteran, devoted himself to my growth like a real teacher should. He did his best, patiently getting me through as many lessons as the small, lifeless campus would provide. With his help, I eventually overcame the mistakes that no one else tried to correct with a simple word of encouragement. By far, my fondest memory while I was a police officer was the night my FTO and I accompanied two other officers in a quick tactical search through a condemned chemistry building in response to several intruders. My corporal took point and I followed closely as we moved smoothly down the stairs and around the corners, our flashlights steady, our pistols readied in the Sul position, until we discovered that the "intruders" were only eight college students trying to film a documentary. With my FTO's blessing, I ran the show, ordering them to spread their feet with their hands behind their heads and their noses in the wall. It was my shining moment, my *magnum opus*. It earned my FTO's respect and proved to him that, even as a female, I could hold my own. A fresh breath of hope.

However, with the shifts shuffled around every so often, it was inevitable that I would end up with the cruel sergeant once again. He mentioned the issue surrounding my hair color to every other supervisor I had, making sure that they took me aside and reminded me to "do something" about it. Dying it brown didn't erase the black, but he seemed to leave me no choice but to cut it as short as another officer wore her hair. Frustrated, I revisited the *General Orders* for a possible solution. Sure enough, the sergeant was wrong. The "punk" hairstyle that the *General Orders* referred to was in regard to the actual *styling* of the hair so it didn't interfere with wearing the uniform hat. Nowhere in the *General Orders*—and I mean *nowhere*—did it *ever* mention hair color. (Even if it had, both black and brown are considered "natural" hair colors.) Interestingly enough, when I reported my findings to my FTO, the sergeant never mentioned my hair color again.

It was my phase three FTO's mission to see me succeed, and I made it to my final phase with his complete confidence in tow. I truly believed I could make it through field training, that there was a light at the end of this terribly dark tunnel. Little did I know that the worst was yet to come.

The fourth and final phase of field training is called "ghost phase" because the FTO shadows the trainee, rarely intervening save for an emergency. At first, my ghost phase FTO was the wife of the K9 officer. (I would learn later that *they* were the officers with the domestic violence problem, who frequently brought their fights to work.) The phase was scheduled during the day shift; how the department thought I'd be able to demonstrate all the necessary skills during spring break on a college campus during the day,

I'll never understand. The phase went smoothly enough, mostly because the shifts were slow and boring; my FTO often had me drive her around so she could visit with various people on campus.

Eventually the sergeant for that shift became my FTO instead, most likely because the department was pressuring him to get me to "do something" during my ghost phase. This sergeant was a physically imposing man who insisted we listen to the most disgustingly ignorant, misogynistic, and sexually explicit rap music he could find on the radio. Mariah Carey's song "Touch My Body," was filled with sexual innuendo and some other songs that contained racist lyrics and graphic sexual content overtones were often played. When a song would end, he would find it on another station, and I'd have to listen to it all over again. If I tried to change the station, or at least turn down the radio so that I could hear the dispatch radio, he would bark at me not to. When I could muster the courage to ask him to do so himself, he would ask me why. I would answer that I didn't like that kind of music, and he would remind me that it wasn't my radio anyway.

The uncomfortable silence between us was unbearable. He always seemed in a foul mood. Like my second phase FTO, the sergeant also liked to comment on attractive females he noticed; but while the FTO's comments were playfully flirtatious, the sergeant's were derogatory and offensive. He rarely spoke to me, and when he did, he was very condescending. I remember trying to keep up with him while we walked across the campus one day, my shorter stride putting me a good ten feet behind him. Like the other sergeant, he asked me why I couldn't keep up, asking if I was Muslim, mentioning that his wife was, and that he "hates that [expletive]."

One morning, at the very beginning of the shift, the sergeant demanded I drive around and conduct traffic stops, literally, until I found an intoxicated driver and made a DWI arrest. With the campus nearly a ghost town at 6 a.m. on a spring break Sunday, the dissatisfied sergeant directed me down various streets until I was suddenly on the major interstate highway. After he eventually instructed me to turn around, he insisted I conduct a traffic stop on a vehicle on the highway. I honestly can't remember what trivial equipment violation I stopped the sedan for, but I do remember that the vehicle was completely full of junk—papers, bags, trash, and anything else you could possibly think of—as if this person lived out of their vehicle. The driver took forever searching for his proof of insurance, which was somewhere in the depths of the paper pile, and my sergeant just seemed to snap. He told me to "[expletive] it" and have the driver go on his way, and we returned to campus with the sergeant seething with anger.

Then the sergeant overheard a call on the city police department channel regarding an armed robbery at a local Taco Bueno. Right away, the call was odd. Who would rob a Taco Bueno? Even though the restaurant wasn't near the campus, the sergeant demanded I head in that direction. When I didn't make the U-turn fast enough, he barked at me to get out of the car so he could drive instead. The sergeant sped the Crown Victoria down the 30 mph campus street at a terrifying 90 mph, flying through every intersection regardless of all the red lights. Petrified, I remember the sergeant had mentioned during a previous shift that if he had a choice, he preferred to die in a shootout during an armed robbery. As we blitzed through every red light on the way there without any shred of due caution, I prayed that we wouldn't be slammed by another vehicle. When we arrived at the Taco Bueno, the perpetrators had apparently already fled the scene, and after futilely scouring the neighboring highways for their vehicle, my sergeant returned to the department. I don't even remember what happened the rest of that day.

With hindsight being what it is, I couldn't tell you why I was naïve enough to assume that they might actually promote me from my field training. I knew I wasn't as bad as the black male officer the department had hired just before me, who had already received nine formal written complaints because he repeatedly ignored other offenses so he could make advances toward white females. The department hadn't fired him, so I figured I was safe. As beat down as I was, it still didn't occur to me that I had never been "one of the guys." Not only was he black, he was also male. I was neither. I hadn't even considered the fact that the new recruit who appeared in the department sometime around my ghost phase was probably my replacement—another male officer.

As I completed a theft report one morning, the lieutenant called me into his office and terminated me, explaining that I "didn't meet the standards of their training program." There was no further explanation, something even other departments don't understand. Stunned, I went through the motions, relinquishing my badge and firearm, and I returned all the gear the department had issued me. It didn't seem to matter that there were plenty of blanks in my training book, or that my supervisors had initialed several lessons I understood but hadn't ever had the chance to demonstrate on a small college campus during the holiday season. The department hadn't even given me the chance to resign instead, thereby saving my resume from disgrace. They just chewed me up and, not even a year later, spit me right back out. I was so numb afterward that the rest of that summer is a complete blur.

Afterward, I wasn't sure what to do. I followed the advice of friends and family and submitted an appeal to the department and then the university itself, explaining that my disrespectful treatment had corrupted my training. Neither entity cared, and nothing about my training was even given a second glance. The male CLEAT (Combined Law Enforcement Associations of Texas) representative I spoke with was also very unhelpful, something that discouraged me from exploring other attorneys or pursuing the matter any further. Everywhere I turned was a dead end.

It took me years to shake off the damage done to my psyche, betrayed by people I thought were my teammates, exploited by people I thought were my teachers. The first moment of my recovery began later that year when my parents found an article in a local newspaper detailing the arrest of my ghost phase FTO for violently assaulting his wife.[*] While I was not surprised by the incident, the date on which it happened—not even two months after my termination—made me thankful that *I* hadn't been the victim of the sergeant's brutal rage. It was then that I slowly began to understand that I wasn't a failure, but rather that my department had failed me.

Whether my experience at my department reflects sexual harassment or not is still debatable. I believe that the sexual harassment we discussed in the academy—indeed, sexual harassment as it is discussed anywhere in American society—is a straw man. Though society has changed significantly since the massive influx of female officers decades ago, the problem faced by women in law enforcement has not disappeared; it has merely gone under-ground. Because we acknowledge that society has changed, we assume it has improved, and we assume that sexual harassment is no longer an issue. And based on that fallacy, we ignore its more subtle forms. I was never slapped on the rear or called any derogatory names—not to my face, at least—but I *was* trained under a double standard, intentionally isolated without a support group to help me. I was surrounded by misogynists and people who didn't understand me and didn't want to. Though there was a witness to any verbal counseling I received, he was always a male, and he never seemed to care; I had no female supervisor to turn to. Even though I had always viewed myself as one of the guys, the department saw me as a female and badgered me with every negative connotation that came with it. It's nearly impossible to change such bias in people who have thought that way for their entire lives.

A background investigator for one particular department I applied to recently revealed that he learned that nine people had been training me, *nine* different people with nine different ways of doing things. How on earth was I supposed to please nine people, some of whom hated each other?

I was recently adopted as a reserve deputy within my local constable's office, and my experience there has been a far cry from that at my former department. The constable and the sergeants that interviewed me and read the first draft of this manuscript believed in me enough to give me the chance I have so desperately sought. Every deputy has accepted me and trained me with compassion and dignity. At one of the many early morning breakfasts at a local cafe, one sergeant noticed how tense I was and mentioned, "We're not your former department, you know. It's okay to be yourself around us." In that moment, the pressure and fear and isolation melted from me. Through their guidance and confidence, I am reassured that law enforcement is where I belong.

---

[*] Donna Fielder, "UNT officer charged with assault," *Denton Record Chronicle*, May 29, 2008, http://www.dentonrc.com/sharedcontent/dws/drc/localnews/stories/DRC_UNT_arrest_0529.3c5799b2.html, retrieved March 29, 2011.

I no longer blame myself, nor do I blame anyone at my former department. It's not the fault of any single individual; there are simply too many factors behind my disastrous experience there. I was young and naïve, and I admit that I didn't muster the discipline the job required of me. Then again, my mistakes were those that every rookie (and the occasional veteran officer) makes. When all is said and done, I believe that I just wasn't ready to be an officer at that point in my life. Was I the problem? No, it's more complicated than that. Many officers there had issues in their personal lives that they either visited upon those around them, or which made them cold and indifferent. The department itself is dysfunctional, fostering an atmosphere of apathy and compartmentalization, isolating the administration from the officers, and the officers from each other. There was no camaraderie, no brotherhood, no family in my former department. It is to empathy what a desert is to water; bonds like that simply can't survive there.

There are a lot of things I would have—should have—done differently. But those days are long gone, and the future is an open book. Since the day that I reaffirmed that law enforcement was the path I was meant to follow, it has been a difficult year. My former department seems to go to great lengths to convince other departments not to hire me, a vendetta that I still don't quite understand, something I hope this manuscript can change. I've recently toyed with the notion of meeting with some of my former supervisors at the department, if only to show them what a different person I am today, and maybe to ask for their blessing instead of their condemnation. As I write this, our relationship ended four years ago. There's no logic, nor honor, in sabotaging anyone's future endeavors. It was traumatic for everyone, but it's time to move on.

One damning whisper that eventually came to the forefront of my criticism at my former department was the notion that I had no command presence, and, looking back on my former self, I know that I probably didn't. How could I? After months and months of conflicting instruction and passive-aggressive degradation, I was left with utterly no confidence in my department, my career, or myself. How could I be proud to be a cop when no one around me wanted me there to begin with? Who on earth could succeed in such a stifling environment?

Today the story is much different. Everywhere I go, especially in the security and law enforcement industries, I am asked if I have ever been in the military. And people—even veterans—are stunned to learn that I haven't. Intrigued by the pattern, I finally asked someone what led them to think I might be a soldier. They said that I carried myself like one, that I seemed proud and confident, that I speak to others with respect, that it was obvious I know who I am and what I want in my life. Something in my eyes tells them that I've known and conquered fear.

And they're right. I've plodded through the red tape and the politics, the machismo and the ignorance, the embarrassment and the slander.

Today I am proud to be the woman I am. I still believe with every fiber of my being that I belong in law enforcement. And no amount of roadblocks can keep me from my destiny.

It's 1 p.m., and I've been working out since 9 a.m., running two miles, weightlifting with our gym's MMA (Mixed Martial Arts) fighters, and enduring a grueling boxing workout. I also plan on finishing the day with a hot yoga class this evening. My body aches, and I'll probably have trouble turning the steering wheel on the drive home. But I have energy still—a strength that has grown from within.

The Brazilian jiu jitsu class assembles on the mat, and I refill my water bottle and throw my heavy *gi* (martial arts uniform) over my shoulders, securing it with my belt. As everyone chooses a partner to grapple with, one of the newer guys, a blue belt from another gym, jokes and says he wants to grapple with me because he wants to "take it easy today." Everyone laughs, but they're not laughing at me. I introduce myself with a smile as my fingers take hold of his *gi* collar. He has no idea what's about to happen.

"Silly boys," one of the other women says. "They'll learn soon enough."

Don't Quit*

When things go wrong, as they sometimes will,
When the road you're trudging seems all uphill,
When the funds are low, and the debts are high,
And when you want to smile, but you have to sigh,
When care is pressing you down a bit,
Rest if you must, but don't you quit
Life is queer with its twists and turns,
As everyone of us sometimes learns,
And many a failure turns about,
When he might have won had he stuck it out,
Don't give up though the pace seems slow,
You might succeed with another blow.
Success is failure turned inside out,
The silver tint of the clouds of doubt,
And you never can tell how close you are,
It may be near when it seems so far,
So stick to the fight when you're hardest hit,
It's when things seem worse,
That you must not quit.

—Anonymous

---

* I have carried a copy of this Hallmark card of wisdom in my wallet for over thirty-five years. I still find it as inspirational today as the day I first found it. —D.L. June

It's Not about the Belt: Martial Arts Spirituality—Body, Mind, and Spirit

9

DALE L. JUNE

Contents

When you are not [training], remember, someone somewhere is [training], and when you meet him he will win.

—Ed Macauley, Basketball Hall of Famer

The word Zen has become part of the English language, but what exactly does [Zen] mean? It's much easier to answer the question "When is Zen?" for that answer would have to be "Now!" The whole point of Zen practice is to become fully aware, here and now. To come home to the present moment; this is truly where we live. Thinking verbally takes us far into the past, or into the distant future. But both past and future are fantasies, since the future isn't known and our memories of the past are often quite distorted accounts of what really happened. Zen exhorts one to "Come to your senses!" for when we get lost in thoughts of the past or future, life passes us by. When one mindfully dwells in the present moment, one completely dissolves into whatever activity manifests. One becomes the activity. Most people have had peak experiences, which all involve being so totally involved with life that one's sense of separateness dissolves into the experience.

—Rafael Espericueta*

---

* Rafael Espericueta, "What is the meaning of Zen?" http://www2.bakersfieldcollege.edu/resperic/what_is_the_meaning_of_zen.htm, retrieved August 26, 2012.

Kiaaaaa! The scream, the thrust of the hand or the kick of the leg, a pine board or a cement block is shattered. A martial artist receives his belt as recognition of his achievement. Students congratulate the achievement and spectators applaud. The new belt holder displays it with pride, believing he is now in possession of skill and knowledge to beat back any nefarious attack.

Years of aerobic exercise and strengthening with practice in technique against a rubber knife or gun on a padded surface in a controlled environment have prepared him for this: the moment he receives his new belt. What he is not prepared for is the fifteen seconds when he is surprisingly attacked on a public street, or when he is the "superhero" coming to the rescue of someone else who is being attacked by a "streetwise or prison-hardened thug" who is attacking with a real knife or gun and hard fists and steel-toed shoes.

Do not be afraid to question, as that is one of the keys to knowledge. I have been involved in some form of martial arts of one kind or another since I was eighteen years old. There was judo (in combat boots and fatigues in sawdust pits at Fort Gordon, Augusta, Georgia, on hot, humid summertime afternoons, with sweat pouring from every pore, the sawdust sticking to every piece of wet sweaty clothing and exposed flesh, even getting under the clothing); bayonet fighting (hand to hand and bayonets on a rifle); combat fighting and unarmed defense; personal fighting (use anything that works) techniques for survival and military police "come-alongs" in the Army; boxing, free-form fighting, more judo, and defensive tactics in college; and various other forms of "restraining holds," defensive maneuvers, and take-downs, including hybrid forms of karate during my law enforcement career. I also trained in the art of Tae Kwon Do for just under seven years. My most recent martial arts training is in traditional Wing Chun Kung Fu, including seminars in knife defense and Dim Mak Kung Fu and the "Quick Defense Method" of self-defense. They are all similar in one very important aspect: the philosophy of the longer a fight lasts, the greater the chances of getting injured or killed. The emphasis is on ending the fight as quickly and efficiently as possible (measured in seconds, or hundredths of a second, while also not drawing public attention).

The training I received accentuated a mental attitude toward quick delivery of a disabling blow, strike, or hold. Closely related to the mental attitude is belief of "a strong mind in a sound body," meaning that being physically fit is an integral part of the actual combative training. Fitness training, by definition, is aerobic and strengthening, usually following a regimen of prescribed exercises of stretching, warm-ups, and agility drills. The training time period allowed for the exercises is usually about twenty minutes, sometimes a little less, depending upon the intended time allotment for instruction and practice.

An important, yet mostly forgotten, overlooked, or simply ignored ingredient is the mental phase of martial arts training and learning to overcome the fight-or-flight reflex of the adrenalin "dump" when confronted in a threatening circumstance. This is where the importance of the spiritual characteristic is partially found; having belief in self, judgment of courage, and strength of principles to confront the immediate danger. The remaining portion of martial art spirituality is finding peace or "The Way of the Peaceful Warrior." Spirituality of martial arts breathes within you as calm surety and perfect peace. Thus I have found or developed a few inspirational sayings that seem to sum up the notion of responding to the initial fear brought on by sudden threats while also bringing tranquility and peace:

> A martial artist remembers to relax and breathe, summoning up internal forces and gathering energy from the Earth, Air, Wood, and Water.
> You can't be neutral in combat range.
> Fear makes men forget, and skill that cannot fight is useless. —Brasidas of Sparta
> The Spartans do not inquire how many the enemy are, but where they are. —Agis, 427 B.C.
> I do not love the bright sword for its sharpness, nor the arrow for its swiftness, nor the warrior for his glory. I love only that which they defend. —J.R.R. Tolkien
> Nothing can bring you peace but yourself. Nothing can bring you peace but the triumph of principles. —Ralph Waldo Emerson
> If one seeks peace and can be fiercely honest with oneself and the reality of life, one will undoubtedly find the place of strength, courage, and wisdom to live the life one seeks. —Leslie Moses, student of psychology, National University (Los Angeles)
> The candle that gives the light must endure the burning.

During my first year in college (which coincided with my rookie year as a city police officer), I had a very wise mentor. He told me, "Too soon old, too late smart." That's the time in my life when I foolishly rushed to combat and to fight any lawbreaker or drunk who felt like he wanted to challenge me. I didn't really care for the spiritual side of martial arts, only the mental and physical parts. I was young, fresh out of the Army, and looked like I was sixteen years old. "Give power to a man with an ego or something to prove and trouble will ensue."

My ego (or self-image of trying to be "hard boiled" or to prove to myself and others how "tough" I was) was such that I never hesitated to use a kick, punch, or strike with anyone who thought he wanted to test "that baby-faced kid." As a police officer, I was in a powerful position but yet had to learn the wisdom of using my power wisely, carefully, and "with heart"; always subconsciously thinking I had something to prove (though I couldn't identify what that was or if it was in fact real). I was in a physical fight at least once or twice a week. I had not learned the meaning of what Stan Lee (the creator of the comic book superhero Spider-Man) had Peter Parker's Uncle Charlie tell Peter, "With great power comes great responsibility." Former President George H.W. Bush said, "Use power to help people. For we are given power not to advance our own purposes, nor to make a great show in the world, nor a name. There is but one just use of power, and it is to serve people."* Power must be used wisely, responsibly, and often in ways far removed from physical domination. I was to learn my lessons the hard way.

One night I was working as the booking officer in a county jail. A city police officer brought in a middle-aged family man of Mexican descent. He was drunk and boisterous. As was standard procedure, my duty was to search him before continuing with the booking routine. I had him face a wall and spread eagle his hands against the wall and move his legs way out from the wall in a widespread fashion until his balance was on his tiptoes and the tips of his fingers on the wall. He shouted something and started to move; I kicked his feet out and he crashed face first onto the concrete floor. I then kicked him in the side with my square-toed cowboy boots I was wearing. From that point on, his cooperation was in ample supply. Later I learned I had fractured his ribs. The only thing that stopped him from suing me in a civil court was that as a struggling family man, he could not afford an attorney.

After I learned about his broken ribs, I felt very sorry for him and his family, but I was able to consciously accept my actions when rationalized as "he had it coming anyway," though I knew it was the wrong thing to do. Even today I feel very guilty of my treatment toward that man, attacking and hurting him for no specific reason and without just cause while he was in no position to protect himself. That day, I swore I would never again mistreat a prisoner and would do everything I could to ensure a prisoner wouldn't be beaten during my presence.

A year or so later, I was still only twenty-two, as a city police officer, I was working an "off-duty" assignment at a loud and raucous "rock" dance. There was a disturbance at the entrance where a drunk young man was shouting and threatening the people charging admission. My partner and I confronted him and placed him under arrest. We needed to handcuff his hands behind his back and found that he was so muscular that the handcuffs could only be clicked in the first notch. As we were placing him in the car to be taken to jail, he gave a deep grunt and pulled his hands apart with all his strength. Amazingly, the chain holding the handcuffs together broke and he turned toward me, swinging a strong right hand. The blow caught me by surprise and in the center of my chest. I was knocked backward and actually rolled.

---

* Anthony C. Scire, *The Power of 2* (Possibility Press, www.possibilitypress.com, 2002), 27.

The next day when I went to the doctor for the pain in my chest, I was told that it was a good thing that I was not standing against something and that I fell backward. If not, "He would have broken every bone in your chest."

In an aside of this story, I found out that the people at the admission door had incited the incident by "short changing" him, because they thought he was too drunk to realize he had been cheated. When he went to court to be charged with being drunk and disturbing the peace, I testified in his favor and asked the judge to be lenient and allow him to enlist in the military, which was his desire. The judge dismissed the charges and the young man soon left for the military. Me? I learned a very strong lesson. That night I thought to myself, "There must be a better way than having to fight all the time." I also recalled my father's words given me when I was a boy, "No matter how strong or big someone is, there is always someone stronger and bigger."

Of course, now I see the spiritual side as being the most important part of finding a "more peaceful way." As I got "too soon old," the wisdom of my mentor's words have come back to me and I try to follow this path of spirituality while trying to maintain my "combat readiness" of mind and aging body.

Age is the price one pays for wisdom: "You can read to gain knowledge, but you have to seek to gain wisdom."* Wisdom is spiritual. Wisdom comes from within and must be awakened by the messengers of education, training and experience. "Too often an education imposes other people's thoughts upon the student instead of helping him create his own thoughts" (—source unknown).

Martial arts training brings together the essence of understanding the relationship of education in methods and application, training to employ those methods and applications, and experience to understand the principles of tempering them with compassion and heart. The best way to win a fight is to avoid it. The spirit of martial arts is to learn to deescalate not escalate, as fighting is "physical force against physical force."

The philosophy of Wing Chun Kung Fu is to take control of your life and make the decisions that are right for you. The art of Wing Chun is truly a combat martial art, but it is also much more. Practitioners of Wing Chun will hopefully spend only a small fraction of a percent of time in their lives fighting. It is important, therefore, to be able to use the same concepts and principles used in fighting to better other non-combat areas of your life. Each fighting principle can also be interpreted philosophically. We believe that the practice of Wing Chun, and an understanding of its principles and philosophies, should be a catalyst to putting each practitioner in the driver's seat of his or her life. The development of great fighting abilities should give each of us the ability to

---

* *Llewellyn's 2004 Witches' Spell-A-Day Almanac* (St. Paul, MN: Llewellyn, 2004).

be kind, compassionate, and loving by overcoming the fears that often mani-fest themselves as anger and hate. The truly competent warrior is not boastful. The truly secure person is free from the need to impress others with his or her physical prowess and free from the need to have the approval of others. He or she can be understanding, accepting, and kind without the fear of being thought weak for his or her kindness.

The reason for the philosophy is to help each of you tap into the inner power that we all have and to help you to take control of and responsibility for your own life. It is designed to help you recognize how much more powerful positive energy and accomplishing goals of a positive nature is, as opposed to negative thought and deed. Our worst enemy is often ourselves. Look inside of yourself and overcome your demons of fear and insecurity and you will find a path to a happier life. No matter how many people you can beat in battle, you will find no lasting happiness in bringing harm to others. Competent fight-ing skills are important but should be used to protect yourself or those you love in times of danger. You must choose your battles wisely. Your fighting skills should be a catalyst to enlightenment. By helping you to gain strength of character and confidence, your skills should give you peace of mind, thereby eliminating insecurity and giving you the capacity to be at peace and in har-mony with others.[*]

Sadly, however, I have over the past few years observed much younger aspiring martial artists following only the same two-thirds of the martial arts triad of body, mind, and spirit as I wrongly did, most often focusing on the physical and, to a much lesser degree, the mental while neglecting the spiritual. Their need to learn to fight (or to gain a colored belt) has become their motivating factor, and most probably have never been in a fight in all their lives and will never be, not because of their "temperament," but because of who they are. How would they react in a real confrontation with a "tat-tooed street thug." Would they "freeze or flee" probably not fight because of the suddenness of the appearance of their attacker? This type of person will even treat newcomers as a target for their aggression, never taking into con-sideration that they were once a beginner.

Ego, the appearance of "hard-boiled" toughness and the need to prove something to someone are both reasons too many people enroll in martial arts and self-defense programs. Indeed, the primary focus appears to be more on the body with physical fitness or building muscular strength, and wrongful mindless pursuit of belts, sashes, and "testing" or "grading" with competition being to see who reaches the highest sash the quickest or who scores the highest point total in grading. There is also just something very wrong about a person who goes to lower sashes and brags that "I have been

[*] Philip Holder, "Wing Chun philosophy," Wing Chun Online, http://www.wingchunonline. com/Wingchun/Concepts_philosophy.html, retrieved July 11, 2012.

here about fifteen minutes longer than you" or "I have attended X number of classes in a row (and hold a higher sash or belt) so let me show you how it's done," then goes on to physically attack the new student, arguably to demonstrate his own "advanced" skill.

It's not the quantity of classes a person attends but the quality of understanding and development of ability that is the desired end product derived from training. Many martial arts students come to the mat with a negative attitude, wrongfully believing their sole purpose is to learn to kick and punch a pad several thousand times, which in turn will make them martial artists. They miss the whole concept of martial arts being the way to tranquility and spiritual strength. "Everybody has a plan until they get punched in the face" (—Mike Tyson).

Martial arts were originated as a lifestyle, not a goal or an arrival point. A colored sash was not even used until later in the evolution of the art. In some parts of the world, a belt or sash is still not awarded for mastering a technique or reaching a special level. All it means is where we are on our journey. We never arrive; we are always growing, students for life. All in all, I regret that, maybe by financial necessity and the need for instructors to earn a living, one-third of the body, mind, and spirit philosophy is being neglected by most modern teachers, in and outside of martial arts. Maybe the Western mind is not able to grasp the Eastern philosophy of body, mind, and spirit united.

I personally would like to see a greater emphasis placed on understanding the Zen* or spirituality of "fighting without fighting" for finding a peaceful way to engage the troubles and rants of the more physically inclined. I am convinced the Japanese belief of truth/courage/compassion is a summation of the rightness of martial arts, which is fully expressed in the Bushido code of the Samurai: honesty and justice; polite courtesy; heroic courage; honor; compassion; complete sincerity; and duty and loyalty.

Justice/Rectitude/Right Decision[†]

This is about doing the right thing or making the right decision, not because it's easy, but because it's ethically and morally correct. No matter the outcome or result, one does not lose face if tempering

---

* Zen—Enlightenment can be attained through meditation, self-contemplation, and intuition. http://www.thefreedictionary.com/Zen.

† This section was obtained on September 1, 2012, from Oriental Outpost: Adventures in Asian Arts, http://www.orientaloutpost.com/learn-from-wisdom.php. (Characters may represent both Japanese and Chinese lettering.)

proper justice. This character can also be defined as righteousness, justice, morality, honor, or "right conduct." In a more expanded definition, it can mean loyalty to friends, loyalty to the public good, or patriotism. This idea of loyalty and friendship comes from the fact that you will treat those you are loyal to with morality and justice.

Bravery/Courage

This character can be translated as bravery, courage, valor, or fearless in Chinese, Japanese, and Korean.

This word is about courage; it is bravery in the face of fear. You do the right thing even when it is hard or scary. When you are courageous, you don't give up. You try new things. You admit mistakes. This kind of courage is the willingness to take action in the face of danger and peril. These characters can also be translated as braveness, valor, heroic, fearless, boldness, prowess, gallantry, audacity, daring, dauntless, and/ or courage in Japanese, Chinese, and Korean. This version of bravery/ courage can be an adjective or a noun. The first character means bravery and courage by itself. The second character means "daring" by itself. The second character just emphasizes the meaning of the first but adds an idea that you are not afraid of taking a dare, and you are not afraid of danger.

Benevolence

Beyond "benevolence," this word can be also be defined as "charity" or "mercy," depending on context. The meaning suggests that one should pay alms to the poor, care for those in trouble, and take care of your fellow man (or woman). This is one of the five tenets of Confucius. In fact, it is a subject on which Confucius spent a great deal of time explaining to his disciples. This benevolent-related word has also been translated as perfect virtue, selflessness, love for humanity, humaneness, goodness, good will, or simply "love" in the nonromantic form. In the English translation, benevolence could mean "do no intentional harm."

Respect

We show respect by speaking and acting with courtesy. We treat others with dignity and honor the rules of our family, school, and nation. Respect yourself, and others will respect you. This is also one of the five tenets of Confucius. This character can also be translated as propriety, good manners, politeness, rite, worship, or an expression of gratitude.

Sincerity

誠

This character means truth, faith, fidelity, sincerity, trust, and/or confidence.

This is the true essence of sincerity. It takes strength of personality to be truly sincere without overdoing it. Speaking of strength, this is probably the strongest way to convey the idea of sincerity in the Chinese language without overdoing it. The first character literally means true, real, and genuine, whereas the second character means sincere and honest.

Honor

名誉

This version of honor is about having or earning the respect of others and about your reputation. It is the status of being worthy of honor (not to be confused with doing honorable things or specific actions).

Loyalty/Faithful/Devoted

This is a Japanese way to write "loyalty." It also contains the ideas of being faithful, devoted, true, and obedient.

Filial Piety

This character represents filial piety. Some will define this in more common English as "respect for your parents and ancestors." This is a subject deeply emphasized by the ancient philosophy and teachings of Confucius.

Honesty/Fidelity

This is another character that expresses the idea of honesty. It can also mean truth, faith, believe in, fidelity, sincerity, trust, and/or confidence

Wisdom

When you meet wise people, you should learn from them and be inspired to become as wise as they are. In this case, you should seek wise people to learn from throughout your life.

Always try to learn enough to become equal to them. It also suggests that the process of learning and seeking wisdom is a nonending cycle.

You May Learn from Victory; You Will Learn from Failure

This Chinese proverb literally translates as "[even a general who has won a] hundred victories [may be] hard put to see through the enemy's [strategy], [but one who has] broken [his] arm three [times] [will] be a good doctor." Figuratively, this means: One cannot always depend on past successes to guarantee future success, but one can always learn from lessons drawn from failure.

Courtesy and Respect

"Courtesy is more than good manners; it is a way of showing respect to others" is a cliché I have preached many times over the years. Respect is not won through aggressive action but by honesty, honesty to one's self and honesty to appreciate the other person for being himself as a fellow human; showing sincerity and compassion when another is in distress or having the courage to stand for right.

For me, I have decided that I may never again participate in "on-the-mat testing" for a belt or sash. My testing has come and gone in the form of actual application "in the street" and on the highway of life.

> One who excels as a warrior does not appear formidable;
> One who excels in fighting is never aroused in anger;
> One who excels in defeating his enemies does not join issues;
> One who excels in employing others humbles himself before them*

Performance Degradation

The Mind Is a Target

Performance degradation occurs with (a) person trying to dial 911, the climber who bumbles repeatedly while hanging from his fingertips at the crux of a dangerous route, and a fighter who suddenly realizes that what he knows in the gym is not what he knows in the ring.

The skills you possess in a calm, controlled environment will probably not be the skills you possess when it really matters. The impact of stress may mean the difference between victory and defeat, a clean climb and a jarring fall, or even life and death.†

Fear freezes. "Fear makes men forget, and skill that cannot fight is useless." There's a direct relation between stress-induced heart rate and both mental and physical performance. Too low, such as when you're just waking up, and

---

* Wing Chun Kung Philosophy posted on a bulletin board at the Sifu Rasun Wing Chun Kung Fu Academy, North Hollywood, California.
† Craig Weller, "Combat psychology and sports performance." www.t-nation.com/free_online_article/sports_body_training_performance/combat_psychology_and_sports_performance, retrieved may 11, 2013.

you can't think or react very quickly. Too high, and one's ability to think and perform motor skills degrades.*

A sudden startle, a menacing threat from an antagonist, or an argument suddenly escalated to physical exchange causes what is called an "adrenaline dump." The heart beat rapidly increases, the blood pressure and respiration rise, a dizzying feeling swirls around the brain causing two opposing results, commonly referred to as the "fight or flight reflex." "Researchers determine the brain has two ways of dealing with a stimulus that causes fear: If it's far away, it strategizes; if it's nearby, it's reactive."† When the aggressor is at a distance of precontact the mind or brain of the object of the aggressor's attack devises a plan or strategy to counter the moves of the opponent or attacker. In other words, the brain of the victim forms a game plan of where, how and when to strike. This is when the mental aspect of martial arts controls the physical. The victim takes a deep breath, relaxes, slows his heartbeat and respiration, and prepares for combat, or if the circumstances warrant, he takes flight.

> But the one thing you have total control over is *you*! What if you did not react, but instead you responded to a condition. Now this may sound like cutting awfully fine hairs in the field of vocabulary, but think about it. By responding, you are acting in a totally unprecedented manner—a way in which the "bad guy" did not think about. This causes the bad guy to have to waste precious seconds figuring out how to "react" to you, as it was not in his game book. Suddenly, you are in control. Any emotional edge that the bad guy had has just been neutralized as well, for it is a psychological impossibility to think and be emotional at the same time. If the bad guy has to stop and think how to handle this unplanned event, he automatically becomes less emotional and loses any edge he created for himself when he was pumping himself up for this attack.‡

The average "barroom fight" lasts an average of two seconds, enough time for one attacker to throw one hard surprise opening blow and perhaps a few quick punches before the fight is broken up, giving the victim no time to retaliate. The average street assault lasts approximately fifteen seconds, hardly enough time to score more than three or four well placed punches or kicks, if that, or any at all, especially while experiencing momentary adrenaline paralysis.

---

* Craig Weller, "Combat psychology."
† Nikhil Swaminathan, "The fear factor: When the brain decides it's time to scram," *Scientific American*, August 23, 2007, http://www.scientificamerican.com/article .cfm?id=the-brain-fear-factor.
‡ Michael Corcoran, "Protection agent's guide to identifying the potentially violent subject or threat assessments on the run," as cited in *Protection, Security and Safeguards; Practical Approaches and Perspectives*, 2nd edition, edited by Dale L. June (Boca Raton, FL: CRC Press/Taylor & Francis, 2012).

"The victory is not defeating an enemy; True victory gives love and changes the enemy's heart."*

If you cultivate a sense of your spiritual worth, if you understand that there are greater things in this world than what we have or what others perceive us to be, then there is no reason to fear. When fear vanishes, so does anger. When anger is gone, your thoughts become clear. When your thoughts are clear, you function at your best.

Only lazy people attempt to make themselves look better by degrading others. You can practice being brave by being kind. You can practice courage by being tolerant of the beliefs of others. Accept that there is more than one way to accomplish any goal. What is the right way for one may not be the right way for others. Those who think that theirs is the only way, or that they know all of the answers have condemned themselves to ignorance. When you keep an open mind your potential for growth is unlimited. When you are free from fear, you can experience each moment to the fullest. This focused and centered state of mind will help you to excel in anything you undertake. Only by letting go of fear and casting out anger can one truly experience the joys of life.†

Without martial art spirituality, the martial art mind and body, even trained to kick and punch a pad two or three thousand times, is merely "playground play" or a ripe invitation to bully the less inclined and trained. Many times a black-belt holder has been soundly defeated by someone who never took a martial arts class in his life. This happened for two reasons. First, the street thug has more intent and aggressive attitude than the black-belt holder and he usually strikes suddenly, surprisingly, and with violence and, second, the black belt's mind was more on his/her belt status while training than learning to react to a surprise attack. Being able to kick or hit a pad a thousand times, or break a board with a chop, punch, or kick in the safe environment of a training studio or waving a brightly colored belt or sash will never equal having the capacity to favorably end a life-threatening fight in reality under one minute or less—or using Zen and peaceful avoidance of the fight in the first place.

"The candle that gives the light must endure the burning." A martial artist does not become a martial artist in the truest sense simply by learning to kick and punch. It takes years of study, practice, understanding the philosophy, psychology, and spirituality of all the words "martial artist" implies about going through the fire and becoming stronger in body, mind, and spirit. A piece of steel becomes stronger by its exposure to fire and water.

---

* Morihei Ueshiba, founder of Aikido, as cited by Rick Fields, *The Code of the Warrior in History, Myth, and Everyday Life* (New York: Harper Perennial, 1991).
† Philip Holder "FEAR: Your worst enemy," Wing Chun Online, http://www.wingchunonline. com/Wingchun/Library_article_P2.html, retrieved on July 11, 2012.

A martial artist becomes stronger through exposure to the spirit and intent of what "martial artist wisdom" means.

"A martial artist (police officer or security officer) is a fighter but does not fight out of aggression." The spirit of martial arts is intrinsic to this statement. "Find your source of strength and apply it to the problem at hand." The Zen of martial arts is a reconciliation with the spiritual consciousness of the universe and the purpose of Man's existence. Spirituality is understanding the interconnectedness of the web of life between Man and Nature. It is a "spirit to transform or transcend aggression through peaceful ways, words and demeanor." As the wasp will sting only when frightened or senses fear, a true martial artist, understanding the spirit of his training and confidence will only fight when necessary to protect himself or others when there is no other way out and will maintain courage in the face of threatening forces.

Emptying Your Cup

> The Japanese master Nan-in gave audience to a professor of philosophy. Serving tea, Nan-in filled his visitor's cup, and kept pouring. The professor watched the overflow until he could restrain himself no longer: "Stop! The cup is over full, no more will go in." Nan-in said: "Like this cup, you are full of your own opinions and speculations. How can I show you Zen unless you first empty your cup?"*

Emptying your "cup" is a lesson to be learned by all. It means ridding yourself of all prejudice and bias, and being willing to accept ideas, opinions, and situations of others. On the training mat, whatever the art, including self-defense, it is common to see a new student, having previous experience, bring his biases and prejudices to the session and initially "fight the problem" by continuously stating, "I'd do it this way or that. In my previous training we did it this way." That may be fine but he has not "emptied his cup." He is full of his own opinions and speculations and may not find that possibly there is a better and more efficient way of thinking and doing.

It's not only on the training mat, however, that opinionated people refuse to change their way of thinking, wishing to retain their prejudices and biases and thus disqualifying them from understanding and accepting new people, methods, and thoughts. Being in this frame of thinking leads to failing to see other perspectives and views, maybe leading to a serious breakdown of communication; and as it has been pointed out, failure to communicate is often the precursor to misunderstanding and violence. No respect can be shown nor can a relationship be maintained without communication. Proper

---

* "Empty your cup," http://purifymind.com/EmptyCup.htm, retrieved September 1, 2012.

communication, learning (and training) begins with an emptying of the cup, allowing room for perspective. A way of personal growth, self-development, and self-knowledge begins with "emptying your cup."

Meditation and Stress

A martial artist remembers to relax and breath, summoning up internal forces and gathering energy from the Earth, Air, Wood and Water.[*]

Zen helps a Samurai reach his "absolute." This is done through strong meditation. Their focus becomes so strong that they can handle anything that comes their way. It is also a way to eliminate fear by total concentration.[†]

Fifteen minutes of total relaxation through meditation will restore energy, bring a brighter perspective, and moderate stress and fear. If done properly, with systemic breathing, those fifteen minutes can be equated with an hour of actual unfettered sleep. Earnest meditation is a manner of self-hypnosis releasing all earthly groundings. It originates with relaxing all muscles in the body, beginning with the toes and slowly moving up through the abdomen, the shoulders, neck, around and down the spine. The practitioner closes his eyes and with each muscle relaxation takes in a deep cleansing breath, holds it for four seconds, then takes four more seconds to expel it, waits four seconds then begins another four second deep intake of breath. This should be repeated four times to cleanse the body of residual air and stress.

At first the person may create thoughts of a youth playing in a beautiful sunlit meadow, near a tree-lined brook, perhaps flying a kite in the robin's egg blue sky. There are flowers of all colors abounding and the child is carefree and joyous. As the meditation deepens, all thoughts seem to pass away as the process of "emptying his cup" brings a peaceful, floating feeling or sensation. He becomes the kite, flying freely and dancing on the wind, above the swaying treetops, amid the trace of puffy clouds. The deep intense breathing has now become less concentrated and is similar to a serene undisturbed sleep, yet it continues its pattern of originating deep within, from the abdomen up through the diaphragm, upward over the neck muscles, keeping them and the back and shoulder muscles relaxed. After approximately fifteen minutes, normal breathing will return, the person will slowly open his eyes and feel fully refreshed as though he has traveled through time and space to another dimension of light and purity. Martial arts spirituality is

[*] Stuart Alve Olson, *The Jade Emperor's Mind Seal Classic: The Taoist Guide to Health, Longevity, and Immortality* (Rochester, VT: Inner Traditions, 2003).
[†] Bill Hanks, "Bushido, The Way of the Warrior," April 22, 2008, http://voices.yahoo.com/bushido-way-warrior-1393947.html?cat=37, retrieved September 2, 2012.

meditation, rejuvenation, and strengthening or reawakening of the spirit and can be defined as the way of the small or little thought, being one with the universe.

Self-Actualization

Martial arts training brings one closer to self-actualization as defined by sociologist Abraham Maslow in his hierarchy of Man's needs. From basic physiological needs of air, water, food, and sex as the foundation for his pyramid, Maslow placed self-actualization at the apex of the pyramid because it is the most difficult to reach and the lower steps in the ladder are more important. In martial arts, working within the framework of mastering the whole art, including the mental phase or spirituality, brings the practitioner closer to the top of the pyramid. Maslow's definition of self-actualization may be considered synonymous with "The Spirituality of Martial Arts."

> Maslow loosely defined *self-actualization* as "the full use and exploitation of talents, capacities, potentialities, etc." Self-actualization is not a static state. It is an ongoing process in which one's capacities are fully, creatively, and joyfully utilized. "I think of the self-actualizing man not as an ordinary man with something added, but rather as the ordinary man with nothing taken away. The average man is a full human being with dampened and inhibited powers and capacities."
>
> Most commonly, self-actualizing people see life clearly. They are less emotional and more objective, less likely to allow hopes, fears, or ego defenses to distort their observations. Maslow found that all self-actualizing people are dedicated to a vocation or a cause. Two requirements for growth are commitment to something greater than oneself and success at one's chosen tasks. Major characteristics of self-actualizing people include creativity, spontaneity, courage, and hard work.[*]

According to Maslow, Man reaches or obtains self-actualization through eight steps that are very similar to martial arts training:[†]

1. Concentration—"First, self-actualization means experiencing fully, vividly, selflessly, with full concentration and total absorption."

    When involved in martial arts training, the practitioner, in the words of Wing Chun Kung Fu in the first form, Sholin Tao, (which means "way of the small thought" or "focus on what you are doing

---

[*] http://www.abraham-maslow.com/m_motivation/Self-Actualization.asp, retrieved May 7, 2012.
[†] Ibid.

while you are doing it and nothing else") trains while fully, vividly, selflessly, with full concentration and total absorption.

2. Growth choices—If we think of life as a series of choices, then self-actualization is the process of making each decision a choice for growth. We often have to choose between growth and safety, between progressing and regressing. Each choice has its positive and its negative aspects. To choose safety is to remain with the known and the familiar but to risk becoming stultified and stale. To choose growth is to open oneself to new and challenging experiences but to risk the unknown and possible failure.

    Obviously a martial artist is not of a personality type to seek the known and familiar and to stick with safety. He or she is seeking new challenges mentally and physically. These are the growth choices a martial artist makes the first time he steps onto the mat.

3. Self-awareness—In the process of self-actualizing, we become more aware of our inner nature and act in accordance with it.

    The physical effect of martial arts training is realized immediately or within a very short period; it is the mental—the spirit—that comes with understanding and accepting one's self and igniting a "better" person inside.

4. Honesty and taking responsibility for one's actions are essential elements in self- actualizing. Rather than pose and give answers that are calculated to please another or to make ourselves look good, we can look within for the answers. Each time we do so, we get in touch with our inner selves.

    Honesty is of such great importance, of being honest to one's self and to all others, that it is an important part of the Bushido code of the warrior (discussed earlier). A martial artist cannot be false because the results of his training and understanding suddenly become illuminated with the light of truth the moment he needs to utilize his skills.

5. Judgment—The first four steps help us develop the capacity for "better life choices." We learn to trust our own judgment and our own inner feelings and to act accordingly.

    Another name for judgment is discretion and as the saying goes, "discretion is the better part of valor." A martial artist having the confidence of his training and knowledge uses his discretion to avoid trouble more often than he chooses to fight. Being able to exude courage and confidence shows an aggressor that the person he is about to attack is not a "freebie" and this may be enough to discourage him from the attack. A police officer in full uniform and with his mere presence and confident attitude is able to dissuade a wrongdoer from belligerence and resistance; the martial artist, exercising an aura of courage and confidence, may be able to dampen the enthusiasm of a potential belligerent attacker.

6. Self-development—Self-actualization is also a continual process of developing one's potentialities. It means using one's abilities and intelligence and "working to do well the thing that one wants to do."

   Like most skills, even the martial arts are a diminishing and perishable skill if not practiced and trained. A professional is a person having a particular skill, education, and training, who continuously works to improve his skills and to keep himself ready for the "moment of truth" when he must perform to the highest levels. Many professions, not only martial arts, fall into this category; police officers, nurses, doctors, other first responders and athletes, to name just a few. Continuous self-development and improvement are entities that cannot be overlooked. There was a very interesting television ad a few years ago for the National Football League that seems to say it all about self-development: "The amateur practices a routine until he gets it right; a professional practices it until he can't do it wrong."

7. Peak experiences—"Peak experiences are transient moments of self-actualization." We are more whole, more integrated, more aware of ourselves and of the world during peak moments. At such times we think, act, and feel most clearly and accurately. We are more loving and accepting of others, have less inner conflict and anxiety, and are better able to put our energies to constructive use. Some people enjoy more peak experiences than others, particularly those Maslow called transcending self-actualizers.

   Those nights Kobe Bryant goes for eighty-one points or hits a buzzer-beater to win the game are when he is at his peak performance level. There are many things that are brought together at the same time to lift one to one's peak performance. It may be an adrenaline "high" or a combination of biorhythms, mental attitude, spirit, or an attitude of being ready for "this moment." Some may call it "being in the zone" but by any name, peak performances are those moments when all "pistons are firing."

8. Lack of ego defenses—A further step in self-actualization is to recognize our ego defenses and to be able to drop them when appropriate. To do so, we must become more aware of the ways in which we distort our images of ourselves and of the external world through repression, projection, and other defenses.

   "Leave your ego at the door" reads a sign at many martial arts training centers. The same can be said for most professions, be it law enforcement, medicine, or academia. As stated back in the early pages of this book, "There will always be someone who is bigger, stronger, faster, smarter, etc."

Martial arts are not a "thing we do" but rather a "path in life" that we live by. It is a moral code for the body, mind and spirit. It is not like football, baseball or any other sport. It is a path to bring us to a higher level of consciousness and teaches us immortal virtues to live by.

It connects us to the Forefathers and Foremothers dating back thousands of years ago. One of the main reasons They have passed the Art on to us is so that we would keep the Art alive within our generation and pass it on to the generation after us.

The Art is always superior to the practitioner and therefore must be held above even our own esteem. It is important to take what we know and empower others with our knowledge as others have empowered us. This is probably the greatest spiritual attribute of living the martial way of life. I hope that you will stay true to your Art, your path, and to yourself, and continue to improve not only your own skills but to empower others who a "Power Greater Than Yourself" will send across your path.*

Spirituality of Martial Arts and the Power of Three

The number "3" is a unique yet popular number. In martial arts, we have the combination of body, mind, and spirit, which encompasses the physical, mental, and spiritual makeup of a human being. We have three stances or forms (we connect our center line with two points on the Earth). Punches come in combinations of three. The time is now (present), not a second ago (past) nor a second from now (the future). In Japanese culture (as well as martial arts tradition), there are the Three Treasures: truth, courage, and compassion.

The following are a few interesting things I found on the Internet relative to the number "3" and are in some way connected to the world and spiritual aspect of martial arts, which is as important as the physical and mental. Obviously there are many more, but I leave those to your imagination or your own research.

> The number three is used in the Torah to mediate between two opposing or contradictory values. The third value mediates, reconciles, and connects the two. Three is the number of truth.
> Time is divided into three portions: the past, the present, and the future. The position in time that is most expressive of the no-physical is the present, because it is so fleeting and instantaneous. The function of that time, the present, is its service as connector. The number three expresses connection.

* Martial Arts Dim Mak Grandmaster Dr. Joseph Bannon, Bannon Institute, e-mail to author, June 3, 2012.

According to Jewish law, once something is done three times, it is considered a permanent thing. Once we have done something three times, we have connected to it and connected it to this world. In Christianity we have the Father, the Son, and the Holy Spirit.

The number "3" represents permanence. That's why we do things in threes, because it adds strength to our acts (i.e., three strikes and you're out).

"3" is the first geometrical figure. Two straight lines cannot possibly enclose any space, or form a plane figure; neither can two plane surfaces form a solid. Three lines are necessary to form a plane figure; and three dimensions of length, breadth, and height are necessary to form a solid. "3" therefore, stands for that which is solid, real, substantial, complete, and entire.

God's attributes are three: omniscience, omnipresence, and omnipotence. We have been encouraged to live with (the cardinal virtues of) faith, hope, and charity. Thought, word, and deed complete the sum of human capability.

In the Taoist tradition, we have the Great Triad of Heaven, Human, and Earth.

Have a healthy, safe, and spiritual martial arts life. See the magical combination of three?

Positivism and Negativism

A positive attitude breeds positivism; a negative attitude fosters negativism. It is up to each individual to cultivate and embrace an attitude cohesive to his or her education, training, experience, and emotion. A negative attitude drains the life from a positive spirit.

The spirit of martial arts is intrinsic to a martial artist. It can be seen in several contexts of his demeanor. He has kind words to say, makes eye contact with people, uses a gentle tone of voice, maintains a relaxed but structured and balanced posture with conservative body movements, shows interest in and attention and sensitivity to others in conversation and facial expressions, and keeps in touch with his own feelings as well as the feelings of others. His personal manners show a graciousness to others and his positive attitude shines through with humility, patience, and gratitude.

In martial arts traditions, we strengthen whatever we focus on and give our energy to. Martial arts are a pathway to personal and spiritual development. People are said to have a fighting spirit, spirit to live, free spirit, happy spirit, or brave spirit. Others may be dispirited, have a broken spirit, or be spiritless. A positive spirit is like an invisible hand; you can't see it but you can feel it. The soul mirrors the spirit of a person. A losing (or negative) spirit will have a weak soul; a winning (or positive) spirit will have a strong soul. Therefore, we can conclude that martial arts bring equal unification of body, mind, and spirit, creating forces that guide and strengthen our soul, with the soul being the full essence of a person.

Life Lesson Experience 10

KEILA ALVARENGA

My name is Keila Alvarenga. I was born January 29, 1976, in San Miguel, San Salvador. I am thirty-six years old, and my hobbies are listening to music, going to the gym, yoga, and spending quality time with my daughter Savannah. She is six years old. I am a registered nurse specializing in surgery.

I lived in El Salvador the first 4 years of my life. Then my parents sent for me in 1980 to come to the United States. It was a drastic change for me. I only spoke Spanish, and the first 3 years of my schooling were very challenging for me, due to the language barrier and my parents only spoke to me in Spanish at home, but I finally caught on in second grade.

Even though we were in America now, my parents still practiced their cultural beliefs and ways of living. My mother worked a full-time job, but it was understood that women should be at home, cooking, and tending to the kids. Girls were not allowed to voice their opinion. I was not allowed to socialize with the adults or talk to boys. The expectations for me were to finish school, set me up with a nice young man, and get married when I turned eighteen and form a family.

As I learned, here in America, I had a choice for my future, and what my parents had planned for me was not what I wanted for my life. When I turned eighteen, I joined the United States Navy and that has been the most valuable and cherished life lesson experience for me, one that I will never forget and will carry with me until I die.

I will never forget July 17, 1994—my first day at boot camp. It was 3 a.m. when we arrived at the naval base in Orlando, Florida. As the bus parked, the yelling of the company commanders began. It was like a dream or a movie that I had seen. I thought I was mature enough and wise enough to handle what I had signed up for, but I realized very quickly that I had a lot to learn.

Eighty girls in one big room, ages ranging from eighteen to the oldest at thirty-one. We were all from different states, cultures, and races. We spent two-and-one-half months together. In the beginning of boot camp, it was very stressful: Learning to live with eighty girls, and getting us all to be in the same state of mind, mentally and physically. I thought some of the girls were not going to make it. There was a lot of crying in the beginning and girls trying to commit suicide just to try to get out of there.

My company commander, Petty Officer Class Trent, an intense woman, cut us no slack. She was tough but fair. We started our day at 5 a.m. with physical training and then activities all day until 10 p.m., nonstop. If one of us didn't pass an inspection or test, she would make it known to the company and we all paid the price for not being good teammates. First lesson learned: Teamwork. Our company learned quickly what we had to do, and what the company commander was trying to teach us. After the first 3 weeks, the morale changed in our company. The girls were coming together making sure we were always squared away, from uniforms to academically and physically. By the end of boot camp, I had learned about teamwork, honor, courage, and commitment.

Our company was awarded first place out of five companies that graduated that year. We were the last graduating class in Orlando. Joining the Unites States Navy taught me that I did have a voice; that women were just as equal and strong as men; and, more important, I learned teamwork, honor, courage, and commitment. It was the best life lesson experience for me. It shaped my life, career, and future.

Tough Love: The Overpowering Addiction of Cocaine

11

CHEYANNE HILL

No one intends to become addicted to drugs. Unfortunately, many of us do. The pattern of addiction begins with an individual, who, like most people in our society, is well intentioned and has hopes, goals, and dreams for the future. My husband had hopes, goals, and dreams. His addiction was not planned; it usually never is. The general attitude is "I can stop anytime I want to" or "I won't get addicted, other people do."

I married young, right out of high school to a wonderful man. I was seventeen at the time I met the man who later became my husband. I felt like the luckiest woman in the world when we married. He was a few years my senior when we met and was attending a university. By the time I graduated from high school, he was ready to graduate from college with a law degree. After his graduation, he landed a job in a small law firm, becoming partners with an old friend from law school.

During my second year of college, I withdrew from school to go to work with my husband. It was a very foolish mistake. At the time, I thought it was the right thing to do. I was young, in love, and so willing to do whatever I needed to do to help my husband succeed in his endeavors to become a successful criminal attorney.

After his first year in practice, everything was running smoothly. We worked around good people, his partner was exceptional, and business looked very promising. Things were going so good we began to plan a family and our future. We figured that in two years, business would really pick up and we could have our family and live in peace and happiness forever. Well that time never came and things for us made a 180-degree turn when cocaine plagued our lives.

During the second year of my husband's business, we attended a party where there were trays of drugs (cocaine, marijuana, alcohol, etc.) being passed around. To my surprise, when the tray came to my husband, he took it and proceeded to snort a few lines of cocaine. I can't imagine how to begin to express how shocked I was and he knew it. I angrily voiced my opinion on how I felt, as what he had done was entirely against all we believed in.

Because I knew a few people who had gotten involved with drugs and saw that it had totally ruined their lives, I was fiercely opposed to any type of drug usage. That included recreational use as well, for recreational use could and has led to more serious problems. A couple of people I knew lost jobs, careers, and relationships all because of drugs. The thought of something like that happening to my husband and me was not even imaginable. I really had a dislike for drugs because of those factors.

Even though he knew how angry, upset, and disappointed I was, he continued to get high throughout the evening. He assured me he was just having a little fun and for me to relax. I was irate with his behavior and wanted to leave but did not want to leave him alone with those people and all those drugs. Right at that moment, I stereotyped him as a druggie but for some reason I felt I had to stay and protect him. We ended up staying several more hours than what I had intended because every time I suggested we leave, he stalled by getting another drink or taking another hit of cocaine. When we finally left, he was as high as the dark clouds in the sky and I ended up driving us home because he was too intoxicated.

That night was the beginning of the end of a good marriage and the beginning of a hellish nightmare. I can't find the words to explain how much in love and happy I was prior to that particular night of the dreadful party. I felt so lucky to have such a terrific husband; he made me feel special all the time until drugs became the center of his life. Anything that was of importance to him—family, friends, business—became secondary to him. It's alarming what drugs can to do an individual. I saw for myself how cocaine changed my husband into a person I no longer knew.

The next day after that particular party, we had a long discussion on what had taken place at the party. He assured me that it was just recreational, that he was just having a little fun, and for me to not worry about anything. For about a week after our discussion, things went back to normal with our daily routine with work and general activities. Then one night he came home with a vial of cocaine. I confronted him, asking him what he thought he was doing. He stated he needed a little something just for that evening only. I totally went off verbally on him and he again reassured me that it wasn't anything I had to worry myself over. After that evening, he continued to bring home vials of cocaine every night. The vials turned into grams and then bigger qualities.

When the weekend came, he would get high and stay high all weekend. As the effect of the cocaine wore off, he would crash and sleep, often for several days. I badgered myself over and over again, wondering why he started getting high so late in life. He was twenty-five, educated, had a wonderful career, and had everything going for him, including a happy marriage. It made me wonder if it was me that he was unhappy with; had I caused his addiction? All this continually ran through my mind.

At first I was in denial, thinking his drug use would soon come to an end, but it got worse as time went on. About a year after his initial use at the party, our life was starting to fall apart. He began neglecting his responsibilities at work, around the house, and with relationships in general. I found myself covering for his actions, making excuses why he couldn't appear at his scheduled court appearances. He was neglecting his clients; totally out of control by the end of the year. Our life was becoming a horror show.

I confronted him one day about my concern; it was driving me crazy not knowing why he started using drugs. He admitted that he and a few of his buddies snorted quite a bit of cocaine during their college days and he had stopped before leaving school because he realized he was using too frequently. Finding this out answered my questions and I better understood his situation. Because he had used before, it was easy for him to fall back into the groove of using. The use of cocaine rekindled those feelings of euphoria that he experienced in college. He craved those feelings again, craving for more.

Cocaine is a stimulant, it's a powerful drug. Heavy use may produce paranoia, hallucinations, aggression, insomnia, anxiety, agitation, and depression. Cocaine stimulates the reward or pleasure pathways in the brain, which use the neurotransmitter dopamine. With continued use, the reward systems fail to function normally, and the user becomes incapable of feeling any pleasure except from the drug. The main withdrawal symptoms are psychological—the continued craving for more cocaine and the inability to feel pleasure.*

My husband had reached this point in his addiction. It was a heart-wrenching situation. I felt obligated to stay because of the love and time we had invested in each other. There was always a hope that he would soon stop using. I had become an enabler, always making excuses for him and covering up his behavior.

One thing he did not do was anything to get the drug, such as stealing, lying, or committing crimes, though he would spend our hard-earned money to pay for his habit. He did work, but all his money went to drugs, which left me trying to keep up our finances, which was a struggle when I was accustomed to his sizable income. He lived to get high. To have met this man one would never have known he was an addict. He was good looking, spoke well, educated, and kept himself groomed no matter how high or low he got. We were having financial problems and almost lost our home. We were real close to filing bankruptcy at one point but were able to rise above it. His addiction was causing too many problems, something that I was not accustomed to and I finally had had enough.

I was ready to get the help we needed with counseling or psychological therapy of some type. I couldn't handle this drug scene any longer. I was sick

---

* S.E. Wood and E.G. Wood, *The Essential World of Psychology* (Boston: Allyn & Bacon, 2000), 219.

and tired of it, and what it was doing to our lives. I wasn't an addict, so why was I subjecting myself to this abuse? All because of love, I felt an obligation to help him through this disease. I may not have been addicted to a substance, but I had a personal addiction that I manifested, and it was my love for this man. I had to tear myself away and do something about the situation I was in. I could no longer be the enabler.

It reached the point that I couldn't cover for him any longer and came to terms that he needed help. I didn't know exactly what I was going to do but I needed to do something. I was hiding his addiction and it was too much for me to handle. My first thought was to contact a specialist who handled cocaine addiction patients. Instead, I did research on my own. The first thing I did was to find all the information I could about cocaine addiction by making a few calls to various treatment centers and speaking to some of the specialists about the addiction. I gathered pamphlets, brochures, and whatever other information I could find on the subject. I wanted to share this information with my husband, hoping he would listen. I was trying to make an attempt to do something before our life was totally destroyed.

I shared with him the information I had gathered. It gave both of us an insight into the cocaine addict and what could become of him if he didn't stop before our life together was completely destroyed. I also suggested to him about going to a therapist but he did not want to hear of it or anything else I was saying. I didn't want to continue pressing the issue right then because I saw that he was becoming irritated and angry, a side of him I had never seen before. In some of the literature I had picked up for him, I read that cocaine abuse could cause one to develop a violent behavior and I didn't want to bring that out in him. Already I had made up my mind that he was addicted and could be capable of anything. I had all sorts of crazy thoughts when it came to someone using drugs. All I knew then was that the gentle, bright, highly professional man I had married was changing right before my eyes. It was scaring me and making me feel helpless. I just didn't understand why he was doing this. He came from a very loving, caring, middle-class family that would be devastated to learn their son was involved in drugs.

One day, my husband's business partner came to my husband and me and wanted to know what was happening with us, because it was obvious to him that something was going on that needed to be addressed. He had been trying to buy time before confronting us in hopes that whatever was taking place would soon pass, but it wasn't passing soon enough and he felt that it was time to confront us because our behavior was affecting the company. I made up my mind that I was not going to hide my husband's addiction any longer. I was tired of covering up for him. I told his partner everything. I needed to get this adversary out in the open in hopes my husband would finally want to get the help he so desperately needed.

My husband's partner gave him some alternatives but it boiled down to get clean and stay clean, or the partnership would be dissolved. Because my husband was so darn stubborn, he refused to get the help he needed. He left, claiming that he would get another job somewhere else. Actually, he was in denial, thinking he could overcome his problem without any help. What I didn't understand was how he was going to overcome his addiction when he didn't stay clean long enough to overcome anything. It had gotten to the point where he needed a hit every day in order to get through the day.

He was now without work and his income had been the main source of our survival. I continued to work while he claimed he was trying to find a job. I knew better, for he was too involved in his addiction that nothing else seemed to matter except the next high. It was consuming all his time. I threatened to leave him and when I did that, he had a job within a week. The job lasted only a very short time before he quit, claiming he didn't like the work environment. The truth was he couldn't stay sober long enough to stay in a job. I had reached the point where I couldn't take living like that any longer. I attempted to leave him but he pleaded with me to stay. I stayed because I felt I would be abandoning him if I left.

By now our families and friends knew what was going on. Too much was wrong in our lives that I had to share it with my loved ones. Everyone was devastated with my husband's behavior, because this was not the person they knew, nor was he the person I knew. I couldn't believe this was the man I married, but I still stuck with him despite everyone's wishes for me to leave him. I felt that maybe he and I could work through this. So I set out to find a therapist.

I found a good one. I got my husband to agree to see the counselor with me, but he reneged at the last moment, stating he wasn't ready yet. After several attempts to get him to go to counseling with me and he reneging every time, I came to terms that he was not going to get the help he needed. One day, he came to me and suggested we move out of state for a while, thinking that may be a solution to his recovery. I didn't want to move, yet I was willing to try anything because of my love for him. I was willing to try almost anything to spare my husband from his addiction. There was a part of me that really didn't want to move because of all my ties within the community; it meant leaving behind all my immediate family and friends. It was a tough decision for me. Tough love is what I had for him and it was breaking me down mentally, emotionally, and spiritually, but I couldn't leave him and moved out of state with him. He was lost in his addiction and I was lost in him.

We both needed help for different reasons. He would promise me repeatedly that he was going to quit and each time was his last time. This went on for year after year and never a change. Even though a part of me wanted to let go, I continued to feed into his sickness.

One day as I was sitting and thinking over my life, something came over me. I had an awakening. I looked back over my life and wondered how I let his addiction affect my life for so long. I flashed on what had become of all our dreams; everything we planned and hoped for together was gone. I became angry with myself when I thought about how many years I had wasted on this man. We never had any children together because I refused to bring a child into this world not knowing if my husband would ever overcome his addiction. As much as I loved children, I refused to have any in my current position. As I sat there, I continued to think about my life and how prior to meeting my husband I had big dreams. My dreams were my destiny and they got shattered along the way with my becoming a caretaker for my husband. I had potential, possibilities, and I just let it go for the love of a man who was not willing to change.

My whole life flashed before me that particular day and I finally came to terms with my life. I was now ready to get the help I needed, which was long overdue. I couldn't take this road by myself any longer. I was emotionally, mentally, and spiritually shattered. Because of the mixed emotions I was having, I called my best friend and she immediately flew in to support me. I had finally said something she had wanted to hear years before, and she wasted no time getting to me. She never gave up hope that maybe one day I would overcome this love I had for this man. I had a very strong support system throughout the entire episode with my husband. I told her I was ready to leave but first wanted to see a counselor because there were things I need to vent and I felt a counselor would understand my situation better than someone who didn't have any inclination of what I was going through.

I found a wonderful counselor who helped me see that I was a work in progress. She helped me see that I did do everything in my power to try to make a difference, but it was time for me to let go. I had to come to terms with the things I couldn't change and these were facts I had to realize. I had to make changes in my own life—something I had control over—and that meant leaving him to waddle in his own madness. I had been putting myself second in my own life since my husband's addiction, it was time for me to stop and start putting myself first, which meant leaving my husband.

I didn't leave him right away. I had to go through several months of counseling before getting the nerve to leave. The counselor I was seeing was very patient, attentive, and an excellent listener. Over the years I had stressed myself out trying to cope with an addicted husband and along the way I became addicted to him.

Finally I was able to leave my husband and not feel guilty about it. It was the best thing I could ever have done for myself. It was finally over and I was gaining control of my life again. I moved back to California as soon as I made up my mind to leave. I must admit it was extremely difficult at first but as time passed I felt like a new person—free of the overpowering addiction of love for an addict.

My husband chose not to get help at the time I did and continued his addiction for another year. He finally felt the heat and wanted professional help. I was able to find him an excellent counselor that specializes in drug addiction and he began his counseling sessions. Counseling seemed to be the answer for him. He's been clean for several years now. It's a constant struggle for him each day but he's making it, living a drug-free life. Fortunately, my husband and I found the right treatments and they were effective. Changes took place within us and our lifestyles. Improving and developing new coping skills was essential for our change to occur. The overpowering addiction of cocaine has not plagued my husband for several years.

Today we are divorced and dealing with life on a positive note. It really makes me happy to see him doing so well after so many years. We were able to remain friends in spite of his many attempts to reconcile our marriage. He finally came to terms that he and I would never be together again and accepted our friendship. At this time in my life, I am very happy, at peace with myself, and have no regrets about leaving my husband.

A very positive thing I did after my divorce was to decide to go back to school. Of all the things to study, I am studying psychology and addictions. Because of all the things I endured in the past, I became very interested in the study of addiction. Ironically, I went against everything I believed in by staying with my husband for as long as I did; my parents raised me better than that. I was raised with very good ethics and morals, yet I put them aside because of the love I had for a man. I lived in that relationship for many years and believe me, it will never be forgotten. It impacted my life tremendously and his too, each for different reasons. Love is tough and can make one do many foolish things. It's the most powerful addiction ever.

Yes! Life is great!

SEE IT THROUGH

When you are up against a trouble,
Meet it squarely, face to face;
Lift your chin and set your shoulders,
Plant your feet and take a brace.
When it's vain to try to dodge it,
Do the best that you can do;
You may fail, but you may conquer,
See it through!
Black may be the clouds about you
And your future may seem grim,
But don't let your nerve desert you;

Keep yourself in fighting trim.
If the worse is bound to happen,
Spite of all that you do,
Running from it will not save you,
See it through!
Even hope may seem but futile,
When with troubles you're beset,
But remember you are facing
Just what other men have met.
You may fail, but fall still fighting;
Don't give up, whate'er you do:
Eyes front, head high to the finish
See it through!

—EDGAR A. GUEST

Posttraumatic Stress Disorder (PTSD)

12

DALE L. JUNE

"Posttraumatic stress disorder (PTSD) is a mental health condition that's triggered by a terrifying event. Symptoms may include flashbacks, nightmares, and severe anxiety, as well as uncontrollable thoughts about the event."[*]

Over twenty years ago, there was a term "afterburn"[†] describing the psychological aftereffects of a traumatic incident involving a life-threatening situation or physical violence. The physical reaction may occur within a very short period, perhaps immediately after the event, for example, a gunfight, or it may manifest itself several years later. It has been observed that the instant the shooting has ended and a body is lying on the ground, the shooting officer may suddenly burst into tears, vomit, lose control of his bladder and bowels, or begin shaking so badly that he may go into shock.

> Most often though, the impact is not so swift for the officer. It's likelier to set in days, weeks, even months after the shooting, through a phenomenon some therapists call "after-burn." This refers to the tendency of the human mind to dwell on unpleasant, emotion-charged events in the wake of their actual occurrence. In after-burn, you relive and react to an experience, churning over what you and others did and what you might or should have done differently. This continual reminding and reassessing can be as vivid as the original event and even more psychologically upsetting.[‡]

Reactions after a gunfight (or life-threatening incident) differ. Sometimes the shooting officer has been hailed as a hero, high-fived, and congratulated for "becoming a man" and "making your bones." The officer may continue the rest of the shift and report to work the next day, continuing his normal routine and activities and responsibilities. But when he has reflective moments, he may fall into depression, begin drinking alcohol to excess or ingesting drugs, or experience sleeplessness and anxiety dreams. He may entertain suicidal thoughts or, worse, he may act out those thoughts.

---

[*] http://www.bing.com/health/article/mayo-MADS00246/Post-traumatic-stress-disorder-PTSD?q=post+traumatic+stress+disorder&qpvt=post+traumatic+stress+disorder, retrieved June 10, 2012.
[†] Ronald J. Adams, Thomas M. McTernan, and Charles Remsberg, *Street Survival: Tactics for Armed Encounters* (Evanston, IL: Calibre Press, 1980), 283.
[‡] Ibid.

Today, the more modern term is *posttraumatic stress disorder*, and psychiatry and police departments are recognizing it as a severe disorder that must be attended to and addressed.

The Mayo Clinic (MayoClinic.com) lists several symptoms of posttraumatic stress disorder grouped into three types: (1) intrusive memories, (2) avoidance and numbing, and (3) increased anxiety or emotional arousal (hyperarousal).*

Intrusive memories may include

- Flashbacks or reliving the traumatic event for minutes or even days at a time
- Upsetting dreams about the traumatic event

Symptoms of avoidance and emotional numbing may include

- Trying to avoid thinking or talking about the traumatic event
- Feeling emotionally numb
- Avoiding activities you once enjoyed
- Hopelessness about the future
- Memory problems
- Trouble concentrating
- Difficulty maintaining close relationships

Symptoms of anxiety and increased emotional arousal may include

- Irritability or anger
- Overwhelming guilt or shame
- Self-destructive behavior, such as drinking too much
- Trouble sleeping
- Being easily startled or frightened
- Hearing or seeing things that are not there

My personal PTSD-defining moment occurred while accompanying my then-fifth-grade son's school class trip to Catalina Island in 2003. (See dedication page in the front of this book.) One of the fun recreational and instructional events was an opportunity for all the kids to paddle a kayak around in a specified area a short distance into the ocean near the loading dock.

I was one of the adults assigned to assist and watch the kids and not let them stray out of the assigned safe zone. Things were going smoothly

---

* "Post-traumatic stress disorder (PTSD)," Mayo Clinic, April 8, 2011, http://www.mayoclinic.com/health/post-traumatic-stress-disorder/DS00246/.

until I noticed that two girls had allowed their kayak to float beyond the limits. I paddled to them and gave them a push back into the direction they were supposed to be heading. The energy of my push caused my kayak to capsize and threw me out. I attempted to upright the kayak but because of the bulkiness of my life jacket I was wearing and my inexperience with a kayak, I was unable to turn the kayak over and climb back in.

Coincidental to this time, a large cargo ship with its engines running was unloading supplies at the nearby pier. The churning of the engines began to draw me closer and closer to the ship. I was swimming as hard as I could to get away from the ship but the undercurrent was too strong and I was being drawn closer and closer to the ship. A seaman saw me and came to the rail of the ship and shouted, "Hey you, get away from the ship!" My wife was on shore shouting "Help him, help him, he can't get away." I was swimming hard and getting exhausted. My legs had lost their kick and my arms were heavy from tiredness. By this time, the draft of the ship had pulled me up against the waterline of the ship.

Just in time, Nicole, a camp councilor heard my wife's shouts for help and paddled to my rescue. She brought her kayak up close enough for me to grab hold and hang on as she paddled to shore. When I was close enough to walk to shore, I stumbled out of the water and fell face first into the sand, completely drawn and exhausted. I was fine … for the time being.

Shortly thereafter, when I was alone, I began to shake and tremble thinking of what-if. What if Nicole hadn't made it to me in time and I was sucked under the ship with its propellers? I could image the horrific death of being shredded to pieces.

I regained my composure and continued as though nothing had happened. I never spoke of the incident again until I began experiencing many of the symptoms listed earlier. When I finally went to the doctor, it took many sessions before I was able to express what I had felt and gone through. Whenever the topic came up about the Catalina trip and my wife began to tell the story, I either left the room or tried to change and avoid the subject. I have only recently been able to tell the story. I have related it only twice as to what I felt and was feeling, once to my doctor and once to one of university classes consisting entirely of registered nurses. This is the first time I have been able to write about it and make it public (though with difficulty; my hands are shaking and trembling with anxiety). It is a thought I try to avoid.

General Life Lessons

II

Combat Psychology and Sports Performance

13

CRAIG WELLER

Contents

One of the first lessons a police officer or soldier is taught when he is learning to shoot accurately is to take a deep breath and exhale slowly while squeezing the trigger ... A hard lesson to learn in martial arts is to relax and breath but doing so increases the practitioner's reflexes, power and speed ... a basketball player shooting a free throw takes a deep breath and slowly releases it as he shoots the ball toward the basket ... to overcome the adrenalin rush when being accosted on the street, take a deep breath and exhale...to overcome stress, breathe deeply and exhale slowly. The secret, the commonality, lies in proper breathing.

—Editor

Everybody has a plan until they get punched in the face.

—Mike Tyson

Picture a large plastic zip tie about an inch wide. The smaller versions are sometimes used to tie garbage bags; soldiers and police officers use the large ones to restrain people. Anyone could figure out how to thread a zip tie: You put the little end through the hole and pull on it.

In 2001, psychologists from Yale and the U.S. Army imposed this task as part of a scenario conducted in a study with a group of Army Special Forces soldiers. During the scenario, the soldiers who had not prethreaded their flex cuffs in advance found themselves almost incapable of using them.

What went wrong? Surely this wasn't an inept group of men. They're some of the toughest, most highly trained in the world. The reason for their failure couldn't possibly be inability. Something beyond physical skills comes into play.

Come out Fighting

If you're a mixed martial artist, you'll know how to do an arm bar and a triangle choke. If you're a football player, you know that you can catch a football or tackle an opponent in your area of the field. If you're a climber, you know how to pull gear off your harness with one hand, place it, and clip your rope into it. You've done these things thousands of times and know how to do them well.

Yet numerous people have found themselves suddenly incapable of doing something as simple as dialing 911. They forget the tiniest details, like the need to dial 9 for an outside line, or they inexplicably call 411 over and over.

In my first MMA (mixed martial arts) fight in San Diego, I found myself repeatedly locking my opponent into a guillotine choke, yet I was unable to finish the choke and submit him. I lost the fight by a single point after going into overtime.

Only afterward did I realize that I'd been keeping my opponent's arm inside the choke and leaving one side of his neck open. It was a mistake that I'd probably made countless times in training but had always had the presence of mind to correct.

I could lock out choke smoothly in a training environment, so why couldn't I think well enough to do the same thing during the fight, in front of thousands of people? Why couldn't the Special Forces guys figure out how to thread their flex cuffs? How could a person possibly forget how to dial 911?

Performance Degradation

The scenario being conducted by the Special Forces soldiers was a close-quarters combat (CQC) simulation. It involved urban warfare with their real weapons loaded with paint bullets, hand-to-hand combat with role players wearing impact-reduction suits, an overwhelming noise stimulus, and poor, macabre lighting. At random intervals throughout the scenario, the Special Forces operators would, without warning, receive a significant pain stimulus to the upper body via an electric shock to simulate a gunshot wound. Under this level of stress, the warriors were incapable of performing unrehearsed complex motor skills, such as threading their flex cuffs to subdue their adversaries.

The same performance degradation occurs with the person trying to dial 911, the climber who bumbles repeatedly while hanging from his fingertips at the crux of a dangerous route, and a fighter who suddenly realizes that what he knows in the gym is not what he knows in the ring. The skills you possess in a calm, controlled environment will probably not be the skills you possess when it really matters. The impact of stress may mean the difference between victory and defeat, a clean climb and a jarring fall, or even life and death. The good news is that the effects of stress can, to some extent, be controlled.

Your Body under Stress

> Fear makes men forget, and skill that cannot fight is useless.
>
> —**Brasidas of Sparta**

The sympathetic nervous system mobilizes the body's energy reserves during times of stress. It neutralizes processes controlled by the parasympathetic nervous system, such as digestion, while ramping up secretion of adrenaline and noradrenaline, dilating bronchial tubes in the lungs, tensing muscles, and dilating heart vessels. It also causes one's heart rate to increase.

There's a direct relation between stress-induced heart rate and both mental and physical performance. Too low, such as when you're just waking up, and you can't think or react very quickly. Too high, and one's ability to think and perform motor skills degrades.*

Dave Grossman, a psychology professor at the U.S. Military Academy at West Point, former Army Ranger, and author of the book *On Killing,* uses a color-coded graph to categorize the effects of heart rate on performance (Figure 13.1). Grossman calls the earliest stages of this spectrum Condition White. The boundary between here and the next stage, Condition Yellow, is more psychological than physiological. We first see major physiological changes around 115 beats per minute (bpm). Between here and roughly

---

* As part of Secret Service training experienced by the editor of this book was a two-phase requirement. The first was to run a timed quarter mile in street shoes and suit, ending at a protective position walking alongside a moving limousine through a simulation of a city street scene with loud crowd noise and bands playing. The second immediate phase was to walk beside the limousine through a judgment shooting course with various situations of pop-up targets. The agent had to decide if the situation was a "shoot or don't shoot" scenario before the target disappeared. Agents were scored on judgment and shooting accuracy while experiencing a high heart rate and stress.

Heart Rate (Beats per Minute)	Condition	Effects
60–80	White, Yellow	Normal resting heart rate
115		Fine motor skill deteriorates
115–145	Red	Optimal performance level for complex motor skills and visual and cognitive reaction time
>145	Gray	Complex motor skills deteriorate
145–175		Black-level performance degradation may begin
>175	Black	Cognitive processing deteriorates, blood vessels constrict, loss of peripheral vision, loss of depth perception, loss of near vision, auditory exclusion

Figure 13.1 Grossman's chart to categorize effects of heart rate on performance.

145 bpm is Condition Red, which is the range in which the body's complex motor skills and reaction times are at their peak. Next is Condition Gray, which is where major performance degradations begin to show. Above 175 bpm is Condition Black, which is marked by extreme loss of cognitive and complex motor performance, freezing, fight-or-flight behavior, and even loss of bowel and bladder control. Here, gross motor skills, such as running and charging, are at their highest.

Remember, these effects are the product of *psychologically* induced stress, not physical stress. An increased heart rate doesn't necessarily mean that you're under psychological stress. You can run a few sets of wind sprints and get your heart rate up to around 200 beats per minute without forgetting how to use your cell phone.

These lines, however, aren't drawn with a permanent marker. It's possible to push the envelope of complex motor skill performance under stress right up to the edge of Condition Black. It's also possible to reach Condition Black for its gross motor skill performance benefits, such as sprinting or deadlifting, and then quickly recede to a calmer state to allow nervous system recovery.

This generally occurs with specific, well-rehearsed skills. For example, studies done on top Formula One drivers found that their heart rates averaged 175 bpm for hours on end. These drivers perform a limited set of finely tuned skills with extraordinary speed under a good deal of stress.

Likewise, the top performers in the Special Forces study had maximum heart rates of 175, while those who were slightly less proficient typically had maximum heart rates of 180 bpm. In both cases, 175 is the maximal rate before high-level performance drops off.

At a certain point, an increased heart rate becomes counterproductive because the heart can no longer take in a full load of blood, resulting in less oxygen delivered to the brain. That, in theory, could be the cause of the performance decrease seen above 175 bpm.

Stress Inoculation

No man fears to do that which he knows he does well.

—Duke of Wellington

As defined by Dave Grossman in another of his books, *On Combat,* stress inoculation is a process by which prior success under stressful conditions acclimatizes you to similar situations and promotes future success.

In a classic stress inoculation study, rats were divided into three groups. The first group was taken directly from their cages, dropped into a tub of water, and observed with a timer. It took sixty hours for all of them to drown.

The second group was taken out of their cages and held upside down to create stress. After the rats gave up on kicking and squirming and their nervous systems went into parasympathetic backlash, they were placed in the tub of water. This group lasted twenty minutes before drowning.

The last group was given the same upside-down stress treatment, and then placed back into their cages to recuperate. This was repeated several times until the rats became accustomed to the stressor. Finally, the rats were taken out, given the stress treatment, and placed immediately in the water. They swam for sixty hours.

The repeated bouts of stress allowed the rats to become inoculated against the stressor. Even with an event that had cut the lifespan of the previous group down to twenty minutes, the third group was able to perform at the same level as the group that faced no stress at all.

Immunizing Your System

There are many forms of stress inoculation, and to be most effective, they must be precisely geared toward one's chosen activity. Fighters inoculate themselves by simulating a fight through sparring. Firefighters are inoculated against fire by being exposed to it repeatedly. Skydivers eventually develop a high level of familiarity and comfort with great heights.

As a member of a U.S. military Special Operations force, I know that we wanted our training to be as realistic as possible. Military training has improved steadily since World War I, moving toward increasingly realistic targets. The closer the training scenario resembles the real thing, the greater the performance carryover will be.

This is called *simulator fidelity:* Switching from simple bull's-eye targets to silhouettes and then to 3D pop-ups was one such evolution, but we would take this a step further.

The first time I jammed a magazine loaded with blue paint bullets into my assault rifle, dove out of an ambushed car, and fired them at a living person while sprinting for cover, it scared the hell out of me. I had such tunnel vision that I could barely see the person I was shooting at, let alone aim. After several repetitions, however, I was able to stabilize myself, turn toward the oncoming fire, and hit my target.

Despite the necessary specificity, there's still a general carryover. Adapting yourself to a stressful situation seems to create a sort of "stress immune system," which allows greater tolerance and more rapid adaptation to other stressful situations.

In *On Combat,* Grossman cites an example of a full-contact fighter who joined his team for CQC weapons training in a kill house. During the first engagement, the fighter's heart rate shot up to 200 bpm, and he dropped his weapon. However, his background in facing other stressful situations allowed him to adapt relatively quickly. By the end of the day, he was performing superbly.

Learning a Motor Skill

The field of neuroscience has a variety of theories on how learning occurs and exactly how the brain functions to create a conscious, intelligent human. Jeff Hawkins, author of *On Intelligence* and inventor of the Palm Pilot®, has developed a theory that the brain is not a computer (a commonly attempted analogy), but in fact a system that stores experiences in a way that reflects the true structure of the world. The brain remembers sequences of events and their nested relationships, and then makes predictions based on those memories. These memories are stored in the neocortex, a two-millimeter-thick sheath that coats the brain. Its 30 billion nerve cells contain all your skills, knowledge, and life experiences. (Fun fact: For all the similarities in brain structure across the animal kingdom, mammals are the only ones with a neocortex. Take that, reptiles!)

Now let's talk about how you learn and remember motor patterns so you can understand what's happening when someone throws a ball at your head and you grab it without having to perform physics calculations to figure out that it's on a collision course with your teeth.

The neocortex is divided into six layers that function in a hierarchy. Each layer attempts to store and recall sequences, with higher layers having the ability to put together more comprehensive sequences or concepts than lower layers.

For instance, say you're grappling in a jiu jitsu match. You see an opening, and "triangle choke" flashes through the upper level of your neocortex. This command is passed down to the next layer, which breaks down the concept into the further sequences: "Drag one arm, throw leg over neck, shift hips."

At the next layer in your cortex, these commands are broken down further: "Tighten fingers around opponent's wrist, and pull in such a way as to prevent him from posturing up and escaping."

Now let's say that your opponent pulls out of the triangle choke. The predicted sequence being performed is supposed to end with your opponent being choked and submitting, but it doesn't match the reality. So the new sensory data are passed back up the hierarchy until a suitable sequence is found and passed back down again.

Too Much Information

If you've ever taught someone a movement in the weight room, you've probably been frustrated by the process. Teaching someone a kettlebell swing involves a number of cues that for an experienced lifter are ingrained so well and so low in the cortex that they can be carried out without conscious thought.

Not so with the newbie, whose upper neocortex is at full tilt processing and associating commands like "keep your heels on the ground," "neutral spine," and "fire your glutes." This is often when you'll hear the trainee say things like, "There's so much to remember at once."

Within the newbie cortex, the uppermost level is occupied just trying to ingrain one of those completely foreign commands. This doesn't leave room for much else, as the higher a pattern must go to be recognized, the more regions of the cortex must become involved. The sensory feedback in response to those actions is completely novel, so the patterns from something as simple as putting one's heels on the ground create countless new associations.

After a while, the cortex will be able to associate a variety of new sensations with expected forms of feedback. Now, when the trainee hears the command, his cortex will be able to predict what it will feel like to carry it out.

The command can now be relegated to a lower level of the hierarchy, freeing the upper levels to process other commands. The more associations brought on by repetitions of a movement, the lower in the cortical hierarchy the pattern can be relegated.

Think of the first time you ever rode a bicycle. It took all of your conscious energy. But after countless repetitions under varying conditions, you can do it while talking to your buddy about the world's dirtiest strip club (it's in Mexico, in case you're wondering)—even if something unexpected comes up, like grandma walking in front of your bicycle.

This is why repetitions are so crucial in learning a motor skill. More repetitions equal more associations and a more strongly ingrained motor pattern.

Quality Matters

We know that repetitions create autoassociative memories within the cerebral cortex, which in turn dictate behavior. This process happens for everything, from shooting a basketball to lifting a barbell to throwing a punch. Because you're ingraining a pattern with each repetition, it's crucial that any sort of technique be drilled flawlessly. Even in a controlled environment, with a punching bag for an opponent, poor technique in training will be reproduced when it matters. You can't train sloppy and then expect to perform well.[*]

Even if two different motor patterns are ingrained, the act of deciding between the two and discarding the poorer one will slow reaction time and performance. A study conducted in 1952 by W.E. Hick found that increasing the range of potential responses from one to two slowed down reaction time by 58 percent.[†]

This is why running backs are taught to cover and protect the football at all times, even when they're just practicing and nobody's trying to strip it away. For the same reason, a shooter in the military or law enforcement will never place his finger on the trigger of his weapon until he's made the decision to fire.

When the trained motor pattern is relegated to subconscious thought, there can be no question that it will be carried out correctly.

Navigating a New World

So let's say you've been training, practicing, and grooving the necessary motor patterns for your sport or profession. You're ready, and you step into the ring, onto the field, or into the kill house. You've just entered a new world.

The patterns ingrained in your cortex will be largely unassociated with this new, stressful environment unless it's been simulated using stress inoculation. The higher stress levels and the overwhelming sensory feedback from the ongoing situation are going to occupy the highest regions of your cerebral cortex. Your only available motor patterns will be those that have been relegated lower in the hierarchy. If you've just learned a new skill, now would *not* be the time to rely on it.

Complex motor control is going to diminish as your heart rate increases; the exact heart rate at which this happens will depend on your level of fitness and the degree to which you're inoculated against stress.

As motor control drops off, the first patterns you'll lose are those that haven't been strongly ingrained low in the hierarchy. This applies to the ones

[*] Practice does not make perfect ... *Perfect* practice makes perfect performance. —Unknown
[†] W.E. Hick, 1952. "On the rate of gain of information." *Quarterly Journal of Experimental Psychology.* 4(1): 11–26.

with the most variations, the ones you've rehearsed with the fewest repetitions, or those you've learned in environments that least resemble this one.

During my first MMA fight, my immediately available motor patterns were only the simplest: punch, kick, charge, clinch. Even something as elementary as a guillotine choke took on sudden complexity. In my adrenaline-fueled state of mind, I kept making the same mistake as hard and fast as I could.

The same thing occurred with the Special Forces soldiers who found themselves clumsily trying to jam a flex cuff together. The pattern hadn't been rehearsed well enough to be recallable under high stress and was temporarily lost. Those who wanted to dial 911 and found themselves listening to a 411 message over and over again were repeating the pattern of keys most heavily ingrained. Their cortex knew they had to dial a three-digit number and went with what it could immediately recall. The 911 pattern hadn't been ingrained through physical repetition. This is why it's actually a good idea to have your family members practice this. (Just remember to disconnect the phone first!)

The Sixteen-Second Solution

There are three basic ways to combat the effects of stress on physical performance:

- Stress inoculation
- Quality motor skill repetition in an environment of high simulator fidelity
- Biofeedback

I've already discussed the first two, which brings me to biofeedback, the process of consciously regulating the body's normally subconscious functions.

In *On Combat*, Grossman teaches a technique called tactical breathing. Next time you're under stress and feel your heart rate picking up uncontrollably, take four full seconds to draw a deep breath. Hold that breath for four seconds, and then exhale for the next four seconds. Pause for another four seconds before repeating the entire sixteen-second sequence at least three times. This practice will immediately slow your heart rate and bring your stress response under control. You'll feel mental clarity and manual dexterity return, and it'll be easier to recall previously ingrained motor skills.

Grossman's protocol entails a four-second inhalation with a four-second hold, followed by a four-second exhalation and another four-second hold. This is referred to as square breathing, meaning that equal time is given to the inhalation and exhalation phases. A factor to consider here is the alternating predominance that occurs in central nervous system output during the respiration cycle.

Using Condition Black to Your Advantage

Gross motor skills like sprinting, charging, and picking up really heavy stuff are at their peak in Condition Black, as I've mentioned. That's why you see powerlifters slapping each other, yelling, and generally making a ruckus before a big lift. It's intentional nervous system arousal.

According to a study coauthored by Grossman, these performance benefits peak within ten seconds. That is, if you need to perform your task within ten seconds of reaching Condition Black, with your heart rate exceeding 175 bpm, you'll get 100 percent of the benefits. But after thirty seconds, you get just 55 percent. It's down to 35 percent after sixty seconds, and 31 percent after ninety seconds. It takes a minimum of three minutes of rest for the nervous system to fully recover from this ordeal.

Prior to a big lift, you can maximize your gross motor skills by artificially inducing stress and creating sympathetic nervous system arousal. For the greatest benefit, you'll have to time it well so that you take your position on the bar right around the ten-second mark. Afterward, in order to prevent subsequent drops in nervous system arousal, allow for at least three minutes of rest. This is where tactical breathing can come in handy, as it can bring back your arousal levels to normal and speed recovery.

Wrapping Up: Preparation Is Power

Sun Tzu wrote, "If you know the enemy and know yourself, you need not fear the result of a hundred battles."* In this case, the enemy is stress, which, as you now know, comes in a variety of flavors. You'll enjoy peak performance in complex motor skills and reaction time at Condition Red, when your heart rate is between 115 and 145 bpm. But even then, your fine motor skills are starting to diminish, meaning that you might struggle to tie your shoe even though you're at the top of your game.

As your heart rate rises above 145 bpm, you might see a real drop in your ability to do the things you can do perfectly well in practice and other less stressful situations. And when you get past 175 bpm, you might not be able to do anything precisely the way you've been trained to do it. But even then, in Condition Black, you could hit a personal record in the bench press or deadlift, as long as you start the lift within ten seconds of reaching that state of nervous system arousal.

And you can mitigate the negative effects of all these states of stressful agitation by practicing your skills and your craft within the parameters in which they'll be most difficult to perform. That's why coaches whose

* Sun, Tsu, 2013. Simon & Brown. Hollywood, FL, (e-book).

teams are about to play in notoriously hostile arenas will try to simulate that environment in practice by bringing in noise machines or deliberately throwing distractions at their players. And it's why elite military units go as far as they can to simulate battle zones before the soldiers are forced to perform their duties inside a real one.

But, as Sun Tzu wrote, "It's not enough to understand the conditions in which you'll have to perform. You have to understand how you react to those conditions. That takes more than practice. It takes the right kind of practice."

The reward? When you perfect your game under properly simulated conditions, you'll be invincible.

Addendum

For our purposes, the nervous system is divided into two main components:

- Autonomic nervous system. Controls the body's functions necessary for survival such as breathing, digestion, heart rate, blood pressure, and organ control.
- Voluntary nervous system. This is consciously controlled and allows you to perform daily functions like lifting weights, running, or picking up a coffee mug.

Within the autonomic nervous system there are two subsystems that coexist in a push-pull relationship.

The first is the *sympathetic* nervous system, which creates the "fight-or-flight" response. This increases physiological performance when a stressor is introduced. The second subsystem is the *parasympathetic* nervous system, which counters the body's response to the sympathetic system and helps create an environment conducive to rest and recovery. Don't think of them so much as a gas and brake pedal because they don't fight each other. Rather, consider them in terms of a continuum, working in unison to varying degrees. Your heart doesn't beat in a perfectly steady, metronomic fashion. Rather, the frequency of your heart rate varies with respiration. Each time you exhale, within milliseconds the brain sends an inhibitory parasympathetic signal to the heart that slows it. As soon as you inhale, that signal drops away and sympathetic tone increases, causing a slight increase in heart rate.*

* Excerpted from "Heart rate variability training," Tmuscle.com, January 2012, http://www.tmuscle.com/free_online_article/sports_body_training_performance/combat_psychology_and_sports_performance.

When we're trying to actively recover from stress, the goal is to increase the influence of the parasympathetic nervous system. This is done by emphasizing the exhalation phase. Do this by taking a deep, diaphragmatic inhalation through the mouth and then exhaling slowly through the nose. The goal is to increase the ratio between exhalation and inhalation as much as possible by dragging out the slow, relaxed exhalation phase while maintaining rapid, full inhalations. This will typically result in an inhalation of one to three seconds followed by an exhalation lasting as long as fifteen seconds as the parasympathetic tone picks up and the heart rate settles down.

During intense stress, an exhalation of this length will, of course, not come easily or immediately. I suspect (but haven't confirmed) that this is one of Grossman's reasons for using square breathing to mitigate stress-induced heart rate during tactical situations. One's respiration rate is likely to be so rapid, and conscious thought so limited, that simple square breathing will be the easiest to remember and apply under those circumstances.

You may find this to be the case, and if so, it's far better to go with whichever method you're actually capable of applying in the moment without distracting yourself from the task at hand. As you practice tactical breathing, though, keep in mind the effects of emphasized exhalation on parasympathetic tone and its ability to mitigate stress and experiment with using it. You will likely find that a lengthened exhalation begins to come naturally and will become increasingly easy to transition into, even during intense training scenarios. As this habit becomes ingrained, you'll develop more effective reflexive stress coping mechanisms and see more reliable performance when it counts.

Observation, Listening, and Perception 14

DALE L. JUNE

Contents

Introduction: Perception, Observation, and Other "Tools of Thinking"

Perception is a tool of thinking, a form of intuition (more about the other tools of thinking later). It is knowing something without knowing how you know it. Perception and intuition can be learned. The first lesson is understanding how to use your five basic senses (hearing, seeing, touching, smelling, and tasting) plus two extra: *perception* and *balance*.

First, let us examine *balance*. Everything in the world is a matter of balance and circles. If something is out of balance, it must recycle until it comes into balance or stasis. One way of looking at it (for law enforcement, military, and personal protection) is "if it doesn't belong, it is wrong." If you know and understand the standard or normal balance or stasis, your perception will tell you when something is wrong (the normal situation is out of balance). Perception is a way of looking at something or point of view in addition to the "feeling" you get when something is out of place or wrong. Therefore, we must view things from several perspectives and not fixate on just one objective and lose sight of reality and "assume" or rationalize the wrongness.

Now let's turn to *perception*. Perception begins with *observation*. Observation is more than seeing or watching. It is seeing, recognizing what we are seeing, and reacting to it. The key words are seeing, recognizing, and reacting. So often we see something, even something simple like a stop sign. We see and read the sign, even recognize the red shape, but fail to stop because of other things on our mind (failure to react or register the recognition). When we react, it is too late. The same can be said of an environment, crowd, or individual. Usually our first reaction is failure to recognize what we are seeing and failure to put it into mental awareness if we are not previously alerted to the possibility of something being wrong or out of place.

153

Plato discussed perception as a point of reason, reality, and intuition. According to Plato: The essence (makeup and composition) of things and appearances of things are not the same. (A picture of a horse is not a horse. If you show a photo of a horse to a young child and convince him that "this is a horse," imagine his confusion and wonderment when placed beside a real horse!) The essence of things doesn't change but the appearance does (point of view[ing], i.e., how a person sees things); the reality of things resides in their essence, not in their appearance; in other words, reality is unchanging, what changes is not reality. (Many studies of perception have been conducted, resulting in conclusions that although different people view the same object, their perception of it changes. An example is the analogy of the six blind men identifying an elephant. Each man touched parts of the animal and described it as a snake, a rope, a wall, spears, a fan, and a tree.) We do not have sensory access to reality. Appearances are all we have sensory access to; therefore, the senses can't supply the content of any thought we have about reality.

For that reason, observation is a key precursor to perception. Observation and knowledge of things in a routine state and being able to recognize the normality allow for recognizing an abnormal state. This process of recognition is a subconscious reception of subtle signals or reception of indicators telling the conscious mind that something is out of balance. Equally important to realize is that if a person is accustomed to seeing everything in one perspective, he may fail to see subtle changes. For example, a person uses the same route to go to work every day, turning left at the traffic signal. He becomes conditioned to seeing the green light, then making his turn after oncoming traffic has cleared. Then one day he is stopped by a police officer and cited for making an illegal left turn (the same turn he has been making for years). The driver failed to notice or see the "no left turn" sign that was posted over the traffic light the day before. Key to understanding this phenomenon is recognizing when something has varied from the routine or has changed.

Subtle signals are identified through the basic five senses (the weakest of which is smell; how do you describe the smell of bacon frying over an open campfire at six in the morning). Translation of those indicators is the job of the senses relaying the information to the brain for recognition and reaction.

Factors That Influence Observational and Perception Skills

Mindset of the person observing—Often we fail to see the obvious because we are too absorbed in looking for something else (e.g., someone seeing a rose may look at it simply as a flower, another may see it as a beautiful painting or photograph, or a subject of a poem or song, another may see it as a symbol of his passion or love of another person). In other words, the thing being observed is evidence or purpose of the person's thinking at the time.

Setting—What is the context of the thing being observed? If we are watching a horror film, the creeping monster will frighten us; if watching a comedy, the same scene may make us laugh (see the film *Scary Movie*).

Was the person paying attention—Often, a witness will be standing right next to a crime being committed and not even realize something is going down.

Education and experience—A well-educated person will see something and because of his education and experience will recognize patterns similar to what he has learned or previously experienced.

Social status—An upper-class social person will be familiar with events commensurate with his status, such as recognizing a name brand, the price and value of real estate, jewelry, and so on of someone in the same class but will be unable to describe a person of a lower class except to describe him as a "ruffian" or "scrubby," or a "gang-type." However, a person of a lower class might be familiar with graffiti, slang, and meanings of distinctive clothing (colors, style, how displayed, etc.).

Male/female and age—Again, this comes from experience and interests gained and judged by the age of the observer.

Bias/prejudice/stereotypes—Race, color, religious or political belief, sexual orientation, gender, social and economic standing, beauty and thinness/fat, and frumpy are only a portion of the biases, prejudices, and stereotypes a person may consciously or unconsciously carry. We often see and hear only that which we want to see or hear. Anything else is colored by bias/prejudice and stereotype.

Time of day/lighting—Sunshine, shadows, and darkness change the appearance of things (but not the essence).

Health of the observer—A fever, physical pain, or a sickness may have a very strong negative influence on the observer.

Sound and movement—Sound draws attention and movement makes "invisible" objects "visible."

Color—Contrasting color is easily seen and remembered.

Drugs/alcohol—Use of drugs or alcohol will have various effects, such as hallucinations and forgetfulness.

Intelligence—Is the person doing the observation capable of knowing what he has seen?

Obviously there are several factors that will impact an observer's points of view, including a literal point of view, and political and religious affiliations. It is for the investigator or analyst to consider all the various factors and make a realistic conclusion of the observer's perception.

Patterns

The next step is identification of patterns (another tool of thinking). Even looking at faces, we recognize the person we are looking at because we are able to place all patterns in perspective. We can detect when someone is angry, happy, sick, and so on merely by understanding the normal facial patterns. We can also sense when a person is about to attack by the facial muscles and often by his speech. The second he stops talking, especially if his facial pattern displays anger or hate, he will be attacking.

We also develop perception through our experiences, education, and a long litany of other aspects too much to delve deeply into here (see earlier), but it suffices to mention experiences and education. Experiences of our own and through discussion and sharing of the experiences of others give us a point of reference when encountering indicators of something out of place. Gaining experience from others is a side effect of after-action reviews (AARs).

An AAR is an opportunity to examine what went right but more importantly what went wrong and how to correct it in the future. When a similar situation arises, the people who have read the AAR will respond accordingly because their "mind" has already visited the situation, and recognize the pattern and are ready to react. If the pattern is similar, it may also have slight or greater differences. Pattern recognition then must question what is different and why.

Another way to mentally prepare our minds for pattern recognition of an emergency is to participate in a game we call "What if…" This is visualization of any particular given scenario, problem or puzzle and ask "what if…" The point is to solve the problem within a specified time (stress factor). The scenarios must be as realistic as possible: "What if you are accosted on a dark street, at night, by a person with a gun and he says he intends to kill you?" "What if you wake up at night with your smoke detector buzzing and you see smoke coming under your bedroom door?"

Pattern recognition is a primary "color" or element of thinking; however, it is not always reliable for several reasons. The pattern of a person's face may remind us of someone (perhaps Aunt Ethel but the differences tell us that it is not Aunt Ethel, but it could be Aunt Lizzy). Differences are sometimes subtle or they may be obvious, but the situation may be different; thus the reaction might call for a different reaction and conclusion.

Now to address crowd body language. Crowds are made up of individuals, and each crowd is different yet very similar (a given). By observing and identifying characteristics of individuals in a crowd we can "read" the crowd regarding mood, intent, and overall disposition and demeanor. We must also understand crowd dynamics and contagion. An individual will react differently and will in fact indulge in hostilities as part of a crowd contrary to what he will do as an individual.

For the military, law enforcement, and others who, in the course of their routine, encounter crowds, to learn and develop that extra sensory ability to read a crowd depends on observation, experience, and education. Experience is another tool of thinking and is accumulative over a lifetime, bringing in yet another tool of thinking: memory. Memory resets the mind to accommodate understanding and associating a present circumstance with past experiences. Education and memory help focus past experience into understanding the present experience. One cannot possess the ability to "know something without knowing how one knows it" as an inexperienced soldier, police officer, or agent, but it will develop over time and practice. The earlier in life a person begins to understand the importance of intuition (perception), the greater his ability to observe and recognize subtle indicators and to react appropriately.

Anyone familiar with the adventures of Sherlock Holmes will know he solved mysteries through observation and deduction and will understand the importance of observation, reasoning (another tool of thinking), recognition of patterns, and so on, and will actively work to develop his sixth and seventh senses.

Some advice to actors is to be able to display up to thirteen emotions in each scene. A convincing actor is able to convey feelings and emotions through facial expressions without the use of words. Facial expressions emote so much, simply by the twitch of an eyebrow or facial muscle, looking in the direction of the eyes, opening and closing of the eyelids, and so forth. An excellent method to learn the emotions an actor is portraying is to watch a movie or television program in a completely foreign language set in a culture of which you have no knowledge and attempt to follow the storyline merely by interpreting the facial expressions, body movements, and tenor and tone of the spoken word, along with the breathing pattern.

As the mind is similar to a computer, wherein "input" is an exacting feature, input is yet another feature in the thinking toolbox. Input is those sights, sounds, and feelings that are fed to the brain for interpretation (recognition).

Things are not always as they seem, and our eyes (and mind) will trick and fool us into believing something else based on all of the above. It is the experienced officer, soldier, doctor, nurse, or other responder to an emergency who will process the entire scene quickly and act accordingly. An untrained person, for example a witness to a traumatic event, will be influenced by many things, with their way of seeing and recognition of what they are witnessing distorted by the quickness and trauma of events. When interviewing a witness or responding to an emergency or other stimuli, consideration must be given to the finer points of perception, observation, and listening.

The Importance of Effective Communication*

15

JARED AXEN

As a registered nurse, I love to share my stories with the nursing (police) students. In nursing (police) school, as you drown in a sea of medical (law) books, exams, and dosage calculation charts, you are never really taught what real-world nursing (policing) entails. You cannot acquire many of the skills that you use in nursing (policing) from a book. And it would be unfair to expect it to be otherwise. Nursing (Police) students are, rather, given the basic tools that they will need in the diverse and ever-changing career of nursing (policing). What they later grow and mold into will depend on what specialties they choose and what life experiences they gain from their patients and work environments. And so, when my nursing students come onto the floor with wide eyes and open hearts, eager to learn what being a nurse really means, I am all too eager to share my experiences, practices, and life lessons learned, as a mentor already nursing in this field.

One of my favorite topics that I frequently share with the nursing students is the importance of having proper communication with a patient. Education is everything between a patient and a nurse. Even though my daily responsibilities are vast and can include delivering medications, coordinating care between medical specialists, and various physical tasks, I spend at least half of my shift providing education to my patients and just getting to know them better as individuals so that I can better serve their needs. All of this requires good open communication with my patients. This was a skill, however, I obtained by consequence rather than by inherited wisdom from my instructors or colleges. This is the story that I share with my nursing students.

I was taking care of an elderly gentleman one evening on the telemetry unit (a hospital unit where the heart is usually monitored). He was primarily Spanish speaking, and my Spanish was very limited. This was however, a

---

* Although this chapter is from the point of view of a registered nurse, the importance of effective communication cannot be emphasized strong enough. In the instance of a law enforcement officer reading this section, all that is necessary is to substitute the word "nurse" with the word "police officer" to see the relevance. The words "police" and "policing" in the first paragraph have been added by the editor for effect. "No relationship can exist without effective communication."

patient with whom I had worked for several nights now, so I felt that we had a pretty good understanding of each other's roles and of the plan of care that lay ahead for that shift. I had noticed over the past few evenings that he had woken up on several occasions because that he felt he could not breathe. I knew that he had been recently diagnosed with chronic obstructive pulmonary disease (or COPD). I understood from my training and experience that most patients with COPD breathe better, and consequently sleep better, when they are sitting upright. So I told him in my very broken Spanish to sleep sitting upright for a while to see if that helped him, and he trustingly obliged me. Mind you, this short conversation took place entirely in Spanish. I turned out the lights and left his room feeling proud of this accomplishment, as the Spanish language was still very foreign to my repertoire of boasts.

I knew that I was going to be busy for a few hours with a new patient I had just received on the floor, so I left my Spanish-speaking acquaintance to sleep. I had confidence that the technician who was monitoring his heart would alert me by phone if my patient was in distress during my absence. At about two in the morning, several hours had passed since I last saw my patient, so I made my way to his room to see how he was sleeping. My assistant, who spoke Spanish very well as it was her primary language from birth, stopped me outside of the room and asked me if the patient could sit back down. I echoed curiously, "Sit back down?" "Yes," she replied. "I went into his room to check his vital signs and I found him standing in the far corner of his room with his eyes closed. He was rocking back and forth trying not to fall over. He said that you told him to sleep standing up." I apologized profusely to my patient—only this time with my assistant as an interpreter. I learned from him that I had accidentally asked him in Spanish to sleep standing upright rather than sitting upright. He never questioned the reasoning behind this order as I was the medical professional, and he was the patient. But I thanked him for listening to me and encouraged him to always ask questions if he had concerns or doubts about his care plan. My patient and I communicated well for the rest of that shift through our common interpreter, but I was not without pause or remorse. This was a small and lighthearted mistake with a humorous consequence. But what if my lack of proper communication had led to some lasting effect? What if I was providing education about the proper way of dosing a medication at home or the restrictions of a new diet? The end result could have been much more severe under a different circumstance.

This has been a life experience that I have since incorporated into my nursing skills and in my interactions with patients. The communication that I have with my patients and their families is to be strong, proper, and clear. Anything less than that would not only be unprofessional as a registered nurse, but it could be dangerous for the people who trust me to care for them. "No relationship can exist without effective communication."

My Life or His: Shoot or Don't Shoot

16

DALE L. JUNE

To survive on the streets, you must live by a whole different set of rules. The first 3 rules of gun safety and survival: (1) All guns are *always* loaded. (2) Don't point a gun at someone or something unless you intend to kill. (3) All guns are *always* loaded.

Just after ten o'clock at night, the first call of the night. "Domestic disturbance … gun involved. Car Eight handle," the dispatcher's voice crackled over the radio. Just as we arrived at the given address, a middle-aged man carrying a shotgun ran out the front door and around the house into the backyard. My partner ran around toward the right to try to head him off in the alley behind the house. I ran directly after the man, gun in my hand.

There was little ambient light and what little light there was cast dark shadows across the yard. As I entered the backyard, my flashlight in my left hand, my .357 in my right, I saw the man stopped by a six-foot-high wooden fence. I shined by light at him and ordered him to drop the gun. He was holding it at port arms.

My vision narrowed so that I was encircled in total blackness with the only things I could see through the tunnel of darkness were my rear sights aligned perfectly with the front, pointing directly at his forehead. My visionary senses were so focused that my only feeling was a tingling through my body, like there was no other stimulus. I couldn't hear anything but time seemed to have stopped. I know it was only a heartbeat or two, maybe a couple of seconds, but in the slowed down movement of time, the standoff seemed like a longer time, maybe a lifetime.

The man looked toward me. I know he looked in my direction, perhaps he was blinded by my flashlight or he saw the gun in my hand. My finger was in the trigger guard; only a layer of air between my finger and the hair trigger I had an expert gunsmith customize so that the slightest touch would have sent a .357 magnum round spiraling into his head. I took a deep, cleansing breath and slowly released it as I relaxed my body to make the aim go straight. One more time, in a calm voice, I commanded, "Drop the gun!"

His hands opened, the gun dropped to the ground, and the man burst into sobs of tears. The darkness of my tunnel vision opened, and time of the world seemed to begin moving again. I quickly moved to secure the gun and take the man into custody. To my surprise and delight, I found the gun was unloaded.

By this time my partner had entered the yard and we began to talk to the man. His story made me grateful that I had not made that fatal decision to squeeze the trigger of my gun. He and his wife were going through a very acrimonious divorce, and he had gone to the house to retrieve the shotgun that had been passed down to him from his grandfather and had been in the family for at least three generations. There was no other intent in the mind of the man for anything other than to get his gun that his wife had refused to give him.

Why didn't I shoot? I had every right and would have been justified. After all, every gun is always loaded. I could have said, "I felt endangered and was afraid for my life." Later as I recalled the scene, I remembered thinking, "He is holding the gun at port arms. To shoot me, he has to drop the barrel of the gun down toward me and in that slight movement I will have time to make the first shot." I also realized that my hesitation could have possibly meant my death, but for some reason, still unclear, that at that critical instant I didn't have that thought. Since that night I have always been thankful I didn't exercise my discretion to end that man's life.

In a threatening life-or-death situation, time may seem to stop, but it can be measured in thousandths of a second. An officer must have full perception of the moment, evaluate the level of the threat of danger, and make a final decision. A bullet cannot be recalled. The time it takes for a bullet to be discharged and travel the short space between the shooter and the target is about the time an officer has to make a shoot-or-don't-shoot decision.

The key to making that decision is evaluating the level of the threat of immediate danger, and time is being counted as quickly as it takes an electrical impulse in the brain to see, recognize, and react. Not much time for second-guessing. A wrong or hesitant calculation can mean the difference between life and death for the officer.

The primary test for analysis of the situation is, "Is a human life in imminent danger, and is the potential threat level high enough to justify taking a life?" The question to be asked, though it usually comes much later, is, "Was the use of deadly force *reasonable and necessary*?"

Officers have been quoted after an officer-involved shooting resulting in death of another person as saying, "I saw him move his hand toward his waistband and believing he had a gun, I was in fear for my life." There was a case several years ago in Los Angeles in which a homeless woman pushing a shopping cart with all her belongings was confronted by police. She pulled out a screwdriver and made threatening gestures toward the officers. "Fearing for their lives," the officers shot her dead. The question coming first to mind is, "If the officers were afraid for their lives by an older woman with a screwdriver, what were they in the police business for anyway?" They know that death is a potential every time they put on their uniform and step out into the street. There were perhaps several ways the officers could have handled the situation without shooting the woman. But they were ruled justified because they expressed concern for their lives.

In another recent Los Angeles case, after a brief car chase of a suspected drunk driver, the passenger of the vehicle jumped out of the car and raised his hands. The officers then shot him fourteen times. The officers' explanation was that they saw him raise his arms from his waist and, fearing he had a gun, opened fire. No gun was found. There are any number of cases where the shooting of a person by the police has been questioned and the rule of thumb for judgment has been, "I was in fear for my life." There are also cases where the officer made a mistake and hesitated or made the wrong decision, and it did cost him his life.

Never point a gun at someone or something unless you intend to shoot. That is good, sound advice for gun safety, but the best answer an officer can make to the question of his intent is, "I shot him with the intent to *stop* him. I believed I was following my department protocol and training procedures."

Cultural Pluralism

17

JENNIFER J. SCHNEIDER

When someone thinks of the word "discrimination," it is automatically assumed one is speaking of a minority group; African Americans, Latinos, Asian Americans, and possibly women. As the United States gains cultural diversity, the typical Anglo-Saxon Eurocentric culture seems to be ironically dissipating. The United States was founded on the principles of religious freedom from "The Mother Country." In gaining those freedoms, the "white man" essentially wanted to create a land of the "free." However, creating the "land of the free" only included Caucasians, thus eliminating almost a whole race: the Native American Indians. The white man pushed the Mexican Indians out as well, essentially "in the creation of our national identity."

"American" has been defined as "white." Not to be white is defined as "other."* As the country grew, many immigrants wished to come to America to create a new life, a better life in the land of the free, but arrived in the United States to find something else: a land of missed opportunities. As time has passed, different cultural groups still are discriminated against. However, more opportunities are arising and awareness is increasing. Interestingly enough, being on the declining Anglo-Saxon Northern European side of things, we too, so it seems, are now being discriminated against; we are becoming the minority. It certainly is an eye-opener, not to mention it makes one take a step back and analyze how this came to be.

I was raised in a typical middle-class, predominantly white neighborhood in a suburb north of Los Angeles. My ethnic makeup includes English, Irish, Scottish, French, Dutch, German, and Polish with both Protestant and Jewish parents. I wasn't raised to be racist. I was raised to treat others with respect regardless of their ethnicity, socioeconomic status, religious beliefs, or sexual orientation. I was never the type of person to be judgmental of other ethnicities. I had and continue to have friends of all nationalities, religions, and sexual orientation: I have Christian, Muslim, Jewish, and Agnostic friends. I have straight friends and gay friends. I have Ethiopian, Iraqi, American, Japanese, Egyptian, Mexican, British, and Jamaican friends (to name a few). As a young adult, I went on dates with an Indian, a Columbian, a Mexican, an African American, a German, a Vietnamese American, and, of course, your standard-issue white guy. I always saw them for what they were as a person, not by what their background was.

---

* R. Takaki, *A Different Mirror: A History of Multicultural America* (New York: Back Bay Books/Little, Brown & Company, 2008).

Not until my more recent years of adulthood have my opinions potentially been skewed. Perhaps it was living in the city of Chula Vista in San Diego with a predominantly Latino culture that made me fall astray? Maybe it was my re-entering college and finding that I did not qualify for any scholarships because I was white, married, had no "minority" backgrounds, and apparently made too much money (although it was a struggle to make ends meet at times) to qualify for assistance.

Living in almost the southernmost point of Southern California (we lived four freeway exits from the U.S.–Mexico border), I certainly experienced reverse discrimination. I cannot recall how many times my family and I would patronize a local restaurant or store and not be helped because we weren't Latinos. Unfortunately for them, I understand some of the Spanish language. It can be disheartening and sometimes amusing when you can understand another language that no one thinks you are able to speak. Listening to the comments of why we were not being served or last to be seated, although it was our turn, was a revelation. I had never not helped someone because of their ethnicity and now here I was, as white as white could be, being discriminated against. This was certainly something I was not accustomed to or had ever experienced.

Almost every time I entered certain stores, the staff would speak Spanish to me. Out of frustration, I would pretend to not speak Spanish. I remember sitting at one of my favorite breakfast restaurants with two of my dear friends, one from Ethiopia and the other from Jamaica. I discussed with them what was happening. Without me realizing what I was saying, they both looked at one another and chuckled. They told me, "You'll get used to it." Here I was preaching to the choir. This only happened because, again, I never saw people by the color of their skin. These were my dear friends Astier and Sherry. They weren't just two black women to me. So with that thought, I had a very difficult time understanding how I or anyone else could be discriminated against. It certainly heightened my awareness.

Upon conducting research on this topic in search of statistics that show I am not alone in my thoughts, I was actually surprised by many of the articles I came across. At one point, I started to believe my thinking was only among a select few. Many of the articles I came across were discussing reverse discrimination, but then someway, somehow still made the article about discrimination of whatever background the author was. However, more studies are being published regarding this topic.

In an article composed by Esther Cepeda, institutions such as the Harvard Business School and Tuft's Department of Psychology Department are concluding that "whites believe that as bias against blacks decreased in the last six decades, intentional discrimination against whites has increased. Whites now see anti-white bias as a bigger societal problem than anti-black bias."* Many of the articles I have researched blamed the defunct economy for this bias. I personally don't see how that pertains to the bias. Possibly the roles are reversing in society.

The numbers of lawsuits regarding reverse discrimination have significantly increased also.† In the Supreme Court case of *Ricci et al. v. DeStefano et al.* (2009), a group of twenty city firefighters sued the City of New Haven, Connecticut, because allegedly the city had discriminated against them regarding promotions.‡ Apparently all the firefighters had tested and passed the examinations required for the positions but because none of the black firefighters who tested passed, all the results were thrown out, not allowing the promotions to take place. A 5-4 vote (Supreme Court) stated that the City of New Haven violated Title VII of The Civil Rights Act of 1964. Fourteen of the twenty firefighters were promoted in their positions after the case closed and were awarded $2 million in damages. It appears that in the arena of public servants such as fire, sheriff, and police departments, fewer whites are being hired due to affirmative action. It is not unheard of to hear white applicants being passed over for a position because the organization needs to fulfill a quota of a certain amount of minorities. I feel that it shouldn't matter what ethnic background you are; if you are qualified for the position, then you should be hired for the position. The examinations should not be altered or thrown out as in the case of *Ricci v. DeStefano*. There should be strict guidelines that will ensure a competent force. This should be instilled in every job available in the United States.

According to an article written by John Blake of CNN, "'The idea that we're losing our country is something that's not going to have a lot of resonance for someone under 30,' [author Tim] Wise says. 'These are white folks who don't remember the country that their parents are talking about.'"§ I suppose I fall in to this category. I am thirty-seven years old and remember what it was like growing up in the relatively small community of Valencia, now the City of Santa Clarita. The City of Santa Clarita has always typically been a middle- to upper-class neighborhood with a predominantly white makeup, typically Republican by nature. Growing up in the Santa Clarita Valley, I can remember as a child in elementary school that in my graduating class, there

* E. Cepeda, "Now Whites are feeling discrimination," *The Sacramento Bee*, June 6, 2011, http://www.sacbee.com/2011/06/05/3679561/cepeda-now-whites-are-feeling.html.

† S. Fontaine, "Many whites filing reverse discrimination lawsuits," *News* One for Black America, April 29, 2009, http://newsone.com/165891/many-whites-filing-reverse--discrimination-lawsuits/.

‡ *Ricci et al. v. DeStefano et al.* (07–1428), http://www.supremecourt.gov/opinions/08pdf/07-1428.pdf.

§ J. Blake, "Are whites racially oppressed?" *CNN U.S.*, March 4, 2011, http://www.cnn.com/2010/US/12/21/white.persecution/index.html.

were two or three African Americans, maybe half a dozen Latinos, two or three Asians, and the rest were Caucasian.

Today, especially in my workforce, I'm noticing a decrease in the number of Caucasians; there are maybe seven Caucasians and the rest are Filipino, Latino, and a very small number of other ethnicities on my working unit at the hospital. I go to work and hear a multitude of languages being spoken among staff, English being one of the least spoken. It's not uncommon for a co-worker to speak a different language to you, only to realize you don't speak that language and had no idea what they just said. I embrace cultural diversity. I would love to learn to speak as many languages as I can. I love to learn about the different cultures surrounding us. But sometimes others aren't open to teaching you.

Our population is forever changing. According to the U.S. Census Bureau for the City of Santa Clarita (2010), the total population was 176,320.* Out of those, 56.1 percent were white, not of Hispanic decent; 29.5 percent were of Hispanic origin; Asians held 8.5 percent; Blacks held 3.2 percent; and others comprised the remaining 2.7 percent. In the state of California, however, the rates vastly differ: whites comprised 40.1 percent, Hispanics were 37.6 percent, Asians were 13 percent, Blacks were 6.2 percent, and the remaining 3.1 percent were of other origins. In the state of California, there are less than 50 percent whites. Granted, whites are still considered the majority at 40.1 percent in the state of California, but that number continues to dwindle. Even authors such as Ronald Takaki state that "within the life-time of young people today, Americans with European ancestry will become a minority."[†]

Currently there are numerous organizations in support of every other minority and none for the Eurocentric American. If a white man established a group for Caucasians only, they'd be considered racist. They'd fall into the same class as the Ku Klux Klan. The white man is not allowed to have a group to discuss their ancestry. Another minority group would call it bigotry. At times, I feel that by being Caucasian, one just can't win. I am still being blamed for the slavery movement, for American Indians being desecrated, and for the socioeconomic problems of other ethnicities.

I can assure you, I personally did not contribute to those problems. I embrace my fellow Americans with arms wide open. I only ask that you in return accept me for being white.

Maybe the white man had it coming to him? Trying to take a land from some other group of people to make it their own, then state that only the white man has rights could have contributed to this. Maybe it was the brutal

* U.S. Census Bureau, "State & County QuickFacts: Santa Clarita (city), California," 2010, http://quickfacts.census.gov/qfd/states/06/0669088.html
† R. Takaki, *A Different Mirror*.

treatment of slaves and segregation of the black people that contributed. Maybe it was the incomprehensible treatment of the Japanese Americans placed in internment camps that contributed. I'd say it is irony at its finest. America was founded on freedoms. Although the statement that "all men are created equal" was a foundation for the United States, the founding fathers certainly didn't mean it literally. One could hope that one day those words will ring true. In the future, maybe diversity classes will discuss the cultural mores, struggles, and contributions of European Americans, who once constituted the majority of Americans. Granted, no matter what happens in my lifetime or lifetimes afterward, there will always be biases and discrimination of some sort. Every person is unique. Each person is an individual. What one person believes in is not what another believes. But, just maybe we will have more tolerance. In the coming decades, European Americans will no longer be the majority. Just maybe diversity classes will one day be held celebrating the contributions of white people.

Life Is Situational

DALE L. JUNE

18

The Zen of fear—Misperception produces fear. To use the metaphor of the rope and the snake; though all the time there is only a rope on the ground, if you pass by it at dusk, you misperceive it as a snake and become frightened. The rope never turned into a snake. It was only misperception that produced fear. Every moment is new and when we have no past, we have no reason to fear.

We are often prisoners of the moment, captive to the circumstances or stuck in a situation. Sometimes the position in which we find ourselves is of our own doing or it may be a consequence of an event, a condition, or an accident. Whatever may be the facts, the only constant is change depending upon the experience.

Issues surrounding us often condition our decisions. What may call for action in one instance may call for passiveness in an identical or nearly identical setting. In other words, we can say, "It all depends..." Let's examine a couple examples.

Killing another human being is morally and legally wrong. But, depending on the situation or circumstances, the killing of a human may not always be wrong and can be justified as excusable. Homicide is generally defined as the wrongful killing of a human. The key word here is wrongful. It usually is accompanied by other words such as "malice aforethought," "lying in wait," or "premeditated"; the perpetrator will be prosecuted and face a possible death penalty or a life of imprisonment. However, absent the key words and intent, the circumstances may dictate that the killing may be excused as "reasonable and necessary," for instance, to save the life of oneself or others. In other words, killing another in self-defense is justified and is not a crime; it is excusable and the killer will not be prosecuted.

Then again, a person having a very strong sense of morality may view even a self-defense killing as wrong and will not find it excusable. A jury won't judge him guilty but he will feel guilty in his own eyes. He may go as far as to seek some type of punishment for what he believes is a breaking of the code of God—The Ten Commandments. He may also suffer pangs of guilt leading to posttraumatic syndrome disorder (PTSD) or other related neurosis, perhaps leading to abuse of alcohol or drugs, further compounding his mental anguish.

There are other crimes the courts recognize as "affirmative defenses," for example, the breaking of a lock or window to gain entry into a building to get out of life threatening weather (i.e., a blizzard). This would not be a burglary, that is, breaking and entering, a crime, but an excusable entry based on the circumstances. Same action, differing situations.

Relative (Relativism)	Majority Average	Absolute (Absolutism)
Very liberal		Ultra conservative
Extremely tolerant		Zero tolerance
Mitigating circumstances		No mitigating circumstance
What will be, will be		Cause and effect
Innocent until proven guilty		Guilty, must prove innocence
Enforce spirit of the law		Enforce strictly "by the book"
Politically to the left		Politically to the right

To view another example, let us think of the world as relative and absolute. No one can be one-hundred percent relative or one-hundred percent absolute. Although some people are always on the left or on the right, their degree of leaning will be adjusted according to the situation but will remain on their side of the dividing line. Even in their liberalism or conservatism, they may hold beliefs that are stronger in one area than in another, and sometimes even a strong belief may weaken with variable circumstances. The bulk of the majority or the average population will fluctuate back and forth, being on the left sometimes and on the right other times, all according to the situation and their perspective of the circumstances.

In the words of the great Basketball Hall of Famer Bill Walton, "It's only minor surgery when it happens to someone else." Or as a hard rock star once remarked, "You are not a rock star in the eyes of your family."

Lesson learned: It's all a matter of perspective, situation, circumstances, and whose "goose is being cooked."

K-9 Partners: True Stories

19

JASON JOHNSON AND OTHERS

Contents

Introduction

Jason Johnson

When I was asked to contribute to this book, I thought that this would be a great opportunity to share the stories of lessons learned from experienced K-9 handlers out in the field.[*] I wanted to create a chapter that could benefit those who think they may want to be a K-9 handler one day, may be new

---

[*] Some of these stories appear in *Protection, Security, and Safeguards: Practical Approaches and Perspectives*, 2nd ed., edited by Dale L. June, Boca Raton, FL: CRC Press, 2012, reprinted with permission of the publisher. The stories are repeated by popular demand as they are entertaining as well as educational.

to the K-9 field, or just love stories about dogs. Instead of sharing a chapter of entirely my own stories, I decided the readers of this book would be best served by reading stories from multiple K-9 handlers in the police, military, and federal service not only in the United States, but from around the world. Therefore, I reached out to a variety of K-9 handlers to make this chapter as diverse as possible. This chapter includes stories from several seasoned and highly respected K-9 handlers from places such as Denmark and the Philippines, as well as many stories from K-9 handlers in the United States. My goal in putting together this collection of stories was to show potential police officers or K-9 handlers the joys, trials, and tribulations of being a K-9 handler. I have included photos of some of the dogs and their handlers to help bring a face or muzzle to some of these stories. Being a K-9 handler has been the highlight of my career, and I have had the pleasure of handling over fifteen partners operationally and being involved in the training of hundreds of working dogs for law enforcement, military, and force protection entities at all levels worldwide. It has been by far the most rewarding thing I have ever been involved with professionally. I hope you enjoy these stories and lessons learned gathered from the field and maybe hold a newfound respect for our four-legged partners.

Training the Handler to Stay out of the Way

Jason Johnson

I was a recent graduate of a six-week narcotic K-9 school, and my young K-9 partner and I had only been out working the streets for a few days. In the first week out of school, we had several good finds for the local patrol officers, the drug task force detectives, and the Drug Enforcement Administration (DEA) agents. In one instance, we were asked to do a search on three seized vehicles that had been in a police impound yard for months. The vehicles were getting ready to go to public auction when one of the agents on the case was informed that the arrested party had been sitting in prison bragging about how the DEA had missed his stash of drugs in one of the seized vehicles.

The agents then tore apart all three vehicles in the impound lot and when they were unable to locate anything, they called me and my dog to come investigate further. Once we arrived, I looked over the three vehicles, which had the hoods open and parts everywhere. I started my first search on an early 1990s model Honda Accord. We started on the front passenger headlight and worked our way around the vehicle clockwise.

Once we made it to the driver's door, my K-9 Flash (Figure 19.1) jumped through the open driver's window on her own with no direction from me, which was a clear change of behavior. Flash went directly to the rear seat and showed increased sniffing on the rear seatback and alerted to the area where the back

Figure 19.1 Jason Johnson and Flash.

of the seat and the bench meet. I immediately put her up in the car and began searching that area. After just a minute or two of hand searching, I located a man-made false wall between the rear seat and the trunk of the vehicle secured by a locking mechanism that had been overlooked until this point. Once we opened it, we found several pounds of marijuana and heroin that would have been let go at auction with the vehicle to an unsuspecting buyer.

This immediately gave me a strong sense of confidence in Flash, and it was my first substantial find; I was very excited and proud of my dog. A few days later, I was called to do my first knock-and-announce narcotic search warrant with the local drug task force on a residence at 4 a.m. I was excited because I knew my dog was doing great after our big find with the DEA, and I was focused and ready to find what I was expected to, which was a large amount of heroin hidden somewhere in this residence.

Once the tactical team made entry and secured all of the suspects, I deployed Flash on the interior of the house. We started in the master bedroom, where we located some drug paraphernalia. I then moved on to the living room, searching for the large amount of heroin that was supposed to be hidden somewhere in the residence. I located nothing in the living room and transitioned to the kitchen. While in the kitchen, Flash pulled me directly under the stove. I pulled out the bottom storage drawer and my dog lunged toward the open drawer. I looked at the ground and I observed several old greasy fried onion rings scattered about the floor. I was certain my dog was trying to get at the food on the ground, and I forcefully pulled her out of the area and continued searching.

I had a few other small finds in the residence but I never located the big stash of heroin that was supposed to be in there. I went outside, put my dog up, and let the detectives know I was finished with my search and what I had located, but made no mention of the kitchen. A few minutes later, I was informed by the sergeant of the task force that they had just located a very large amount of heroin in the residence on a hand search, all hidden behind the stove in the kitchen. The exact area my dog pulled me to, but I removed her from it because I thought she was interested in the onion rings.

I immediately felt horrible and the consensus among the task force was that my dog had missed the heroin on the search, which wasn't the case at all. She was a great dog and she didn't deserve any discredit for us not locating that heroin that day. I tried to explain that it was strictly handler error and how I made the mistake, but it's one of those chances you can't get back.

The lesson learned in this story is that I had a world of confidence in my dog from our great find earlier in the week and just a few days later I showed no confidence in her at all. What I should have done, since I saw the food on the ground, was allow my dog a little more time to see if she was actually going after the food or if she was taking me directly to the heroin. Other options would have been to remove the food and continue the search, or declare that area as an area of interest to an agent and let them hand search it in my presence to clear it of any narcotics.

It took me a little extra time for the drug task force to rebuild their confidence in K-9 Flash, even though I knew she was great and it was her handler who was still learning. Over the next several years, we totaled over 732 finds as a K-9 team for multiple agencies at the state, local, and federal levels. I learned a hard lesson that day: not to assume or think I know what the dog is doing and just allow them to work. We missed a huge find because of it and took a little hit on our reputation. Years later, Flash would become well known as one of the best K-9s in the state. It just took a little while for her to train her handler to stay out of her way.

Advanced Warning

Jason Johnson

I had worked with explosives dogs in the States for a few years before I took my first assignment in Iraq as a tactical explosive K-9 handler for high-threat dignitary protection details for the U.S. Department of State Diplomatic Security Service. My very first K-9 partner I had in Iraq was K-9 Uran. He was a beast of a dog, a long-haired Czechoslovakian shepherd who weighed 103 pounds. He was known as Fuzzy because of his long hair, but I just called him Big Fuzz (Figure 19.2). In our living conditions in a regional U.S. embassy in Al- Hillah, Iraq, we did not have kennels, so our assigned K-9 partners stayed in our already small 12-by-10 rooms with us.

Sharing a room with a 103-pound, long-haired shepherd was challenging but had its advantages. Big Fuzz would stay at the end of the bed patiently

Figure 19.2 Jason Johnson and his dog Big Fuzz in Iraq.

while I worked on my computer or watched TV when we weren't out running missions outside of the wire. At the end of the night when I turned out my light, Big Fuzz would get up from the end of the bed and go lay down in front of the only door to the room, blocking it with his big body so it could not be opened in the middle of the night without him knowing.

After a few weeks of being in Iraq, Big Fuzz continued to show me that he meant more to me than just being able to detect bombs with his nose. He showed me he could do it with his ears as well. I was sitting at my desk one night working on my computer when Big Fuzz quickly came over to me barking as loud as he possibly could, which was very loud in a twelve-by-ten-foot metal room. I looked at him and he got low on the ground down on all fours, barking uncontrollably and whining. About three seconds later, I heard the loudest boom I had ever heard in my life for the very first time.

Al-Qaeda was known for launching mortar attacks on the regional U.S. embassy in Al-Hillah late at night, and this was my first time being mortared, but it wasn't my partner Big Fuzz's first time. Big Fuzz was able to give me just enough warning to take quick cover or prepare for an oncoming attack. It was one of the most incredible things I had ever had a K-9 partner do that was unrelated to searching.

Big Fuzz and I lived together for quite some time and we survived several Al-Qaeda mortar attacks together; and every time, without fail, he would give me a few seconds warning before the mortars hit the ground. It took me a while to figure it out, but I came to the conclusion that Big Fuzz could hear the high-pitched whistle of the mortar in the air that was undetectable to the human ear and he was associating that noise with the loud boom that followed, which he really didn't like very much. I look back at our time together in that small room in Iraq and I will always be thankful for Big Fuzz and the advanced warnings he gave me even though it may have just been a few seconds. In combat, a few seconds can be the difference between life and death.

Second-Guessing Every Move

Jason Johnson

In the spring of 2009, I was working on special missions for the U.S. Government in Iraq as a tactical operator and an explosives dog handler. On this particular mission, I was supposed to move with a tactical team to an Iraqi police academy located in the south-central region of Iraq. Due to staffing issues, I was the only dog handler available for this mission and I was going to be tasked with clearing the entire venue, which was probably a total of several acres.

At this point in my career, I was a very seasoned operator and handler, and had conducted over one hundred red-zone, high-threat missions so I was comfortable with this particular assignment. I fully understood that with the 120-degree heat there was no way I was going to be able to successfully clear all parts of the academy that I wanted to. I also knew that there were a large number of high-ranking American military officers and government officials coming to the graduation and that this venue would be a high-value target for Al-Qaeda terrorists.

I was lucky enough to have several highly trained explosives K-9s assigned to me and with whom I was used to handling on a daily basis. For this mission, I decided to take K-9 Bundas with me as my primary K-9 to sweep the drop area, the parade field, the VIP seating area, bathrooms, and a meeting room. Bundas was the youngest dog assigned to me. He was a three-year-old big, strong German shepherd but he had plenty of stamina and was a hard worker (Figure 19.3). However, he was the least experienced dog I had, so I thought that this would be a great mission for him to go on. I chose to bring K-9 Sientje as my secondary K-9 to conduct a search of the parking lot and the vehicles that would be arriving at the ceremony before they sealed off the location. K-9 Sientje was a very experienced seven-year-old Belgian Malinois that had been in Iraq for the previous five years and was accustomed to all kinds of searches and venues.

Upon the team's arrival, I immediately deployed K-9 Bundas with my overwatch and began to search, starting with the most primary areas first and working my way into the secondary and tertiary areas that I previously outlined. In 120-degree Iraqi heat, I could usually get between twenty and thirty minutes of continuous search time out of my highly acclimated dogs. In one of the meeting rooms, K-9 Bundas had a positive alert on a large

Figure 19.3 Jason Johnson and Bundas in Iraq.

wooden crate, but I was immediately informed by the Iraqi police officials that it contained known secured explosive munitions that are used for the training. I accepted that as a valid answer and returned to my search as I had a lot left to do and not much time. I completed most of the areas I wanted to search, but due to the sheer size of the academy grounds, I had to leave many areas unsearched by my K-9. I then informed the agent in charge that I had completed that portion of my mission and I then placed K-9 Bundas back into an air-conditioned Suburban and retrieved K-9 Sientje, who had been waiting patiently in the air-conditioning for her turn.

I deployed K-9 Sientje to the main entrance of the academy and searched all of the vehicles, outbuildings, and other applicable places in that vicinity such as trash cans, guard shacks, and anything I felt an explosive device could be concealed in. K-9 Sientje did an excellent job as always and once we completed searching all of those areas, we searched any additional cars entering into the secured parking lot.

Once we secured the entire venue, the high-ranking American guests arrived via helicopter and motorcade. At this time the venue was sealed off and my team, which did the advance, was released to return to our home base. The drive back was about forty-five minutes and during the drive, I had an additional duty as a door gunner so I was still highly focused on us getting back safely, but overall I felt good about both K-9 Bundas and K-9 Sientjes' performances.

Once I returned to my room, I shut off my radio, put away all my equipment and firearms, and took off my body armor of which I was soaking wet underneath. As I was changing, I turned on the television in my room and immediately on the news channel I see an updated news flash on the bottom ticker that read "over 150 wounded or killed in Iraqi police academy explosion." I immediately felt sick to my stomach and scrambled to turn my radio on again to find out more about this recent development. The tactical operations command was a few minutes away and I didn't want to tie up the radio channels. We didn't have phones so I jumped on the Internet to see what I could quickly learn about this deadly explosion.

While I was frantically trying to find the details of this incident, I had started to replay in my mind everything that I had just completed. Over the next several minutes, I started to think about the positive alert that K-9 Bundas had in the meeting room on the munitions, every presentation I made to my dog, and every presentation I didn't make. I thought about every area I wanted to search but I couldn't because I didn't have the man-power to do so. I was beginning to feel nauseated as I was having trouble finding details of the incident because the event had just occurred. To think that I could have been responsible for the deaths of 150 people was something I had a very hard time accepting because of the pride I took in my job. Within a five-minute time frame, I second-guessed everything to the detail on what I had done on that search in slow motion, including the dogs I chose to bring and the order in which I worked them.

After a short period of time, I learned that the cause of the explosion was a vehicle-borne improvised explosive device also known as a VBIED that rammed the front gate of the academy. This was a vehicle that approached from outside of my search area from the street that was totally inaccessible to me, plus it occurred at the police academy in Baghdad that was having a graduation on the very same day. Even though it was tragic that so many people died, I felt relieved that their lives did not rest on my shoulders, but for five minutes I was led to believe that that was quite possibly the reality I would have to live with.

In the time it took me to receive the details of the explosion, everything I did instantly came back to me and was replayed in my mind over and over. Time slowed for me and the fact that I was second-guessing my every move was realistic, but it was unfair to my dogs and me. We were both highly trained and highly prepared for that mission that day. We were selected to do it alone because we were capable of doing it. I could say that with 100 percent of my heart that I did that search the best I could and my dogs gave me all they had that day until they were physically exhausted. It was not right for me to second-guess every look they gave me, every pause or extra sniff they had in a certain area, but I did just that, repeatedly wondering what we missed and where it could have been located. I trusted in my dogs on the scene that day, just as I should have once I heard of the explosion. From that day forward, once I completed my search and I knew my dog and I were both 100 percent, I never looked back on that day again. Since that time, I have gone on to take on greater missions in Afghanistan with the U.S. ambassador; and no matter what happened, I never had that feeling in my stomach ever again. I have trusted all of my dogs with my life; therefore, anyone I perform a search for can do the same, and I will never second-guess my dogs' performance again.

Sometimes You Have to Search the Police Car

Jason Johnson

I was at home sleeping at about 2 a.m. when I received a late-night call from the city police department dispatch for an agency assist with the local sheriff's office. I gathered the details of the traffic stop the deputy was on, along with the location. I quickly got dressed and loaded up my K-9 partner and responded to the location of the traffic stop where the deputy was still on scene with the suspect detained in his marked patrol car.

Upon arrival, the deputy informed me that he had stopped the driver for a minor traffic violation, but when he got up to the car, he smelled a very strong odor of marijuana coming from the vehicle. The deputy then placed the subject under arrest for having a suspended license and did a search of his vehicle due to the strong odor of marijuana coming from the car but came up with nothing. It is common for marijuana or other drugs to be hidden in a vehicle that is difficult for an officer to find without the use of a K-9 to pinpoint the location.

Once I was finished talking to the deputy, I went back to my patrol vehicle and got my K-9 ready for the search. The deputy stood in front of his car and watched as we did our thing. I had never done a search or worked with this deputy before because I was a city officer, so I could see he was interested in seeing what we were all about as we had a very good reputation in the state as a K-9 team and he was referred to call us out before giving up on the search.

As we were walking up to the traffic stop, my K-9 pulled me over in the direction of the deputy who was standing in between his patrol car and the suspect's car waiting for us to find what he had been searching for all this time. I regained my K-9s' attention back to the suspect's vehicle and attempted to do an exterior search of the vehicle before I moved on to the interior, which was our standard search pattern. Once again, my dog pulled me directly over toward the deputy, and I used the rule that if my dog pulled me in a direction twice, I would go search that area to eliminate it, then come back to what I was originally going to search.

I then asked the deputy to move away from his car and to stand over to the side, as I wanted to search his patrol vehicle. The look on his face is one I will never forget. He reminded me that the smell of marijuana was coming from the interior of the suspect's car and here I wanted to search the exterior of his car. I told him I realized that and I again asked him to step aside so

I could search his patrol vehicle, as that was the area my K-9 was trying to pull me toward. With hesitation and shaking his head like I had no idea what I was doing and I was wasting his time, he moved out of my way.

I started my search on the front passenger headlight of the deputy's car, and by the time we made it over to his push bars, my K-9 showed a change in behavior and increased respiration on the front grill toward the radiator and gave me a quick sit. I told the deputy to open the hood of his vehicle, and by now I could see that he was curious as to what was going on.

Once he opened the hood we located approximately half pound of marijuana stuffed on the inside of his grill in front of the radiator. The look of surprise on the deputy's face was priceless when I asked him if he had the handcuffed suspect sitting on the front push bars of his vehicle at any time, and he stated he did, at which time he must have removed it from a place hidden on his body and stuffed it in the deputy's grill.

The deputy's attitude about our abilities quickly changed and he talked us up to every member of his department for a long time. As a result, we got a lot more searches and great finds due to our increased number of late-night callouts. From that point on, I was never afraid to search the police car if that is what my dog was telling me to do.

Avoiding Outside Experts

Kyle Day

I have been a police canine handler for six years. One of the main things we were taught as we got toward the end of our class is to trust our dogs. What they didn't tell us was to always work the pattern that you have trained and not listen to officers on scene.

One incident that has really stood out in my mind occurred while deploying my partner for another agency while they happened to have a film crew following them as they patrolled. I was called to assist in a narcotics search of a vehicle after it was stopped and the odor of cocaine was coming from the vehicle. At the time, I had a couple years as a handler and felt pretty confident in my dog and my ability. As I got to the vehicle, I looked inside as I always did and scanned the vehicle for any items that might hurt my dog.

I noticed the car was extremely clean; however, one of the officers walked up to me and said there was a box on the floorboard under the passenger seat. Now I knew they had been at the scene for a few minutes prior to my arrival and figured they had done an initial scan of the car. So I thought he must be trying to give me a heads up that I need to check the box, especially since a camera crew was filming the deployment.

So I got my partner (Figure 19.4) out of the car and ran the exterior of the vehicle like we always did; and when we got to the open passenger door,

Figure 19.4 Officer Kyle Day and Dingo.

I had him check the door panel and then right to the box under the seat. The dog sniffed the box and moved on, wanting nothing to do with it. I brought him back to check it again and this time he sniffed again and moved on. At this point with the camera rolling and several officers around, I am getting upset at the fact that my dog is not indicating to the drugs. I brought him by the box for a third time and this time he stuck his nose in the box and showed no interest in the box at all.

At this time, I started the pattern I had always trained and watched my partner as he tried to crawl under the passenger seat past the box and begin sniffing where the console meets the floor. I watched as he sniffed the entire center console from the back to the front where the cup holders and radio come together. I could see that he was very intent on sniffing this console area and he increased respirations and had changed his body posture. This was followed by a quick sit on the driver seat. This sit was his passive indication to the odor of narcotics.

I advised the officers that he was indicating to the center console and that would be the place to start looking for the narcotics. The cup holders were removed at that point and we found one and a half pounds of cocaine hidden throughout the console. I then picked up the box and realized it was an animal cracker box that was empty. The officer had not searched it. He just thought that was where the drugs would be since that was the only thing in the car. He told me he wanted to be sure that I knew it was there.

So the lesson that I learned from that incident was not to worry about what the officers on scene were doing, had done, or what areas they thought I should check. Officers may check something or think a certain area would be a good hiding spot, but that is why we bring the dog in the first place.

Instead, no matter what the situation, I needed to work the pattern the way we train and as long as it is consistent and we cover all the areas needed, we would be successful.

Clear and Concise Communication

Kyle Day

One of the things that I have found when training dogs is that you have to be clear as to what you want from the dog. Obviously we can't just tell them to sit or stay or search where we want them to. We have to use repetition and generally set up a winning situation for the dog. I recently watched as a handler talked about having a dog that kept coming up the leash (handler aggression) when he tried to get the dog to perform a detailed search.

I watched as the handler began to work and noticed that when the dog did not search what the handler wanted it to search, it was time for the dog to be corrected. These corrections were to yank the dog off its feet in a harsh correction. The handler was asking the dog to check light switches on a wall.

When I asked how many times they had checked light switches, the handler replied maybe one or two times in the year they had the dog. So we continued on and watched again as the dog did not check an area. The handler would hammer the dog, and in response, the dog would get upset and come up the leash. This was not an overly aggressive or even particularly hard dog. She just did not know why she was being hammered and in response went into defense drive. It was apparent the dog was doing what it had been taught and then when the handler wanted something outside the training scope done, the dog got corrected without knowing what it was supposed to be doing.

Finally when the dog got into odor and was about to sit (passive indication), it was not fast enough for the handler, so again the dog got corrected, brought back to the source of odor, and then corrected again until it finally gave a sit. This dog had been working for nearly four years on the street and the handler still had to call the sit because the dog did not understand what to do. When the dog started to sit, it would get corrected. When the dog got back to the odor again, it got corrected, and finally the handler would yell, "Sit!" This happened on the first 3 finds; essentially, the handler had built that entire interaction into the final response.

At this point it was time to actually teach the dog what it was supposed to do and what was being expected of it. We placed training aids in three light switches in the first 3 rooms. The dog was asked in a high, happy tone to check the light switch in the first room and when it did, it encountered odor, and without being hammered on was allowed to give a final response, at which time the reward came in at the exact moment the dog's behind hit the ground. This same setup took place in the next two rooms, each with a positive response, and the dog clearly began to realize that checking where the handler asked could have a positive outcome and by sitting faster, the toy would come in faster.

When we got to the fourth room, sure enough the dog was following the handler and when it came to checking the light switch, the dog actually beat the handler to it. This one did not have any odor and the dog moved on and wanted to check where the handler was asking. The other thing that happened, the dog never came up the leash as there were no more random corrections being given. The dog was doing what was asked because of the positive environment it was now in. The dog understood that checking the areas the handler was asking could result in finding odor and ultimately getting the toy.

By changing the training to a positive and encouraging environment with proper timing and voice commands, the dog was able to understand what was being asked of it. This is an important aspect when trying to get the dog to demonstrate a behavior or perform a task, such as searching a specific spot, compared to when we are trying to stop a behavior.

In training, if you are clear and consistent, generally you will have more success and the dog will be willing to repeat the behavior because of the positive experience and understanding of what it is supposed to be doing.

When to Call off a K-9 Search

Jes Poppelvig

We were sent to an armed robbery at a gas station downtown. It was rush hour and we got there approximately forty-five minutes after the robbery. The gas station had not closed for business and no one had thought to secure the scene. Between the customers and police officers trampling around, there were about fifty people present when we arrived.

I really didn't see how K-9 Paco could be effective in such a situation. (See Figure 19.5.) I got Paco out just to try and he picked up a track right away. He actually tracked in between two people who had to step apart. We followed the track down some busy roads into an apartment area. We went between two apartment buildings, over a fence, and onto a lawn. Here, the dog found a cap that was secured for DNA by a fellow officer.

The track continued behind one of the apartment buildings, where we found a shirt that the dog alerted strongly on. We had to wait for this to be secured. We then continued between some bushes and out onto a very busy main road. The dog hesitated, but then took me down a side street. He was not pulling on the line nearly as much as he had been and the track was now two hours old in the downtown area. I made the decision to call him off.

Figure 19.5 Officer Jes Poppelvig and Paco.

I doubted that it was possible to follow the track under those difficult conditions.

I didn't want to take a great success with finding the track and clothing, and then throw it away. The dog was young and inexperienced, and ending on a positive note when the dog was still very sure and pulling hard was important. From a training perspective for the future, it was a sound decision; however, I sure came to regret it later.

On our way back to the gas station, I had the dog do an evidence search along the escape route. He found the gun in some bushes about twenty yards from the track. Through DNA analysis of the cap and shirt, we got the name of the suspect. The gas station attendant later identified the man in a lineup. When he was interrogated, the man outlined the escape route he had taken, including the side street he had turned on to where he had continued another quarter mile to a friend's apartment. If I had only continued up that side street, we could have gotten the suspect that day. The suspect admitted that he was worn out at that point and was hiding in the apartment, hoping the police had given up.

My years of experience worked against us that day. I had seen colleagues end up with dogs that would half-heartedly walk in a direction to please the handler because they had lost the track and were unsure. When the handlers followed these dogs, the behavior became ingrained; the dogs became less trustworthy and difficult to read if they really were tracking or not. I made the decision to stop to avoid potentially teaching my young dog that behavior in circumstances that I thought must have already taxed his abilities to the limit. On the other hand, the boost that my dog could have gotten that day from actually catching the bad guy, and maybe even getting a bite, is unfathomable. The dog is not always correct, but they are correct more often than the handler.

Let the Dog Tell You Where to Go

Jes Poppelvig

Very early in my career as a police dog handler, I got a callout that opened my eyes to what a dog really can do on track; the importance of trust; and the value, or lack thereof, of firsthand witness accounts. A patrol unit was in hot pursuit of a stolen car late one night. They reported that the car was found abandoned on a road with fields on both sides.

When I got there, they told me that the suspects must have run south because otherwise they would have seen them. I searched for a track on the field south of the car with no luck. Still believing my fellow officers, I searched a farm nearby that was also south of the car. We still could not find the track or the suspect.

Finally, I went back to the car and let the dog search north of the car. He found a track immediately and followed the track over a field to a creek. We crossed this creek three times at different intervals. The water was waist high with a lot of current and it was pitch dark out. I really thought at this point that the dog was having a lot of difficulty on the track or was just taking me for a walk.

Finally, we followed the track over some more fields and found the bad guys shivering in a ditch. Being from another town, they were completely lost and had no idea where they were. They also admitted that they had crossed the creek three times in their panic. My dog was young and I still had to learn to trust him. We wasted a lot of time in the beginning because I believed what I was told by the witnesses. It's better to let the dog tell you which way the bad guys went.

Imagination: A Dog's Only Limitation

Jes Poppelvig

One of the most amazing tracks I have ever done was with my five-year-old German shepherd Paco. It was after an armed robbery in a downtown bank on a Friday afternoon. I arrived forty to fifty minutes after the robber had fled the bank. I was asked to search for evidence along the escape route. About three hundred yards from the bank, my dog found the robber's cap. My dog picked up a track and another officer followed us for our safety. It was my impression that the robber had fled on foot.

We followed the track on hard surface roads through rush-hour traffic. After about a mile, we came to a sports stadium. Here we found the sawed-off shotgun, clothing, and some money covered with red dye. We had to wait for other officers to come to secure the evidence before we could continue the track. The track now led to an area with ponds and a golf course. My dog stopped at a pond and bit into the water without drinking. Later, I found out that the bad guy had tried to wash the red dye from the money off his hands.

My backup officer was falling behind and I told him to hurry up if we were going to catch the suspect. I then received one of the biggest shocks of my career. He looked at me oddly and asked, "Didn't they tell you? The guy is on a bicycle! We're not going to catch up with him!" If I had known that, I would never have attempted the track.

After another thirty minutes, the track wound back into town. By then, we had found more evidence along the way such as gloves, coveralls, and the bike. We came back to a road that we actually had been on before. My backup officer was keeping our colleagues constantly updated on our location. Two guys were arrested a few hundred yards in front of us who were on one bike. It was determined that one of them did the robbery. The robber had driven away from the bank on his own bike and later was picked up on another bike by a friend. We had covered about two and a half miles in total. The bad guy suffered from psoriasis, and maybe that made it easier for the dog to follow his track. I don't know. I am sure that human beings have absolutely no idea what a dog can do with his nose. The only thing that limits their use is our imagination!

Taking the Bus

Jes Poppelvig

One afternoon, I was called to an area with farm fields and a small forest. Two men had run from a stolen car after a minor traffic accident. We got there approximately one hour after the accident. My dog, Nikon, a two-year-old German shepherd (Figure 19.6), found the track and we followed it over some fields for about two miles. After crossing a schoolyard and playground, we got to a busy asphalt road where we lost the track near a bus stop.

While we were searching for the track, a bus came and let some passengers off. I talked to the driver and he told me that he had earlier picked up two people that fit the suspects' description. He let them off the bus at a little harbor in the town nearby.

I drove there immediately and found and arrested the two suspects. They were very surprised, to say the least. At that point, they were more than fifteen miles away from the stolen car.

Figure 19.6 Officer Jes Poppelvig and Nikon.

The Dog's Nose Knows

H.C.S.

I was working with the Joint Terrorism Task Force on a search warrant and advised that I would be looking for peroxide-type explosives. Since I do not normally have peroxide-type explosives on hand, I contacted another federal agency that had access to some. The morning of the search, I hid some TATP and HMTD in a garage to ensure that my K-9 partner was up on her peroxide-type explosives. I let her do about ten hits on the explosives.

I headed out to the house that I was to search. After the SWAT team cleared the house, I walked through the house ensuring that the house was safe to search with my K-9. I grabbed my K-9 partner out of the vehicle and we entered the house. Behind me was a bomb technician in case we found anything. Within a few seconds of entering the house my K-9 partner pulled me to a drawer in the kitchen and alerted by sitting. I looked at the bomb technician and he did not have to say anything. I took my K-9 partner outside the house for our safety. A few minutes later, the bomb technician came outside and told me that the only thing in the drawers was a hand blender. I was sure that there had to be something there. My K-9 partner had a big change in her behavior by digging in and dragging me to the kitchen. I was lucky to be paying attention or she could have pulled my arm off.

I went back into the house and continued my search. I had to divert my K-9 away from the kitchen so I went to the other side of the house. After completing my search, I was standing in the living room, looking around to make sure that I had searched everything. Once again, my K-9 partner started pulling me toward the kitchen. I followed her to the kitchen and once again she alerted on the same drawer. I asked the bomb technician which drawer had the hand blender inside it. He told me that same drawer that she is alerting on. The bomb technician showed no concern that she was alerting on the drawer again. In my short time as a K-9 handler, I knew that with her change of behavior and her alert, she could not be wrong. As I looked down at her, I could see the saliva dripping from both sides of her mouth (shoestrings). I was not about to give up. As the bomb technician started walking away, I asked him if there was a way for him to test the hand blender or drawer, and he said yes. He left the house to grab some things from his vehicle and came back to the kitchen and swabbed the hand blender. He said that if there were any explosives on the hand blender, then his swab would turn colors.

Unfortunately, the swab did not change colors. Feeling very disappointed, we both walked outside the house. While walking to our vehicles, the bomb technician sat the swab on the porch. I placed my K-9 partner back into the vehicle and walked back over to the house. While walking past the porch, I had noticed that the swab was a different color. I asked the bomb technician what color the swab would turn if it was positive for explosives. He told me that it would depend on the explosive. I told him that the swab was a bright pink. He told me that it meant that it was positive for a peroxide-type explosive. I could not express how happy this made me, and I was glad that I did not give up on my K-9 partner.

Word of my K-9's find spread like wildfire through the different agencies, and it has led to us being called out for many search warrants dealing with explosives. An important lesson that was learned was one that you hear over and over: trust your dog. I would like to expand on that: to know your dog. If I did not trust or know my K-9 partner then this crucial piece of evidence would had never been found. (See Figure 19.7.)

Figure 19.7 Bomb Sniffing dog emblem.

Thinking Outside the Box

Murray Cox

I was at our headquarters office for a meeting, a bit of a dog-and-pony show, when we got a request from the county task force on a case that it picked up from the prison system several months earlier. The task force needed a dog to try to identify a storage unit rented to a now-known drug dealer.

This was my first search for law enforcement outside the prison. My dog Rowdy was, and still is, one of those dogs that would allow me to pick him up and work from any position as long as he could move his front feet. The detective was kind enough to give me a range of fifteen doors to search. During the first pass across the door fronts, Rowdy showed a little interest but nothing I would pin my hat on. This unit is fairly close to the freeway so there was lots of noise and it was windy.

After looking at the search a second time, I realized that the gap at both the bottom and top of the doors was fairly large, at least two inches top and bottom. One of the detectives was a smoker so I asked to use his lighter. I held the flame to the bottom of the door only to have the flame blow to the direction of going into the unit. I checked the same way at the top of the door. This time the flame blew out as if the breeze was coming from inside the unit. Luckily, Rowdy is only about fifty pounds and a very willing worker. He sat on my shoulder and put his front feet on the door and gave a hard sniff on the top of the first two doors. I can only imagine what the detectives thought of this sight.

The third door was a direct hit. He couldn't get off my shoulder fast enough so he could sit. He was rewarded instantly and the detectives all gave high fives to one another. At that instant I knew Rowdy was a stud. They got a warrant and I found out the next day they recovered one pound of tar heroin and a half kilo of powdered cocaine. The detectives learned that the wife of the dealer also had a storage unit in the facility and they recovered several thousand dollars in stolen property. The case ended with the seizure of two businesses, ten cars, one plane, and over $100,000 cash. They found another pound of cocaine at one of the businesses. The dealer pled guilty and received ten years' federal time.

The lesson is to never give up and don't be afraid to think outside the box. The job is easy as long as you don't think with your brain alone; think with your eyes, experience, and brain. Most of all, expect your K-9 partner to make you feel a little stupid once in a while. It feels good later when he is right, and it never hurts to fail once in a while; it helps you think next time. It also helps to have a partner you trust and one who trusts you.

Know Your Limitations and Capabilities as a K-9 Team

Larry Mayberry

Shortly after returning home from my deployment to Iraq, I was afforded the opportunity to work two explosive/patrol dogs due to manpower issues in our kennels. While working both dogs, I realized the younger dog, Dax, a small-stature German shepherd, was very proficient with bite work. Dax's demeanor was very relaxed and he was more than willing to do what I asked of him. However, there were a few issues with him not outing when given the command.

My other dog, Eddo, was a large German shepherd (Figure 19.8). He was older and we had worked together longer as well as deployed together so we had a very close bond (Figure 19.8). His bite work was proficient as well. As for his demeanor, he was a very aggressive and he was a handler protective dog.

A few months later, we had an incident on base where someone brought a gun into the base mechanics shop and threatened to shoot himself. Because the base did not have a full-time SRT (special reaction team), the military equivalent to police SWAT, a local SWAT was called to handle the situation. After arriving, they requested K-9 assistance, and I was asked to be the handler providing the support.

This left me with a decision of which dog to bring: Eddo, the dog I deployed with, who was very vocal during aggression and bite work; or Dax, who was very proficient and didn't bark when asked to bite. I chose the older dog for a few reasons: (1) being I had worked him longer and we had a very close bond; (2) the attachment I had with him made me want him to make the entry with the team as a confidence builder for us as a team; and (3) I did not realize at the time, but after reflecting on the incident, I realized that arrogance and pride played a large role in the decision of which dog to take.

Figure 19.8 Larry Mayberry and Eddo.

After exiting the control van, we began our approach to the rear exit of the building because the front of the building had a glass front and the individual with the gun could be seen pacing around in the front. On the approach, Eddo started barking, which gained the gunman's attention toward us, thus giving away our position. Due to Eddo's barking and our position being given up, the approach and entry had to be cancelled.

My mistake was that my attachment to this dog caused me to overestimate his abilities and our capabilities. The limitations we had as a team made us unqualified for the mission, which could have jeopardized lives. The correct choice would have been to use the younger dog because his capabilities were better suited for the situation at hand. Another option would have been to defer the mission to another handler within our kennels or make it known that this mission requires more than our capabilities allow. The negotiator, which was also being utilized to bring a solution to the situation, eventually talked the gunman out of the building and the local police made their arrest. But I feel if I had made the correct choice regarding the deployment of the K-9, we could have successfully completed this mission as originally asked to do.

More than Just a Tool

Derrick Perez

The bond between handler and K-9, I believe, begins the first day they meet. I can still remember the day my K-9, Chevy, and I met (Figure 19.9). I received

Figure 19.9 Officer Derrick Perez and Chevy.

a call from a fellow K-9 handler who said he had found a dog at a local dog shelter, so I packed up my kennel and drove up to test the dog.

When I arrived, I met with the dogcatcher who had caught Chevy eating out of a trashcan behind Burger King® and she stated, "I sure hope you can find a place for this dog." As she opened the kennel, out ran this black and brown German shepherd and Rottweiler mix. He appeared to have been enjoying the burgers from Burger King, because he was a little on the heavy side.

After running Chevy through a few tests, we decided that he would be able to be placed into the canine school. I loaded up Chevy in the back of my Tahoe and took him home. When we arrived at my house, I opened the car door thinking he would get out, but he wouldn't. Apparently, Chevy thought we were back at the shelter. After a few dog bones and some water, he got out and I introduced him to his new family, and that's where our bond began.

Chevy and I attended an accredited local narcotics canine course and a few weeks later we were introduced to the narcotics detection world. Our days started out early and ended late. Cleaning kennels, setting finds, and feeding dogs were just a few of our daily activities. I remember one day of training in particular when a supervisor from another agency came in to talk to us about a handler who had lost his K-9 for reasons unknown to us. The supervisor who was just that—a supervisor with zero K-9 experience— proceeded to tell us that getting attached to a K-9 is unacceptable. And we should treat our K-9s as tools that we use in the field and nothing more than that. I thought to myself that was a little strange since I had already formed somewhat of a bond with Chevy and it would be hard for me to give him up.

The class went on without a hitch and after a few months, we graduated. Our first real-world find was a kilo of cocaine and a little over $ 100,000, which was located in a hidden gas tank compartment. I continued to work Chevy, and our bond grew with every deployment. However, that supervisor's comment stuck with me over the years and I've come to realize that he was wrong. K-9s in any field, whether it is narcotics detection, explosive detection, tracking, or apprehension, all share something very special when it comes to the bond between handler and K-9.

Our story begins on a late summer afternoon after we just finished an instruction block at a school where we had been teaching. I was on duty and received a call of domestic violence that had already occurred. I cleared the training site, and arrived at the call and contacted the victim. While I was talking with her, I noticed that several items in the house had been broken. I advised the victim that I needed to photograph the damaged property and that I needed to retrieve my camera from my patrol car. As I was exiting the residence, I observed a silver truck driving past the residence. The vehicle caught my attention because it was only traveling at about five miles an hour.

I noticed that as the driver passed me, he was fixated on a house across the street from where I was. As I watched the driver, I noticed he was fumbling with something on the front seat. I continued to watch as he passed my location; I observed him level a rifle out of the driver's side window and take aim at the residence across the street from where I was. The driver's rifle appeared to malfunction and he pulled it back into the vehicle. It took a few seconds to register what I had just witnessed. I got into my patrol vehicle and advised my dispatch of what I had observed. As I pulled out onto the street, the driver saw me and a vehicle pursuit ensued.

After traveling a distance of approximately two miles, the vehicle's motor gave out and came to a stop. Before I could exit my patrol vehicle, the suspect had already opened the door, exited, and taken off running with the rifle in hand. I also exited, drew my service weapon, and took cover behind my patrol vehicle. As I looked up to see where the suspect had fled, I noticed that Chevy had also exited the vehicle and was sitting right next to me. I scanned the area to locate the subject, who had run into a heavily wooded area but was unable to locate him or any movement. As I looked down, Chevy's ears were back and he was staring straight ahead with his head moving from right to left. I looked in the direction he was looking and I observed the subject's white shirt protruding from behind a row of trees, which were approximately twenty to twenty-five yards away. I maintained my position of cover while continuing to observe the subject's movement. Additional units arrived and we carefully approached the subject, who had now discarded his weapon that had malfunctioned and took him into custody without further incident.

After the incident was over, I walked back over to my patrol vehicle to see how Chevy had gotten out. Apparently, I had only partially closed the partition separating Chevy and me. Somehow he had pushed the partition open, jumped through and then out the window that I had left rolled down. After a debrief of the incident, I had some time to reflect on what had actually happened. I realized that had it not been for Chevy, I would never have seen the subject and may have easily walked into an ambush where my fellow officers or I could have been seriously injured or even killed.

In conclusion, I firmly believe that a handler views his K-9 as much more than just a tool. When you spend the majority of your time on and off duty with your K-9, you can't help but become attached, and thus they become more than just a tool. They become your best friend, family member, and, most important, your partner.

A Real Cat-Tastrophe

Joel P. Altman

Let me start off by saying what a rewarding career I have had as a federal law enforcement officer and K-9 handler. I began my career with the FBI police in Washington, D.C., in 2004. I took advantage of every training opportunity that came along, including becoming a certified mountain bike patrol officer, field training officer, executive intelligence briefer, and, what I consider my greatest accomplishment, K-9 handler. I attended the Bureau of Alcohol, Tobacco, Firearms and Explosives (ATF) K-9 Training Academy in Front Royal, Virginia, in the fall of 2006 and graduated with my K-9 partner Kurt in December of that year. For me, at age twenty-five, it was surreal to represent the Federal Bureau of Investigation (FBI) and to take so much pride in my partner. Over the years, with the help of the ATF staff in Front Royal, Kurt and I have worked hard to become a competent and thorough working team. It has been an honor to serve both the FBI and ATF, and I will look back at the time I had with Kurt as one of the greatest times in my career and life.

Working downtown in Washington, D.C., Kurt and I were always found next to FBI Headquarters. We worked six blocks from the White House and ten blocks from the U.S. Capitol Building. So over the years we saw our fair share of crazy things happen. In July 2010, I had one of the crazier events of my career take place. It was a hot, humid day, not unlike any other summer day in downtown Washington, D.C. People were out and about, and Kurt and I were at our usual spot, waiting for deliveries to come into the building. While we were waiting, another officer came up to me and asked me to assist him in checking out a "crazy-looking car" that was parked just north of FBI headquarters across the street. So I put Kurt in my truck and off we went to check it out. As we approached I saw a car that looked like something out of the 1960s television show *Beverly Hillbillies*.

It was a four-door early 1990s model sedan that had huge baskets overflowing with lord-knows-what strapped to the roof with ropes. The trunk was bungeed down because it was packed and overflowing with all sorts of junk. Inside the car was packed and stacked with everything you could imagine. I thought that this was totally bizarre but not so much for downtown Washington, D.C. As we approached the car, a woman popped up from the passenger seat. We asked if there was anything we could do for her and that is when she started rambling about all sorts of nonsense. I asked if there were any weapons in the vehicle and she stated that "the guy I am with has a pistol somewhere in the car." We scrambled around and tracked down the owner about a block away and found out he had just attempted to enter FBI headquarters on the opposite side of the building from where we were and was turned away by the officers at the door. While he was not 100 percent mentally focused, he seemed to genuinely not have any hostile intentions. He was from Texas and trying to find information about some kidnapping case and decided to stop by our building on his way back down to Texas.

After securing the driver, I asked permission to search his vehicle. He told me where the pistol was and I retrieved it from under the driver's seat.

Now it was time to put Kurt to use and utilize him to find any other guns, ammo, or explosives that might be in the vehicle. Before starting my search with Kurt, as I looked around the vehicle I realized the crates in the backseat weren't crates to hold clothing or other items. The crates were stacked on top of each other and were loaded with seventeen live cats!

I thought there was no way that Kurt was going to search this vehicle once I bring him out of my truck. But I had to search and put him to work. Now Kurt hates all small animals, but especially cats. However, on that day, he went right to work, searched the vehicle, and ignored the cats in the backseat. He showed a lot of interest in the center armrest of the vehicle and after the search was complete, we opened the armrest and found a pistol magazine and more ammo that was buried underneath a bunch of other garbage.

It was 90-plus degrees with an equally high humidity on that day and the cats looked like they were about ready to die. Luckily, D.C. animal control officers came and took the cats to a shelter. We learned the female passenger was wanted for animal cruelty in Maryland and had a warrant out for her arrest. We believed she was trying to leave town with this poor old guy from Texas. They were both arrested and processed.

So in the end it was a positive conclusion for both Kurt and the cats. I would never have thought that Kurt would search a vehicle that was loaded with live animals, but sticking to our search pattern and training he did exactly what he was trained to do. I would add that we train our dogs on different distracter odors all the time, but I do not recall training my dog to search around live animals (especially cats) during the academy. Perhaps it is something that can be utilized in the future to keep the dogs focused. Perhaps during training after the academy, working with your partner in situations that involve animals or people would be very beneficial to any K-9 team.

In conclusion, I want to add that my favorite part of the job and what I miss most about my work was simply interacting with the public on a daily basis—something I do not get to do in my current position. I took great pride and satisfaction when people, especially young people, would walk by and be amazed that they were next to the FBI building. I was an ambassador for the FBI and Kurt was the best ambassador the bureau could ever hope for. I would bring Kurt out to meet tourists, children, and families, and they would pet him and he might give them a paw and shake hands. I met thousands of people during my five years working there as a handler. I miss it more and more every day. It was a great time and I will always look back on it with fond memories and pride. Kurt is eight years old now and he is still working as good, if not better, than ever. I moved on from the bureau in 2011 for another K-9 position, but looking back I wouldn't have traded it for the world.

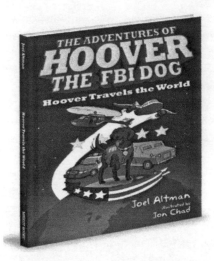

Figure 19.10 Officer Joel Altman and K-9 Kurt's book.Mascot books, 2011.

A Special Bond

Rommel R. Aclan

I had this habit of not putting the dog back into the kennel after the training day was complete when I was doing my initial K-9 training with the Philippine National Police Special Action Force Unit. I would just notify the training instructors that the dog would be staying with me in the barracks. So me and my K-9 partner Spike were always together between our training and our free time. Spike and I had a lot of good times together. We would trek the mountains near the training center; we would play and run in the rain until we dropped in the mud. At night, Spike slept in my room underneath my bunk. We developed a very strong bond between training and playing, which I could see as a direct positive effect in his performance.

Our training was focused on explosive detection so we spent much time imprinting on explosive odors and searching. Some of the training exercises as the course progressed were very stressful on our dogs. Therefore we ultimately lost some of our K-9 classmates due to the stress. However, K-9 Spike was still on point with his training and willing to face and undergo the most difficult of training exercises.

K-9 training is a science, and many aspects of the desired response are the result of a behavior modification. It is also about conditioning, approximation, and many more theories in behavioral science. It seemed to me that a great deal of training a K-9 is mechanics; that is, when you do this, the reaction of the dog will result in that. Later on with K-9 Spike, I realized that it's not all about the mechanics of reward and punishment. I realized that

K-9 Spike did good in training because we became friends, partners, and we had developed mutual trust and confidence in each other. I believe it was a mutual friendship and our respect for each other that made Spike perform better than any of the other K-9s in our class.

During that time, I learned that a dog has an intense sensitivity to human emotion and you can't fool the dog with an insincere verbal praise or gesture. The dog can sense what's going on inside you and will be able to respond accordingly to those feelings. Spike was a black male Labrador retriever. He was playful and very friendly. I never saw any aggression or a violent reaction from him.

However, there was an instance when a companion of mine was fooling around the barracks playing jokes on the others in the class. This particular classmate attempted to sneak up on me with a bandana covering his face and growling real low like a monster. He put his hands on me and began choking me around the neck in an attempt to scare me. We were shocked when Spike jumped up, barking fiercely at my classmate and then lunged toward him. It was a good thing his leash was tied on my bunk so Spike was somewhat restrained. He barked loudly and intensely until my classmate walked away from us out of the barracks room. That is when I realized that this dog is so willing to sacrifice his life for the sake of his friend, in this case me, his handler.

Since that time and long since we graduated from our training academy and have deployed and worked together on many different cases and scenarios. I will always remember this lesson that was taught to me during my junior class handlers. The concept that a good bond that is developed through mutual trust and confidence can result in a very good K-9 partner that is able to withstand all kinds of testing and stress.

Above all, I believe that not just anyone can make or train a good K-9 until the handler or assigned trainer has made peace with him. There must be devotion and a sense of goodness to what that handler or trainer is doing to the K-9. There is no room for hatred, short tempers, or other ill-mannered behavior in K-9 training. A sense of peace and love must start inside the heart of the handler, and the dog will sense it and become an effective agent of peace.

The Power of a Dog's Eyes

Jason Johnson

Over the past several years, I have researched the idea of training K-9s specifically to help those veterans returning from war with posttraumatic stress disorder (PTSD). Being a former soldier and having had many friends in combat, I have had direct experience with the effects PTSD can have on the mental health of a hero. As I was starting back up my company, K-9 Solutions International (K-9SI), I developed a comprehensive program where I would rescue certain breeds of K-9s from humane societies nationwide. I wanted to find K-9s having the right qualities we were looking for and then train them in an in-depth, several-weeks course. The goal would be to get them to a certification level of a service animal and place them in a home with a veteran.

The idea is that the veteran would have a companion with them 24/7 that they care for and can take with them wherever they go, such as restaurants, movies, airline flights, and so on. The dog would be in an official harness and be labeled as a service animal or as a wounded warrior K-9 if the veteran so wished. Studies in this area have taught me that if that soldier has someone or something that they have agreed to take care of, a sense of loyalty and duty to that animal, then they are less likely to harm themselves in any way because of that oath of responsibility they took when they committed to that K-9. I wrote up a detailed business plan and training regiment for this program to try and implement this program. I was aware that there were already a few programs like this out there but I wanted to take this to a national level and I still do.

My first thought was to contact the Wounded Warrior Project because I know they are greatly involved in programs assisting with PTSD and they also have ways of receiving funding to help get the dogs trained, certified, and placed with veterans. After several correspondences with them, I was shot down, so I moved on to the Department of Veteran Affairs. The Department of Veteran Affairs had been looking into doing a pilot program, which I contacted them about and threw my name into the mix for the project, but they stated that for now they were simply researching the idea and were not ready to move completely forward yet.

I spent the next couple of months talking with various veterans and some who suffer from PTSD to see if this was a program that they would like to participate in or help get started. Thus far, the response has been nothing but positive, and I think veterans would like a national program that helps place PTSD companion dogs with them at little or no cost to them. This program took on a whole new meaning for me when I visited with an old military friend of mine whom I had known for several years. He had done some very hard time in Iraq as a military police officer and had lost many friends in combat over the years from acts of war. I remember spending time with him after his deployments, and I knew that this was something he was going to deal with for the rest of his life. After a few years of being out of the Army, he contacted me about helping him adopt a retired military police working dog that belonged to one of his old partners. I made the appropriate calls and wrote a letter of reference and soon he drove down to Texas to pick up his new companion, K-9 Fulles (Figure 19.11), to live with him on his ten-acre piece of land. I was very pleased I was able to help him out with adopting a military working dog because I knew how much he loved animals and I knew that he lived alone so this would give him great companionship.

Figure 19.11 U.S. Army Military Police K-9 Fulles (J201).

Over the past few years, he would thank me for helping him adopt his dog, and one day I stopped in to visit him as I was passing through his area. We got to talking about dogs and my company K-9 Solutions International, and I started to tell him about the program I had developed in reference to placing trained rescue dogs with veterans suffering from PTSD solely for a mental health purpose as a companion. This is when he shared a personal story with me that I will never forget. He told how great an idea that was and how he wanted to help and get involved too. He explained to me that the previous Memorial Day was a sad day for him, as he sat on his front porch thinking of all the friends he had lost in combat. He described his feelings of anger and hurt, and how he had suicidal thoughts himself that day and was considering taking his own life. He had all but made up his mind to do so when his adopted retired military working dog came up to him and put his muzzle on his lap, and he told me that when he looked into his dogs eyes, all of those thoughts left his mind instantly; and it was because of his dog that he is still alive today. He also conveyed to me that this isn't the only instance that K-9 Fulles had helped him when he was down, but it was the most significant. He was sure to point out to me that owning that dog has been nothing but a positive influence in his life and that the dog could sense any time he was down and would attempt to cheer him up on a frequent basis.

I shook his hand as he thanked me for helping him adopt his dog, and right then I knew not to ever give up on the idea of taking the program I had developed to help veterans with PTSD and to keep trying to promote it and get stories like this out there so we can make it a nationwide program. For more information or comments on how to help with this program, you can visit us at www.K-9si.com and send a message through the "Contact Us" page. My goal is to train dogs to be companions to help save the lives of many veterans after they sacrificed so much to save the lives of many Americans.

I wrote this story on behalf of a veteran who told it to me in confidence and I'm thankful to him for sharing it with me. I was given his full permission to share his touching experience with all of you. I would like to dedicate this story to the men and women of the U.S. Army Military Police Corps on his behalf for the ultimate sacrifice you have made for our freedom. Assist, protect, and defend. You are not forgotten!

*   *   *

The last story of this chapter is another true story. Unfortunately, it doesn't necessarily have a happy ending, but it reflects the poignant association between man and dog and the sad truth of war.

*   *   *

"Finding Your Passion"

Chan Follen

Foreword

On the morning of August 6, 2011, a group of U.S. Army Rangers was on a mission to kill or capture a senior Taliban leader in a remote location of Afghanistan. When the mission did not go as planned, the rangers, finding themselves in a very precarious situation and immediate danger, called for a quick reactionary force (QRF) to assist them with the mission. It was the members of the U.S. Navy's Gold Squadron, formerly known as Seal Team Six, who got the call at 0100 hours to assist that morning.

While responding to assist the rangers via a Chinook CH-47 Helicopter, call sign "Extortion 17," they encountered an attack from Taliban insurgents and were struck by a rocket-propelled grenade causing the helicopter to go down and crash in the Tangi Valley of the Wardak Province. The crash left zero survivors, tragically killing thirty-three passengers, five crew members, and one military working dog.

Among the thirty-eight killed in what was the deadliest U.S. military incident since the start of the war in Afghanistan in 2001 were twenty-two U.S. Navy Special Operation Forces personnel, twenty of whom were attached to Seal Team Six and two from a West Coast-based Seal Team; five U.S. Army Aviation crew members from the 158th and the 135th Aviation Regiment; one U.S. Air Force Combat Controller and two U.S. Air Force Pararescuemen from the 24th Special Tactics Squadron; seven Afghan Special Operations Soldiers; one Afghan interpreter; and one

U.S. Navy military working dog, K-9 Bart, whose handler was John "Jet Li" Douangdara.

John Douangdara was a U.S. Navy Gold Squadron member. He was a very well-respected K-9 handler and loved by many. His untimely and tragic death was a huge loss to the K-9 and Special Operations community, and he will not be forgotten. Submitted by a close family member, the following story is about John, who he was as a person, and his love for his profession as a handler.

—Jason Johnson

My name is Chan Follen. I am the sister of the late John Douangdara. He was the lead dog handler for the Elite Seal Team Six. John and his military working dog, Bart, were both on a Chinook helicopter shot down on August 6, 2011. I want to share with you a more personal side of John. (See Figure 19.12.)

My parents fled Laos, a small landlocked country situated in Indochina, back in 1980, with only me in tow. Born December 29, 1984, in Sioux City Iowa, John was the third child of five. Our family actually grew up on the Nebraska side of the Missouri River in South Sioux City. For my family, Nebraska was quite a change from communist Laos and our Buddhist foundation, but it was an opportunity we always appreciated.

As a child, Johnny, our family's nickname for him, was the typical boy. Watching him grow into a teenager, I noticed early on that he was not a follower. While countless local kids were often pulled into gangs and drugs or the much lesser evil of skipping school, Johnny remained steadfast; he was simply not susceptible to peer pressure or influence.

Figure 19.12 John Douangdara and Bart.

While other boys were romancing girls all night, Johnny was working on computers at home. He was pretty much a computer geek, a well-loved computer geek. He excelled at school activities and enjoyed the challenges of debate team, an activity that bolstered his skills in research, public speaking, persuasion, teamwork, and finding opponents' weaknesses.

He had tons of friends and I never once heard of any of his friends being mad at him or talking bad about him. He was the friend that you could always count on and that trait stayed with him throughout his life. When his friends were deployed, he would step in and help them out. One of his friend's daughters was distraught that her father was unable to attend a father–daughter school function but was ecstatic when Johnny stood in for her dad. He sometimes also would babysit for friends so they could make the most of their time at home by taking their wives out on a date night.

From as far back as I can remember, my father was always trying to get one of his kids into the military. My mother's father was a captain in the Laotian army. My father knew that the military would add discipline and structure to our lives so we always stopped at the recruiter's office every time we went to the mall. We even had an Army bumper sticker that read "Army— Be All You Can Be" on our front door that reminded us that it would make him proud if one of us would join, and this is what we saw every day when we walked out of our home.

Toward the end of Johnny's junior year in high school, he started weighing the options of what he wanted to do after high school. He started going to see recruiters and by the beginning of his senior year, he had made up his mind to enlist in the Navy and specifically wanted to work in the Navy's nuclear program. In fact, his plans were to graduate from high school a semester early, so he would be heading to boot camp in January.

Our brother Pan and I, being older siblings, sat Johnny down and asked if the Navy was what he really wanted to do. I couldn't see my geeky little brother making it in the military. He was small, standing 5'5" and maybe 115 pounds; I thought he would probably have to prove himself to make it. We offered to pay for his college even if that meant taking out personal loans for him. But he was adamant about going into the military and that was that, debate over. John graduated midterm in 2002 and headed to Great Lakes, Illinois, for Navy boot camp in 2003.

John went in as a Master at Arms (security and force protection) and after completing his school, he headed to Sicily. In his calls and letters, we could tell he was homesick and it broke my heart hearing my baby brother so unhappy. It appeared it was going to be a long three-year tour for all of us.

Weeks passed and I noticed his mood had changed. Johnny would call me, but instead of being muted voices, the background noises were now barking dogs. I asked what he was doing at the kennels and he told me he was watching the dogs that were retired but unadoptable. They would stay in the

Navy until their last breath. I asked him if that was a hard thing to do, and he told me he spent time giving great care to these K-9s before they had to go. You could tell in his voice that he loved being around the dogs.

Then, a wonderful surprise came when Johnny called me to tell me that he would be in San Antonio, Texas, for canine school. I was ecstatic because I lived in Dallas and was going to see my baby brother more often now. It was not until after Johnny was killed and I met Billy, a kennel master for the Navy, that I learned the full story of Johnny being drawn into the kennel. Billy shared with me that, indeed, Johnny was miserable in Sicily. Billy felt badly for him so he invited Johnny to stop by the kennels and hang out with him. Billy felt like he needed to take this young kid under his wings and make his stay a little easier by befriending him. That is when Billy discovered that Johnny loved being in the kennels and being with dogs. Johnny would work ten- to twelve-hour shifts at the gate, then go to the kennels and volunteer his time at the kennel for a couple of hours. Once Billy realized that Johnny loved being with the dogs and that he had a natural understanding of them, Billy put in a word for Johnny to head to canine school in San Antonio.

After canine school, Johnny loved his job, and he never stopped talking about his dogs. His first deployment to Iraq scared me; he had a bomb-sniffing dog and they worked the gates searching vehicles and deliveries. I told Johnny that he needed to call or e-mail me to let me know he was safe. We never talked about how it was over there, because we both knew it was dangerous and our phone conversations were more of getting his mind away from this dangerous place. He was the type of guy to make the best of things in any situation.

An example of that are the pictures he would send me. He would e-mail me pictures of his dogs and he always had them wearing silly accessories. He had bunny ears on one dog for Easter. On his twenty-first birthday, he had to celebrate it in Iraq, but he sent me a picture of him and his dog wearing a Hawaiian lei and a bottle of sparkling grape juice celebrating the occasion.

Going through all of Johnny's personal belongings after he died, one could tell how much each and every dog he handled meant to him. He had all kinds of pictures of his dogs all over his house and on his cell phone. Most especially, he had Toby's ashes in his room. Toby was a dog he had on deployment on his second tour in Iraq. Tragically, Toby was killed in action in 2008, the only time Johnny ever called home crying. The action remains classified, but we do know that Toby had saved six Canadian lives that day, and our family was gifted with a plaque from the Canadian military to honor Johnny and Toby after Johnny's death.

We also heard of stories from many fellow handlers of how great a handler Johnny was, from taking the most difficult dogs and being able to work with them, to how he would baby his dogs by carrying them around the kennel over his shoulders. I can honestly say that these dogs were his passion. So dying beside his dog and fellow comrades, those in whom Johnny trusted his life, would have been, to Johnny, an honorable way to leave this earthly life. Johnny had found his passion and died among friends in a war against terrorism and worldly violence.

John was a selfless and loving man; he had the chance to touch many lives, and so they grieve with us. With an electric smile and an unforgettable laugh, John lived life to the fullest. We will miss our beloved John, but his memory will carry on in our hearts until we meet with him again. John's hometown, South Sioux City, Nebraska, has named the dog park that is part of Freedom Park in honor of John: the John Douangdara Memorial War Dog Park (Figure 19.13). The park is to honor all military working dog handlers as well as their faithful companions—past, present, and future.

To keep his memory alive, a statue of Johnny and his always-faithful companion, Bart, will be donated to Freedom Park (Figure 19.14). With his passion for his loyal canine partners that went into battle with him, we would like to honor all military working dogs and their handlers. Internationally known Susan Bahary is working on the sculpture. She is the same sculptor who worked on "Always Faithful," the monument dedicated to twenty-five Marine dogs on base in Guam.*

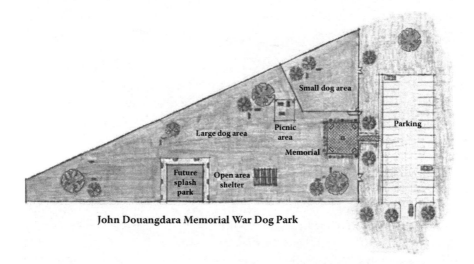

John Douangdara Memorial War Dog Park

Figure 19.13 The John Douangdara Memorial War Dog Park in Freedom Park in South Sioux City, Nebraska.

---

* To learn more information about the John Douangdara Memorial War Dog Park or how you can donate to a statue of John and K-9 Bart, visit www.inmemoryofjohn.com.

Figure 19.14 A statue of John and Bart will be added to Freedom Park.

Addendum

In answer to a Facebook question to David Marris, a soldier in Afghanistan: "I see your photos of dogs. Are you a dog handler?" He replied, "Negative, Sir, I am in security, but I haven't worked with handlers and their dogs. We have a dog section on my current base. They do a great job for us, and I would trust my life to those dogs." —D.L. Jane

Conflict of Time, Priorities, and Family

20

RUTH STORTROEN

There are many types of conflicts. Conflicts can manifest between family members, between colleagues and co-workers, between the people of a nation and the governing leaders, and between countries. A personal conflict that most Americans face is the conflict between time, priorities, and family.

We've all heard the sayings "There's just not enough hours in a day" or "There's so much to do with so little time." In America, where everyone is hustling and bustling, we must all feel that way at least once a day. Whose idea was it to add so many tasks or obligations to each of our schedules? Was it the invention of electric appliances that freed up our time to do more? Was it the motto of the U.S. Army that states: "Be all that you can be?" Could it have been the march of the feminists who declared that women can do it all and have it all? However it began, the conflict of doing so much with so little time has affected generation after generation ever since.

In her article titled "Time Management and the Affects It Can Have on Your life," Jennifer Foote states, "Improper time management can have a negative impact on the workplace, the home, and everyone else around you. … It is possible for improper time management to cause family disagreements and unnecessary tension."* Families have to find a balance between work, school, home, and play in order to value quality time with each other. That is an ongoing conflict for so many of us, and it affects each and every family member.

When parents have careers that take them away from home for extended periods of time, their spouses and children suffer. The person who is absent the most misses out on critical milestones in their children's development. She may have missed the first steps her one-year-old took. He may have missed his daughter's first lost tooth or her first crush on a boy. They may find that their spouses have met emotional or sexual fulfillment elsewhere in their absence. This is an issue that my husband and I have faced continually for the past fifteen months.

Since I have been enrolled in the National University Cohort for my B.A. courses, my husband and I have had to "find" time for each other. It sounds cruel in a way that I would have to find time for him, but my schedule

---

* Jennifer Foote, "Time management and the affects it can have on your life," April 11, 2006.

is very hectic and we work different hours. He leaves for work at four in the morning while I am still asleep. I come home to him cooking so that I can eat dinner and begin the task of homework or paperwork. I also have the added responsibility of memorizing our son's schedule due to practices and performance dates for band. I often have to stop to pick him up on my way home from work. By the time I come home, I am dead on my feet. My husband has been home for at least two hours and has had time for himself. He allows me time to settle in and eat dinner. It is then that we converse and share our day. Sometimes we only get one hour to talk and then he is off to bed. I have to make time for him on the days we do have more time together. I have to be very careful of his feelings and not express the attitude that spending time with him is just "one more thing I have to do." I make a conscious effort to be considerate of him. I must also make time for my children.

Even though my children are grown and two are adults, they still crave my attention and affection. My youngest son is almost as busy as I am. We all try to get together at least once a month and more in the summer months when I am home full time. Sometimes it's just a few hours lounging around watching movies. My children will still climb into bed with me on those not-so-frequent, exceptionally gloomy, lazy days as we enjoy much-needed snuggle time. Yes, my grown, adult children love snuggle time with their mommy. Like I said before, we are creative.

Most parents that I speak with always say the same thing after their kids have grown up: "I wish I had spent more time with them when they were little." My point is that you can't get those years back. Is it impossible to have a quality relationship later? No. Is the damage irreparable? No. There is still time with the strategy of "managing time" to fit your family into a very busy schedule and make the most of that time spent together. One of the best strategies is to cut down on activities outside the home that take too much time away from home. Some children are overwhelmed by a hectic schedule from the time they are very young. They may be involved in Girl Scouts, Boy Scouts, organized sports, organized academics, music lessons, tutoring, art lessons, and many other activities that serve to enrich their knowledge and skill level, yet do not allow for time to bond with their families. Children must not be hurried to do too much too soon for fear of early stress and burnout.

In his book *The Hurried Child*, David Elkind describes the use of technology to "hurry" a fetus to become accustomed to the world around him by simulating the sound of a mother's heartbeat via a small device attached to the pregnant mother's belly.* The purpose of this product is to introduce the baby to sound patterns that will later relate to his sequential learning process.

---

* David Elkind, *The Hurried Child: Growing Up Too Fast Too Soon* (Cambridge, MA: De Capo Press, 2011).

In the world of early childhood development, this is a skill a child will fully develop at approximately four years of age. There is no need to hurry an unborn fetus. With the proper adult–child interactions in the first 3 years of life, the child will succeed on time. The author also mentions a video product aimed at introducing infants and toddlers to the world of sports. As these young tykes watch a series of images and role-playing puppets, they are supposed to gain an interest in soccer, football, basketball, tennis, and golf that will instill in them the desire to become all-star athletes. Really? Early childhood development teaches that children learn and become interested in activities through hands-on knowledge. Again, there is no need to rush infants and toddlers into making a lifelong career choice or athletic preference.

As I think about this conflict, this dilemma, I need to find ways to combat the effects of being overwhelmed with too much to do in so little time. For me the problem is an everyday occurrence. I can't remember a Saturday morning or a Wednesday evening when I wasn't in a classroom with fifteen of my colleagues. Since January of 2010, I have missed every band performance that my son has been part of, except for two. My last birthday was celebrated with friends I hadn't seen in over three years. If I compare these facts with other busy people, I may not have it so bad, but one fact remains too hard to dispute. If I had put down my work files and spent more time with my mother, I would have gone to visit her the day before she unexpectedly passed away instead of saying to her, "I'll see you tomorrow Mom." That is an opportunity I will never get back.

As I write this chapter, I am reflecting on the consequences of my conflict as it relates to my extended family. My mother-in-law has actually resorted to writing my husband and me a letter asking for forgiveness for whatever she has done for us to neglect her. At first, I was angry at this. Now I can see and recognize that she is feeling left out. Although we have always told her she does not require an invitation and can drop by anytime, she is actually asking for our undivided attention when she does visit. I get that now. If she were to come over tonight, she would find me sitting at the computer in my dining room among fifteen months of clutter. My husband would be sitting in front of the television enjoying a movie alone, and our youngest child would be in his room practicing beats on his drum pad. That is not quality time.

Being caught up in my own world of work, school, paperwork, homework, the Internet, the telephone, and Facebook have been cause for disagreements in my home. No one understands the demands on me due to my career choice or because of the requirements to earn my B.A. The deadlines my colleagues and I suffer through are unrealistic to say the least. They are sometimes torturous, causing me to stay awake past midnight and to go to work the next day with little or no sleep. I often distract myself from these pressures by spending a few minutes texting or talking to friends or checking updates on my Facebook page. Now it's time for me to make some changes. To do that, I must isolate the conflict and deal with it head-on.

In reevaluating my tools of thinking, I realize that the language I have used to communicate my frustrations and stress to my family has been rich with sarcasm and guilt. I have downplayed their needs and their frustrations in the same breath I use to excuse myself for not being there for them. It is true that I do have mandates and requirements to consider in my hectic schedule, but I didn't have to strive for the perfect letter grade or the perfect evaluation from my supervisor. In retrospect, I could have done less and still passed every class while maintaining my relationships at home. I can associate myself with my own father growing up and how I felt as a kid. He worked six days a week all year long. It was an exciting adventure to spend one or two days each summer in his old work truck as he made his rounds to landscaping nurseries to deliver exotic plants and to reload. I will never forget the soda machines that he dropped coins into to dispense a cola in a small glass bottle. That was the best way to drink it! These little moments are what I cherish of my time spent with my dad. I now try to spend one day a week with him before he is no longer part of my life here on Earth.

I also suffered some neglect from lack of time with and attention from my mother. Yes, she had six children to bond with, nurture, teach and care for, but I was her baby girl. I should have been more spoiled. I actually don't recall much of a relationship with my mom as a young child. I had two sisters who dressed me, combed my hair, and watched over me. They taught me the facts of life and how to behave like a lady. I found out in junior high school that my mom had been sick since the time I was three years old. She suffered through her last pregnancy and subsequent birth of my baby brother to the point of becoming diabetic and suffering through a hysterectomy. She also had gallbladder surgery and was in bed recuperating a lot. When I was five years old, she began to spend time teaching preschool and attended night classes at UCLA. I never realized the workload she had on her because I witnessed her still having time for all of her children and my father. She woke up before five in the morning and went to bed very late. Yes, she managed a household, worked, studied, and volunteered her time, but all of this contributed to her poor health that led to her leg amputations and her early death at the age of sixty-eight.

My perception of what I have to do as a mother, a wife, and as a financial contributor to my household is influenced by my childhood, my moods, my stress level, my experience as a member of a lower socioeconomic class, and by my attitude. In hindsight, I should have resolved this conflict of time versus priorities versus family a long time ago. Understanding the root of my conflict is key in making the decision to change. I believe the root of my conflict is thinking that I *have* to do everything well. With the knowledge I have gained in this class, I realize that my family must be my first obligation.

I must plan my day and manage my time better in order to leave "work" at work. When I come home, I must turn off my cell phone and resolve to spend only one hour at the computer while I research information for a class or for work. I believe this is reasonable. I may need to revisit this time limit if I find myself falling behind on a project. The desired outcome is for my family to get me back and for us to reconnect, have some fun, share some laughter. I have made the decision not to continue with this cohort as it evolves into a master's program. I already know that I will be of no good use to anyone if I continue at this pace. I will fail personally and professionally if I allow myself and my family to be burdened any further. With that said, I have said all I can say. It is time to retire this chapter and give my family some much-needed and much-deserved attention.

Marriage and Conflict

21

YESENIA VEGA

Contents

Introduction

Can you remember how you felt the day you "tied the knot"? The bride dressed in white and the groom dressed in a black tuxedo. All the bridesmaids dressed in the same color dress and groomsmen dressed in the same suit with the same colors. The preparations for the wedding started the day the groom popped the question and the bride said yes. The day of the ceremony arrives and the priest will ask the magic question: "Do you take this man/woman to be your lawful wedded husband/wife?" The bride and groom say I do, and they are married for their rest of their lives, "through sickness and health and till death do you apart." Then comes the honeymoon stage and still everything is perfect between the couple.

Life goes on and then some marriages fall apart. The couple is having problems and is thinking about D-I-V-O-R-C-E. The way a couple solves its problems can affect or enrich a marriage. Therefore there are several issues that can lead to divorce, such as miscommunication, trust, infidelity, and stress. However, marriage can also survive with counseling, proper communication, and respect for one another.

Miscommunication and Marriage

There are many barriers in communication between a couple that can affect a marriage. For example, without interaction there is no communication. Lack of communication can occur when one person in the relationship cannot make the other understand how they feel. Therefore, this means that the other party is not exercising his or her listening skills. To communicate effectively, the husband and wife must be able to listen to one another and acknowledge the other's feelings. According to James Park, "The longer that this practice of non-communication lasts, the harder it becomes to break down the pattern. It is often easier to keep quiet and let the relationship drift along."* For example, most couples reach a point in their relationship where communication is only used when necessary. Therefore, these couples start to form a pattern of miscommunication because this is what they are immune to as conflict arises.

As other couples use communication, they use it in a harmful way that will affect the partner and the whole relationship. Couples can find themselves complaining about everything. For example, they can argue about problems such as broken household items, finances, or household duties. Dr. Laura Schlessinger reinforces a key concept in communication: "Communication is just not about complaints! Forgetting to keep love fresh is the worst communication mistake of all."† A good example of this can be an unappreciative husband who demands everything but might not even tell his wife thank you for what she does for him or just give her a kiss. In addition, Schlessinger states, "Don't think that all communication is with words; do realize, accept, and enjoy that there are little things you're both doing for each other that say 'I love you.'"‡ As couples we need to keep in mind the different communication methods that we use with our partner to express the way we might feel.

Marriage and Trust

A key term that can also affect a marriage is *trust*. *Webster's Dictionary* defines "trust" as to rely on somebody or something; to place confidence in somebody or in somebody's good qualities, especially fairness, truth, honor, or ability. If either spouse does not trust the other the marriage can suffer negative consequences. Lauer and Lauer add, "When trust declines or is lacking, the relationship is likely to deteriorate and may sink into a series of severe arguments."§ For example, I recall trust issues in a relationship between my cousin and her spouse who always seem to worry about each other's whereabouts and would express their feelings of mistrust to other family members but not with one another. This situation made them feel they could not trust each other so they had many arguments that led to a divorce. According to

---

* James Park, *New Ways of Loving: How Authenticity Transforms Relationships*, 6th ed. (Minneapolis, MN: Existential Books, 2007), 220.
† Laura Schlesinger, *The Proper Care & Feeding of Marriage* (New York: HarperCollins, 2007), 127.
‡ Ibid, 129.
§ Robert H. Lauer and Jeanette C. Lauer, *Marriage and Intimacy: The Quest for Intimacy*, 5th ed. (New York: McGraw-Hill, 2004), 256.

Lauer and Lauer, "If you don't trust your spouse, if you don't have a firm sense that your spouse is honest, supportive, and loyal, you will probably find yourself continually challenging your spouse on a variety of issues."[*] Therefore, the real dispute in the relationship will not be how, what, where, and who the spouse is with, but it will be the lack of trust in the relationship.

Marriage and Infidelity

Infidelity can be more then sexual unfaithfulness in a relationship (p. 256). For example, a spouse can have a different lover, like his career, interest, or friends, and he will place all these things before the wife. This can be seen in relationships were the husband has not had a sexual relationship with someone else but he is not fulfilling the wife's needs and the vows they both said at the altar. Other types of infidelity are extramarital affairs and adultery. These infidelities are some of the major factors of marriage desolation. Brad Lewis adds, "Well, definitive numbers are hard to come by, but most polls and estimates typically report that more than one-third of men and about one-quarter of women admit to having had at least one extramarital sexual act."[†] Betrayal in a marriage is very hurtful and can cause lots of damage for the whole family. For example, my father was unfaithful to my mother many times, and my mother had low self-esteem so she felt as if there was nothing she could do about it. Although my parents would talk things over, my father seemed to not understand how much he was really hurting my mother. One day she was brave enough to ask for a divorce and explained to my sister and me that things were no longer working between my father and her. A year and a half later, my parents divorced and my mother brought my sister and me to Los Angeles to live. According to the Holy Bible, in Hebrew 13:4: "Have respect for marriage. Always be faithful to your partner, because God will punish anyone who is immoral or unfaithful in marriage." Marriage is sacred and one should respect their vows and their marriage.

Marriage and Stress

Stress in a marriage can be affected by many factors such as miscommunication, finances, infidelities, and careers. Stress can also affect the health of the couple if there are too many problems that cannot be solved. Rick Roepke

---

[*] Ibid.
[†] Brad Lewis, "An all-too-common affair," Focus on the Family, 2002, http://www.focusonthefamily.com/marriage/divorce_and_infidelity/affairs_and_adultery/an_all_too_common_affair.aspx.

states, "Lifestyle choices are negatively impacting not only the family life, but also the physical, spiritual, and emotional health and well-being of couples."[*] Therefore, a married couple under stress can face many challenges like health problems, bad moods, and sleepless nights. In addition, no couple going through chronic stress can actually feel fulfilled and happy together. Roepke adds, "Marriage and family life are particularly affected by stress. Under stress, we tend to snap at our children or spouses, pushing them away as our minds become preoccupied with our stressors."[†] Thus, stress can really affect the family and this can lead to depression or divorce. One way that a couple can try to work out their problems and stress can be marriage counseling.

Marriage Counseling

Marriage counseling can be beneficial for all couples, especially those who are going through difficult situations like the ones mentioned in this chapter. According to the Mayo Foundation for Medical Education and Research, "Marriage counseling, also called couples therapy, helps couples, married or not, understand and resolve conflicts and improve their relationship."[‡] Therefore, marriage counseling can bring couples to understand one another's feelings and how to solve their problems in a healthier way. The Mayo Foundation adds, "Marriage counseling gives couples tools to communicate better, negotiate differences, problem solve and even argue in a healthier way." In every relationship, couples might experience different ideas or might not be able to solve their problems effectively without arguing. Thus, marriage counseling is a great asset to use if a couple wants to save their marriage and learn how to communicate, trust, love, and respect one another.

Conclusion

There are several issues that can lead to divorce, including miscommunication, trust, infidelity, and stress. However marriage can also survive with counseling that offers exercises for proper communication, understanding, and respecting one another. The issues that affect a marriage can be suppressed if the couple works together and fights against all odds. Marriage will never be perfect, but we can gain the knowledge to make it work. Communication

---

[*] R. Roepke, "Stress and your marriage," *LifeWay*, November 4, 2003, retrieved from http://www.lifeway.com/article/?id=155422.

[†] Ibid.

[‡] Mayo Foundation for Medical Education Research, Rochester, MN. www.mayo.edu.

is one of the most important aspects of a marriage, and couples should know how to use it in order to solve problems and understand each other's feelings, beliefs, and opinions. According to Robert Anderson,* "In every marriage more than a week old, there are grounds for divorce. The trick is to find, and continue to find, grounds for marriage." Therefore, no marriage will ever be perfect or fairy tale; but if one looks for reasons why they fell in love in the first place, they will understand why they want the marriage to work. *No relationship can exist without communication.*

* Robert Anderson (1861–1939) American Economist. Robert Anderson Quotes; ThinkExist.com. http://www.thinkexist.com/quotes/Robert_Anderson/

The Need for Ethics 22

DALE L. JUNE

Contents

Introduction

This chapter examines how personal and moral beliefs influence the relationship between criminal justice and social justice, and how professional beliefs and principles sometimes conflict with personal instincts for "doing right." In a conflicting dilemma, the choice (often not by personal preference) is made in favor of professional obligations overriding personal principles of virtue. Law enforcement officers and agents are confronted daily with temptations and ethical decisions in addition to judgments allowing a great degree of discretion for addressing issues of ethical, moral, and constitutional concerns. A study of normative judgments as applied to contemporary human problems such as the uses of power, practices, and the right to live and to die are ethical principles applied to choices and decisions that arise in professional, personal, and social lives that reflect membership in a subculture of a democratic society.

The Need for Ethics

Some synonyms for ethics are *principles, morals, beliefs, moral principles, moral values,* and *having a moral code.* Other synonyms for ethics include ethical, conscientious, decent, honest, honorable, humane, integrity, moral, noble, (of good) character, proper, respectable, scrupulous, and trustworthy. What more can we ask of criminal justice officers? One thing we can ask is for them to understand and practice the elements of ethics in their professional and personal lives. A more complex meaning in eight words: "the choices people make between right and wrong."

Journalist Edward R. Murrow (1908–1965) said, "Most truths are so naked, that people feel sorry for them and cover them up, at least a little bit."

The American criminal justice system is far from perfect but in a democratic world, it is considered one of the best for maintaining rules of society. Our Constitution is a written guarantee that everyone, whether they can afford legal representation or not, will be treated fairly and equally in matters of criminal liability. That is the ideal. That is the ethical approach. The reality is, in spite of all good intentions, that from the moment a bill is proposed in Congress to the actual enforcement of a law and carrying out of sanctions, equality and fair treatment are sometimes trampled.

We know that human decisions play a major, if not the key, role in how the system is dispensed. It has been said that our justice system is like a metro transit system. As the train starts from the originating station (an arrest), it begins collecting passengers and making several stops along the way, with some getting on and some getting off, until it finally arrives at the last stop—prison—with all appeals spent.

Imagine for a minute, if you will, that according to all statistics, a "typical" criminal encounters the power of the law when initially faced by a police officer and is taken into the criminal justice system. From that first confrontation he is afforded all the protections extended by the Constitution. That should not be too hard to imagine because that is the intention of the system. Does it always work as intended? No. Why? Very simple: Decisions, decisions, decisions.

Decisions are matters connected to ethics. Everyone has some system of ethics (morality) or code they live by. Looking at accepted ethics and codes of conduct, we see that legislative law often reflects personal morality prescribing how the system ought to work. When placed in the light of actual events, we find that what ought to be is not what is. This is because of the human factor that plays into the formula.

Now imagine you are a special consultant whose job is to examine the American criminal justice system and provide a lesson plan that could result in a more fair system that must be ethics based. You recognize as a given that police officers potentially face a life-threatening crisis with every contact they make. What rules should they follow: their unwritten personal values, their professional conduct rules (not written but heavily enforced by a "wall of silence," peer influence) or The Law Enforcement Code of Ethics? Also, never discount the influence of prejudice, bias, personal goals, consequences, and conscience. When evaluating the system, examine the criminal justice transit analogy and focus your attention on the question of personal and professional ethics, and to whom do they apply and how they are important in a democratic society. There is a hidden trap in this lesson because it is also controlled, influenced, and conflicted by your own ethical beliefs of morality and what is right.

It is obvious, even to the disinterested casual observer, that there is a serious flaw in the American educational system—a lack of ethics training. This defect appears and is multiplied in the criminal justice system. We are talking about the dearth of a common-sense approach and applicable material in ethics, and how they are applied by officers of law enforcement, the courts, and corrections. Police have a very wide range of discretionary power, from a simple traffic stop to taking of a life. When influenced by prejudice, bias, personal goals, consequences, conscience, and personal ethics, decision making may be flawed, especially if the decision involves a dilemma between two conflicting potential outcomes. The correct approach is to decide what gives the greater good and less harm. In other words, ethics is about doing the right thing. Every walk of life has some form of code of behavior or what can be considered a code of ethics for that particular endeavor. Nearly every culture and religion has a code that is similar in meaning and direction: "Treat everyone as you would want to be treated," as an example of the universal Golden Rule.

Codes of Ethics

Every profession, business, and person should have some form of a code of ethics. Simply put, a code of ethics means "a standard to live by." For example, an ancient code written in antiquity for physicians and one of the oldest binding documents in history is the Hippocratic Oath, written by Hippocrates in 400 B.C.E.

The Oath

I SWEAR by Apollo the physician, and Aesculapius, and Health, and All-heal, and all the gods and goddesses, that, according to my ability and judgment, I will keep this Oath and this stipulation—to reckon him who taught me this Art equally dear to me as my parents, to share my substance with him, and relieve his necessities if required; to look upon his offspring in the same footing as my own brothers, and to teach them this art, if they shall wish to learn it, without fee or stipulation; and that by precept, lecture, and every other mode of instruction, I will impart a knowledge of the Art to my own sons, and those of my teachers, and to disciples bound by a stipulation and oath according to the law of medicine, but to none others. I will follow that system of regimen, which, according to my ability and judgment, I consider for the benefit of my patients, and abstain from whatever is deleterious and mischievous. I will give no deadly medicine to any one if asked, nor suggest any such counsel; and in like manner I will not give to a woman a pessary to produce abortion. With purity and with holiness I will pass my life and practice my Art. I will not cut persons laboring under the stone, but will leave this to be done by men who are practitioners of this work. Into whatever houses I enter, I will go into them for the benefit of the sick, and will abstain from every voluntary act of mischief and corruption; and, further from the seduction of females or males, of freemen and slaves. Whatever, in connection with my professional practice or not, in connection with it, I see or hear, in the life of men, which ought not to be spoken of abroad, I will not divulge, as reckoning that all such should be kept secret. While I continue to keep this Oath unviolated, may it be granted to me to enjoy life and the practice of the art, respected by all men, in all times! But should I trespass and violate this Oath, may the reverse be my lot!*

In modern times, developed and adopted by most police departments, is the Law Enforcement Code of Ethics. Second to the oath to "protect, defend, and preserve the Constitution of the United States" and to "protect and serve," a law enforcement officer must know and follow the tenets of the Law Enforcement Code of Ethics, written, endorsed, and adopted by the International Association of Chiefs of Police.

The Law Enforcement Code of Ethics

As a Law Enforcement Officer, my fundamental duty is to serve mankind; to safeguard lives and property; to protect the innocent against deception, the weak against oppression or intimidation, and the peaceful against violence or disorder; and to respect the Constitutional rights of all men to liberty, equality and justice.

I will keep my private life unsullied as an example to all; maintain courageous calm in the face of danger, scorn, or ridicule; develop self-restraint; and be constantly mindful of the welfare of others. Honest in thought and deed in both my personal and official life, I will be exemplary in obeying the laws of the land and the regulations of my department. Whatever I see or hear of a confidential nature or that is confided in me in my official capacity will be kept ever secret unless revelation is necessary in the performance of my duty.

I will never act officiously or permit personal feelings, prejudices, animosities or friendships to influence my decisions. With no compromise for crime

---

* This version was translated by Francis Adams in 1849. http://classics.mit.edu/Hippocrates/hippooath.html, retrieved September 1, 2012.

and the relentless prosecution of criminals, I will enforce the law courteously and appropriately without fear of favor, malice or ill will, never employing unnecessary force or violence and never accepting gratuities.

I recognize the badge of my office as a symbol of public faith, and I accept it as a public trust to be held so long as I am true to the ethics of the police service. I will constantly strive to achieve these objectives and ideals, dedicating myself before God to my chosen profession … law enforcement."

One of the oldest codes of conduct is the Bushido* (The Way of the Warrior) code of the Samurai established between the ninth and twelfth centuries. The samurai were medieval warriors or soldiers of fortune who swore allegiance to a Shogun (Daimyo, feudal lord, or high-ranking nobleman). A Samurai's duties were *to protect* his lord, the shogun, from any and all enemies *and serve* in any way the shogun dictated. He would sacrifice his life for the shogun, even committing suicide if he in some way brought dishonor to himself or the shogun. The Way of the Warrior is a universal code of personal conduct as relevant for today's living as it was when Samurai were the elite class of warriors (or protectors and servers) for Japanese shoguns and royalty.

The code is resplendent with principles of ethical, moral, and character instruction. A modern criminal justice practitioner should learn and embrace these concepts and make them a way of life. In the Code of the Samurai, the word "samurai" could very easily be substituted with the words "modern

* The term *Bushido* was not used until the seventeenth century and was codified under the Tokugawa Shogunate. Prior to that there was a much looser concept of what honor was but it didn't become Bushido until the seventeenth century and even then the term was rarely used. It, like so many of the things we think of as ancient Japanese history, was a relatively modern concept codified in the peaceful (relatively) Edo period. Things were much less chivalrous during the Sengokku Jidai (Warring States period). Most of the West understands that Samurai culture comes from writings done during the peaceful period beginning in the early seventeenth century and ending with the Meiji Restoration. In other words, a lot of chivalrous concepts were retroactively applied to Japanese history. Even books like the *Hagakure* (*Hidden in Leaves*), which was sort of a collection of concepts about what it meant to be a Samurai, often contradicts itself.

The beginning of what would become what we understand as Bushido is most often attributed to the daimyo Kato Kiyomasa, who basically had a book of guidelines as to what he expected as far as his soldiers' behavior, "The Precepts of Kato Kiyomasa." He was very much a death before dishonor sort and drilled this into his vassals. Several other house codes and writings preceded and followed but a written version didn't happen until 1965 when it was put to ink by Yanaga Soko. Up until this time, Bushido was more of a loose code established and interpreted as house rules by various lords with a strong focus on Confucian ideals and the emperor being the focus of the loyalty. Historically, interpretations that focused on loyalty to the emperor caused conflict with the de facto rulers, the Tokugawa Shogunate, which came very much into play during the closing days of feudal Japan when Shogunate forces and Imperial forces battled for the future of Japan. The Shogunate forces believed that Bushido was about what was best for Japan and its class system, while the imperial forces believed loyalty to the emperor was their duty. Don Gaffney, Japanese historian, private conversation January 21, 2013.

criminal justice practitioner (police officer, prosecutor, judge, parole or probation officer, and corrections officer)." These codes are the ideal that should be sought and pursued by all who participate in a democratic criminal justice system. The key words bear repeating: honesty and justice; politeness and courtesy; courage in the face of danger; honor; compassion; sincerity; and loyalty.

Principles

Take a sad song and make it better.

—The Beatles, "Hey Jude"

Character

What is character, and how does one develop "good character"? Good character means doing the right thing for the right reasons. It means being true and honest, coming through when the road is rocky, hard, and tough. In other words, it means principled and ethical behavior. The words *principled*, *ethical*, and *moral* are often used interchangeably. When there are choices, we decide the best course based on what does the most good, and the least harm. In that pathway we establish personal and professional values.

Principles are man's beliefs, values, and character shaped by inheritance (family values passed from one generation to the next), environmental factors, and psychological makeup. Call it by any name you wish—virtue, morality, ideology, philosophy, or ethics—but the doctrines of character and principles are powerful forces in the universe. Some people are said to have "saintly virtues," meaning they feel their mission in life, their reason for being, is to make the world a better place for everyone to live. They believe in "taking a sad life and making it better." They do this by self-sacrifice, helping those who can't help themselves, and literally doing good for the mere sake of the goodness they bring, asking for nothing in return for themselves. This can be dubbed the "Mother Teresa syndrome,"—tending the poor, sick, and hopeless at the expense of self.

At the opposite end of the Mother Teresa spectrum are people who are said to be morally bankrupt. This has been called the "Hitler syndrome." They are void of any emotion except personal goals of power, influence, and wealth. Everything they do begins with I, me, and mine. Their only care for the rest of humankind is "What can you do for me?" The web of the unprincipled, the uncaring, and the emotionless includes the antisocial personality, the sadistic rapist-murderer, serial killers, stalkers, and a large body of others who may not reach the level of the evil types just mentioned but who could be considered because of their lust for power, influence, and wealth. A petty thief and a morally corrupt officer of the court have many things in common, primary of which is a desire of personal gain without consideration of those who may be hurt in the process.

Values

Family life, values, and biology of gene inheritance are often wellsprings of principled or unprincipled conduct. A study of sociology renders us the conclusion that many familial traits are passed from one generation to the next. This includes norms, values, socialization, and formation of character. A family that provides care and loving relationships with appropriate guidance and discipline forms a security ring around a child that will shape his personal values and beliefs of morality. It is not to say that a "bible thumping, preachy, highly disciplining, unloving parenting style" will create ethical principles in the child so he will grow to be an "ideal" and contributing citizen. Nor will a laid-back, undisciplined, uncaring, perhaps even overloving parental relationship create ethical-driven children. The ideal of family life is one in which a middle ground of compassion, understanding, and love are on equal terms, tempered with a belief in good role modeling of helping others, a strong knowledge of the difference between right and wrong, and a conviction of the goodness of doing good.

The environmental factors in a person's life help shape his principles, values, and morals. All across the land, from the largest city to the smallest rural town in farm country, ethics and principles of fair play are being learned on the baseball and soccer fields. The "code of the playground" is perhaps one of the first elements taught, often learned the hard way by peer pressure and influence. There is no room in a game, either a sanctioned league or a pick-up sandlot game, for cheaters. It is in this crucible of youthful justice that the first inklings of a career in criminal justice may be born with a sense of justice and equal treatment for all.

The playground is fertile field for bullies and cheaters. The bully is usually the one demanding his own way, calling "balls and strikes"; when he is batting, every call is a ball unless he happens to hit it, and when pitching (which he insists on doing), every call is a strike; or crying foul and attempts to get away with roughshod play in a soccer or basketball game. Members of the team will simply tolerate his activities because he is a bully, but there is usually one player, believing in fairness, who will step forward as an individual and take on the bully.

In an entirely different type of environment, a neighborhood infested with gang members and drugs, and where misery is compounded by violence, poverty, and unemployment, a young person quickly learns the "code of the street": don't be a snitch, the hood belongs to the strongest, and look out for number one and your homies." It's a code enforced by street justice, usually a beating or revenge executed by a drive-by shooting. Live by the code or suffer the consequences and die by the code.

Through all this muck and mire, one individual is usually respected for his stance against these social conditions. This person has an innate sense of justice and will often place himself between danger and a potential victim of violence. His native feel for right and wrong often places him at odds with his friends and peers, but the strength of his convictions earns respect for his belief in justice and helping those who can't help themselves. He is truthful, honest, and trustworthy, contrary to his living environment. He may come from a broken family or have alcoholic parents who also are drug abusers. He may have a violent and abusive parent; possibly both parents are uncaring and unloving. Yet his principles and feeling for justice and doing good for no other purpose than to help others overcome all other obstacles.

Family and environment are two factors incubating a person's character. The third is his psychological makeup or inner strength. Character results from integrity, moral fiber, individual spirit, personality, and attitude. A person born into a family with a tradition of good family values and having access to all the advantages of wealth, education, and employment may not possess strength of character or a good reputation for treatment of others. He may lack genes for fair play and see no reason or advantage to place himself in the line of danger for somebody else, especially a stranger. He may lack compassion, possibly a conscience, and willingly seeks to take advantage of others for his own benefit. These are not characteristics that would lead him into a life where he would be expected to want to look out for the protection of others and to make sure all their Constitutional guarantees are honored. Surely this type of person, in spite of his advantageous environment and biological background, is psychologically weak of character and unfit for a career in criminal justice, which, by definition, requires integrity, honesty, moral strength of character, compassion for fellow man, and high ethical standards.

"Even in a permissive business environment, it is possible to be honest. You need to have strong moral values ... An honest person has a clear conscience, an inner calmness, and self respect. He can be a positive influence on those around him."*

Attitude

Much of our time is accounted for by the demands and wishes of others, often requiring us to tolerate their manner and philosophy, which can be polar to ours. We acknowledge that and move forward with a personal attitude of "I'm

---

* "Is it possible to be honest in a corrupt world?" *The Watchtower*, October 1, 2012.

not going to permit your dogmatic negativism ruin my day." We shouldn't allow the down or negative attitude and dictates of others dampen our enthusiasm for living and looking forward to the day and the endeavors ahead. An optimist has no room or time in his life for doomsayers, because he is too busy giving of his time for spreading smiles, good wishes, and lending a hand to those who cannot help themselves. Spending time doing good for the sake of doing good is a healthy application of positivism.

An old anecdote tells the story of a person's attitude early in the day. A person should wake up in the morning, throw open the windows and shout, "Good morning, Lord. Most people wake up, hit the snooze button, and mutter, 'Good Lord! It's morning.'"

Idealism

Do one spontaneous good thing every day for someone and expect nothing in return, and you will come to know the true joy of happiness, giving, and sharing. This is a very explicit example of ethical beliefs of an idealistic person with an attitude directed toward concern for fellow man. Is that not one of the primary reasons an individual seeks to become a police officer? He has a strong concern for his fellow man. He is idealistic, believing the role of a police officer is to help those who are in need and who cannot help or defend themselves.

Idealism—A strong belief in the way things should or ought to be.
Realism—The way things are, never reaching the point of the ideal.

Making Choices

Every day from the time we wake up until we go to sleep at night, our world is made of decisions, from the very simplest of what to have for breakfast to life-changing choices. This section provides information relative to how to make the right choice, especially in times of conflicting choices.

The world as we know it is made as a result of choices of humankind. There are many simple examples of wrong choices, such as wearing stripes with plaid; most choices are of free will (free will meaning choices made without influence either from within or without). Some choices are choices of no choice at all, for instance, a "Hobson's choice."

Hobson's Choice

Hobson maintained a large stable of rental horses. Anyone wanting to rent a horse could choose any horse in the stable as long as it was the one closest to the door. As horses were rented and returned, Hobson placed the return horse in a stall farthest from the door and moved all the other horses up one stall. In this way, no one horse became overused. Thus "a choice but no choice."

One accepted definition of ethics is "the choices people make between right and wrong." For most people, choosing between right and wrong is a Hobson's choice. There are many sociological and psychological factors involved in making free will choices, but to be ethically, morally, and legally correct, there should be but one choice: the difference between right and wrong. When dealing with people, sometimes it's not a bad idea to spend a minute in the other guy's shoes to visualize how a choice will affect others.

One good way to decide a choice is to ask, "What gives the most good and the least harm?" When there are two equally poor choices, the question becomes one of deciding which of the two brings the least harm to the least number of people. This is a true dilemma because both choices offer a harmful consequence. This then becomes another example of Hobson's choice.

When a public servant, such as a law enforcement officer, makes a decision, he must use great discretion and choose carefully. One test is the "film at eleven" test. How will his decision and words be perceived when shown on the eleven o'clock news? In other words, decision making must be accomplished through sound and ethical means. Will his decision stand up to investigation and evaluation by others? Often an officer must make a life-threatening decision in hundredths of a second that will take attorneys, juries, and judges years to decide if it was the right decision.

Ethics of Silence (Police Culture)

"If you are not one of us, you are one of them, and in this world it's us against them." Unfortunately, that has become an unwritten rule along with the "blue code of silence" in many or most law enforcement agencies. Law enforcement is a closed brotherhood with its own standards of conduct and beliefs. These paragraphs address many of the factors and stresses facing an idealistic officer or agent attempting to maintain his own values, principles, and idealism as they conflict with professional unwritten codes.

"The blue wall of silence" and the code of "Omertà" are similar though from opposite poles. Omertà is the code of silence of the Mafia and the blue wall of silence (not officially sanctioned but enforced by peer pressure and influence) is a standard that one police officer doesn't rat out his fellow officers. "No one likes a squealer" is first learned as kids on the playgrounds and neighborhoods. The standard is set as the tattletale is sanctioned by being shunned or cast out from the group. In the real world of cops and robbers, a whistleblower who informs on fellow officers may not receive backup when required, or he may even be set up by fellow officers. It is in this type of culture (or subculture) that corruption festers and grows. An idealistic officer, holding to his personal and professional principles of honesty and integrity, may find he is alone in upholding such standards. He is then faced with a dilemma of compromising his values and morality, or breaking the blue code of silence.

An outstanding example of holding to one's moral beliefs and ideology of honesty in the face of opposition from fellow officers who were very corrupt is the story of Frank Serpico, an officer on the New York City Police Department in the 1960s, who broke the code of blue silence and testified against the corruption in the department. His testimony led to an investigation by the Knapp Commission, but also led to his being shot in the face when his backup failed to assist him in making a drug arrest. (Serpico survived the shooting.)

Corruption

"There is no such thing as a free lunch." This is a cliché but the wisdom of it is undeniable. Many restaurants offer and provide officers with free or discounted half-priced meals as a thank-you for their presence. Even car dealerships and home sellers often discount prices to police. This may sound innocent enough, and the intentions are good. But there may also be a hidden agenda. The question a professional officer must ask himself: "At what price would you sell your integrity?" Would it be for the price of a meal or a monetary bribe? It's not the amount offered, but the price to be paid later. Corruption begins with free lunches or half-priced meals to stealing drugs from the evidence room and dealing it. Accepting favors or special treatment is easily justified and rationalized until the conscience is no longer a factor, and corruption is well ingrained as an expected way of life in the form of "pay to play" by the corrupted officer.

How to corrupt personal values by professional conduct: accept gratuities (bribes), show disrespect, manipulation of others, us versus them, trust only the "us" attitude, accept or demand discounts, learned behavior institutionalized from veterans, intoxicated with police power (power corrupts), occupational deviance (criminal and noncriminal behavior) including improper behavior that is not illegal, and abuse of authority.

Honesty and Integrity

Principles, ideals, values, and morality are guidelines for living your life. What do you stand for? This section explores some basic principles and provides students with sociological and psychological explanations of how values and principles are formed and maintained. Should professional values corrupt personal values? Personal values equal honesty, truthful, loyalty, thoughtful of others, selfless, respectful, self-disciplined, of good character, integrity, noble, and fairness.

The number-one idealistic reason a person chooses to become an officer of the law is "to serve and protect ... to help those who can't help themselves" with the key words being "to help." As a career progresses, a criminal justice practitioner will find that a successful career and personal satisfaction will come their way if their idealism and the principles of honesty and integrity are not compromised. Maintaining institutional high-performance principles while remaining grounded in acting ethically is crucial.

It has been said that honesty and integrity are like pregnancy. You cannot be "half pregnant." You either are or you aren't. Very simply stated, the same may be said for honesty; you either have it or you don't. You cannot be honest only some of the time. A lie or dishonest act must not compromise honesty and integrity. In a few words, honesty and integrity mean being ethical or simply "doing the right thing."

The following essay, written by E. Alan Normandy, a lieutenant in the South San Francisco Police Department, and at the time a student at Henley-Putnam University, appears in the book *Introduction to Executive Protection*, 2nd edition, by Dale L. June (Boca Raton, FL: CRC Press, 2008). It is included in the book (and this essay) with the permission of Normandy, and is a very excellent example of the meanings of honesty and integrity in criminal justice.

Honesty and Integrity: A Values Conversation

It is impossible to spend any time in law enforcement, the military, or personal protection without hearing about at least two values: honesty and integrity. We hear about these values early in our careers. Virtually every presenter at an academy graduation will incorporate those words into his or her speech. Honesty and integrity are powerful, and they mean more to us than mere words. Still, do we really understand what honesty and integrity mean? More importantly, how do we live our lives with both of these values in them?

In my opinion, dictionary definitions mean very little. In this industry, we use these terms so often they sound clichéd. As such, they have lost their meaning. Worse yet, I imagine that most of us explore these concepts only superficially. Perhaps we only scratch the surface, because we don't understand the material. It is likely we're just too embarrassed to admit it.

So, how are we to lead our lives with honesty and integrity when we aren't really sure what these qualities are? Personally and professionally, I have noted that most people cannot tell the difference between honesty and integrity. We use the terms synonymously. Although inevitably intertwined, honesty and integrity are demonstrably different.

One cannot have integrity without honesty; yet, one can be honest and have no integrity. Personal intentions apply, but integrity matters only when we share it with others. Honesty may be individual, but integrity is applied to our relationships.

Honesty and truth are elements of integrity. Integrity, however, is often not as sound, solid, or steadfast as we wish it were. One merely needs to ask others for the definitions of these words, and one will find this conversation is as clear as mud. In the end, both values are only as important as they relate to trust. Trust must be shared. As I mention often, whether the trust be public or personal, life is about relationships. Without trust, real relationships do not exist.

Definitions

To illustrate my point, we'll start with *Merriam-Webster's* definitions:

Honesty—1. *obsolete*: Chastity; 2. a: fairness and straightforwardness of conduct; b. adherence to the facts: Sincerity. Synonyms: Honesty, honor, integrity, probity mean uprightness of character or actions. Honesty implies a refusal to lie, steal, or deceive in any way. Honor suggests an active or anxious regard for the standards of one's profession, calling, or position. Integrity implies trustworthiness and incorruptibility to a degree that one is incapable of being false to a trust, responsibility, or pledge. Probity implies tried and proven honesty or integrity.

Integrity—1. firm adherence to a code of especially moral or artistic values; Incorruptibility; 2. an unimpaired condition; Soundness; 3. the quality or state of being complete or undivided; Completeness. Synonym: see honesty.

If honesty and integrity are synonymous, how are they different?

Connotations

At the Sherman Block Supervisory Leadership Institute (SB-SLI), where I serve as an auditor, we discuss honesty and integrity ad nauseam. To attend SB-SLI, one must be a sergeant for at least two years. Just to attend SB-SLI, the selection process is very competitive. Selection and graduation are considered quite prestigious. Students must volunteer to be selected, and not everyone is chosen.

Yet consistently, in my own class and those I have audited, I watch in awe and dismay as SB-SLI students struggle with these two terms. Dismally, we demonstrate a distinct and disappointing lack of compassion for them. For me, at least, it is hardly encouraging, watching sergeants struggle in this way. I fear we cannot teach what we do not understand. More important, I feel we cannot live in a manner which we cannot explain.

In my humble opinion, honesty means commitment to the truth, particularly at personal cost. True honesty is measured by difficulty factor. The harder it is for one to tell the truth, the more trustworthy one becomes by the telling of it.

The truth is invaluable, when measured by selflessness. We can be trusted, but only by admitting our mistakes. When we do this, we sacrifice our safety. We must never forget that all of us make mistakes. We are human. Yet, when it comes to mistakes, we are deplorably ruthless when it comes to confessing the sins of others. At times, we even seem to enjoy holding others accountable. Nothing is easier than pointing the finger at someone else. So how many of us will "cowboy up" when that finger is pointed in our direction, especially when life, finances, and reputations hang in the balance? Why is it so easy for us to be such hypocrites?

Walking the Talk

Without personal cost, honesty is easy. We can tell the truth if we don't have to sacrifice. So, what if the truth can harm us? What if the truth endangers our position? What if the truth includes revealing facts that are less than flattering? Will we tell the truth then? Aren't these the specific scenarios when telling the truth is most important?

The selfish part of our human nature motivates us to lie, to escape negative consequences. The more negative we perceive the consequence to be, the more likely we will lie. We believe we are protecting ourselves. Self-preservation is the very foundation of selfishness.

As selfish youngsters, we all considered lying. In truth, we did it. If we met success the first time we lied, we were encouraged to do it again. That's why lying is so dangerous. Lying is based in fear. We are afraid we will be rejected or punished if we tell the truth.

When we tell the truth fearlessly, even at personal cost, we can be trusted. For goodness' sake, we are human! We're never perfect. Still, trust is necessary in good relationships, and trust is critical to this industry. If we cannot be placed in faith and confidence, we are useless. Everything unravels and comes apart. That's how honesty relates to integrity. Honesty breeds trust. Together, both give birth to integrity. Trust completes our relationships.

More Than the Sum of Our Parts

Integrity is about completeness. If honesty is keeping the truth, then integrity is keeping our word. To whom do we give our word? Are we bound by our word, thus fulfilling the expectations of our relationships?

Integrity is a commitment to a comprehensive, all-encompassing value system, and ultimately how we measure our character. We either commit, or we don't. To measure integrity in others, we must begin with an honest self-evaluation. We ought not make promises we cannot keep. Promises are not meant to be broken. Oaths are not necessary for men of integrity.

In truth, self-evaluation is where we fail most often. Yet without it, there is no integrity. Unfortunately, our integrity is attacked constantly. Convenience, comfort, and complacency abet such attacks. If we are not careful, we don't even realize the attack is coming.

Entropy

Rarely is our integrity threatened in one fell swoop, as if it were a brand-new building suddenly demolished with a wrecking ball. Usually, human character is eroded by a series of seemingly insignificant acts or omissions that, together, combine to create a person who is unrecognizable in the mirror.

Our character edifice is whittled away, after being subjected to worldly threats, both real and imagined, as we weather the elements. Ultimately, situational ethics cause us to rationalize away this behavior. Moral relativism does not help us relate to each other. If we are fortunate, life will humble us. With humility, we may come to understand that whatever we try to protect by compromising our integrity is hardly worth saving.

Most dangerously, when we get away with such behavior, the more frequent it becomes. We must be vigilant to avoid it. Vigilance demands we admit our own flaws first. By admitting our humanity, we can earn the trust of other humans.

Personal Values and Personal Ideals of Protection and Service

We cannot protect and serve if we cannot be trusted. Trust is born by our telling the truth unabashedly, humbly, and fearlessly. I would never consider having someone protect me if he or she could not be trusted.

Ironically, I have found that others are able to forgive us, provided we admit our mistakes in the first place. When we lie, we fatally assume others will not forgive us, or that somehow they are incapable of forgiving.

I wouldn't want to work under those conditions. Good relationships preclude negative fantasies. Integrity is only significant as it relates to other people. People are important and life is about relationships. Without people with whom to share it, integrity *is* just a word.

Idealism, Cynicism, Absolutism, and Relativism

Idealism means the way things should or ought to be. However, reality intervenes and what should be falls short of what is. Cynicism is pessimistic, looking at the dark or down side of things and being critical. Absolutism means there are no other options or mitigating circumstances. It is the final stamp with no alternatives; whereas relativism is a nonjudgmental, hands-off approach.

In this chapter we have discussed idealistic principles and stated they should be followed in the professional world as well as in personal life. At this point we will address characteristics that offer freewill choices and compare them for an ethical life.

Idealism—Positivism (bright and positive attitude)
- Shoulds and oughts (the way things should or ought to be; an ideal)
- Doing good for goodness sake and expecting nothing in return
- Role model
- Moral values
- Ideals
- Honesty and integrity
- Obligations

Cynicism—Negativism (dark and negative attitude)
- Burnout
- Skepticism
- Scorn

- Distrust
- Sarcasm
- Egoism

Absolutism

- No exceptions
- Zero tolerance (no mitigating circumstances)
- Strictly by the book
- Extremely conservative
- Enforce the law as written
- Judgmental
- Leads to cynicism and negativism

Relativism

- Exceptions are made (discretionary allowances)
- No zero tolerance (room for mitigating circumstances)
- Liberal
- Nonjudgmental
- Enforce spirit of the law
- Leads to idealism and positivism

The concepts of idealism–cynicism and absolutism–relativism can easily be understood when placed in a diagram like the figure concluding Chapter 18. Similarly, the average person is in the middle of the axis and may fluctuate back and forth between the two poles.

Women Who Bully

23

VEDA HALL

Contents

This chapter defines women and bullies, as well as discusses the various types of bullies, including women who bully in the workplace, women who bully their spouses, moms who bully other moms, and women who bully their children. It will also explore how bullies select their targets, in addition to the long-term emotional damages caused by bullying.

Introduction

Historically, women had few or no rights, and were considered second-class citizens. In fact, they were looked upon as weak, having very little intellect, and were deemed inferior to men. They were actually forced into matrimony, and were prohibited from working, owning property, voting, and so much more.* That was then, and this is now; fast forward to the twenty-first century.

Details

A woman is the female of the human species. According to the *Merriam-Webster Dictionary*, a woman is defined as "a woman belonging to a particular category (as by birth, residence, membership, or occupation)—usually used in combination <councilwoman>."† But if we asked ten different people to define a woman, we would probably receive ten different answers. Some will define a woman as being complex, vulnerable, dependable, confident, strong,

---

* "Women's Rights Movement in the United States," Buzzle.com, 2010, http://www.buzzle.com, retrieved November 22, 2010.
† "woman," Merriam-Webster.com, 2010, http://www.merriam-webster.com/dictionary/woman, retrieved November 22, 2010.

determined, patient, empathetic, compassionate, kind, generous, funny, hardworking, loving, and so forth. Others might define women by gender (mother, daughter, sister, wife), or by occupation (female lawyer, female doctor, female teacher, female police officer, female office holder), and the like. And yet, despite all the progress made by women, the Women's Rights Movement, for example, it is surprising to know that women are also on the other end of the spectrum. Whereas men were known for bullying women, likewise, women are now bullying others. In fact, women are not only bullying in the workplace, but they are bullying their spouses, their children, and other moms as well.

What is a bully? As defined by Dr. Kenneth Rigby (adjunct research professor, University of South Australia), "Bullying involves a desire to hurt + hurtful action + a power imbalance + (typically) repetition + an unjust use of power + evident enjoyment by the aggressor and a sense of being oppressed on the part of the victim."[*]

Research shows that bullies are extremely calculating. For some bullies, once their target has been selected, like a lion stalking its prey, they carefully watch every move the victim makes. They observe when he comes and goes, whom he associates with, and times when he is alone. For most bullies, there is no rhyme or reason for why they attack. The victim may not even be aware he is being targeted or for what reason. Simply put, the target could just be at the wrong place, at the wrong time. The type of bully encountered determines how the victim will most likely be treated.

Interestingly enough, there are more than ten types of bullying. Some of the more familiar types of bullying are corporate (or workplace) bullying, cyber bullying, organizational bullying, gang bullying, client bullying, serial bullying, and institutional bullying. Types of bullying that may not be so familiar are "pressure bullying or unwitting bullying, where the stress of the moment causes behavior to deteriorate; the person becomes short-tempered, irritable and may shout or swear at others."[†] When the pressure stops, the bully retreats from his behavior and may even show remorse. Pair bullying is another form of bullying in which a serial bully works with a partner. Usually, the serial bully intimidates the person, while the partner takes notes. There is also vicarious bullying. "An example of vicarious bullying is where the serial bully creates conflict between employer and employee, participating occasionally to stoke the conflict, but rarely taking an active part in the conflict themselves."[‡]

---

[*] "What is bullying?" Kenrigby.net, from http://www.kenrigby.net/define.html, retrieved November 22, 2010.

[†] "Bullying: what is it?" Bully Online, April 2003, http://www.bullyonline.org/workbully/bully.htm, retrieved November 22, 2010.

[‡] Ibid.

Now that we've discussed bully types in general (mostly referring to men who bully), women are also bullies. As previously mentioned, women do some of their bullying at work.

"While men tend to target male and female employees equally, women bosses are likely to aim their hostility toward other women more than 70 percent of the time, according to a survey by the Workplace Bullying Institute."* And the reasons women bully vary. Some women bully for competitive reasons. If the bully is a manager who is up for promotion and she finds out that another female manager is being considered for the same position (and there is only room for one promotion), the bully will do or say anything to prevent her competition from being considered. Women bullies in upper-level management may ask a subordinate to work on a project, and once the project is complete, the bully accepts praise for completing the project as if she did the work herself. In addition, a female administrator may decide to sabotage the reputation of one of her female employees by telling others that she is too difficult to work with, is uncooperative, her work is unproductive, and so on.

There are also moms who bully other moms. Because of the Internet, moms who bully can hide behind their computers and tell other moms (in not so kind words) where to go and how to get there. As stated by Catherine Connors, a Toronto blogger and writer, "Moms—and parents in general—feel more free to express their opinions aggressively when they don't have a face-to-face relationship with those on the opposite side of the debate."† Therefore, if the bully mom did not agree with another mom's opinion, the judgmental bully mom would hurl venomous insults. The subject matter could be on just about anything, for example, parenting.

There are numerous debates online, including how to raise children, whether breastfeeding should be done in public, co-breastfeeding someone else's baby, the negative aspects of micromanaging your children, nursing and the appropriate time to start or stop nursing, and so on. Chances are that if a mom has an opinion and posts it online, women who bully will be waiting to strike. But that is not all that women are waiting on. Women bullies also enjoy striking their husbands.

Historically, men have mentally and physically abused women. However, there are reports (though this type of abuse usually goes unreported) indicating that, in some households, the roles have reversed. Men

---

* Anna Wild and Jonann Brady, "Women bullies often target other women," ABC News, February 24, 2009, http://abcnews.go.com/GMA/story?id=6943347&page=1, retrieved November 22, 2010.
† Amy Hatch, "When moms bully moms, online and off," Parent Dish, February 4, 2010, http://www.parentdish.com/2010/02/04/when-moms-bully-moms-online-and-off/, retrieved November 23, 2010.

are now walking on eggshells for fear of their bullying wives. Some wives will not hesitate to bully their men in public. For example, the wife will yell and scream at her husband in front of his friends. Then there is the bullying wife who enjoys the blame game. For instance, if the wife forgot to pick up their son, she would find a way to blame the husband by saying, for example, "If you weren't so stupid, you would have reminded me to pick up our son." Another bullying wife may abuse her husband through physical violence and intimidation. While enraged, the wife will either throw things at her husband, such as knives and sticks, or she will punch, kick, or slap her husband.

Some women bully their children. "When you think of bullies, you probably think of kids teasing other kids at school, at the playground or even on the Internet. But what happens when children are terrorized in their home by the one person who is supposed to nurture and protect them the most: their mother?"[*] For example, Nikkie (mother of a five-year-old), admitted on the *Dr. Phil Show* to abusing her daughter by saying, "If you don't eat that, I swear to God, I will kill you," "Eat your lunch or I am going to shove it down your freaking throat," and so on. In addition, when describing her five-year-old, she stated that her child is "out of control," "a brat," and "maybe she'll run into a wall and kill herself."

As disturbing as all this is, what are the reasons women bully? Yes, women may bully for slightly different reasons than men, but what is interesting are the commonalities that bullies share. "Bullies usually have a sense of entitlement and superiority over others, and lack compassion, impulse control and social skills. They enjoy being cruel to others and sometimes use bullying as an anger management tool; the way a normally angry person would punch a pillow."[†] Bullies are controlling, manipulative, unwilling to accept responsibility for their actions, and are focused on taking as much as they can get. They also lack understanding, are selfish, and needy. Bullying is a learned behavior influenced by different home environments and neighborhoods. In addition, those who bully have typically been (during childhood) on the opposite end of the spectrum, and have either been bullied by other children or abused by their parents.

As a result, what are the long-term effects of bullying? As stated by Mark Dombeck, Ph.D., "Bullying causes long-term emotional damage."[‡] Lasting harm does not have to be physical; the words used by bullies are enough. What is most debilitating to victims is the damage to their self-concept; they lose

---

[*] Dr. Phil Show, "Mom's who bully," *Dr. Phil Show*, May 4, 2010, http://drphil.burrelles-luce.com, retrieved November 23, 2010.

[†] Jane St. Clair, "What causes bullies?" By Parents for Parents, http://www.byparents-forparents.com/causesbullies.html, retrieved November 23, 2010.

[‡] Mark Dombeck, "The long term effects of bullying," July 24, 2007, http://www.mental-help.net, retrieved November 23, 2010.

their uniqueness and individuality. And the cost of being repeatedly targeted by bullies is high. There are two undesirable outcomes that negatively affect your view of self. The first is depression, angriness, and bitterness. Bullying teaches the victim that he is unwanted and unattractive, and he has no control against bullying. Also, by constantly questioning motives for not fighting back, the victim starts to believe there is no hope, and thus becomes discouraged and dejected. He may also start to believe that everyone, including the bullies, have him pegged as fragile, useless, and a loser. What is more damaging is actually starting to believe that the bully is justified in his or her negative treatment of the victim. The second undesirable outcome is that because self-concept is damaged, the target begins to give up more easily during difficult situations.

Following is a list of the short-term emotional damage the victim may feel:

- Anger
- Depression
- Anxiousness about certain areas where bullying occurred
- Frequent illness
- Poor grades
- Suicidal ideations

Over the long term:

- Less opportunities for employment
- Persistent feelings of rage and resentment
- Thoughts of revenge
- Difficulty trusting people
- Inner conflict, isolation, low self-esteem, and other negative emotions

Summary

With the amount of bullying that is being perpetrated by women, where did they lose their natural instincts to nurture? What are the reasons behind women bullies? Are they aware of the pain and confusion they are inflicting on their co-workers, spouses, children, and other moms? When people are bullied, they are shaken so much at their core, they begin to lose their self-concept, and they lose confidence in their abilities, and are forever changed by the experience. Yes, women's roles have changed and they have taken on family and career, but does it mean that they have become so busy, tired, frustrated, and overwhelmed that they resort to bullying others?

Conclusions

Women bully for all kinds of reasons, but ultimately it is because there is a need that has not or is not being met. Perhaps the bully does not feel validated at home or does not feel accepted at work. The bully could be feeling power-less, hopeless, and actually be crying out for help. To illustrate, if a women is bullying her spouse, it may be because she feels overwhelmed that her husband is not helping with the chores, or the bills are not getting paid on time, and so on. With this type of lack of respect (in her mind), it makes her feel tired, confused, uncomfortable, and these unmet feelings cause her to start bullying her husband. In many instances of spousal abuse, it is the wife who commits the aggression against her husband, for no other reason than to express power over him, but men are often reluctant to mention or acknowl-edge it for various reasons, including misconceptions of his manhood.

However, although I understand what motivates bullies, I completely disagree with the behavior. It is never right to take advantage of others, under any circumstance. Bullying is actually a negative reflection on the person who is perpetrating the act.

Until bullies acknowledge they have a problem, their behavior will simply continue until someone gets hurt, someone goes to jail, or someone ends up dead. But for those who are willing to and do take a look at themselves, they should accept counseling, support groups, self-help groups, and the like. There are obviously inadequacies that need to be addressed. And gender is of no consequence—wrong is wrong.

Humorous
Lessons

The Fifty-Miles-an-Hour Parking Ticket

24

DALE L. JUNE

I had to pick up my daughter at the Buffalo, New York, airport. Her plane was a few hours delayed so she didn't arrive until after midnight. It was approximately ninety miles to my home where we were staying. Once you leave the immediate airport area of Buffalo, in just a few miles you are in a more rural area. One small town I had to pass through was the village of Arcade, New York.

Arcade is a picturesque 1880s-type country community. The buildings have false fronts and trees planted along the main street running through the center of town. The town could be an ideal setting for a Mark Twain *Tom Sawyer* adventure, right down to the whitewashed picket fences in front of the old Victorian houses lining the streets. The feeling one gets is that this place could be straight from *Mayberry, RFD.*

The New York State speed limit in that area is a posted fifty miles per hour. Just a few feet from the village line I saw the fifty mile per hour speed limit sign posted very clear and easily visible. Approximately two car lengths beyond that sign was a sign saying, "Welcome to Arcade Speed Limit 25 miles per hour." At the same time as I saw that sign, I happened to see an Arcade police patrol car parked to the side in the parking lot of a hardware store. There were no other cars parked on the street or in sight. I let off my accelerator and touched the brake pedal to slow down to twenty-five from the fifty I was going. Within a block I saw the red lights of the police car pulling me over.

The officer approached my door and asked for my driver's license and registration. I was driving my car that was registered in New York, but I had a California driver's license. He said he had me speeding at 50 miles an hour as I entered the village and went past the posted 25 miles per hour sign. He also wanted to know why my car was registered in New York and I was holding a California driver's license.

I explained that my mother lived in a small town approximately sixty miles away and I would leave my car there when I was in California where I lived. He was very nice and understanding (country police officers are like that). He said, "Mr. June, I have to cite you for something because I stopped you, so what I'll do is issue an illegal parking ticket so you won't have a moving

* Mayberry is a fictitious town made famous by *The Andy Griffith Show* of the 1960s.

violation on your record because here in New York should you get a certain number of points, your driving privileges will be canceled in your home state and your insurance company will be notified of the moving violation." That sounded reasonable to me so I agreed that was a great option.

A little over an hour later I arrived home and after all the family greetings were finished and we were just catching up on all the local family news, I told the story of the officer citing me for a parking violation. Then I looked at the ticket and in the violation section he had written "Illegal Parking." My eyes were drawn to the section heading of "Approximate speed." Here I read 50 miles per hour.

The next day I called the magistrate/judge in that small town and told her I wanted to pay my parking ticket. She said, "Oh, yes, illegal parking. That will be one hundred dollars."

"What! For a parking ticket?"

"You were going fifty miles an hour. That will be one hundred dollars."

Lesson learned: If you are cited for illegal parking while driving fifty miles per hour and must pay a fine, the way things are, aren't always as they seem and country police officers get the last laugh.

Lessons in Life: The Mom Keaner Story

25

RICHARD REPASKY

The first time I ever talked with United States Secret Service Assistant Special Agent in Charge (ASAIC) Dale E. Keaner was early in 1971 when I heard my home telephone ring about 9 p.m., and I answered to hear the question, "Why did you lie about your arrest record?"

I had served three tours in Vietnam as a Navy diving officer, and when I returned to Columbus, Ohio, I bought a pizza shop and also applied for a teaching job as I was certified to teach math and science. I was hired to teach seventh and eighth grade at an inner city school, where I was one of four white teachers out of thirty. A few months of making pizzas at night and teaching during the day convinced me that I needed something more. So, I took the Treasury Law Enforcement Examination at the Federal Building in Columbus. Leaving the testing area, I picked up some brochures about the Drug Enforcement Agency (DEA), the Internal Revenue Service (IRS), U.S. Customs Service, and the United States Secret Service (USSS). In about a month, letters started coming to me, requesting that I complete a Standard Form 86 (SF86), a questionnaire for a background investigation to obtain a top-secret (TS) clearance. The form requested my history back to my sixteenth birthday, and required all residences, employments, and personal references I could come up with to complete the investigation. Luckily, having spent years in the government as a Navy officer, I was familiar with these kinds of forms and had assembled most of the information required. I had also learned long ago that the government tends to lose things, so I always kept several copies for myself.

After reading through the brochures that I had picked up, I decided to complete the SF86 for the United States Secret Service, as it sounded the most interesting and afforded me a chance to meet interesting people and go places that I had never been. Upon completing the SF86, fingerprint cards, and release forms, and sending them into Washington, D.C., I had no idea that the clock would start ticking on a one-year wait for a further response, which would see me change schools to the suburbs, expand my pizza store staff, and have a baby on the way. My mind had put the thought of this job out of sight, and I had focused on my other endeavors and written off ever becoming a U.S. Secret Service agent.

The ringing of the telephone after 9 p.m. usually meant that something was wrong at the pizza shop, so I picked it up, expecting to hear my store manager say they had run out of cheese or someone had cut themselves on the meat slicer. Instead, I heard the stern and official voice of ASAIC Dale E. Keaner asking me about my arrest record. Now it was not like I had never been arrested. Several times in Vietnam I had been taken into custody by the military police and thrown in what they called a jail, but which was really a metal conex (shipping) container. Once I was accused of speeding as I was driving my Chevy Bronco in the jungle, and one other time I was accused of stealing the idling Jeep belonging to a Special Forces sergeant, who was visiting his girlfriend in the local bar. Each time I was taken before the provost officer, an Army captain, who was the same rank as me since I was a Navy lieutenant. Each time, he ordered that I be picked up by someone in my command senior to me, but there was no one, so my chief had to come and get me released. But as far as I could recall, I had never been taken into custody by any civilian authority. So, when I was asked the question, I stammered, "What are you talking about? I did not put down any false answer that I can recall." It was then that Keaner stated, "We have checked the records of the Canton, Ohio, Police Department (my hometown), and you are of record there." I said, "I was never arrested by the Canton Police; that is a mistake." Keaner responded, "What happened on January 19, 1959?"

I was momentarily taken aback. January 19, why that was my birth date. And 1959? Wait a minute, that was my sixteenth birthday, and why should that be memorable? Well, let's see. I turned sixteen on that date and had my mother drive me to the Bureau of Motor Vehicles (BMV) where I picked up a temporary driver permit and a rules of the road booklet. We then practiced parallel parking for a few minutes and I read through the booklet, and we drove back to the BMV, and I took the written and road tests, and was issued my State of Ohio Driver's License. I was so excited because I had made arrangements to apply for a job as a bag boy at Fishers Market, which only hired those sixteen and older, and I had a meeting with Mr. Fisher, who interviewed all his staff personally at his law firm in downtown Canton.

My meeting was at 4 p.m., and at 3:30 p.m. I was driving down an alley behind the law offices, looking for parking. There were three high schools in downtown Canton at that time—McKinley, Timken, and Lincoln—and all three got out at 3:30 p.m., so the sidewalks and streets were filled with kids. As I tried to take the alley and cross a main street into the connecting alley, my mother's car was surrounded by high-school students banging on my fenders and distracting me. I stepped on the gas to get across, then bam; I hit a car coming down that street, a car that I never saw until I hit it.

Within seconds, a Canton police cruiser was on the scene. The officer came to my car and ordered me to get into the police cruiser and had the driver of the other vehicle also get into the police cruiser. I explained to the officer that I never saw the other car, as he wrote his report. The officer looked at the other driver and said, "How long have you been driving, sir?" The driver responded, "Twenty years, officer." The officer looked at me and said, "And how long have you been driving, son?" I looked at my watch, and stated, "About two hours, sir." I received a ticket to appear in juvenile court and went on to meet with attorney Fisher. Yes, I got the job and kept it throughout high school.

I related this tale to Agent Keaner, and he replied, "Okay, but don't let it happen again." I said, "What, the car accident?" And he replied, "No, the falsification." I got off the telephone thinking that I had screwed up this application, and the job was gone.

But in March 1972, I again received a call from Agent Keaner, who said that he wanted to personally interview me in the Federal Building, Columbus, Ohio. We arranged an appointment for late afternoon, since I was still teaching school. I walked into the Secret Service office and was introduced to Assistant Agent in Charge, Dale E. Keaner, later to be known as "Mom" Keaner. He was a big man, about 6'2", on the portly side, with orange-red thinning hair. I noticed that he spoke very clearly and was very affable. He explained that the agent in charge, Robert Foster, was not in and he was going to make the decision on hiring in Foster's absence (which would lead to further problems), and after the interview, ASAIC Keaner made me a job offer.

The offer was that I was to start in two weeks, but I explained that I had a teaching contract that went to the end of the school year in May and I did not want to screw the school district. Keaner said, "These offers do not come along often; start in two weeks or forget it." I pondered for a few minutes and then said, "I will take it." Of course, I now had to break my contract with the school system, which did not endear me to the administration.

Two weeks later, I happily entered the Secret Service offices in Columbus, eager to begin my new career. Upon entering the waiting room, I was greeted by the administrative assistant, Doris Lamp, who advised me that special agent in charge Robert Foster wanted to see me, and I was led into his office. Foster was a tall lean man with silver hair. He had served on the Kennedy detail and as bodyguard to the Kennedy kids, and he was very close to that family. He had also served under President Johnson, and I never heard him utter a kind word about that man.

I put out my hand to shake, but it was ignored. The first thing out of Foster's mouth was, "Keaner hired you when I was gone, and I never would have hired you because you're too short. You could only protect pigmies." Obviously, I was shocked by this statement and the obvious candor of the man. It told me a lot about Foster and also a lot about the relationship between those two men. One thing about SAIC Foster was that he was a man of his word. He sent a memo to headquarters stating that I was a former Navy diver and was too short for anything but pigmies, so I found myself in later years sent to protect any dignitary that wanted to go scuba diving and was also sent to protect President Bongo from Gabon, a pigmy.

I went home disappointed with this welcome from Foster but confident that at least Keaner liked me.

Time passed swiftly as I was sent to Washington, D.C., for basic training and then onto Beltsville, Maryland, for real Secret Service training in firearms, executive protection, detection of counterfeit currency, and arrest procedures. I returned to Columbus, Ohio, full of confidence. That Monday when I returned, I entered the office and bid hello to the staff. I received a grunt from Foster but a hearty handshake from Keener, who advised me that he was taking me under his wing for field training.

A few weeks passed and I got to shadow some of the senior agents on their assignments. I was kind of surprised when Agent Donald C. Burger took me to the Lazarus Department Store Men's Department and commenced to try on several three-piece suits. As Burger told me, "An agent must look good out there in the public eye," and so I too became a clotheshorse. I filled my closet with three-piece suits and ordered a special shoulder holster for my Smith & Wesson® .357 Magnum™.

Then came that fateful Friday morning. I went to work, and Keaner called me into his private office. "Sit down," he said. I took a seat. He related to me that he had been after a check thief for months and just found out that the man was going to be in Columbus that afternoon, drinking at a local pub favored by the Kentucky crowd. Keaner told me that I was to accompany him on this arrest, so that I could get some experience in arrest situations. I said, "Great, I look forward to it."

About 4 p.m., Keaner gathered me up and we went to the garage and got his government car. He drove and handed me a picture of the suspect. Within a few minutes we were cruising by the bar, which was filled with construction workers starting their weekend celebration. We drove by several times and Keaner pulled down on the brim of his Stetson (he was one of the few agents who still wore a hat) to shield his eyes from the sun.

All I could see was a swarm of men in the place, but Keaner growled, "There he is, playing pool." I still did not see the man. We then pulled to the rear of the parking lot. Keaner turned off the engine and related his strategy to me. "Look," he said. "This place is full of bad guys, many of whom, we must assume, are armed." I nodded in agreement. "So," he said, "this is what I want you to do. I will go in the front door and as he pulls back on the pool stick, I will snap the cuffs on him and take him out the front door and bring him back here to the car. I want you to go in the back door and make sure that none of those guys pull a gun on me and plug me while I am making the arrest. Can you do that?" Like a puppy, I nodded my head in agreement.

So we opened the car doors and moved toward the bar. I gave Keaner a few minutes to get set, and then I went in the back door and through the kitchen. The place was jammed with bodies swilling draft beer and shots of whiskey and yelling at each other; then I saw that familiar Stetson hat come through the front door.

All I could think of was keeping Keaner safe, as he requested. I needed to control this group of half-drunken construction workers. So, without too much thought, I reached inside my suit coat, feeling my own sweat on the leather of my holster. Out came Mr. Smith and Mr. Wesson, and with all the vocal power I could muster over that din, I shouted, "Everybody put your hands up. Reach for the sky." Immediately the place became deadly quiet and all eyeballs were locked on that .357 Magnum. All hands went skyward, and I observed Keaner place his handcuffs on the suspect and lead him out the front door. No one else in the bar appeared to have even seen the arrest. They were all glued to me.

As soon as I could see that Keaner was clear of the bar, I said, "Thank you very much. Have a nice day." And I backed out of the bar, put back my gun into its holster, and raced for the car. Keaner had the suspect in the backseat and I drove back to the Federal Building. What a success! We had made the arrest and got away clean, with no one hurt. We were all smiles as we entered the office and started for the processing room. Suddenly, Foster's voice boomed out, "Keaner, Repasky, get in my office." We handed off the prisoner to another agent and went into Foster's office.

"What's the problem?" Keaner asked, as Foster turned from looking out the window. "What's the problem? What's the problem?" Foster said. "I just got off the phone with the mayor and the chief of police. You two just held up a bar with fifty patrons in it. That is the problem." I was in shock, as I thought we did such a great job. A terrible argument ensued, and I have to give this much to Mom Keaner; never once did he blame me or hand me over to the wrath of Foster. Mom Keaner stuck with the story that I had done what I did just to protect another agent.

My adventures and training with Keaner would continue, but he did show me one method of conducting cold weather surveillance that I am sure is not taught in any training division. It was late in January 1973, and once again Keaner was on the trail of a young check thief, who was following the postal carrier around on Social Security check day, and removing the checks from the mailbox a block behind the carrier. Keaner had a confidential informant who told him the young man would be visiting his mother's home that very morning, and Keaner wanted me to go along and back him up. Plus, if the kid ran, I was younger and lighter, and could catch him.

So off we went to the east side of Columbus and drove around until we found the mother's house. The snow was several feet deep and the temperature was in the 20s when Keaner slid the car into a curbside parking space a half block from the house. He immediately turned off the engine, which also turned off the heat in the car.

I said, "What the heck are you doing? It is freezing out there!" Dale replied, "The first rule of surveillance is that you do not want your vehicle spotted. If we keep the engine running, the suspect can look out the window and see that someone is sitting in a car down the street, perhaps looking for them. So, the engine goes off." Of course, within a few minutes, our breathing had fogged up the windows so badly that nothing could be seen through any of them. I sat there thinking that this is really dumb, and I turned to make a comment to Keaner. But, as I observed him, Keaner took his gloved hand and cleared off two little holes on the fogged-over driver's side window and then pressed his face against the window so that his eyeballs were lined up with the clear spots. Of course he had to hold his breath, or the window would fog over once again.

After about an hour of this, Keaner exclaimed, "I see a young boy going into the house. That has to be him." So we finally started the engine and got some heat. My fingers were unmovable. We watched the house for a few minutes and Keaner said, "Let's go get him." So through the snow we trudged; up to the front door went Keaner, and I went to the back door. Keaner talked to the lady who came to the door, and she denied that anyone was there but her. He asked if we could look through the house, she said OK, and so in we went. We spent about half an hour looking from room to room, and found nothing.

Keaner said to me, "I don't understand this. We saw him come in and nobody went out, so he must be here." We then went into the kitchen and talked with the mother, explaining that her son was a check thief, and that he was taking money from her neighbors on Social Security check day, and it was taking them months to get the checks replaced. She started crying and sat down at the table. Then Keaner said, "Do you have a broom?" The woman got up and went to a closet and got a broom. Keaner took the broom and pushed aside the panels in the ceiling of the kitchen and out dropped our check thief. His mother's crying had made him move around and Keaner heard the sound. Later he would tell me, "I knew that kid was up there, or that that lady had really big rats."

My adventures and training with Keaner would go on for the five years I was in the Columbus office, and they would be great learning experiences. Sometimes crazy, sometimes funny, but always thoughtful, and Dale (Mom) Keaner would always be one of those people who shapes your life and your thoughts and who you can consider to be always a gentleman. Kind, professional, and thorough. I was lucky to know the man. Oh, yes. Lest we forget SAIC Robert Foster. Did he mellow with age? I think not. I went to a luncheon with him several months before he died in the home his former wife and kids placed him. His last comments to me: "You're too short for protection."

I Knew You Were Federal Agents

26

DALE L. JUNE

It was a very complex and convoluted case. A person or persons unknown were forging and cashing U.S. Naval reenlistment bonus checks at various banks throughout San Diego. All the checks in amounts of several thousand dollars (from three to six thousand) were used to open an account at the banks by a person who stated he had just reenlisted in the Navy and needed to set up an account at the bank. He provided very little identification, saying he had "just arrived in San Diego and left my military ID aboard ship." Eager to help (or get credit for opening an account), bank personnel immediately opened the account and returned cash to the individual.

During the investigation I found that several checks had been stolen from the back of a payroll checkbook in the safe of the payroll officer on a ship in the bay. The payroll officer didn't even know the checks were missing because they were taken from the back of the checkbook. I also found that the checks were written on computers at San Diego State University and stamped with the signature of the payroll officer. The rubber stamp had misspelled the word "naval" as "navel." This was a clue that led to a rubber stamp store in Tijuana, Mexico.

Eventually, two girls and three men were arrested and charged with the crime. One of the men had served aboard the ship and had stolen the checks. However, the forger and passer, although identified, had managed to elude arrest. He had never been in the Navy but his intellect was so high that he managed to talk the talk when questioned by bank officials opening the accounts. As an aside to the story, when he was eventually arrested and interviewed, he cooperated and related how he had managed to fool the banks. He also was able to recount the check numbers and the places where he had passed each one. Quite an amazing feat!

Then he went on to fill in the blanks on another aspect of the story. I had narrowed down the search to one possible location where he would be on a specific date and time. My partner and I established surveillance up the street from the house where he would be. After about an hour, we saw him in the front yard and then turn and run into the house. My partner ran to the back of the house to make sure the fugitive didn't run out the back. I went to the front and asked for admittance as I was searching for a federal fugitive I had seen run into the house. The residents allowed me to enter, let my partner in through the back door, and allowed us to search the house because, "There is nobody here."

253

We began our search, looking everywhere. I opened one bedroom door and saw two mattresses on the floor with a baby asleep atop of them. I quietly looked around the room and opened the closet door. No one was in the room except the baby. After looking in every nook and cranny of the house and speaking with the residents, we had to conclude he was not in the house and swallow our pride and leave.

About two weeks later, the man was arrested, without incident (as the papers say), in a motel in Chula Vista, a suburb of San Diego, California. When I asked him about that night we saw him run into the house, he said, "I was hiding between the two mattresses the baby was sleeping on. I knew you were federal agents and wouldn't want to disturb the baby."

April Fools, Motherf___ers

27

DALE L. JUNE

One day several years ago, I was working an assignment as a bank robbery suppression agent in Los Angeles. LA at the time was the bank robbery capital of the country, with several bank takeovers by groups of two to ten armed robbers. One day, my partner, a retired LA police officer, related this story:

The city had been experiencing a series of armed robberies of mom-and-pop convenience stores. On a particular night, two officers were assigned to establish surveillance inside a store and arrest the culprits if and when they attempted to rob the store. The officers were armed with shotguns and hid behind a curtain in the back of the store. Two young men entered the store, pointed guns at the frightened storeowner, and demanded all the cash in the register.

In an attempt to arrest the men, one of the officers shot and killed one of the robbers. The survivor was taken into custody.

During the ensuing trial, one of the officers took the stand and testified: "We were on surveillance at the store when two people came in to rob the store. They pointed their guns at the store clerk and demanded money. My partner and I stepped out from behind the curtain, identified ourselves as police officers, our badges were in plain sight on our belts, and told them they were under arrest and began to explain their rights. One of the men turned toward me with his gun and I, unfortunately, being afraid my life or my partner's life was in imminent danger, I fired and shot him. He died at the scene."

The defendant took the stand and testified, "We went into the store, not intending to hurt anyone, just to scare them and take the money. As we asked for the money, two men with shotguns stepped out from behind a curtain and shouted, 'April Fools, Motherf___ers!' BLAM!"

Mentis Incompitus (Tripped up by Bad Planning)

28

DALE L. JUNE

Jesse's car was stolen. The car was a "distressed" 1990 model Honda. Jesse reported the theft to the police and his insurance company, but wasn't very optimistic about getting it returned, at least with the wheels and other easily removed parts still intact.

Two weeks later, he received a call from the police, who told him the car had been retrieved and those responsible were locked up in jail. Good police work? No. It was simply a matter of luck, the awareness of an impound lot attendant, and the mental incompetence (*mentis incompitus*) of the offenders.

Three boys in their late teens driving a 1990 model Honda arrived at a police impound lot in Los Angeles to attempt to sell the car to the attendant. The attendant told them to wait with the car. While they were waiting, he went to his computer to research the history of the car. Immediately, when checking the license plate number, he discovered the car was stolen. He electronically closed the high-security gates to prevent the boys from leaving; he then called the police, who arrived and took them into custody.

When Jesse retrieved his car from the police, he learned the thieves had given the car a major tune-up and replaced the torn cloth interior with all new upholstery.

Patriotic and Immigration Lessons

IV

From out of the past come many contemporary lessons in life no longer taught in most schools, academies, or institutions. When looking at history with its wars, politics, and sociological impacts, it is only a matter of interpretation of the intent and importance of the words spoken and written that chronicles come alive with meanings for succeeding generations. Today's sons and daughters are often so involved in material and technological matters that they often overlook the basic concepts of liberty and freedom, which are the cornerstones of our free and democratic country, "The Golden Door" to the world.

The following essays were written by university students as an assignment in a cultural pluralism course who, by looking back at one of the most powerful speeches in history, Lincoln's Gettysburg Address dedicating the cemetery at the site of the most bloody battle in American History and the "Lady" holding the "Torch of Freedom and Welcoming" in New York harbor, were reminded of what this country means and stands for in terms of "life, liberty and the pursuit of happiness."

The students were career-oriented registered nurses dedicated to caring for the sick and injured, regardless of the person's race, color, ideology, or ancestry. Although they all graduated from nursing schools and have been exposed to every aspect of the human condition, none were ever exposed in their training to an examination of the true meaning of historical antecedents that have given them (and others aspiring to live free, and perhaps have traveled from "far and distant lands" to gain a better life) insight into the rights and freedoms they have taken for granted.

Interpreting the Meaning of the Gettysburg Address

29

NICOLE TYE

Abraham Lincoln's Gettysburg Address is such a powerful message to all whose eyes fall upon reading it. The field on which the famous Civil War battle of Gettysburg was fought is extremely symbolic of our nation's advancements toward obtaining freedom and equality for every individual. Approximately 50,000 soldiers lost their lives at the Battle of Gettysburg July 1–3, 1863. In Lincoln's address to the nation, he wanted to honor those who died defending this right by leaving a lasting memory and legacy behind for future generations to embark on, preserving for years following the battle of Gettysburg. Although America has come quite a long way since this memorable event and people desire to live in this country because of such advancements, we still struggle with violence among different racial groups, and I will continue to do my part in upholding the mission of preserving equal rights and freedom to all with whom I interact within my daily life.

Four score and seven years ago, our fathers brought forth upon this continent a new nation: conceived in liberty, and dedicated to the proposition that all men are created equal.

Now we are engaged in a great civil war ... testing whether that nation, or any nation so conceived and so dedicated ... can long endure. We are met on a great battlefield of that war.

We have come to dedicate a portion of that field as a final resting place for those who here gave their lives that that nation might live. It is altogether fitting and proper that we should do this.

But, in a larger sense, we cannot dedicate ... we cannot consecrate ... we cannot hallow this ground. The brave men, living and dead, who struggled here have consecrated it, far above our poor power to add or detract. The world will little note, nor long remember, what we say here, but it can never forget what they did here.

It is for us the living, rather, to be dedicated here to the unfinished work which they who fought here have thus far so nobly advanced. It is rather for us to be here dedicated to the great task remaining before us ... that from these honored dead we take increased devotion to that cause for which they gave the last full measure of devotion ... that we here highly resolve that these dead shall not have died in vain ... that this nation, under God, shall have a new birth of freedom ... and that government of the people ... by the people ... for the people ... shall not perish from the earth.

We are very fortunate to live in a country that offers us so many liberties. For example, we have the freedom to choose where we want to live, what career to pursue, how to dress, what religion to follow, who we decide to marry, what gender we associate more with, just to name a few. People come from all around the world to indulge in the delectable idea of making decisions as simple and as much taken for granted as those listed here.

Even today there can be some tension at times between members of certain racial and ethnic groups, and this may be evidenced in the greater Los Angeles area. We can turn on the news and, as an example, see or hear about the violence committed on others purely based on skin color. For instance, different gangs primarily made up of one single race may display violence upon members of a different gang of another ethnicity and/or skin color. While our country has taken many steps forward in progressing toward the demonstration of equality and respect for all, there remains some degree of regression.

In my nursing career, I care for sick and injured individuals who fit into all different categories of race, gender, and ethnicity. I take it upon myself to demonstrate cultural sensitivity, compassion, and respect toward my patients and their families at all times. Moreover, it is extremely important that all my patients and families be treated equally and be given fair and equal rights to education on medications, prophylactic care, and resources to assist them upon discharge from the hospital. Oftentimes, the hospital receives inmate patients from the local jail, and it is especially important that we turn off the emotions of any fear or judgments perceived about these certain individuals and treat them as the human beings they are, regardless of the crime they have committed. I might not like the crime they have committed, but my duty is to act the role of a nurse, not a judge or jury. Furthermore, the methods in which I care for and convey verbal messages to a ninety-year-old patient is the same as that which is portrayed to a convicted felon under my care. Not only do I uphold these values in my nursing career, but I do so in my personal relations as well.

While we may never see the day when all members of our nation come together to convey mutual feelings of respect and equality as Lincoln emphasized the importance of in his Gettysburg Address, we are doing well if we continue progressing forward with these issues instead of staggering backward. Freedom did not come for free but came at the heavy price of bloodshed and tears shed by the heroes who fought for the American dream, so that we may enjoy the privileges and rights we have this present day. In Lincoln's Gettysburg Address, he states, "It is for us the living, rather, to be dedicated here to the unfinished work which they who fought here have thus far so nobly advanced." Now it is up to our generation and future generations to uphold, preserve, and optimize ways in which we can maintain our nation's freedom and equality for all, and by doing so, honor the deceased who went to war defending it all those years ago and to those who continue that fine tradition today.

The Golden Door

30

CARLY JENNINGS

"I lift my lamp beside the golden door" was written in the poem "The New Colossus" by Emma Lazarus and engraved on the famed Statue of Liberty in 1903.* But what is the golden door? It is the symbolization of the United States' welcoming arms. Offering freedom and a new life to people suppressed by darkness and tyrannical leaders in their homelands; it is the metaphorical open door to the land of golden opportunity.

Holding high her ever-glowing lamp and the Declaration of Independence, a broken chain at her base, she welcomes those who have sought refuge from being bound by chains, tied by the hands of selfish governmental powers (Figure 30.1). "Not like the brazen giant of Greek fame, with conquering limbs astride from land to land," the female silhouette of the Statue of Liberty depicts warmth for those who need nurturing. What a

Figure 30.1 The Statue of Liberty. (Courtesy of Derek Jensen (Tysto), September 26, 2004.)

* E. Lazarus, "The New Colossus," http://www.libertystatepark.com/emma.htm.

monumental sight to see when arriving on the shores of a dream-fulfilling land. And what an encompassing poem that welcomes strangers to walk through her golden door of prosperity as she lights the way. Despite hardship, war, hatred, or great depression, she holds her peace-representing torch high for the world to see that freedom is the true American dream.

The New Colossus: What It Means to Me

31

STEFANIE WINKLER

It is no mystery that the United States is made up of millions of people from all over the world. No matter what country they come from, those who come to America do so because we are a country founded on freedom and equal opportunity for all. Since 1886, those who have sailed into New York Harbor have been able to gaze at the Statue of Liberty, the ultimate symbol of freedom and democracy. Engraved on the pedestal of the statue is a poem by Emma Lazarus, whose words represent more than just freedom and liberty.[*]

The New Colossus

Not like the brazen giant of Greek fame,
With conquering limbs astride from land to land;
Here at our sea-washed, sunset gates shall stand
A mighty woman with a torch, whose flame
Is the imprisoned lightning, and her name
Mother of Exiles. From her beacon-hand
Glows world-wide welcome; her mild eyes command
The air-bridged harbor that twin cities frame.
"Keep, ancient lands, your storied pomp!" cries she
with silent lips. "Give me your tired, your poor,
Your huddled masses yearning to breathe free,
The wretched refuse of your teeming shore.
Send these, the homeless, tempest-tost to me,
I lift my lamp beside the golden door!"

—Emma Lazarus

In Lazarus's poem about the Statue of Liberty titled "The New Colossus," she ends by saying, "I lift my lamp beside the golden door." This eight-word phrase puts into perspective the whole idea of immigration. This is because since its arrival, millions have come to America, or the "golden door," entering it so they can make a better life for themselves. In the final verse

---

[*] Emma Lazarus, "The New Colossus," http://www.libertystatepark.com/emma.htm, retrieved May 4, 2012.

of the poem, Lazarus continues to personify Lady Liberty herself, writing, "Give me your tired, your poor, your huddled masses yearning to breathe free." Thus, many have come to see the Statue of Liberty as a symbol of immigration. Immigrants themselves saw it as a welcoming sigh of relief as they reached America, and the idea that the hardships they may have suffered in their home country were over.

Although the idea of freedom and immigration is the universal meaning of the poem, when I start to think about the United States today and all the chaos with immigration, I cannot help but wonder if America's golden door still holds that welcoming feeling. To those immigrants who sailed into the harbor decades ago, the Statue of Liberty was a promise of hope, a woman urging them to come forward away from oppression and persecution.* Even long before the Statue of Liberty, many made their way over for the same reasons. Today, many people come to this country with the same hopes and dreams in mind, but unfortunately many are not greeted the same way. People of different cultures are greeted with suspicion and often discrimination. When Americans feel like certain people do not belong, there is a great deal of hypocrisy, because, as we have come to learn, America was first settled by those who did not necessarily belong either. Since then, nothing but immigrants have come here to inhabit America and have essentially made it what it is. I guess the point I am trying to make is that people have always come to America for economic, social, political, and religious reasons, so why now is it such a shock to so many that the white, Caucasian race is becoming the minority. Granted, I myself do not know all of the issues surrounding each side of the immigration debate, but I do know that immigration is inevitable despite personal beliefs on the issue.

Overall, I think that final verse of the poem does represent what America is founded on and that is a nation of people from all over, cultural diversity if you will. There are many people today who argue this meaning, claiming that the Statue of Liberty is in fact the statue of liberty, not the statue of immigration. However, the words "I lift my lamp beside the golden door," implies that America really is a door of opportunities, and there is no specification as to whether or not those opportunities apply to just Americans or to anybody wishing to come to America.

---

* Julie Redstone, "Message of the Statue of Liberty: The promise of the golden door," WorldWatch, 2011, http://www.lightomega.org/worldwatch/, retrieved May 4, 2012.

Ideology and Philosophy

V

Don't Be Afraid; Listen to and Use Your Intuition

32

JANINE FRANCOVICH

When you are afraid of anything, you are acknowledging its power to hurt you. In your fearlessness, you acknowledge your invulnerability.

Did you ever feel the hair on the back of your neck stand up or have the feeling someone was watching you? This is one of your senses, the sixth sense, intuition, or extra sensory perception. My story takes place in a beautiful mountain resort called Lake Arrowhead, located at the top of a mountain above San Bernardino, California. My husband, Mark, had taken me there for our anniversary. It was a beautiful inn with a panoramic view of the lake.

Our first day there was pleasant: shopping in the village, relaxed conversation, walking hand in hand. It all started to change when we returned to the resort. We stopped at the hotel bar for a drink before getting ready for dinner. There was a man at the bar who was extremely intoxicated and wanted to talk about his reason for being there. My husband, being kind, listened to the man's story, and this is where it all started. I was standing next to my husband and this man, and I suddenly became extremely uncomfortable. Unfortunately, I am the type of person who cannot hide my feelings. If I am upset or angry, everyone knows it.

Mark, seeing I was getting upset and agitated, excused us from this man. I didn't know why the man made me so uncomfortable until the next day. He told us he was there with his wife visiting his son who was in a drug rehab program. Harmless enough, right? Mark and I then went back to our room and got dressed for dinner. We decided to walk back into the village and go to Coyote, a staple restaurant in town. The walk is about three blocks from the hotel; it is dark at this point, and we are busy talking and laughing until we turned a corner. Suddenly, I began to have shortness of breath and become extremely frightened. Mark was confused about my sudden agitation, but in his normal reaction, he tried to distract me with humor. I told him I had a horrible feeling of dread and that I was frightened. He refers to a Nike™ commercial, telling me I could outrun anyone; you see, I was a runner. However, this did not quell my feeling of impending doom. We finally made it to the restaurant where they sat us in the bar area. Again I became apprehensive and felt it difficult to breathe. Mark asked if they could move us away from the bar, which they did, and this made me feel only a little better. My husband at this point was irritated to say the least, but I could not rationalize my feeling of sheer terror and the inability to get a good breath of air until we left the bar. On our walk back to the hotel, we saw flashing red lights and a swarm of police and detectives, with their yellow tape in hand, taping off the exact location where my internal nightmare began. I approached a detective and asked what was going on, but he told me it was official police business and to keep moving.

The next morning we returned to the village for breakfast and my nightmare continued. We saw the coroner's car. I spotted a "townie" and asked him to tell me what happened, but he said they couldn't talk about it. This is a village that makes its living on tourism, so they couldn't afford to have crime. I grabbed this young man's arm and told him I felt something in that area and I needed to know what happened. Meanwhile my husband, now in the uncomfortable seat, tried to make me let go. I would not back down until I got my answer! The young man saw the determination in my eyes and began to talk. Apparently, the victim was a woman who was visiting with her husband to see their son who was in rehab. The couple had a fight, she ran to the local bar Coyote and met an unsavory soul, a man recently released from prison and hiding out in the mountains. Apparently, she left with him willingly, but her willingness changed once his intentions were made clear. He then choked the life out of her on the shoreline below the very road where we had been walking the night before; the road where I too could not breathe. My seemingly irrational fear was due to the murder that was happening at that time we were walking by. The victim was the wife of the man who we had met that night. It was now clear to me why that man made me feel so uncomfortable earlier that night. My sixth sense knew of the impending tragedy that would shatter his life. Mark, with a look of sadness, could only say he now understood the reason I felt all those feelings.

As disturbing as it is for me to recall this dreadful experience, it was a life lesson. If you ever have that unexplained feeling or sensation, that is your sixth sense. Even if your instinct is to ignore that feeling, it is better to believe that it is your subconscious trying to keep you safe. We all have it, but we don't all believe it.

What I Should Know about Islam: A Basic Primer

33

MOHAMAD KHATABLOO

Contents

Islam is the second-largest and fastest-growing world religion, with minority populations in fifty-six countries spanning North Africa to Southeast Asia, and significant minorities in Europe and the United States. Despite its more than 1.2 billion adherents, many in the West know little about the faith and are familiar only with the actions of a minority of radical extremists. Islam has had a significant impact on world affairs, both historically and in the contemporary era. Therefore, it is important to understand not only what it is that Muslims believe, but also how their beliefs are carried out both privately and publicly, both as individuals and as members of the Muslim community. We will see that Islam is not monolithic. Although Muslims share certain core beliefs, the practices, interpretations, images, and realities of Islam vary across time and space. The multiple and diverse images and realities of Islam and Muslims are in a number of phenomena worldwide:

- The many cultures in which Islam is to be found, from Africa to Southeast Asia, Europe to North America.
- Women's dress, educational and professional opportunities, and participation in mosques and societies differ widely from country to country.
- In politics, from Turkey to Algeria to Malaysia, Islamic activists peacefully press for the implementation of religion in state and society, and have been elected to parliaments.
- Islamic associations provide educational, legal, and medical services in the slums of Cairo and Algiers, Beirut, Mindanao, the West Bank, and Gaza.
- Terrorists, in the name of Islam, attacked the World Trade Center and the Pentagon. The hijackers reflect a religious radicalism that has threatened many regimes in the Muslim world and Western governments.
- The geographic, cultural, and religious diversity of Islam reflects its status as a world religion with a global presence and impact.
- Islam is the second-largest and one of the fastest-growing of the world's religions. It has more than one billion followers, and multiple languages, ethnic groups, tribes, and cultures.
  - Only twenty percent of the world's Muslims are Arabs.
  - The majority of Muslims live in Asian and African societies.

- Islam is a visible presence in the West as the second-largest religion in Europe and soon to be the second largest in America.

The Contemporary Resurgence of Islam

In the last decades of the twentieth century, a series of political events and economic realities led to the desire of many Muslims to achieve greater authenticity and self-definition through a revival of Islam. This revival was reflected both in private life (greater mosque attendance and concern with Islamic dress and values) and in public life through political and social activism. Whereas reformist movements have worked within mainstream society for change, extremists have resorted to violence and terrorism to achieve their goals.

Despite the Islamic community's size, global presence, and significance, myths, stereotypes, and misinformation about Islam and Muslims abound. The study of Islam today is often motivated by and cannot escape the threat that radical Islam— Muslims extremists and terrorists—has posed to their own societies and to the West. Significant interest in Islam in recent decades was not driven by Islam as the second-largest and perhaps the fastest-growing world religion, but by the challenge and threat of political Islam or Islamic fundamentalism.

This is especially true after September 11, 2001, in the context of the war against global terrorism and in particular, Al-Qaeda.

Islam at the Crossroads

Like members of other faith communities, contemporary Muslims face the challenge of defining the role, meaning, and relevance of Islam in both private and public life. Often we focus on radicalism and extremism, but a more pervasive struggle exists. At the heart of this "struggle for the soul of Islam" between conservatives and reformers, mainstream Muslims and extremists, is the question of who should interpret Islam and how reform should be achieved. Its major issues include the relationship of religion to state and society, the role of Islamic law, the status of women and non-Muslims, the compatibility of Islam and democracy, and relations with the West.

Who Are the Muslims?

For a fifth of the world's population, Islam is both a religion and a complete way of life. One billion people from a vast range of races, nationalities, and cultures across the globe—from the southern Philippines to Nigeria—are united by their common Islamic faith. About eighteen percent live in the Arab world. The world's largest Muslim community is in Indonesia. Substantial parts of Asia and most of Africa are Muslim, although significant minorities are to be found in the Soviet Union, China, North and South America, and Europe.

What Do Muslims Believe?

Muslims believe in one, unique, incomparable God; the angels were created by Him; the prophets received His revelations to mankind; the Day of Judgment and individual accountability for actions; and God's complete authority over human destiny and in life after death. Muslims believe in a chain of prophets including Adam, Noah, Abraham, Ishmael, Isaac, Jacob, Joseph, Job, Moses, Aaron, David, Solomon, Elias, Jonah, John the Baptist, and Jesus. According to Muslim belief, God's final message to man, revealed to the Prophet Muhammad, was a reconfirmation of the eternal message and a summing up of all that has gone before.

How Does Someone Become a Muslim?

Someone becomes a Muslim simply by saying, "There is no God apart from God, and Muhammad is the Messenger of God." By this declaration the believer announces his or her faith in all God's messengers and the scriptures they brought.

What Does Islam Mean?

The Arabic word *Islam* simply means "submission," and is derived from a word meaning *peace*. In a religious context Islam means complete submission to the will of God. "Mohammedanism," as used in earlier generations, is thus a misnomer because it suggests that Muslims worship Muhammad rather than God. The Arabic name for God, used by Arab Muslims and Christians alike, is "Allah."

Why Does Islam Often Seem Strange?

Islam may seem exotic or even extreme in the modern world. Perhaps this is because religion does not dominate everyday life in the West today, whereas Muslims have religion always uppermost in their minds, and make no division between secular and sacred. They believe that the *Divine Law*, called the *Shari'a* must be taken very seriously and strictly interpreted according to the Quran, giving Quranic law precedent over "laws of Man," thus explaining why issues related to religion are so important to a devoted believer.

Do Islam and Christianity Have Different Origins?

Islam and Christianity do not have different origins. Together with Judaism, they go back to the prophet and patriarch Abraham. The three primary prophets descended directly from his sons: Muhammad from the oldest son, Ishmael; Moses and Jesus from the younger son, Isaac. Abraham established the settlement Makkah (Mecca) and built the *Ka'ba* with his sons, toward which all Muslims turn when they pray.

What Is the Ka'ba?

The *Ka'ba* is the place of worship God commanded Abraham and Ishmael to build more than 4,000 years ago. The building, made of stone, was constructed on what many believe was the original site of a sanctuary established by Adam. God commanded Abraham to summon all mankind to visit this place, and when pilgrims go there today, they say "At Thy service, O Lord."

Who Is Muhammad?

In the year 570, the child Muhammad, who would become the prophet of one of the world's great religions, Islam, was born into a family belonging to a clan of Quraysh, the ruling tribe of Mecca, a city in the Hijaz region of northwestern Arabia.

Mecca had with the decline of southern Arabia become an important center of sixth-century trade with such powers as the Sassanians, Byzantines, and Ethiopians. As a result, the city was dominated by powerful merchant families, among whom the men of Quraysh were preeminent.

Muhammad's father, Abd Allah ibn'Abd al-Muttalib, died before the boy was born; his mother, Aminah, died when he was six. The orphaned, Muhammad, was consigned to the care of his grandfather, the head of the clan of Hashim. After the death of his grandfather, Muhammad was raised by his uncle, Abu Talib. As was customary, Muhammad was sent as a child to live for a year or two with a Bedouin family. This custom, followed by noble families of Mecca, Medina, Tayif, and other towns of the Hijaz, had important implications for Muhammad. In addition to enduring the hard-ships of desert life, he acquired a taste for the rich language so loved by the Arabs, whose speech was their proudest art. He learned the patience and forbearance of the herdsmen, whose life of solitude he first shared and came to understand and appreciate.

In 590 CE, Muhammad, then in his twenties, entered the service of a widow named Khadijah as a merchant actively engaged with trading car-avans to the north. Sometime later, Muhammad married Khadijah, with whom he had two sons, who did not survive childhood, as well as four daughters.

During this period of his life, Muhammad traveled widely with the merchant caravans. In his forties he began to retire to meditate in a cave on Mount Hira outside of Mecca, where the first of the great events of Islam took place. One day, as he sat in the cave, he heard a voice, later identified to him as that of the Angel Gabriel, who ordered him to "Recite 'In the name of thy Lord who created, created man from a clot of blood.'"

Three times, Muhammad pleaded his inability to do so but each time the voice he heard repeated the command. Finally, Muhammad recited the words of what are the first five verses of the 96th *surah* or chapter of the Quran—words that proclaim God the creator of man and the source of all knowledge.

At first, Muhammad divulged his experience only to his wife and his immediate circle. As more revelations and voices enjoined him to proclaim the oneness of God universally, his following grew, at first among the poor and the slaves, then as time passed his following also included the most prominent men of Mecca. The revelations he received at that time and those he received later are all incorporated in the *Quran*, the scripture of Islam.

How Did Muhammad Become a Prophet and a Messenger of God?

At the age of forty, while engaged in a meditative retreat, Muhammad received his first revelation from God through the Angel Gabriel. The revela-tions, which continued for twenty-three years, came to be written and known as the Quran.

As soon as he began to recite the words, "In the name of thy Lord who created, Created man from a clot of blood," he heard from Gabriel to preach the truth that God had revealed to him. He and his small group of followers suffered bitter persecution. It grew so fierce that in 622, God gave them the command to emigrate. This event, the Hijra, or "migration," in which they left Mecca for the city of Madinah some 260 miles to the north, marks the beginning of the Muslim calendar.

After several years, and much warfare, the Prophet and his followers triumphantly returned to Mecca, where they forgave their enemies and established Islam definitively. Before the Prophet died at the age of sixty-three, the greater part of Arabia was Muslim, and within a century of his death, Islam had spread west, to Spain, and as far east as China.

How Did the Spread of Islam Affect the World?

Among several reasons for the rapid spread of Islam was the simplicity of its doctrine; Islam calls for faith in only one God worthy of worship. The Quran also repeatedly instructs man to use his powers of intelligence and observation. Within a few years, great civilizations and universities were flourishing, for according to the Prophet, "seeking knowledge is an obligation for every Muslim man and woman." The synthesis of Eastern and Western ideas, and of new thought with old, brought about great advances in medicine, mathematics, physics, astronomy, geography, architecture, art, literature, and history. Algebra, the Arabic numerals, and the concept of the zero (vital to the advancement of mathematics) were transmitted to medieval Europe from the Islamic countries. Sophisticated instruments, including the astrolabe, the quadrant, and good navigational maps to make the European voyages of discovery possible, were developed.

What Is the Quran?

The Quran is a record of the words revealed by God through the Angel Gabriel to Prophet Muhammad. Muhammad memorized the words and dictated them to his companions, and they were written down by scribes, who cross-checked it during his lifetime. None of its 114 chapters (*suras*) has been changed over the centuries, so that the Quran is in every detail the same unique text revealed to Muhammad fourteen centuries ago.

As a literal, eternal, uncreated Word of God, the Quran enjoys authoritative status among Muslims as the most important source of Islamic faith and practice. The Quran confirms the truth of the Torah and Gospel of the Bible. Muslims believe that the Quran represents both the original and final revelation of God to humankind, making Islam the oldest, rather than the newest, of the monotheistic faiths. The Quran reveals the compassion and justice of God, the role and responsibilities of human beings, and relations between men and women. It also addresses issues of sin and repentance, social justice, and religious pluralism.

What Is the Quran About?

The Quran, the last revealed Word of God, is the prime source of every Muslim's faith and practice. It deals with all the subjects concerning humanity, wisdom, doctrine, worship, and law, but its basic theme is the relationship between God and His creatures. At the same time, it provides guidelines for a just society, proper human conduct, and an equitable economic system.

Are There Any Other Sacred Sources?

Other sacred sources include the *Sunna*, the practice and examples set by the Prophet. It is the second authority for Muslims. A *Hadith* is a reliably transmitted report of what the Prophet said, did, or approved. Belief in the *Sunna* is part of the Islamic faith.

What Are the Five Pillars of Islam?

The Five Pillars of Islam are the framework of the Muslim life: faith, prayer, concern for the needy, self-purification, and the pilgrimage to Mecca for those who are able. All Muslims accept and follow the Five Pillars of Islam:

- Making the declaration of faith
- Engaging in prayer five times a day
- Tithing
- Fasting during the month of Ramadan
- Making the pilgrimage to Mecca at least once in a lifetime

These pillars are the core beliefs that unite all Muslims across time and space, and are the hallmarks that distinguish Islam from all other faiths. The Five Pillars reflect Islam's emphasis on practice and action. Although it has no such official status, *Jihad* is sometimes referred to as the Sixth Pillar. Jihad, "meaning to strive or struggle," refers to the obligation incumbent on all Muslims, as individuals and as a community, to exert (jihad) themselves to realize God's will, to lead a virtuous life, to fulfill the universal mission of Islam, and to spread the Islamic community. Jihad has also come to define the struggle for or defense of Islam, popularly referred to as "Holy War," Despite that Jihad is not supposed to include aggressive, offensive warfare, as distinct from defensive warfare, that has occurred throughout history. The two broad meanings of Jihad, nonviolent and violent, are found in the Quran and expressly contrasted in a well-known prophetic tradition. This tradition reports that when Muhammad returned from battle, he told his followers, "We return from the lesser jihad (warfare) to the greater jihad." The greater jihad is the more difficult and more important struggle against one's ego, selfishness, greed, and evil.

Faith

According to Islam, there is no other god worthy of worship except God, and Muhammad is His messenger. This declaration of faith is called the *Shahada*, a simple formula that all the faithful pronounce. In Arabic, the first part is *la ilaha illa Llah* (there is no god except God). Ilaha (God) can refer to any-thing that we may be tempted to put in place of God, such as wealth, power, and golden idols. Then comes illa Llah, that is, except God, the source of all Creation. The second part of the Shahada is *Muhammadun rasulu'Ll ah* (Muhammad is the messenger of God), a message that guidance has come through a man like ourselves.

Prayer

Salat is the name for the obligatory prayers performed five times a day and is a direct link between the worshipper and God. There is no hierarchical authority in Islam, and there are no priests, so the prayers are led by a learned person who knows the Quran, chosen by the congregation. These five prayers contain verses from the Quran and are said in Arabic, the lan-guage of the Revelation, but personal supplication can be offered in one's own language.

Prayers are said at dawn, noon, midafternoon, sunset, and nightfall, and thus determine the rhythm of the entire day. Although it is preferable to worship together in a mosque, a Muslim may pray almost anywhere, such as in fields, offices, factories, and universities. Visitors to the Muslim world are struck by the centrality of prayers in daily life. A translation of the Call to Prayer is

> God is most great. God is most great.
> God is most great. God is most great.
> I testify there is no God except God.
> I testify there is no God except God.
> I testify that Muhammad is the messenger of God.
> I testify that Muhammad is the messenger of God.
> Come to prayer! Come to prayer!
> Come to success (in this life and the Hereafter)!

Come to success!
God is most great. God is most great.
There is no God except God.

The Zakat

One important principle of Islam is that all things belong to God, and that wealth is therefore held by human beings in trust. The word *zakat* means both "purification" and "growth." Our possessions are purified by setting aside a portion for those in need, and like the pruning of plants, this cutting back encourages new growth.

Each Muslim calculates his or her own *zakat* individually. For most purposes, this involves the payment each year of two and a half percent of one's capital. A pious person may also give as much as he or she pleases as *Sadaqa*, and does so preferably in secret. This word is translated as "voluntary charity" but it has a wider meaning.

The Prophet said, "Even meeting your brother with a cheerful face is charity. Charity is a necessity for every Muslim." He was asked, "What if a person has nothing?" The Prophet replied, "He should work with his own hands for his benefit and give something out of such earnings in charity." His companions asked: "What if he is not able to work?" The Prophet said, "He should help poor and needy persons." The companions further asked, "What if he cannot do even that?" The Prophet said, "He should urge others to do good." The companions said, "What if he lacks that also?" The Prophet said, "He should check himself from doing evil. That is also charity."

The Fast

Every year in the month of Ramadan (in the Muslim calendar), all Muslims fast from first light until sundown, abstaining from food, drink, and sexual relations. Those sick, elderly, or on a journey, and women who are pregnant or nursing are permitted to break the fast and make up an equal number of days later in the year. If they are physically unable to do this, they must feed a needy person for every day missed. Children begin to fast (and to observe the prayer) from puberty, although many start earlier.

Although the fast is considered beneficial to health, it is regarded principally as a method of self-purification. By cutting oneself off from worldly comforts, even for a short time, a fasting person gains true sympathy with those who go hungry as well as growth in one's spiritual life.

Pilgrimage (Hajj)

The annual pilgrimage to Mecca—the Hajj—is an obligation only for those physically and financially able to perform it. Nevertheless, about 2 million people go to Mecca each year from every corner of the globe, providing a unique opportunity for those of different nations to meet one another. Although Mecca is always filled with visitors, the annual Hajj begins in the twelfth month of the Islamic year (which is lunar, not solar, so that Hajj and Ramadan fall sometimes in summer, sometimes in winter). Pilgrims wear special clothes: simple garments that strip away distinctions of class and culture, so that all stand equal before God.

The rites of the Hajj, which are of Abrahamic origin, include circling the Ka'ba seven times, and going seven times between the mountains of Safa and Marwa as did Hagar during her search for water. Then the pilgrims stand together on the wide plain of Arafa and join in prayers for God's forgiveness, in what is often thought of as a preview of the Last Judgment.

In previous centuries, the Hajj was an arduous undertaking. Today, however, Saudi Arabia provides millions of people with water, modern transport, and the most up-to-date health facilities.

The close of the Hajj is marked by a festival, the Eid al-Adha, which is celebrated with prayers and the exchange of gifts in Muslim communities everywhere. This, and the *Eid al-Fitr*, a feast day commemorating the end of Ramadan, are the main festivals of the Muslim calendar.

Does Islam Tolerate Other Beliefs?

It is one function of Islamic law to protect the privileged status of minorities, and this is why non-Muslim places of worship have flourished all over the Islamic world. Islamic law also permits non-Muslim minorities to set up their own courts, which implement family laws drawn up by the minorities themselves. History provides many examples of Muslim tolerance toward other faiths: when the caliph Omar entered Jerusalem in 634, he granted freedom of worship to all religious communities in the city. The patriarch invited him to pray in the Church of the Holy Sepulchre but he preferred to pray outside its gates, saying that if he accepted, later generations of Muslims may possibly use his action as an excuse to turn it into a mosque.

Paths to God: Islamic Law and Mysticism

Piety, and the desire for reform, resulted in the development of Islamic law (the *Shariah*) and Islamic mysticism (*Sufism*). Islamic law reflects Islam's emphasis on the orthopraxy (correct practice), rather than orthodoxy (correct belief). Islamic law applies to both the private and public realms and is concerned with human interactions with God (worship) and with each other (social relations). *Sufism*, as the "interior path," has emphasized personal spirituality and the devotion, and has played an important role in the spread of Islam through missionary activities.

What Do Muslims Think about Jesus?

Muslims respect and revere Jesus, and await his Second Coming. They consider him one of the greatest of God's messengers to mankind. A Muslim never refers to him simply as "Jesus" but always adds the phrase "Peace be upon him." The Quran confirms his virgin birth (a chapter of the Quran is titled "Mary"), and Mary is considered the purest woman in all creation. The Quran describes the Annunciation as follows: "'Behold! the Angel said, 'God has chosen you, and purified you, and chosen you above the women of all nations. O Mary, God gives you good news of a word from Him, whose name shall be the Messiah, Jesus son of Mary, honored in this world and the Hereafter, and one of those brought near to God. He shall speak to the people from his cradle and in maturity, and shall be of the righteous.'"

"She said: 'O my Lord! How shall I have a son when no man has touched me?' He said: 'Even so; God creates what He will. When He decrees a thing, He says to it, "Be!" and it is'" (Quran, 3:42–7).

"Jesus was born miraculously through the same power that brought Adam without a father. Truly, the likeness of Jesus with God is as the likeness of Adam. He created him of dust, and said to him, 'Be!' and he was" (Quran, 3:59).

During his prophetic mission, Jesus performed many miracles. The Quran tells us that he said: "I have come to you with a sign from your Lord: I make for you out of clay, as it were, the figure of a bird, and breathe into it and it becomes a bird by God's leave. I heal the blind, and the lepers and I raise the dead by God's leave." (Quran, 3:49)

Neither Muhammad nor Jesus came to change the basic doctrine of the belief in One God, brought by earlier prophets but to confirm and renew it. In the Quran Jesus is reported to say that he came: "To attest the law that was before me. To make lawful to you part of what was forbidden you; I have come to you with a sign from your Lord, so fear God and obey Me" (Quran, 3:50).

The Prophet Muhammad said: "Whoever believes there is no god but God, alone without partner, and Muhammad is His messenger, that Jesus is the servant and messenger of God, His word breathed into Mary and a spirit emanating from Him, and that Paradise and Hell are true, shall be received by God into Heaven" (Hadith from Bukhari).

Why Is Family So Important to Muslims?

The family is the foundation of Islamic society. The peace and security offered by a stable family unit is greatly valued, and seen as essential for the spiritual growth of its members. A harmonious social order is created by the existence of extended families; children are treasured and rarely leave home until the time they marry.

What about Muslim Women?

Islam sees a woman, whether single or married, as an individual in her own right, with the right to own and dispose of her property and earnings. A marriage dowry is given by the groom to the bride for her own personal use, and she keeps her own family name rather than taking her husband's.

Both men and women are expected to dress in a way that is modest and dignified. The traditions of female dress found in some Muslim countries are often the expression of local customs. The Messenger of God said in the Quran, "The most perfect in faith amongst believers is he who is best in manner and kindest to his wife."

Women and Change in Islam

The status of women in Islam is a hotly contested issue, both in the Muslim world and in the West. Muslim women are often viewed through Western stereotypes or the policies of extremists, such as the Taliban. Although some critics claim that Islam oppresses women, others view Islam as a source of women's empowerment. The diversity of practice in the Muslim world is reflected in dress, access to education and professional positions, and the visibility and roles of women across time and space. The veil has become a particularly charged symbol, yet even the wearing of the veil has diverse meanings for wearers and observers. Increasingly, Muslim women today are struggling to forge new paths, reinterpreting the Quran and Muslim traditions, taking their place in education and the professions, and seeking to improve their status both in the family and as professionals.

Can a Muslim Have More Than One Wife?

The religion of Islam was revealed for all societies and all times and so accommodates widely differing social requirements. Circumstances may warrant the taking of another wife. The right is granted, according to the Quran, only on condition that the husband is scrupulously fair.

Is Islamic Marriage Like Christian Marriage?

A Muslim marriage is not a "sacrament," but a simple, legal agreement in which either partner is free to include conditions. Marriage customs thus vary widely from country to country and culture to culture. As a result, divorce is not common, although it is not forbidden as a last resort. According to Islam, no Muslim woman can be forced to marry against her will. Her parents will simply suggest and arrange a marriage with a man they think may be suitable.

How Do Muslims Treat the Elderly?

In the Islamic world, there are no old people's homes. The strain of caring for one's parents in this most difficult time of their lives is considered an honor and blessing, and an opportunity for great spiritual growth. According to Islam, God asks that we not only pray for our parents, but also act with limitless compassion, remembering that when we were helpless children, they preferred us to themselves. Mothers are particularly honored: The Quran says, "the Prophet taught that 'Paradise lies at the feet of mothers.'" When they reach old age, Muslim parents are treated mercifully, with the same kindness and selflessness.

In Islam, serving one's parents is a duty second only to prayer, and it is their right to expect it. It is considered despicable to express any irritation when, through no fault of their own, the old become difficult. The Quran says, "Your Lord has commanded that you worship none but Him, and be kind to parents. If either or both of them reach old age with you, do not say 'uff to them or chide them but speak to them in terms of honor and kindness. Treat them with humility, and say, 'My Lord! Have mercy on them, for they did care for me when I was little'" (Quran, 17:23–4).

How Do Muslims View Death?

Like Jews and Christians, Muslims believe that the present life is only a trial preparation for the next realm of existence. Basic articles of faith include the Day of Judgment, resurrection, Heaven, and Hell. When a Muslim dies, he or she is washed, usually by a family member, wrapped in a clean white cloth, and buried with a simple prayer preferably the same day. Muslims consider this the final service one can do for their relatives, and an opportunity to remember their own brief existence here on Earth. The Prophet taught that three things can continue to help a person even after death: charity that he had given, knowledge that he had taught, and prayers on their behalf by a righteous child.

What Does Islam Say about War?

Like Christianity, Islam permits fighting in self-defense, in defense of religion, or for those who have been expelled forcibly from their homes. It lays down strict rules of combat that include prohibitions against harming civilians and against destroying crops, trees, and livestock. As Muslims see it, injustice would be triumphant in the world if good men were not prepared to risk their lives in a righteous cause. The Quran says, "Fight in the cause of God against those who fight you, but do not transgress limits. God does not love transgressors" (Quran, 2:190). "If they seek peace, seek you peace. Trust in God for He is the One that heareth and knoweth all things" (Quran, 8:61).

War, therefore, is the last resort and is subject to the rigorous conditions laid down by the sacred law. As stated earlier in this chapter the term *jihad* means "struggle." Muslims believe there are two kinds of *jihad*. The other *jihad* is the inner struggle that everyone wages against egotistic desires, for the sake of attaining inner peace.

What about Food?

Although much simpler than the dietary law followed by Jews and the early Christians, the code that Muslims observe forbids the consumption of pig meat or any kind of intoxicating drink. The Prophet taught that "your body has rights over you," and the consumption of wholesome food and the leading of a healthy lifestyle are seen as religious obligations. The Prophet said: "Ask God for certainty [of faith] and well-being; for after certainty, no one is given any gift better than health!"

How Does Islam Guarantee Human Rights?

Freedom of conscience is laid down by the Quran itself: "There is no compulsion in religion" (Quran, 2:256). The life and property of all citizens in an Islamic state are considered sacred, whether a person is Muslim or not. Racism is incomprehensible to Muslims, for the Quran speaks of human equality in the following terms: "O mankind! We created you from a single soul, male and female, and made you into nations and tribes, so that you may come to know one another. Truly, the most honored of you in God's sight is the greatest of you in piety. God is All-Knowing, All Aware" (Quran, 49:13).

Islam in the United States

It is almost impossible to generalize about American Muslims: converts, immigrants, factory workers, doctors—all are making their own contribution to America's future. This complex community is unified by a common faith, underpinned by a countrywide network of a thousand mosques.

Muslims were early arrivals in North America. By the eighteenth century there were many thousands of them, working as slaves on plantations. These early communities, cut off from their heritage and families, inevitably lost their Islamic identity as time went by. Today many African-American Muslims play an important role in the Islamic community.

The nineteenth century saw the beginnings of an influx of Arab Muslims, most of whom settled in the major industrial centers where they worshipped in hired rooms. The early twentieth century witnessed the arrival of several hundred thousand Muslims from Eastern Europe: the first Albanian mosque opened in Maine in 1915; others soon followed, and a group of Polish Muslims opened a mosque in Brooklyn in 1928. In 1947, the Washington Islamic Center was founded during the term of President Truman. Several nationwide organizations were set up in the 1950s. The same period saw the establishment of other communities whose lives were in many ways modeled after Islam. More recently, numerous members of these groups have entered the fold of Muslim orthodoxy. Today there are about 5 million Muslims in America.

The Muslim World

The Muslim population of the world is around 1 billion. Thirty percent of Muslims live on the Indian subcontinent, twenty percent in Sub-Saharan Africa, seventeen percent in Southeast Asia, eighteen percent in the Arab World, and ten percent in the Soviet Union and China. Turkey, Iran, and Afghanistan comprise ten percent of the non-Arab Middle East. Although there are Muslim minorities in almost every area, including Latin America and Australia, they are most numerous in the Soviet Union, India, and Central Africa.

The Future of Islam

At the close of the twentieth century, it appeared that the future of Islam could be one of new opportunities for peace; democracy; expanded human and women's rights; political, social, and economic empowerment; and an increasing acceptance in Western societies of the Judeo-Christian-Islamic tradition. The September 11, 2001, hijacking of Islam by militant extremists shattered the hopes and dreams of many Muslims throughout the world. They found themselves facing a new millennium in which the old stereotypes of Islam and Muslims as a violent religion and people to be feared and fought returned to center stage. Thus, for Muslims, the twenty-first century will be a time not only for self-reflection, self-criticism, and internal reform, both religiously and politically, but also a time for educating, engaging in dialogue with, and finding new ways in which to work with and within the West and many nations around the world.

Summary

The diversity of cultural and religious practices of Islam is reflected by the geographic expanse of the Muslim world. Like Judaism and Christianity, Islam is one of the great monotheistic faiths that trace its ancestry to Abraham. Muslims share certain core beliefs, but the cultural practices, interpretations, and realities of Islam vary across time and space. Although Islam's more than one billion followers live in some fifty-six countries around the world, many in the West know little about the faith and are familiar only with the actions of a minority of radical extremists. Islam is the second-largest and fastest-growing of the world's religions, is part of the religious landscape of America and Europe, and has had a significant impact on world affairs.

Ideology and Philosophy 34

DALE L. JUNE

It is not from the benevolence of the butcher, the brewer, or the baker that we expect our dinner, but from their regard to their own interest. Put simply, your (banker, financial advisor, employer, etc.) is not motivated by a desire to see that your kids have money for college. He is motivated by a desire to see that his kids have money for college.

—**Berry Goldman**[*]

No man can profit except by the loss of others ... If every man examines his own conscience, he will find that our innermost desires are nourished for the most part and bred in us by the loss and hurt of others ... an undertaker profits only when people die ... the practice of religious ministers rely upon our death and vices ... the lawyer by lawsuits and controversies between men ...

—**Michael De Montaigne (1533–1592)**[†]

How do you fight an idea, ideology, or fanatical religious movement? It is the responsibility of every free and reasonable person to resist, through awareness and intellectual analysis, the threats, bombings, kidnappings, assassinations, and intolerant dogma of those fanatics who would end religious freedom and replace it with their own version of world unification through the dictatorial establishment of draconian doctrine, canons, and religious laws. Guns and bullets don't work. For every insurgent killed, another two take his place, passed on to the next generation of terrorists. This has been proven true since the third century. Every person who believes in freedom, liberty, and democracy must be aware of the insidiousness and dangers lurking in principles of religion grounded in the ideas and ideology of a megalomaniac's self-serving pronouncements, fatwas, and blasphemy laws.

Understanding the strength of the forces and the menace of a rigid religious movement arrayed against a free people in a secular world is the first step in developing resistance to that ideology.

---

[*] Berry Goldman, "The Good Time Charley theory of customer relations: Businesses are in business to make money. Benevolence is not the guiding principle," *Los Angeles Times*, February 9, 2010.

[†] Michel de Montaigne, "That the profit of one man is the damage of another," Quotidiana, http://essays.quotidiana.org/montaigne/that_the_profit_of_one_man/ retrieved June 18, 2012.

The purpose of religion is intended to bring a code of humanity based on virtue, love, goodness, tolerance, kindness, and spiritual faith. When any religion is hijacked and corrupted by individuals who purport to "speak for God," establishing rules, laws, and guidelines subjugating other people to their own fraudulent convictions, the true meaning and purpose of religion is lost, replaced by terror, death, torture, and confinement.

A couple of years ago, my astrological stars said, "Do something nice for someone without him or her knowing it ... Watch the excitement you start." Now I don't really believe in astrology or what the stars say, but more often than we like to think, the forecasts and personal characteristics are pretty nearly on the money.

Coincidence? Maybe. But for many years I have preached, "Do one spontaneous good thing every day for someone and expect nothing in return and you will come to know the true joy of giving and sharing." This is a lesson I learned long, long ago when I was just beginning my college days; help out some other person who needs help and expect nothing in return except to ask them to do the same for someone else.

Of all the philosophies and opinions I have (and of course I have many), this is one that I willingly share: "To find true happiness, give a lot of what you have little of and it will come back to you ten times over." Money is important in life but not nearly as important as the intrinsic values of giving, sharing, and caring. Care for your fellow man—after all, he is your brother—and you will be rewarded in many ways you can never imagine. Smiles are free and contagious. Courtesy is showing respect. Why not give a smile and share courtesy? It may brighten someone else's day. Who knows? It could save a life!

A person down on his luck (or maybe out of good luck and hope) and unable to cope with all the trials of life he has had to endure may be looking at the "final solution" or a "permanent solution to a temporary problem." A small unexpected gesture, a smile, a good word of encouragement, or a helping hand may give him the boost he needs to continue and eventually overcome what he thought was the end of his world.

Our karma (destiny) is tied into all mankind. Everything is connected in some way. That is called the "web of life." Shouldn't we have the time and motivation to help others who are less fortunate? Doing good for no other reason than for goodness sake is not a selfish act. It is selfless.

Over the years I have asked criminal justice students this question: "Why do you want or why did you choose this profession?" The number-one answer of all time is, "To help those in need and to help those who can't help themselves." So give spontaneously or do something nice unexpectedly for someone and watch the excitement grow. The more you give, the more you receive in return!

A Look to the Future through Today's Prism

35

DALE L. JUNE

Contents

The future is as close as tomorrow or the next minute. The face of crime has changed throughout the years. What was once never thought of, or never believed would ever occur, (such as identity theft, terrorism, spousal rape, stalking, serial killing, high rates of child sexual molestation and pornography, etc.) have become and are quickly becoming as commonplace as burglary and auto theft once were. Evolving with the onslaught of new features of crime is an advancing evolvement of crime-fighting techniques, methods, technologies, and philosophies.

This chapter reminds us of the present while casting a look at the future that is presently on the drawing boards, currently being implemented, or residing in the imagination of a forward-looking crime specialist of what could become crime-arresting techniques of the future.

The Grim Sleeper

On August 10, 1985, the body of a twenty-nine-year-old African-American woman was discovered a few miles from downtown Los Angeles, California. This was the first reported killing eventually charged to a serial killer who came to be known as the "Grim Sleeper." By 1988 the known body count attributed to the Grim Sleeper had grown to eight.

The commonality of the crimes was that all the victims, except one, were black females. All victims were sexually assaulted and shot, and left outdoors in a radius of one mile from each other. One victim survived after she was shot in the chest and thrown from the killer's car. She described her attacker as a black male in his thirties, but this meager clue was insufficient to help the police.

The name "Grim Sleeper" was bestowed on the killer by a writer for a local newspaper after the killer took a hiatus during the 1990s but began again in the early 2000s. By 2007, through DNA analysis, the number of linked murders had reached twelve. Investigators attempted, to no avail, to identify the killer by DNA comparisons with individuals who had been arrested and were of record in a statewide DNA database.

In a creative investigative technique, police detectives turned to familial DNA comparison, a controversial method of comparing crime-scene DNA to people in the database and using that information to identify potential suspects who are relatives with a similar DNA. Police extended their search to the DNA database of recently arrested persons and discovered a near match. The man whose DNA most closely matched the crime scene DNA was much too young to be the Grim Sleeper.

Looking at family relatives, the police focused on the man's father, who fit the general description furnished by the one victim who had managed to survive the Grim Sleeper's attack over twenty years earlier. Surveillance of the suspected man, Lonnie Franklin Jr. (Figure 35.1), led police to a pizza parlor, where they obtained DNA samples from discarded pizza crusts he had been eating. The match was perfect. A search of Franklin's house provided evidence linking him to at least ten of the victims. Photos of an additional 108 women, all similar to the known victims, were also discovered. Though many of them have not been identified, it is suspected they were also victims.

Figure 35.1 Lonnie Franklin (the Grim Sleeper serial killer). (From http://www. bing.com/images/search?q=images+grim+sleeper&qpvt=images+grim+sleeper& FORM=IQFRML.)

Figure 35.2 Osama Bin Laden. (From http://www.bing.com/search?q=image+o
sama+bin+laden&qs=SC&form=QBLH&pq=imagesosama&sc=8-11&sp=1&sk=.)

In another dramatic use of familial DNA comparison, when U.S. Navy
Seals raided a compound in Abbottabad, Pakistan, on May 2, 2011, and
killed terrorist mastermind Osama Bin Laden (Figure 35.2), they did not
have samples of his personal DNA but they did have samples from close relatives they used to make a positive identification of the body. The comparison
was made with a ninety-nine-plus percent certainty.

From serial killers to terrorist leaders, familial DNA comparison is a new
weapon in law enforcement's arsenal. Though it has proven its effectiveness,
familial DNA comparison remains controversial because it may infringe on
privacy issues, casting suspicion on innocent family members and violating
their expectations of privacy. Some critics challenge the procedure under
aspects of the Fourth Amendment against unreasonable searches or the
Fourteenth Amendment's equal protection clause. The Supreme Court has
not yet ruled on the Constitutional question of the use of familial DNA
comparison, but earlier precedence has allowed the testing of bodily fluids,
hair, DNA, and so on.

Critical Thinking: Why should civil libertarians be concerned about
familial DNA testing?

The ethical issue of placing all relatives of a potential suspect under
scrutiny poses the question of whether the benefits of positively identifying
a suspect outweigh the concerns of invasion of privacy of innocent people.
The person whose DNA is used for a familial comparison is unwittingly
placed in a position of being a witness against his or her parent, sibling,
uncle, or other family member.

The trends indicate, based on successful usage and with several states
signing into law or exploring the concept of allowing familial DNA comparison,
that it will become an accepted law enforcement investigative technique.

Criminal Justice in the Future

Society changes generation by generation. It is only natural that as society changes, the systems created by society also change. The American "criminal justice system exists to improve public safety, provide services for victims of crime, reduce recidivism and promote fairness and justice for all."* Stepping into the future means adjusting programs and systems to meet the evolving needs and circumstances of society. From historic dungeons and torture, to enlightened practices and guaranteed Constitutional rights and protections, the criminal justice system is designed to meet the challenges of the future with strategic foresight and planning, specifying granted rights and guarantees, and protecting citizens from arbitrary laws and an authoritarian government or a dystopian society perhaps arising from unbalanced conflict between freedom and security.

According to Cetron and Davies, "The next two decades will be a trying period for police departments in the United States and in most of the developed world. Yet they need not face the coming tests unprepared. We cannot anticipate everything that will occur in the period ahead. Yet well-informed foresight can make a big difference in how successfully we meet future demands."† In a society of laws, rules and laws are made by representatives of the people, enforced by the executive branch of government and interpreted by the courts, with the Supreme Court ruling on Constitutional issues through a process of Judicial Review. The interpretation of laws, court rulings, precedent, and the will of the people have changed greatly over the years, and will continue to do so in many ways.

Trends and indicators—Recognizable patterns of instances, events, or occurrences over a period of time; a continuing series of coincidental circumstances, activities, events, or occurrences.

These changes are often foretold by trends and indicators, which are ongoing patterns over a period of time pointing to something that is about to occur. "Examining these trends, it becomes clear that the next ten or twenty years will be a trying time for the world's police agencies, and especially for those in the United States. Many changes are under way that will require significant adaptations on the part of law enforcement. These include new

---

* Virginia Department of Criminal Justice Services, "Setting a course for the future of the criminal justice system in Virginia," http://www.dcjs.virginia.gov/research/documents/08EnvironmentalScan.pdf.
† M.J. Cetron and O. Davies, "55 trends now shaping the future of policing," (The Proteus Trends Series), February 2008, http://www.carlisle.army.mil/proteus/docs/55-policing.pdf.

technologies, demographic shifts, changing values, and a host of other forces for transformation."[*]

The Cetron and Davies Proteus Trends study (2008) identified fifty-five trends[†] shaping the future of the world that will have significant impact on the world of criminal justice. These trends are demographic and societal driven. A sample of the trends of the Cetron–Davies report are

1. Technology increasingly dominating both the economy and society.
2. Societal values are changing rapidly.
3. The global economy is growing more integrated.
4. Militant Islamism continues to spread and gain power.
5. Mass migration is redistributing the world's population.
6. Privacy, once a defining right for Americans, is dying quickly.
7. The population of the developed world is living longer.
8. Continuing urbanization will aggravate most environmental and social problems.
9. Specialization continues to spread throughout industry and the professions.
10. The work ethic is vanishing.
11. The economy of the developed world is on a path to grow for at least the next five years.
12. The world's population is on course to reach 9.2 billion by 2050.
13. Life expectancy in the developed world is steadily growing longer.
14. The elderly population is growing dramatically throughout the world.
15. Technology is creating a knowledge-dependent global society.
16. Despite some xenophobic reactions to immigrants, there is growing acceptance of diversity.
17. Young people place increasing importance on economic success, which they have come to expect.
18. Tourism, vacationing, and travel (especially international) continue to grow with each passing year.
19. The physical-culture and personal-health movements are improving health in much of the world, but they are far from universal.
20. The women's equality movement is losing its significance, thanks largely to past successes.
21. International exposure includes a growing risk of terrorist attack.

In 2008 the Virginia Department of Criminal Justice produced a study identifying twenty-one areas of concern for the future. These points are[‡]

[*] Ibid.
[†] Ibid.
[‡] Virginia Department of Criminal Justice Services, "Setting a course."

1. Collaboration and coordination in the criminal justice system
2. Information sharing in the criminal justice system
3. Technology in the criminal justice system
4. Diverting nonviolent offenders from jail and prison
5. Prisoner reentry into society
6. Recruiting and retaining criminal justice system personnel
7. Multidisciplinary training for criminal justice system personnel
8. Standardized training and testing for law enforcement officers
9. Juvenile delinquency and crime prevention
10. Improving the juvenile justice system
11. Preventing crime
12. Security at schools and college/university campuses
13. Domestic preparedness and the criminal justice system
14. Mental health and the criminal justice system
15. The impact of drugs on the criminal justice system
16. Drug prevention and treatment
17. Knowing what works in criminal justice
18. Equality and consistency in the criminal justice system
19. Immigration and the criminal justice system
20. Victims of crime and the criminal justice system
21. Public awareness and the criminal justice system

Rule of Law and Rule of Man

Historically, throughout the world, until the establishment of the United States as a free and democratic representative government, the law of the land was whatever the king, emperor, or church said it was. This is a very brief description of rule of man, as still seen in various parts of the world, with one person or a small group dictating the law to fit a particular moment and their own whims and wishes; for example, North Korea and Syria. In today's world, the law is still by man in countries ruled by dictators or a repressive system disallowing the people from having a say in how the law should be enacted and enforced.

Rule of man—A nondemocratic form of government, usually a dictatorship whose only voice is the single powerful leader or council. He is considered above the law as he dictates the law.

Shariah or moral law—Laws following a strict moral interpretation of religious dogma.

Morality police—Enforcers of a moral code dictated by a conservative religious body.

Inquisitorial law—An accused is assumed guilty and must prove his innocence.

Rule of law—No man is above the law and is presumed innocent until proven guilty beyond a reasonable doubt.

Figure 35.3 A call for Shariah law.

> Adversarial law—Two opposing sides presenting a case. Prosecution
> attempts to prove guilt beyond a reasonable doubt, the defense tries to
> create reasonable doubt in the mind of the judge or jury.

Another example of rule of man is religious or Shariah law, commonly referred to as "moral law," meaning to "do the good" or referencing differences between "bad" and "good" with definitions by man, as the word of God (Figure 35.3). The government, in Saudi Arabia, for example, enforces Shariah by The Commission for the Promotion of Virtue and Prevention of Vice (the Hai'a), commonly referred to as "morality or religious police,"[*] which establishes laws considered in keeping with good morals in accordance with religious dogma, and dictates the behavior of people through repressive discriminatory means, often interpreted by extremely conservative religious groups.

In prosecutions under this type of inquisitorial law, the accused is assumed guilty and must prove his or her innocence. For example, a woman accused of adultery by her husband or the government must prove that she did not engage in sex prior to marriage or with anyone other than her husband (Figure 35.4).[†] Should she not be able to prove her innocence, she will be condemned to death by being half buried in sand and stoned by relatives including fathers, husband, sons, and members of the community.

In 2011, spontaneous uprisings by the people in several Middle Eastern countries led to what became known as "Arabic Spring," meaning the

[*] http://www.msnbc.msn.com/id/29840195/ns/world_news-mideastn_africa/.
[†] F. Sahebjam, *The Stoning of Soraya M.: A True Story* (New York: Arcade Publishing, 1995.)

Figure 35.4 Buried in sand and stoned. (From http://images.sodahead.com/ polls/00512507/polls_sharia_law_muslim_1129821863_poll_slarge.jpeg.)

people were looking for freedom and democracy. Future implications for American criminal justice practitioners may be seen in a rise in "home-grown" terrorism as migrants from dictatorial countries settle in the United States and bring their voices and values to future generations of their culture and religious beliefs, counter to the American criminal justice system.

The rule of law means that no person is above the law. In the United States, "rule of law" may be defined as principles of publicly known codified laws, establishing legitimate government authority, enforced through a Constitutional provision of "due process." Rule of law also means that a person is assumed innocent until proven guilty beyond a reasonable doubt and is applied equally through a system known as adversarial law. The Bill of Rights and the Fourteenth Amendment of the U.S. Constitution and the due process clause guarantee equal protection for all from the government. The Constitution calls for a strict division of church and state, and guarantees equal protection with due process regardless of a person's religious affiliation. As long as the free people of the United States support, defend, and protect the U.S. Constitution, adversarial law will be the means by which criminal justice is meted out.

The Pendulum of Justice

Using an analogy of a pendulum, the pendulum of justice swings back and forth, from a tendency toward leniency to a harsh, nearly draconian philosophy of punishment. As it has since the early 1980s, it has come to pass that the public is quickly accepting, without challenge, laws that are enacted by politicians seeking votes by trading on the public's fear of crime. The campaign platform of many politicians has been "I'm tough on crime." No one will therefore vote against a policy calling for stricter laws and a criminal justice system that calls for quick, decisive punishment equal to or greater than the crime.

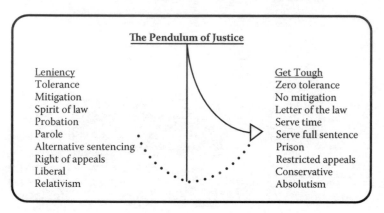

The Pendulum of Justice	
Leniency	Get Tough
Tolerance	Zero tolerance
Mitigation	No mitigation
Spirit of law	Letter of the law
Probation	Serve time
Parole	Serve full sentence
Alternative sentencing	Prison
Right of appeals	Restricted appeals
Liberal	Conservative
Relativism	Absolutism

The people have responded by electing representatives who actively endorse laws calling for swift and harsh punishment for crimes. The "man on the street" has also called for harsher (you could say draconian) punishment for committing a crime after being convicted for two previous felonies and, as in the instances of violators of Megan's and Jessica's laws, registration and tracking of sexual violators. Laws of this nature can be termed "emotional" or "knee-jerk" reactions resulting from some heinous crime like a child abduction, sexual assault, and death without serious consideration of long-term consequences or Constitutional concerns.

No child should be exposed to such things as kidnapping and sexual assault. Even one child sexually assaulted and killed is too many. It affects them and their families for the rest of their lives should they be lucky enough to survive the attacker. The trauma of a sexual attack or infringement can have devastating consequences. A victim of rape (forcible or otherwise) may take years and thousands of hours of counseling to come to grips with the matter. Over ninety percent of sexual attacks come from within the family or with a known and trusted person, such as a neighbor. Not to mention the priests who have preyed on boys. According to the Association for the Treatment of Sexual Abusers, "Most sexual offenders assault victims whom they know. Children are most likely to be assaulted by members of their family followed by acquaintances (e.g., neighbors, family friends); adults are most likely to be assaulted by a current or former husband, a cohabitating partner, or a date."*

---

* Association for the Treatment of Sexual Abusers, http://www.atsa.com/ppTenThings. html.

Many laws have been passed with the good intention of protecting children from sexual predators. But the laws have had some unexpected consequences. The California law that prohibits registered sex offenders from living within 2,000 feet of a school, park, or playground has driven many offenders to live on the streets or underground with their whereabouts unknown and they cannot be checked up on. In Orange County, California, many cities are adopting laws that prohibit a sex offender from visiting a park. This means that a father who is a registered sexual offender can't even take his family to the playground or an amusement park such as Disneyland.

Without serious consideration of long-term consequences or constitutional concerns, laws of this nature are often a public's emotional response, stirred by news media sensationalism, to heinous crimes such as a child abduction, sexual assault and death. Jessica's law was started as a citizen's initiative and was passed with 70 percent of the vote.

Several laws have been enacted in recent years calling for harsher punishment for repeat offenders and sex offenders, including

- Three strikes law—"The Three Strikes law significantly increases the prison sentences of persons convicted of felonies who have been previously convicted of a violent or serious felony, and limits the ability of these offenders to receive a punishment other than a prison sentence."[*]

Three Strikes

The three strikes law significantly increases the prison sentences of persons convicted of felonies who have been previously convicted of a violent or serious felony, and limits the ability of these offenders to receive a punishment other than a prison sentence. Violent and serious felonies are specifically listed in state law. Violent offenses include murder, robbery of a residence in which a deadly or dangerous weapon is used, rape, and other sex offenses; serious offenses include the same offenses defined as violent offenses, but also include other crimes such as burglary of a residence and assault with intent to commit a robbery or rape.

Most state and federal laws impose stiffer sentences for repeat offenders, but they do not impose punishments as harsh as "Three Strikes and You're Out" (TSAYO) laws. TSAYO laws mandate that a heavy sentence be imposed on persons who are convicted of a third felony. The minimum prison sentence required by such laws is typically between 25 years

---

[*] "The three strikes and you're out law," Legislative Analyst's Office, February 22, 1995, http://www.lao.ca.gov/analysis_1995/3strikes.html.

and life. The federal government and more than two dozen states have passed TSAYO legislation since 1992.

TSAYO legislation is designed to protect society from dangerous individuals who show a pattern of lawlessness, incapacitate repeat felony offenders by keeping them behind bars, and deter others from committing similar criminal offenses. National criminal justice statistics show that the number of violent crimes has precipitously dropped over the past eight years. TSAYO legislation is not without its critics, however. In 1998, several studies called into doubt the effectiveness of TSAYO laws. Constitutional challenges have been leveled against TSAYO laws at both the state and federal levels, but courts and legislatures have resisted overturning them.

In 1994, the Congress passed the Violent Crime Control and Law Enforcement Act (VCCLEA). Public Law 103–322, September 13, 1994, 108 Stat 1796. It imposes a mandatory sentence of life imprisonment without parole on defendants who are convicted of a serious violent federal felony when they have two or more prior serious violent felonies or one or more serious violent felony convictions and one or more serious drug offense convictions. The first two convictions may be for state or federal offenses, but the third conviction must be for a federal offense before the VCCLEA three-strikes provision applies.[*]

- Jessica's Law—Jessica's Law is designed to punish sex offenders and reduce their ability to reoffend. Among the key provisions of the law are a mandatory minimum sentence of twenty-five years in prison and lifetime electronic monitoring of adults convicted of lewd or lascivious acts against a victim less than twelve years old.[†]

Jessica's Law

California Proposition 83, also known as Jessica's Law, was on the November 7, 2006, ballot in California as an initiated state statute, where it was approved (70.5 percent to 29.5 percent). Proposition 83 was named after Jessica Lunsford, a nine-year-old girl. She was the victim of a convicted sex offender who had failed to report his whereabouts, in spite of laws requiring him to do so. Proposition 83 is well known for requiring registered sex offenders who have been convicted of a felony sex offense to be monitored by GPS devices while on parole and for the remainder

---

[*] "Three strikes laws," The Free Dictionary, http://legal-dictionary.thefreedictionary.com/Three+Strikes+Laws.
[†] "Jessica's law, California Proposition 83 (2006)," Ballotpedia, http://ballotpedia.org/wiki/index.php/Jessica%27s_Law,_California_Proposition_83_(2006).

of their lives. It included a number of other provisions that increased the legal penalties for specified sex offenses by

- Broadening the definition of certain sex offenses. Under Proposition 83, aggravated sexual assault of a child is defined as including offenders who are at least seven years older than the victim. Prior to Proposition 83, an offender had to be at least ten years older for a sexual assault of a child to be defined as "aggravated."
- Establishing longer penalties for specified sex offenses. Under Proposition 83, the list of crimes that qualifies for life sentences in prison includes assault to commit rape during the commission of a first-degree burglary.
- Prohibiting probation in lieu of prison for some sex offenses, including spousal rape and lewd or lascivious acts.
- Eliminating early release credits for some inmates convicted of certain sex offenses, including habitual sex offenders who have multiple convictions for specified felony sex offenses such as rape.
- Extending parole for specified sex offenders, including habitual sex offenders.
- Increasing court-imposed fees currently charged to offenders who are required to register as sex offenders.
- Prohibiting any person required to register as a sex offender from living within 2,000 feet of any school or park. For specified high-risk sex offenders, the ban extends to 2,640 feet.
- Making more sex offenders eligible for an SVP (sexually violent predator) commitment.

- Megan's Law—California's Megan's Law provides the public with names and addresses of registered sex offenders.*

Megan's Law

Megan's Law, which addresses sex offenders and child molesters, was signed by President Clinton on May 17, 1996. Megan's Law was much needed, despite Washington State's 1990 Community Protection Act, which included America's first law authorizing public notification when dangerous sex offenders are released into the community. It was the brutal 1994 rape and murder of seven-year-old Megan Kanka by a previously registered sex offender that prompted the public demand for broad-based community notification.

---

* Megans-Law.net, http://www.megans-law.net/.

Megan's Law requires the following two components: sex offender registration and community notification.

SEX OFFENDER REGISTRATION

The 1994 Jacob Wetterling Act requires states to register sex offenders convicted of sex crimes against children. Sex offender registration laws are necessary because

- Sex offenders pose a high risk of reoffending after release from custody;
- Protecting the public from sex offenders is a primary governmental interest;
- The privacy interests of persons convicted of sex offenses are less important than the government's interest in public safety;
- Release of certain information about sex offenders to public agencies and the general public will assist in protecting the public safety.

COMMUNITY NOTIFICATION

Megan's Law allows states discretion to establish criteria for disclosure, but compels them to make private and personal information on registered sex offenders available to the public. Community notification

- Assists law enforcement in investigations;
- Establishes legal grounds to hold known sex offenders;
- Deters sex offenders from committing new sex offenses;
- Offers citizens information they can use to protect children from registered sex offenders, child molesters, and victimization.

California Assembly Bill 488 (Nicole Parra), sponsored by the attorney general, now provides the public with Internet access to detailed information on registered sex offenders. This expanded access allows the public for the first time to use their personal computers to view information on sex offenders required to register with local law enforcement under California's Megan's Law. Previously, the information was available only by personally visiting police stations and sheriff offices or by calling a 900 toll-number. The new law was given final passage by the legislature on August 24, 2004, and signed by the governor on September 24, 2004.

For more than 50 years, California has required sex offenders to register with their local law enforcement agencies. However, information on the whereabouts of these sex offenders was not available to the public until the implementation of the Child Molester Identification Line in

July 1995. The information available was further expanded by California's Megan's Law in 1996 (Chapter 908, Stats. of 1996).

California's Megan's law provides the public with certain information on the whereabouts of sex offenders so that members of our local communities may protect themselves and their children. Megan's Law is named after seven-year-old Megan Kanka, a New Jersey girl who was raped and killed by a known child molester who had moved across the street from the family without their knowledge. In the wake of the tragedy, the Kankas sought to have local communities warned about sex offenders in the area. All states now have a form of Megan's Law.

The law is not intended to punish the offender and specifically prohibits using the information to harass or commit any crime against an offender.*

Laws passed with the intention of protecting children from sexual predators have had unanticipated consequences. For example, California law prohibiting registered sex offenders from living within 2,000 feet of a school, park, or playground (Jessica's Law) has driven many offenders to live on the streets or underground with assumed identities. With their whereabouts unknown, they cannot be monitored.† Laws that make the name and address of an offender public can have other unfortunate consequences as well. In a Riverside, California, for example, neighbors posted signs on a registered sexual offender's lawn, picketed in front of his house, and forced the offender to move. In another example, similar signs were posted on the lawn of a well-liked and respected man who had lived in the neighborhood for over twenty years without any hint of his past. A neighboring mother found the man's name on an online database and began picketing the man's property until the community arose against him, forcing him and his family to move.

A twenty-three-year-old man in Wisconsin was harassed by a neighbor posting signs on his lawn that told the town he was a registered sexual offender. His crime? When he was sixteen years old, he received oral sex from his fifteen-year-old girlfriend and according to court records, the girl testified she instigated the sex act. But he still has to register as a sex offender for the rest of his life. The neighbor posting the sign stated she was trying to protect her children. ("WI—Sex offender says neighbors' actions constitute harassment," http://sexoffenderissues.blogspot.com/2007/08/wi-sex-offender-says-neighbors-actions html).

---

* "About Megan's law," State of California Department of Justice, http://www.meganslaw.ca.gov/homepage.aspx?lang=ENGLISH.
† "Laws restricting lives of sex offenders raise constitutional questions," *PBS Newshour*, January 17, 2008, http://www.pbs.org/newshour/bb/law/jan-june08/sexoffenders_01-17.html.

These and other "get tough on crime" laws present a controversial issue for the American public. Proponents believe that these laws help safeguard and protect the public by inflicting more stringent regulations and punishments on offenders. Critics claim that such laws increasingly infringe on individual freedoms. Laws are a means of setting rules for society to live by; as "get-tough" laws are made, restrictions become more inclusive, maybe eventually leading to a society controlled by well-meaning but limiting constraints.

In 2006, prior to the California vote on Jessica's Law, Californians Against Jessica's Law* posted an opinion essay online to denounce the advent of the law and urged Californians to vote against it. An edited version of that essay is reproduced here because six years later, many of the points made in the opinion piece seem to have come to fruition through the "get tough on crime" policy and public fears of crime and the threat to children from "demented" or deviant persons. To be a deviant does not necessarily mean being a criminal because the meaning of deviant is "someone doing, saying, dressing, etc. out of the accepted norm"; being a criminal means being deviant because they are doing something outside the accepted norm.

"In the last three decades the hysteria over sex crimes, both real and fabricated, has become political (with) … the detection, apprehension, prosecution, defense, incarceration, supervision, control, and treatment of the sex offender and those wrongly convicted. … The Sex Crime Witch Hunt Nightmare has caught tens of thousands of innocent men and women in its ever widening web who now must endure the life-long Scarlet Letter of being a convicted sex offender. 63,000+ Californians are now required by law to register with the police as convicted sex offenders and this number continues to grow daily with no end in sight. These tens of thousands must also submit to sex offender community notification that plasters their faces, descriptions, and other personal information all over the Internet warning their communities of their presence. Numerous studies have indicated that these internet postings do little to protect the public from true sexual predators. What California's sex offender notification websites do is (to) create unnecessary fear in the community, mistrust, and promotes violence. Murder, brutal attacks, and other forms of violence have been directed at those unfortunate enough to appear on CA's sex offender web sites. …

"Can you think of a worse nightmare than being falsely accused of a sex crime, being wrongly convicted, unjustly sent to prison, losing your

---

* The Association for the Treatment of Sexual Offenders, "Ten things you should know about sex offenders and treatment," http://www.atsa.com/ppTenThings.html, retrieved June 7, 2011.

reputation forever, losing everything you own, and when you are finally released from prison you are told because of Jessica's Law you will be forced to wear a GPS Tracking Shackle for the rest of your life or be sent back to prison. In a lot of cases, those who are now forced to register with police as convicted sex offenders committed their crime 20, 30, 40, or more years ago and never reoffended or were totally innocent in the first place. ...

"Internet postings, do little to protect the public. What Jessica's Law will do is further stigmatize, punish, and ostracize not only registered sex offenders, but also their family members. Why stop at GPS Tracking Shackles for sex offenders? Why not all ex-felons? Why not everyone who crosses our borders? What about the mentally ill? Why don't we just implant a GPS Tracking Device in every man, woman, and child in California? Then we really will be safe from one another. The State could also collect DNA samples from all Californians to be stored in a police database until needed. Or maybe The State can collect information about all aspects of every Californian and post it on the Internet, so no one in California could "hide" personal information from their neighbors. It's all for our own good. The State only wants what's best for us. Even if we don't know it yet. We sure wouldn't live in the Land of the Free anymore, but we sure will be safe and secure from one another. Who needs rights, liberties, freedoms, or the pursuit of happiness when we could be 100% safe and live in a Police State Utopia. Jessica's Law is just one of the many first steps we are headed toward this U.S. Constitution hating utopia. We must come together and fight Jessica's Law before it is too late. Please, join the fight. If not for yourself ... for your children." (Californians Against Jessica's Law, 2006)

When laws are passed, long-range consequences must be considered and where does it stop? Today it is sexual offenders, tomorrow who knows, maybe adultery? Then maybe drunk drivers, then people with addictions such as gambling, drugs and sex, and/or other "moral" criminals who in the eyes of the public must be registered and providing a residence address with the government very similar to the people of today who are on probation or parole or in the sexual predator and DNA files. Many cities have begun publishing the names and photographs of men who utilize the favors of prostitutes. Should they also be required to register as sexual offenders inasmuch as prostitution is illegal in most states?

This does not mean an advocacy for sexual offenders here; what is being considered is equal justice and guaranteed Constitutional freedoms and protections. We can't discriminate who gets Constitutional protection and who doesn't. A pending bill in the California legislature requires sexual offenders to register their Internet email user name with law enforcement in their community. If this bill becomes law, it may potentially raise several Constitutional questions like freedom of speech, equal protection, and, perhaps, due process and self-incrimination.

As get-tough-on-crime laws are passed, the average person acknowledges it with rationalization and justification, saying, "If you are doing nothing wrong, you have nothing to worry about"; therefore, allowing and tacitly approving laws that infringe more and more on individual freedoms, moving ever closer to the day when there is nothing left to lose, thus potentially creating a society of law by man or rule by a "moral majority." The people who trust that "if you are doing nothing wrong, you have nothing to worry about" overlook the possibility of being falsely accused. As the net is spread and tightened, many innocent people will become ensnared in legal battles to disprove a false claim or accusation. The "scarlet letter" of an accusation will haunt an innocent person for the rest of his life, as do the current sexual offender laws.

Critical Thinking: How is being wrongly accused of a crime a scarlet letter?

The government of the United States will never be forcibly overthrown through rebellion or invasion. However, as government power is more consolidated in the name of security and freedom from fear of crime (for example, the implementation of harsher and more restrictive laws; the creation of Department of Homeland Security through consolidation of twenty-two other agencies; and enactment of controversial laws like certain portions of the Patriot Act allowing roving wiretaps and warrantless searches and creation of military tribunals), individual Constitutional freedoms will slowly be eroded, possibly resulting in an authoritarian state or benevolent dictatorship.

Critical Thinking: Should civil libertarians and freedom-loving people in our democracy be concerned about potential Constitutional rights being eroded in the name of security and law and order?

Police of the Future

It often comes as a major surprise to many people to learn that only approximately ten percent of police work involves crime fighting. The remaining ninety percent of police work consists of service to the community; acting as ambassadors or representatives of the local government, community, and public relations; and being a visible representation of public law and order.

Service to the community is the lion's share of police work. Answering calls for service may have meanings such as quieting a loud party at late hours, settling disputes between neighbors, directing traffic and crowd control, or other mundane services far out of the realm of crime fighting. In the world of police work, officers are arbitrators, referees, coaches, confessors, marriage councilors, ambassadors of good will, and a range of other duties and responsibilities far removed from "police work." Quite often, police officers themselves fail to see their role as ambassadors representing the government of their city, state, or country.

Critical Thinking: What is your image of the role of police officers? Does your image primarily see them as crime fighters? Are police becoming more militarized?

To the everyday citizen, an out-of-state visitor, or a tourist from a foreign country, the police dressed in their uniform with all the accouterments of their position, including a highly visible black-and-white police car, may be the only perceptible element of the political entity they symbolize. In that role, the police might be called to report a street pothole, a broken street sign or light, or simply to give directions. In other words, people call the police when they have a problem or need help. That problem or help may be totally unrelated to crime but yet officers are expected to respond and settle the problem.

In a community-oriented police agency (think community policing), the police spend time getting to know the citizens of the area in which they work and to help with any problems or concerns the citizens may have. This involves a large share of the police's time as they participate in community programs such as neighborhood watch, police activity leagues, or other public relations curricula.

The patrol function of a police department is very often referred to as the backbone of the department and the eyes and ears of the city. It may not be a stretch of the imagination to suggest that the police role of the future will no longer be involved with citizen services or complaints. Those aspects of current policing will be conducted by private neighborhood security patrols who can respond more quickly and cheaply to calls for service and investigation of minor complaints. As private security patrols are paid by subscriber fees, cities will save millions of dollars in personnel payrolls. A neighborhood patrol will be exactly that; a neighborhood patrol, responsible for minor incidents involving prowlers; noisemakers, barking dogs, and other nuisance calls; and taking reports of burglaries, theft, and traffic accidents. Perhaps they will also be given greater powers of arrest in certain misdemeanor incidents matching the current arrest authority of police.

Figure 35.5 Police car of the future? Drones?

Police will be involved only as investigators in the most serious crimes, terrorism, and threats to public officials and national security. Not only will the patrol function of police become a responsibility of private patrols, but the police will also have the capability of monitoring street and neighborhood activity through a network of cameras and pilotless aircraft as we move toward a society of surveillance. There may be a movement toward further militarization of the police with greater powers of arrest, search, and seizure (see Figure 35.5 and Figure 35.6).

Warriors, Public Service, or Government Servants?

The mental image or definition of a warrior is one exemplifying confidence, courage, and training in special skills or attitude usually related to warfare. As a frontline of defense for people who can't defend themselves or their property, a police officer is often regarded in many societies as a warrior. Many officers carry that same self-image of courageous confidence, bravery, and attitude of helping others regardless of the danger to themselves, thus seeing themselves as warriors in the everlasting battle between forces of criminality and their victims. Police officers are the first to step forward when danger calls for intervention. Whenever the public needs help, it is the police who respond with whatever resources necessary or at their command to restore order and normalcy. Whether it is a raging flood, a wildfire, or a hostage situation, the warrior mentality of a police officer makes him step into the line of fire and brave uncertainty.

With movement into a world dominated by technology, police of the future may not be exposed to conditions requiring the warrior mentality. Even wars today, and into the future, are fought from long distances, sometimes half a world away (as the wars in Iraq and Afghanistan have been

Figure 35.6 Police uniform of the future? (From http://www.bigsaltydog.com/pictures/future_of_police_robocop253.jpg.)

waged). The same may be true in the future for police with the ability to maintain surveillance over an entire city with strategically located cameras, even "eyes" in the sky.* The role of the patrol officer, for instance, may be reduced to sitting in a remote location monitoring happenings in every neighborhood. This will produce a severe blow to the imagery of police as warriors.

FAA Has Authorized 106 Government 'Entities' to Fly Domestic Drones

T.P. Jeffrey, CNSNews.com, July 20, 2012

Since Jan. 1 of this year, according to congressional testimony presented Thursday by the Government Accountability Office, the Federal Aviation Administration has authorized 106 federal, state and local government "entities" to fly "unmanned aircraft systems," also known as drones, within U.S. airspace.

"We are now on the edge of a new horizon: using unmanned aerial systems within the homeland," House Homeland Security Oversight Subcommittee Chairman Michael McCaul (R-Texas) said as he introduced the testimony.

"Currently," said McCaul, "there are about 200 active Certificates of Authorization issued by the Federal Aviation Administration to over 100 different entities, such as law enforcement departments and academic institutions, to fly drones domestically."

GAO testified that the FAA's long-term goal is to permit drones to operate in U.S. airspace "to the greatest extent possible." The proliferation of domestic drones, GAO said, raises a number of issues, the first of which is the right to privacy ... as it relates to the collection and use of surveillance data.

Police of the future may have new technological tools at their disposal to help them protect and serve. Police patrol functions could be reduced to responding to incidents visible on camera, and officers will respond accordingly as directed from the central station (Figure 35.7). With the movement away from traditional police service, police of the future may be highly trained in the areas of intelligence gathering and analysis, personal protection of public figures, and counterterrorism.† More simply stated, police will no

---

* T.P. Jeffrey, "FAA has authorized 106 government 'entities' to fly domestic drones," CNSNews.com, July 20, 2012, http://cnsnews.com/news/article/faa-has-authorized-106-government-entities-fly-domestic-drones, retrieved September 2, 2012.
† From an original essay by Dale L. June (2005).

Figure 35.7 Police monitoring an entire city from a central location. (From http://www.bing.com/images/search?q=+images+security+camera+monitoring &view=detail&id=1212EA86F12C247F015AA5595B8E36AC13B71FBF&first=0.)

longer "police" but will become symbols of the government mandated to prevent terrorist acts of horror, sabotage, and assassinations or murder.

Public law enforcement agencies with enforcement, protective, investigation, and intelligence gathering mandates and responsibilities are forming elite special units ranging from SWAT to covert intelligence gathering and analysis as the patrol functions are becoming less important in the evolving global war on crime and terrorism. Perhaps there will come a day when uniformed officers are used primarily for making arrests, seizing property, and controlling the masses.

This sounds very much like George Orwell's prophetic novel *1984*, but the indicators are beginning to fall into place where the out-of-the-ordinary is becoming very commonplace, accepted, and moving into the venue of science fiction turned reality as official policing merges with a public turning its eyes to strict enforcement of laws aimed toward greater safety and elimination from society those who deviate from the norm. When we look at the changes in the world since World War II and the past twenty years, we can see that Orwell was a futurist before his time.

1984 is a dystopian novel written in 1949 by George Orwell depicting a surveillance society introducing a militarized police state of Big Brotherism, political correctness, citizens betraying each other for infractions of minor laws such as a loving relationship, a new language called Newspeak, individuals being called by a number rather than their name, and ruled by an invisible government (Big Brother) maintained through a dictatorial and feared Ministry of Love.

Partnership with Private Security

Colleges and universities are scurrying to forge partnerships with police and law enforcement agencies to bring working relationships that will focus more on antiterrorist research, training, and modeling. They are also providing degree courses and majors in private security and intelligence management and private investigations.

Other trends and indicators see a professionalization of private security companies with advanced training, educational requirements, and experience rivaling that of police officers (Figure 35.8 and Figure 35.9). Business buildings have "security ambassadors" in the lobby to greet and direct visitors, security alarm companies have armed officers in marked patrol cars to patrol neighborhoods and respond to client alarms, and many public figures and celebrities are hiring professional personal protection agents to provide security emulating the best procedures of the most highly trained security professionals in local, state, and federal governments. Private security has become a highly regarded multibillion dollar business, including companies specializing in the gathering and analysis of intelligence data.

Figure 35.8 Security personnel of the future will be known as police security officers and carry similar credentials. This figure as well as Figure 35.9 depict the close relationship between police and private security.

Figure 35.9 The law enforcement/security badge of the future.

Less than thirty-five years ago, private security was looked upon with a skeptical eye by the public and official law enforcement. Individuals working in private security were considered "rent-a-cops" or "wannabe" police, were often undereducated, poorly paid, and had little or no training.

Today, there has come to be a new awakening throughout the world of private security and public policing. With the professionalization of private security, intelligence gathering and analysis, and private investigators, law enforcement has experienced a positive attitude change toward the private sector and has carried out a good working relationship with private security. Information is shared between private patrol operators and private investigators cooperating with police to ensure the safety of a public figure or celebrity. Often—in jurisdictions where it is allowed—off-duty city police officers contract with private security companies to work as personal protection agents as well as conduct private investigations, usually under a strict policy of not using official agency resources and avoidance of conflict of interest. This standard has been created within the past twenty to twenty-five years and may become more prevalent in the future as private/public policing/security become further interconnected in purpose, training, education, and duties.

As the line between professional jurisdictional policing and private security continues to narrow, it brings with it a host of ethical questions and prospective legal issues. What will the future bring? In summation of the ethical questions and prospective legal issues, it is easy to conclude that the line between professional jurisdictional policing and private security is becoming very narrow indeed. What does tomorrow bring? A future of harsh punishment, police and private security as one entity under the banner of "law enforcement," and technology?

Ethics and Professionalism: Off-Duty Police Officers and Private Security

Off-duty police officers working private protection assignments and private investigations can raise many ethical and potential legal questions. The primary question is if an officer is considered to be on-duty twenty-four hours a day, seven days a week, is he or she ever really off duty to work as a private contractor? Should an incident arise requiring forceful action, that is, involving physical restraint or firearms, is the officer acting in his or her capacity as a private contractor or as a police officer? Where does liability lie: with the public agency jurisdiction or the private company? If the assignment requires protective personnel to carry a concealed weapon, can the officer carry his or her official sidearm, and is his or her badge considered a license to carry a concealed weapon? If an officer observes the person he or she is hired to protect committing a crime, must the officer make an arrest?

Professional personal protection agents are highly trained in the nuances and requirements of their specialty. Being a police officer does not necessarily make an officer qualified as a personal protection agent. The officer may be experienced in dealing with various types of circumstances and have excellent interpersonal skills, but dealing with political figures, celebrities, and VIPs requires an entirely different set of skills than simply responding to threatening situations.

Critical Thinking: Should police officers be allowed to work as private investigators and private security? If they work three days a week as police officers and four days as private security, what should be considered their primary job?

In cities where police officers work a twelve-hour, three-day-a-week schedule and work as private security contractors four days a week—perhaps being paid more than their police job—what should be considered their primary job? In states requiring a private investigator license or other requirements as a personal protection agent, are off-duty police officers exempt from those requirements based on their qualifications as a police officer? Is it ethical for a private investigator to ask his police colleague, whom he may have been working with as a private security officer the day before, to conduct name and license identifications from official records? What if the private investigator was/will be the officer's supervisor on the earlier assignment or in future endeavors?

Core Values of Criminal Justice Practitioners: What Are They? What Should They Be?

Police recruiting seeks people with four important *I*'s: intelligence, integrity, interpersonal skills, and imagination. As the future develops, these qualities will become even more important in a very complex and turbulent world dominated by technology and opportunists who exploit every advantage for their own illegal and immoral purposes.

- Intelligence is that feature of the human brain used for critical and creative thinking, and reasoning. Education, training, experience, and emotion are all important ingredients of intelligence.
- Integrity simply means honesty, morality, ethical, and trustworthy. These are favored values forming a person's character.
- Interpersonal skills is the ability to work as a team or to resolve multifaceted situations and problems with and between others. It is being able to diplomatically work with persons of all socioeconomic, ethnic, and political backgrounds.
- Imagination means analytical thinking in the abstract; capable of creating new ideas, solutions, and procedures. Imagination is the genesis of the future.

To Protect and Serve

The public service role of police in today's world calls for the police to be at the call of the public, affording whatever service is required when a person is in need of help. The primary purpose of modern policing is to prevent chaos, maintain peace and order, and to be available when the public calls for help. "We are here to help" should be the motto, if not the dictum, of police. The long-time slogan of the Los Angeles police department, originator of the phrase "to Protect and Serve," means the police recognize the importance of being a public servant (Figure 35.10). Tomorrow's world will change, but the police, following a code of justice and commitment to public service, will remain on the same steady course of protecting and serving.

About the LAPD

JoinLAPD.com

In 1955, a contest was announced in the Los Angeles Police Department's internal magazine, *BEAT*. The contest involved devising a motto for the Los Angeles Police Academy. The motto needed to be something that would succinctly express the ideals to which those who serve as Los Angeles Police Officers are dedicated.

The winning entry, "to protect and to serve," was submitted by Officer Joseph S. Dorobek and served as the LAPD academy's motto until, by City Council action, it became the official motto of the entire Los Angeles Police Department in 1963. It continues to appear on the department's patrol cars (Figure 35.10) as a symbol of commitment to service.

"To protect and to serve" has become one of the most recognizable phrases in law enforcement. Throughout its almost 50 years of use, it has come to embody the spirit, dedication, and professionalism of the officers of the Los Angeles Police Department.

Police and Crisis Management

Tragedies, disasters, and crises, and emergencies manmade and naturally occurring, can happen at any time of the day or night. An emergency or crisis is defined as a disaster or any condition that results in peril to the safety and lives of persons or destruction of property. Examples of natural disasters or emergencies include earthquakes, floods, mudslides, and wild

Figure 35.10 Los Angeles Police motto on door of patrol car.

fires. Examples of man-made disasters or emergencies include civil unrest, terrorist activity, hazardous materials spills, residential or industrial fires, infrastructure failure, and air disasters.

Police, being first responders, must be fully prepared to help mitigate the situation and restore normalcy as quickly as possible. Traffic and crowd control, evacuations, life saving, control of looters, crime scene preservation and investigation, liaison and communication with other responding agencies, and a myriad of other critical responsibilities fall to the police. In proactive planning, police anticipate potential threats and allocate resources according to levels of crisis management preparedness.

Since the terrorist attacks of September 11, 2001, police and other agencies have stepped up planning for future attacks. Police must look to the future and try to determine potential targets and take preventive measures. Police must use every technique, including technology not yet developed or released to the public, to prevent or moderate every terrorist act. In preparation for the future, police have developed specialized antiterrorism units trained and equipped by the military, and receive intelligence information from scattered sources, including national intelligence agencies and the private sector. It is the role of criminal justice researchers and analysts to read the data to reach conclusions and make recommendations for what might occur.

Police Authority: Role, Misuse, and Constraints

Police authority is derived from the political jurisdiction of a city, state, or federal government. Each state and the federal government define a law enforcement officer and his authority in similar terms. The California Penal Code Section 830 defines peace officer as "any person who comes within the provisions of this chapter and who otherwise meets all standards imposed by law on a peace officer is a peace officer, and notwithstanding any other provision of law, no person other than those designated in this chapter is a peace officer." The penal code section includes descriptions of all types of officially recognized and sworn law enforcement officers and then explains the foundations and extent of authority:

> The authority of these peace officers extends to any place in the state, as follows: (1) As to any public offense committed or which there is probable cause to believe has been committed within the political subdivision that employs the peace officer or in which the peace officer serves. (2) Where the peace officer has the prior consent of the chief of police or chief, director, or chief executive officer of a consolidated municipal public safety agency, or person authorized by him or her to give consent, if the place is within a city, or of the sheriff, or person authorized by him or her to give consent, if the place is within a county. (3) As to any public offense committed or which there is probable cause to believe has been committed in the peace officer's presence,

and with respect to which there is immediate danger to person or property, or of the escape of the perpetrator of the offense. (California Penal Code Section 830.1)

To be more explicit, law enforcement authority is codified and explained in terms of arrest, search, and seizure upon probable cause. For example, if a law enforcement officer has probable cause to believe a felony has been committed and he has probable cause to believe he has the person who committed the felony or there is a warrant outstanding for the person, the officer must make an arrest. In the instance of a misdemeanor, it must be committed in the officer's presence (e.g., a traffic violation), but if there is immediate danger to another person or property of a person or if a perpetrator is attempting to escape, the officer has authority to arrest or to use an amount of force that is "reasonable and necessary."

As part of the swearing-in oath, an officer is required to "support, defend and protect the Constitution of the United States"; accepting his role and commandment to adhere to the provisions of the Constitution relegating his power and authority to the stipulations in the Bill of Rights and reinforced by decisions of the Supreme Court. Of greatest examples are the Fourth and Fifth Amendments referring to authority to seize (arrest) and search only upon probable cause and to inform an arrested person of his rights against self-incrimination. When an officer exceeds his authority, for example, conducting a search without probable cause or failure to inform someone of their Fifth Amendment rights, the Supreme Court has ruled that the evidence and the case are tainted and may be ruled as inadmissible.

Since the end of the liberal Supreme Court of Earl Warren, the criminal justice system has become more conservative, partly driven by the political and social consequences demanding a "get tough on crime" policy. This has resulted in an increase in law enforcement authority that may become even more conservative in the Supreme Court of Chief Justice John Roberts. One example is the 8-1 decision of the Court under Roberts on May 16, 2011, in the case of *Commonwealth of Kentucky v. Hollis Deshaun King* (302 S.W.3d 649, Ky., January 21, 2010) (USSC No. 09-1272, 5/16/11).[*]

Commonwealth of Kentucky v. Hollis Deshaun King (No. 09-1272; Supreme Court of United States; 302 S. W. 3d 649) is a decision of the U.S. Supreme Court that police may forcibly enter a private residence without a warrant under the "exigent circumstances rule" if they have probable cause to believe evidence is being destroyed.

Police were chasing a suspected drug dealer who had entered an apartment building. They knocked on the wrong apartment door and

---

[*] 302 S.W.3d 649, Ky., January 21, 2010; USSC No. 09-1272, May 16, 2011.

announced, "Police." Upon hearing noises of "movement," the police forcibly entered (without a warrant) and arrested King, and others, for possession of marijuana.

The Fourth Amendment challenge to the Court was, by knocking and announcing and forcibly entering the wrong apartment, the entry legal under the exigent circumstances standard?

The overriding issue was: In emergency circumstances, police may enter and search a private residence without a warrant. Does this exception apply when police create the emergency circumstances through their own lawful action, such as knocking on a door?

In this case, police chased a suspected drug dealer into an apartment building. The police knocked on an apartment door and identified themselves—although, unbeknownst to them, it was the wrong door. After hearing "movement" inside, police forcibly entered the apartment without a warrant and arrested King and others for possession of marijuana. The case was challenged in the Supreme Court, under the claim that by forcibly entering the wrong apartment, even with knocking and announcing, the police's entry into the apartment was illegal under the Fourth Amendment. The Supreme Court ruled, in a decision written by Justice Samuel Alito, that it is legal for police to enter a residence without a warrant if they hear noises that indicate evidence is being destroyed:

> It is well established that "exigent circumstances," including the need to prevent the destruction of evidence, permit police officers to conduct an otherwise permissible search without first obtaining a warrant. In this case, we consider whether this rule applies when police, by knocking on the door of a residence and announcing their presence, cause the occupants to attempt to destroy evidence. The Kentucky Supreme Court held that the exigent circumstances rule does not apply in the case at hand because the police should have foreseen that their conduct would prompt the occupants to attempt to destroy evidence. We reject this interpretation of the exigent circumstances rule. The conduct of the police prior to their entry into the apartment was entirely lawful. They did not violate the Fourth Amendment or threaten to do so. In such a situation, the exigent circumstances rule applies.

The decision was not without concerns. Justice Ginsburg (Figure 35.11) worried about the precedent set by the Court's decision. In her lone dissent, Ginsburg wrote:

> The Court today arms the police with a way routinely to dishonor the Fourth Amendment's warrant requirement in drug cases. In lieu of presenting their evidence to a neutral magistrate, police officers may now knock, listen, then break the door down, never mind that they had ample time to obtain a warrant

Figure 35.11 Supreme Court Justice Ruth Bader Ginsberg. (From http://www.
bing.com/images/search?q=images+justice+ginsberg&view=detail&id=FBDFEA
1A9E2975340F4D6C5033F3B7D7E6B37FD6&first=0&qpvt=images+justice+gin
sberg&FORM=IDFRIR.)

> … How secure do our homes remain if police, armed with no warrant, can
> pound on doors at will and, on hearing sounds indicative of things moving,
> forcibly enter and search for evidence of unlawful activity?

Expressing the thought that police powers are increasing while limiting protections of the Fourth Amendment, Ginsburg noted that under certain or
"exigent" circumstances, police do not need a warrant to enter a residence.
Ginsburg wrote that the case posed a serious challenge to the protections
afforded by the Fourth Amendment and redefined the "exigent circumstances exception" that police now have the freedom, power, and authority to
"create their own exigent circumstances" even when they have time to obtain
a warrant under probable cause.

The exigent circumstances exception to the Fourth Amendment has been
defined as being able to "excuse a warrant for an in-home arrest when
probable cause exists and there is a compelling reason for not obtaining
a warrant—for example, a need to protect an officer or the public from
danger, [a] need to avoid the imminent destruction of evidence, when
entry in hot pursuit is necessary to prevent a criminal suspect's escape,
[or a need] to respond to fires or other emergencies." (*Fisher*, 509 F.3d at
960 quoted in *Kolesnikov v. Sacramento County*, 2008 U.S. Dist. LEXIS
33155 (E.D. Cal. April 21, 2008))

This very conservative Supreme Court ruling may be a serious body
blow and an erosion of a very important principle of the Bill of Rights so

eloquently and briefly spelled out in the Fourth Amendment of the U.S Constitution—"the right of the people to be secure in their persons, houses, papers, and effects, against unreasonable searches and seizures, shall not be violated, and no Warrants shall issue, but upon probable cause, supported by Oath or affirmation, and particularly describing the place to be searched, and the persons or things to be seized"—that will carry forth into the future as similar rulings build on the precedent setting *King* decision, eventually so eviscerating the amendment that police, at their own discretion, can create their own exigent circumstances and, without a warrant based on probable cause, will enter and search a private residence and arrest the occupants.

Police authority—Power of arrest, search, and seizure allowed to a sworn officer of the law by a political jurisdiction.

Exigent circumstance—A search warrant is not required under an emergency circumstance.

Probable cause (arrest)—The facts and circumstances that would lead a reasonable person to believe that a crime was committed and this is the person who committed it.

Probable cause (search)—The facts and circumstances that would lead a reasonable person to believe contraband is secreted at a particular location.

Reasonable and necessary—The facts and circumstances justifying, but limiting, the use of force needed to effect an arrest or to save the life of someone.

Police Culture and the Average Citizen

As we move further into the twenty-first century, the age of information and technology has already produced a generation of people raised on beliefs that no longer cherish individualism, privacy, or physicality. Through apathy and disinterest, the current and future generations will quietly accept subtle incursions by police and hardliners whose primary concern will be of their own self-actualization and interest. Populations of people have come to forget that a large tree grows by millimeters, and fail to recognize the minuscule erosion of their rights, freedoms, and privacy. "You never miss what you have plenty of until it's gone."* Without the four

---

* "What is the meaning of the Proverb You never miss the water till the well goes dry?," http://wiki.answers.com/Q/What_is_the_meaning_of_the_Proverb_You_never_miss_the_water_till_the_well_goes_dry.

I's (intelligence, integrity, interpersonal skills, and imagination) of individual law enforcement officials who believe in Constitutional protections and public awareness and interest, policing will become a semimilitarized arm of government used to suppress dissenters as well as criminal elements. Realistically it can be imagined that dissenters and "deviates" will be classified and labeled as criminal. Being deviate is not being criminal; being criminal is deviance.

Deviate—Outside the accepted norm.

Culture—The totality of socially transmitted behavior patterns, arts, beliefs, institutions, and all other products of human work and thought. The predominating attitudes and behavior that characterize the functioning of a group or organization. (http://education.yahoo.com/reference/dictionary/entry/culture)

Police culture—The term "police culture" can refer to several different aspects of policing. It can refer to the "us versus them" attitude that is attributed to police forces almost everywhere, whereby "them" can be variously meant as "society at large," "criminals" and "senior police officials." It can also refer to police attitudes towards the use of their discretionary powers, especially where the end (protecting society from criminals) is thought to justify the means (for example, unlawful searches, excessive use of force and untruthful testimony). Finally, it can refer to the strong feeling of loyalty towards and solidarity with fellow officers, a feeling which goes beyond what is normally encountered among employees, even other professionals. (John Westwood, *Police Culture and the "Code of Silence"* as quoted by http://sociologyindex.com/police_culture.htm)

When Police Culture Clashes with Average the Citizen

Notoriously, police culture has fostered an "us versus them" attitude that if you are not one of us, you must be one of them—meaning that police consider themselves apart from the rest of society, an elite of "brothers" (and sisters) dedicated to one purpose: the eradication of an unlawful element in society. According to this belief, an entire subculture has grown around a concept that if you are not a law enforcement officer, you are a potential criminal element. Police have one belief in the trust of only themselves and their fellow officers; no one else is to be trusted or believed. A police culture sees goodness, sometimes inclusive of corruption, only in fellow officers of the badge, adhering to a strict code of blue silence.

Everyone else is seen as outsiders, despicable, untrustworthy, and potentially criminal.

Fortunately, the majority of society does not view law enforcement in this light. It is taken as a given that police are trustworthy and earnest in their intent to protect and serve. People who live their life honestly, with purposes of goodness, rarely, if ever, have contact with the police in a negative manner.

Code of Blue Silence—An unwritten code of honor to remain silent about topics discussed by and activities participated in by fellow officers.

Ethical behavior is sometimes described as doing the right thing. Police departments have begun to embrace concerns about professional courtesy and ethical behavior. Ethical beliefs are, in fact, replacing the concept of professional courtesy, allowing fellow police officers special treatment and adherence to the blue code of silence The police officer's code of ethics is an eloquent explanation of honor that dedicated and professional officers have accepted and should carry with them into the future.

Professional courtesy—Allowing fellow police officers special treatment and adherence to the blue code of silence.

Critical Thinking: How might professional courtesy lead to corruption?

There will always be distrust and animosity when cultures conflict or clash. Though the police culture is, in reality, a subculture, police are still a part of the larger social culture in which they live and work. It is incumbent upon the police, as with any subculture, to manifest the best attitudes and cooperation from the larger social order. It is even more important in the future that police nurture belief in the goodness of people to maintain an equal balance between the good and bad. If there is no trust in the goodness of either element, society will be the long-term loser. If there is trust and understanding, society can and will turn to the police when in times of peril or the victim of an assault or other crime. With the rapid growth of a surveillance society and loss of personal privacy, it will become even more important that the entire criminal justice system adopt restrictions and guidelines preventing police or law enforcement agencies from becoming a subsociety of us versus them.

Critical Thinking: How might law enforcement professional courtesy lead to an us versus them subsociety?

The Role of Women in Modern and Future Criminal Justice Systems

Women work in every aspect of criminal justice, from police patrol officers to Supreme Court justices. Long gone are the days when the primary role of women was in the capacity as "matron," working exclusively with children and female prisoners. Today, women work alongside men on patrol and in investigations and administration (Figure 35.12).

For the last several years, female students have far outnumbered males in college criminal justice courses. This trend would indicate that women are a growing force in criminal justice careers and may outstrip men in numbers of personnel working in the criminal justice field. Where once it was unusual to see one female in a criminal justice class, now it is very common to see more women than men.* Women are now teaching criminal justice courses that were once the province of men only. Women are earning Ph.D.s in criminal justice and becoming university criminal justice department chairs.

Although women have only taken a slight lead, with females earning 50.4 percent of doctoral degrees, the shift is quite significant. This is particularly true when considering that in 2000, women were only earning 44 percent of doctoral degrees. In addition, while the percentage of doctoral degrees going to women has increased, so has the percentage of women earning master's degrees. While women already earned the majority of these degrees back in 2000, the most recent data indicate that women are now earning 60 percent

Figure 35.12 Today's police woman. (From http://i.ytimg.com/vi/Ipjin RTSGNQ/0.jpg.)

* Personal observation as a criminal justice student and professor.

of master's degrees. To that end, Nathan Bell, who is the director of research and policy analysis for the Council of Graduate Schools has said the increased percentage of doctoral degrees being earned by women is "a natural progression of what we have been seeing" in higher education.[*]

Women now work in every aspect of criminal justice; from police patrol officers to chiefs of police, attorneys, and Supreme Court justices; from crime and intelligence analysts to crime scene investigators; from private security guards to high-level personal protection agents (Figure 35.13 and Figure 35.14). The way has opened up for a woman to become the president of the United States, chief justice of the Supreme Court, and leaders for other major law enforcement agencies like the Federal Bureau of Investigation (FBI), the U.S. Secret Service, and the Central Intelligence Agency (CIA). In other words, the way has opened up for women to reach the highest levels of criminal justice.

To What Extent Will the News Media Have an Impact on the Criminal Justice System?

The news media has often earned a negative reputation regarding its impact on the criminal justice process. Media organizations have been blamed for releasing information that should not have been disclosed, and law enforcement officers often complain that reporters interfere with their criminal investigations. The distrust between police and the media is

Figure 35.13 Julia A. Pierson was sworn in as the 23 director of the United States Secret Service on March 27, 2013, in an Oval Office ceremony.

[*] "Women overtake men in terms of percent of doctoral degrees earned," Top-Colleges, http://www.top-colleges.com/blog/2010/09/25/women-overtake-men-in-terms-of-percent-of-doctoral-degrees-earned/

Figure 35.14 Cathy Lanier, Chief of Police, Washington, D.C.

sometimes mutual, as some reporters claim the police try to hide or cover up many aspects of information and data that are of important public interest.

Police–News Media Relations

Despite their occasional differences, the relationship between police departments and the press is not always negative, and in fact the two entities have reached a point of mutual respect over the years. Law enforcement agencies have seen the positive aspects of news media cooperation. Most police agencies have organized press relation units with official spokespersons who hold frequent news conferences to present information about ongoing cases and departmental news that an interested public would want to know. In return, the press has been known to withhold critical and sensitive information until given approval by the police.

Political Concerns; Public Image

But the press has also received hits from other sources. In a speech at the White House Correspondents' Dinner in April 2006, TV humorist Stephen Colbert made the following remarks:

"Over the last five years you people (of the press) were so good—over tax cuts, WMD intelligence, the effect of global warming. We Americans didn't want to know, and you had the courtesy not to try to find out. Those were good times, as far as we knew. But, listen, let's review the rules. Here's how it works: The President makes decisions. He's the Decider. The press secretary announces those decisions, and you people of the press type those decisions down. Make, announce, type. Just put 'em through a spell check and go home. Get to know your family again. ... Write that novel you got kicking around in your head. You know, the one about the intrepid Washington reporter with the courage to stand up to the Administration. You know—fiction!"*

Where does the truth lie, and what is the role of the press? The truth lies somewhere in the middle between press interference and reporting the facts as interpreted by others. The role of the press is to act as the eyes and ears of a free society, not blindly accepting free handouts of information without questioning. The press is the watchdog over government and authority. When a dictatorial government comes to power, the first blow is to stifle the news media.

In the famous George Orwell novel, 1984, the protagonist, Winston Smith, works in the Ministry of Truth. His job is to review past news articles and rewrite them to conform to current thinking of Big Brother. In other words, as Smith was eventually forced to understand, "who controls the present controls the past, who controls the past controls the future," the meaning of which is that revisionism of the past in the present will determine the future.

Critical Thinking: Should the press be forced to disclose their confidential sources as part of the people's right to know?

The people of the United States have a right to openness in government and the freedom of speech, being allowed to speak out as long as what they say does not endanger national defense. As long as the United States has a free press (guaranteed by the First Amendment of the Constitution), the role of the press will be to independently investigate, ask questions, and report information the public has a right to know and should know. The future relationship between criminal justice elements and the press, while greatly improved, must continue along the same evolutional plain to reach a higher degree of trust and sharing in the public interest.

---

* S. Colbert, keynote speech at the White House Correspondents' Dinner, Washington, D.C., April 2006, http://video.google.com/videoplay?docid=-869183917758574879#, retrieved June 28, 2012.

On July 4, 1966, President Lyndon Johnson signed the Freedom of Information Act* into law allowing public access to previously undisclosed government information. The act has been extended to include all levels of government and is restricted only under certain specific statutory exemptions, such as issues related to national security and public safety.

United States Code; Title 5. Government Organization and Employees; Sec. 552. Public information; agency rules, opinions, orders, records, and proceedings

Each agency shall separately state and currently publish in the Federal Register for the guidance of the public:
   (A) descriptions of its central and field organization and the established places at which, the employees (and in the case of a uniformed service, the members) from whom, and the methods whereby, the public may obtain information, make submittals or requests, or obtain decisions.

Secrecy

Governments and police organizations must have some secrets, especially if they are related to national security and public safety. However, in a free democratic republic, the secrecy of many things must see the light of day and not remain hidden in vaults. There is a saying that "things done in the dark will come out in the daylight." That is the role of the press—to shine light on things others would like to see remain in the dark.

Preventing and Solving the Crime

New developments in technology have forever changed the face of crime. For instance, with the installation of high-tech alarms, warning devices, and cameras, property crimes have shown a decline over previous years (Figure 35.15). According to FBI statistics, "The number of property crimes in the United States from January to December of 2010 decreased 2.8 percent when compared to data from the same time period in 2009. Property crimes include burglary, larceny-theft, and motor vehicle theft."[†]

Another type of crime becoming obsolete, though still very prevalent, is auto theft. Tracking devices, shut-off switches, and locking devices built into a vehicle as it is being manufactured means a thief will be instantly tracked

---

* "Freedom of Information Act (text)," About.com, http://usgovinfo.about.com/library/foia/blfoiacode.htm.
† "Preliminary Annual Uniform Crime Report, January–December 2010," The FBI, http://www.fbi.gov/about-us/cjis/ucr/crime-in-the-u.s/2010/preliminary-annual-ucr-jan-dec-2010.

Figure 35.15 No burglary.

and located before he can travel far. Cars without the technology are the first choice of car thieves.

Modern crimes have evolved through technology. The fastest-growing crimes, including identity theft, credit card and security fraud, and stalking, are made possible because of the advancement of computers and related equipment. A criminal may be on an opposite side of the world while committing his crime with a simple click of a computer key. Technology and newer, more devious methods of committing crimes command an evolution in policing methods and investigative procedures. A side effect of the changing face of crime also stimulates a change in police methods of crime prevention and solution.

Scientific methods and futuristic technology, unheard of only a few years ago, are altering police work from old-fashioned footwork to greater physical evidence collection and forensic analysis. As the Bertillon method of criminal identification became obsolete with the advent of fingerprinting, fingerprinting is giving way to DNA analysis. (Familial DNA comparison was discussed earlier). But that is just one of many tools being upgraded, nearly at a revolutionary pace, in police work.

Intelligence Gathering

Intelligence is information and data that have been collected and analyzed with conclusions and recommendations disseminated to operatives with a need to know. Conclusions and recommendations are reached after a process of critical thinking, mapping and diagramming, and measuring all trends and indicators. Traditional methods of obtaining information from informants, news media reports, and other proven sources are still valuable tools, but technology and new threats of terrorism and sophistication of criminals have presented challenges to the old systems and created new methods of gathering intelligence.

Intelligence—Intelligence is information and data that have been collected and analyzed with conclusions and recommendations disseminated to users with a need to know.

Strategic intelligence—For long-range planning.

Tactical intelligence—For immediate use.

Fusion centers—Central depositories for data collection, analysis, and sharing among intelligence and law enforcement agencies.

After the surprise aircraft hijackings of September 11, 2001, investigations revealed that a lapse in procedures and failure to communicate and share intelligence information were major causes of the success of the attackers. The term most often used to describe why there was a failure of intelligence was "failure to connect the dots." Various investigative and intelligence agencies had snippets of information and data, but there were no procedures or communication channels in place to bring the totality of intelligence into the larger picture. As a result, the government created intelligence fusion centers as one of many policy changes to improve national security.

A fusion center houses intelligence from a variety of sources, and analyzes and shares it with all participating agencies (Figure 35.16 and Figure 35.17).

Figure 35.16 The El Paso Intelligence Center.

Figure 35.17 Inside a fusion center. (From http://www.bing.com/images/ search?q=images+intelligence+centers&view=detail&id=BB2CB0C6AAB13AE3 98D55A.)

From city, state, and federal law enforcement agencies and the intelligence community, along with private, for-profit, information gathering, and analysis brokers, fusion centers obtain information and data, analyze it, share it, and make it actionable ready.

Intelligence fusion centers

- Are part of the domestic surveillance system that incorporates private contractors, federal government, military, and local law enforcement
- Were originally organized by the Department of Homeland Security and the Department of Justice
- Provide federal authorities with access to local databases and legally protected information concerning law-abiding citizens
- Often function with military liaisons and integrate with National Guard units and generally will have private post office boxes as physical addresses

As of July 2009, approximately seventy-two fusion centers existed nationwide with several others in strategic allied countries.

The concept of consolidation of intelligence resources has seen great success, but there may be a central moral issue and potential for exploitation. The issue of concern is one of Constitutional questions. A private security company is not regulated by Constitutional protections like the Fourth and Fifth Amendments. There is no requirement of probable cause or warning against self-incrimination. A private-sector agent can search and obtain information by questionable means; he can then provide it to his co-intelligence police counterparts who can readily say in an affidavit for a search or arrest warrant that information was from a "reliable source." The questioning trend of the future is one of very interesting proportions. Is the partnership between official law enforcement intelligence gatherers and analysts just another step in the direction of public–private consolidation?

Critical Thinking: Should private intelligence brokers be included in governmental fusion centers as part of a working team? Should national security issues take precedence over Constitutional issues?

Technology

In the 1940s there was a newspaper and comic book police detective character named Dick Tracy. His advanced technology consisted of a two-way wrist radio (Figure 35.18). In those days, many, or most, police patrol cars didn't have radio communication. The idea of Tracy's creator and writer was good; only seventy years ahead of his time. Technology has come a long way since then with breakthroughs even science fiction or comics writers couldn't conceive.

Today the world has become dependent on cellular telephones for instant communication. Nearly everyone, including young children, owns a cell phone. With the ever-increasing sophistication of phones, there are so many options available as "apps" or applications (for example, instant research, GPS locations, etc.) that the phones have become the primary dependent link to human interface.

Every generation of phones contains newer features that border on the limits of intrusion and raise questions of privacy and potential illegal wiretapping. With GPS tracking, an individual telephone user can be located within a meter of his actual location. The phones, even when turned off can become listening devices when remotely turned on from another phone without the knowledge or permission of the phone holder. Law enforcement and others can instantly listen in on conversations meant to be private by this method of instant wiretaps.

Today's Dick Tracy two-way wrist radio sends instant messages around the world in text as well as pictures taken with the phone. Complete files can be received in a matter of seconds. In the future, challenges to police use of these instant "wiretaps" may be a central issue in a question of constitutionality before the Supreme Court.

Anyone who has traveled through an airport since the airplane skyjackings of September 11, 2001, has encountered more and more security features

Figure 35.18 Dick Tracy's wrist radio. (Scanned from a comic book, circa 1946, http://www.tomheroes.com/Comic%20Ads/classic%20ads/dick_tracy_wrist_radio.Htm.)

and methods of preboarding searches of the person. The latest is a system of full-body scanning. A passenger will walk through a scanner that will identify an outline of the person's body, detecting anything secreted under the clothing. Utilizing the same technology as body scanners, a company in Massachusetts is producing surveillance vans that can scan the contents of cars, vans, and trucks as they drive along a city street.*

---

* A. Greenberg, "Full-body scan technology deployed in street-roving vans," *Forbes*, August 24, 2010, http://blogs.forbes.com/andygreenberg/2010/08/24/full-body-scan-technology-deployed-in-street-roving-vans/. The accompanying photos depict the current state of vehicle scanners.

Currently the vans can't identify a human in a vehicle but will have the capacity over time. The system will also be developed that can scan the interior of buildings to identify a human form. Perhaps the technology will be included in gun telescopes, as laser beams are today, allowing police (or an assassin) to spot and shoot a target within a building.

Justification for the technology includes statements of being able to identify vehicle bombs, hidden or smuggled humans, and even contraband cargo (Figures 35.19 to 35.20). Building, vehicle, and body scanners open a whole range of potential questions regarding searches without the probable cause and warrant requirement of the Fourth Amendment.

In *Kyllo v. United States,* a heat-sensing device was used to detect unusual heat radiating from Kyllo's house. Police entered without a search warrant and found Kyllo was growing marijuana plants.

In a related case involving questionable use of technology in lieu of a probable cause warrant, *Kyllo v. United States* 533 U.S. 27 (2001), the U.S. Supreme Court ruled that thermal imaging of the interior of a residence was indeed a search and required a search warrant. Adhering to that reasoning, it could be argued that technologically scanning a body, building, or vehicle is also a search, and therefore any evidence obtained would be inadmissible as the result of an illegal search. On the other hand, it could be argued that security purposes outweigh expectations of privacy, as in antiterrorism and airport passenger screenings where a warrant is not required to search persons and baggage.

Figure 35.19 Truck scanner.

Figure 35.20 Truck scanner.

Predictive Policing

Predictive crime detection and prevention—Crime analysis and mapping combined with a mathematical formula to predict when, where, how, and what type of crime will be committed.

Science fiction of the future comes to the present-day police department. Predicting a crime before it happens may seem like the premise of a science fiction movie, but it has become a reality sooner rather than later. While not yet fully arrived, it is in the refinement and implementation stages at several police departments, including the Los Angeles Police Department.* Working with scientists from the University of California–Los Angeles (UCLA) and other universities, the LAPD has pioneered a program that has had extreme early success. The Los Angeles Police Department is the largest agency to embrace an experiment known as "predictive policing," which crunches data to determine where to send officers to thwart would-be thieves and burglars. *Time* magazine called it one of the best inventions of 2011.

Early successes could serve as a model for other cash-strapped law enforcement agencies, but some legal observers are concerned it could lead to unlawful stops and searches that violate Fourth Amendment protections.

---

* G. Risling, "LAPD embracing 'predictive policing,'" Associated Press, July 1, 2012; http:// lapd.com/news/headlines/lapd_embracing_predictive_policing/, and various other sites found using key words "predictive Crime prevention" and similar wording.

In the San Fernando Valley, a suburb of Los Angeles, where the program was launched in 2011, officers are seeing double-digit drops in burglaries and other property crimes. The program has turned enough in-house skeptics into believers that there are plans to roll it out citywide. "We have prevented hundreds and hundreds of people coming home and seeing their homes robbed," said police Captain Sean Malinowski.*

In predictive crime detection and prevention, crime analysts and mathematical researchers work to develop mathematical formulas in an attempt to predict the time, date, location, and type of crime where a crime will be committed. The crime analysts will identify and map types of crime, where and when they were committed, who committed them, how they were committed, and who the victims were. Working with these mathematical formulas it may be possible, with a high percentage of accuracy, to predict a crime prior to its occurrence. Police will then be able to flood the area with officers, preventing the crime or being near the scene for a quick and rapid response.

Police will also access local, state, and federal crimes databases to identify previously arrested, convicted, or accused persons living in a particular area fitting the crime profile identified by crime mapping and the mathematical formula. Preventive crime prevention may have beneficial consequences of lowering the crime and victimization rate, but there may also be harmful consequences. The window could be opened to questionable citizen stops, searches, and arrests. The public may have conflicting emotions, feeling both secure and intimidated by the sudden increase in the number of uniforms and undercover lawmen in a neighborhood.

Unfortunately, most people will acquiesce with an attitude of "I'm not doing anything wrong, so I don't have to worry" and are thankful to the police for stopping a crime before it occurs.

Training and Education

Law enforcement officers are expected to make decisions in time factors measured in thousandths of a second. The same decision may take lawyers and judges years to decide and sort out. Education, training, and experience constitute the isosceles triangle of a well-rounded police officer. Education is obtained by reading, lectures, research, and writing. Police are expected to resort to their educational level when dealing with persons from all walks of life and socioeconomic groupings. Training and experience increase an officer's reflex ability to respond instantly to challenging and changing circumstances that their education prepared them for through intellect and academic achievement. A few short decades ago, police were required to have

* Ibid.

an eighth-grade education, then a high-school degree; later, many police agencies required an associate's degree; and today, a bachelor's degree is a standard requirement in many departments. The very near future will see front-line officers being required to obtain a master's degree with promotions predicated on a doctorate-level degree.

Evolving technology, procedures, and complex equipment demand that an officer be trained and educated in every aspect and skill necessary to complete his duties. An officer not staying current with the latest trends and changes will quickly no longer be a positive asset to his agency. Police departments are setting educational standards very high with expectations that officers will continue their education throughout their career. Training has become more demanding and varied, covering aspects such as sociology, psychology, and human behavior, as well as the standard police training topics of fitness, arrest and defensive tactics, and laws of arrest, search, and seizure.

Police training and education in small towns and large cities must also focus on the politics and workings of terrorism. Ingredients for bomb making such as nitrate fertilizer can be purchased in small farming communities, plus with immigration of various cultures into smaller towns, "homegrown" terrorism is a grave possibility. And there are many militant militias utilizing terrorist tactics centered in small towns. The U.S. Military has extensive training in suburban and terrorist warfare, making them ideal for training police in anti-terrorist procedures and suburban warfare tactics. Though police have their own training facilities, it can be expected that the military will provide resources, equipment, and training facilities to give police the highest level of expertise, training, and scenario experience.

DNA Testing

DNA analysis helps investigators identify victims and perpetrators of crime. Every crime scene tells a story. The crime scene investigator and analyst must decipher the story to help lead to a successful prosecution. Everything at a crime scene is potential evidence, even the smallest speck of dust, hair, or fingernail clipping. A shift in criminal investigation techniques from fingerprinting to DNA analysis has given police investigators advanced tools for identifying the victims and perpetrators of crime.

Every living thing with cells has a DNA pattern. A technician can test an object and produce the DNA chain. As in the case of fingerprinting during the police booking procedure, DNA samples are routinely collected and stored in databases. The databases are available to investigators for comparison with known suspects in an investigation. Eventually, newborns may be identified through DNA processing as they are now fingerprinted or footprinted.* It is also conceivable that a person may have to provide a DNA sample when applying for a driver's license or maybe getting married. As a person comes of record through birth, police arrest, hospitalization, licensing, and so forth, his DNA will be added to the database until the entire population's DNA is databased. Familial DNA testing and comparison, while still controversial, will come to be accepted as a legitimate police investigative tool, providing investigative leads where nothing else did, solving many "unsolvable" crimes. With DNA tools, police departments have established cold-case investigative units with the responsibility to reopen and solve previously unsolved crimes using new technology. Revisiting old crimes has resulted in many cases finally being solved, even after many years, bringing closure to victims and survivors. In one example, a 25-year-old murder was solved in Los Angeles when police retrieved a coffee cup the suspect had discarded at a fast-food restaurant. Her DNA matched a DNA sample found at the crime scene.†

A Colleague's Arrest on Suspicion of Murder Stuns the LAPD

Los Angeles Times, June 6, 2009

Police allege veteran detective Stephanie Lazarus, 49, shot her ex-boyfriend's wife in 1986, then harbored the secret for more than two decades. ...

Calling it an apparent "crime of passion," Deputy Chief Charlie Beck said Lazarus allegedly beat and fatally shot Sherri Rae Rasmussen, a 29-year-old hospital nursing director, two years after joining the department.

Three months after they were married, Rasmussen's husband returned to their Van Nuys condominium on the evening of Feb. 24, 1986, to discover his wife's badly beaten body on the floor in the living room. She had been shot several times, Beck said.

Days after the slaying, two men robbed another woman in the area at gunpoint. Homicide detectives suspected that the pair had also killed Rasmussen when she came upon them burglarizing her home. ... The search for the men led nowhere. ... With homicides in the city falling to historic lows, LAPD detectives have had unusual freedom in recent months to revisit cold cases. Detectives returned to the Rasmussen killing in February, testing blood or saliva samples from the crime scene thought to have been from the killer. The DNA tests showed that the

---

* http://www.bing.com/search?q=DNA+recording+of+newborns&go=&qs=n&sk=&first=2 1&FORM=PERE1
† "A colleague's arrest on suspicion of murder stuns the LAPD," *Los Angeles Times*, June 6, 2009.

attacker was a woman, disproving the theory that a man had killed Rasmussen.

Detectives scoured the original case file for mention of any women who could have been overlooked during the investigation ... they found a reference to Lazarus, who was known at the time to have had a romantic relationship with the victim's husband, John Ruetten. Ruetten allegedly broke off the relationship and soon after became involved with Rasmussen. ... Last week, an undercover officer surreptitiously trailed Lazarus as she did errands, waiting until she discarded a plastic utensil or other object with her saliva on it, police sources said.

The DNA in her saliva was compared with the DNA evidence collected from the murder scene. The genetic code in the samples matched conclusively, police said.

Futuristic speculation tells us that, over time, criminals will be so sure of getting caught that they will reconsider whether to commit a crime in the first place. Naturally there will always be crime, but types of crime and ways of committing it will evolve to more sophisticated means.

DNA testing and comparison, while still controversial, are increasingly being used as a legitimate police investigative tool, providing investigative leads and helping solve many unsolvable crimes.

Profiling

"A pattern is a trap." With a high rate of accuracy, an individual's movements can be anticipated if several factors are known. Among these factors are the individual's residence, place of employment, schedule, favorite recreation and hobbies, and route of travel. It is a good investigative technique to learn as much about a suspect as possible, especially during the course of trying to locate the suspect or to anticipate his or her movements. Included in building the suspect's profile is his or her psychological makeup and social habits. How is the suspect's family life? Who are his or her friends and associates? What is his or her background, habits and patterns, and modus operandi?

Profiling—Building a "picture" of a person through psychological, sociological, and human behavior patterns.

Profiling is still in its infancy with roots based in the mid-1970s. As advancements are made in the fields of psychology, human behavior, and social science, profiling will become an important adjunct to predictive crime analysis. Used as a part of predictive crime prevention and detection, police can build a profile of potential suspects and use that as a basis for identifying persons who are most likely to have committed a crime or who will commit a crime.

The Changing Face of Crime

Cybercrime—Crime committed through computer-related technology.

The development of new technologies has changed not just criminal investigations, but also crime itself. The term "cyber" means having to do with computer technology. Crime rates of traditional crimes such as burglary, for example, have declined over the past half decade as the rate of cybercrime has steadily increased. Cybercrimes are the direct result of the computer information revolution since the 1980s and are quickly redefining the meaning of crime as it moves from crimes we would traditionally think of, like burglary, to newly conceived and defined crimes that can be committed by computer from half a world away. Some traditional crimes have become obsolete but many have become more complex and difficult to detect.

Counterfeiting of currency, for instance, remains a traditional crime, but the method of producing fake money with computers and high-resolution copiers and printers has become easier with a higher-quality end product, making it very difficult to detect even to the trained and expert eyes of the U.S. Secret Service, charged with the responsibility of investigating currency crimes since 1865 (Figure 35.21).

Figure 35.21 Comparing counterfeit and genuine currency. (From http://cache. gawkerassets.com/assets/images/17/2010/12.)

The United States Secret Service is a federal law enforcement agency with headquarters in Washington, D.C., and more than 150 offices throughout the United States and abroad. The Secret Service was established in 1865, solely to suppress the counterfeiting of U.S. currency. Today, the agency is mandated by Congress to carry out dual missions: protection of national and visiting foreign leaders, and criminal investigations. See http://www.secretservice.gov.

Cyber Stalking

Social networking is an online way of reconnecting with long-lost friends, making new friends, and "staying connected." Unfortunately, carried beyond the bounds of friendship, it is also a way of executing a campaign of fear, intimidation, and invasion of privacy through various techniques such as e-mail, hacking, and incursion into the life of a selected victim(s).

Criminal stalking is generally defined as harassing someone by inappropriate, persistent, and unwanted attention. It is being stealthy and invasive, attempting to attract the attention of the stalker's center of interest. It may be a former spouse or lover, a fanatical celebrity worshipper, a mentally deranged person, or a disgruntled employee. Stalkers know no bounds of privacy and will commit any act they think will gain the attention of their victim. With the proliferation of personal information readily available through modern technology, a stalker can easily determine and predict the exact location and movements of his prey.

Cyber stalking—Creating fear, intimidation, and invasion of privacy through the use of computer technology.

A cyber stalker doesn't necessarily need to make his physical presence seen or felt; in fact, he may be totally bedridden and unable to physically stalk his victim but through his bedside computer he can cause the same effect as though he were shadowing his target (Figure 35.22). Cyber stalking will increase as more private information is available through Internet channels. Pedophile stalkers will also increase the use of cyber "friendships" to lure potential victims.

Financial Crimes

A cyber financial crime is a crime of fraud or theft through the manipulation of accounts, securities, and other monetarily related devices by computer technology. Types of cyber financial crime may include, but not be limited to, money laundering, money theft directly from a bank customer's account by gaining access to the account with stolen passwords, securities fraud, identity theft, and a host of other related illegal financial transactions.

Figure 35.22 Computer + motivation = stalking victimization.

Cyber financial crime—A crime of fraud or theft through the manipulation of accounts securities, and other monetarily related devices by computer technology.

With a move toward elimination of cash, banks are turning to electronic representation of transactions. No actual money is ever moved; only its representation is instantaneously moved electronically. Without actually having cash on hand, banks and law enforcement will witness a downturn in the number of bank robberies committed with a note and gun. A robber will simply key in the correct sequence of words and numbers into his computer and instantly he will have harvested somebody else's account.

Software and Copyright Piracy

No longer do kids steal music by placing a cassette or CD under their jacket. With a few clicks of a computer mouse, books, movies, music, and computer software programs are instantly downloaded. With that click, the crime of

Figure 35.23 Copyright pirates work in the shadow.

copyright piracy has been committed if made without the permission of the copyright owner. Often, movies are on a disk on the "gray or black market" and sold ahead of general release to movie theaters.

What is lost on the minds of people downloading the movies, songs, and software is the simple fact that their act is a crime called "bootlegging" and is theft. It is stealing the copyright royalties that would normally flow to the rightful recipient. Because it is done through computer technology, often from distant parts of the world, the person doing the downloading or buying makes no connection to the victim of his crime (Figure 35.23).

Copyright piracy—A form of bootlegging; illegally making, marketing, and distributing copyrighted material by computer technology without proper authorization of the copyright owner.

Bootlegging—Historically and commonly mentioned in reference to alcohol or tobacco. The illegal making, marketing, or distribution of something without payment of taxes or proper payment to the legal copyright holder.

With every new technological breakthrough and innovation, people motivated to committing some form of crime will adapt their efforts toward utilization of the latest revolution, finding victims as easily as turning on a computer and clicking a mouse. The entire purpose of their intent is nothing as new as the technology. The intent, as historically verified, is to separate a victim from his money or property, or to cause fear and intimidation.

Police will also continue to upgrade their own anti-cyber crime equipment, knowledge, and expertise to stay abreast or ahead of cyber criminals, and the cycle will continue, with each side attempting to outpace the other.

Hate Crimes

Hate crimes are a recent addition to criminal penal codes. For as long as there has been prejudice, bias, hate, and intolerance of somebody's nationality, religion, race, or sexuality, there have been crimes of assault, intimidation, terror, and murder against the person of differing culture or subculture. The first definitions of "hate crime" began to surface in state penal codes during the late 1980s relating or attaching a crime to religious beliefs, racial background, and homophobic attacks. "Hate crime is a social concept that has proven to be very difficult to define since its formal recognition in the US Hate Crime Statistics Bill of 1985. The term was created in the 1980's but, while not officially termed, hate crime has been around as long as people have."[*]

Today most states and the federal government have statutes defining the crime, including an enhanced penalty for any crime proven to be motivated by hate, prejudice, or intolerance of somebody's religion, ethnicity, or sexual orientation. It is possible that future definitions of hate crime will include crimes of rape and sexual assault if there is sufficient evidence the crime was motivated by a hate of women. Perhaps elderly or child abuse and any other crime to which hate, prejudice, and intolerance can be attached will become defined as a hate crime. As the criminal justice pendulum swings in the direction of "get tough on crime," it may become more realistic to believe future laws will be enacted calling for similar definitions of hate crime. (Of course this is speculation but looking at all aspects of the future is speculation; what was once science fiction is now fact. What evidence did the writers of science fiction have of their predictions? It was by analysis of trends.)

Terrorism

Terrorism is not a new crime; it has been used for centuries, whether by a single person or by organized groups. What is new—developing within the past thirty to forty years—is the escalation of bombing attacks, kidnappings,

---

[*] A.P. Taylor, "Hate crime," Yahoo!Voices, http://www.associatedcontent.com/article/5682134/hate_crime.html?cat=7.

and assassinations. The number of incidences has decreased, but the over-all body count has continuously risen. Law enforcement agencies across the world have, and will continue to pour resources into detecting and preventing terrorist plots. Terrorism will likely never be completely eradicated; there will always be those who want to resist or overthrow their enemies in the form of violence. In turn, police will increase their efforts to control it. All the crime prevention and detection tools previously discussed and many not yet conceived will be necessary in the "war on terror."

Understanding the psychological aspects of terrorism from the point of view of the terrorist as well as the victim will help formulate policies and procedures leading to advances in terrorist deterrence, detection, and elimination.

- Suicide terrorism is not caused by religion (or more specifically, Islam). Many suicide terrorists around the world are secular or belong to religions other than Islam. Suicide terrorists are moti-vated mainly by political goals usually to end foreign occupation or domestic domination by a different ethnic group. Their "martyr-dom" is, however, frequently legitimized and glorified with reference to religious ideas and values.
- Terrorists are not insane or irrational actors. Symptoms of psychopa-thology are not common among terrorists. Neither do suicide terror-ists, as individuals, possess the typical risk factors of suicide. There is no common personality profile that characterizes most terrorists; they appear to be relatively normal individuals. Terrorists may fol-low their own rationalities based on extremist ideologies or particu-lar terrorist logics, but they are not irrational.
- What causes terrorism? The notion of terrorism is applied to a great diversity of groups with different origins and goals. Terrorism occurs in wealthy countries as well as in poor countries, in democracies as well as in authoritarian states. Thus, there exists no single root cause of terrorism or even a common set of causes. There are, however, a number of preconditions and precipitants for the emergence of vari-ous forms of terrorism.[*]

Many states have adopted laws making a hate crime or shouting a hate-filled threat a felonious act of terrorism. Street gangs and "outlaw" motor-cycle gangs advocating and participating in violence and racial attacks and intimidation have been, or will be, designated as terrorists.[†]

---

[*] Randy Borum, *Psychology of Terrorism* (2004) Tampa, FL: University of South Florida.
[†] "California's civil and criminal laws pertaining to hate crimes," February 25, 1999, State of California Department of Justice, http://ag.ca.gov/civilrights/htm/laws.php.

Women in Crime

Through twentieth century American history there are a few women who stand out in notorious criminal files: Bonnie Parker (Figure 35.24), Kate "Ma" Barker (Figure 35.25), Aileen Wuornos (Figure 35.26), the Charles Manson "family" women, and a few others. Still, the overwhelming majority of criminals who become historically notable are men. Throughout history, men have been more criminally active than women.

Today, and moving into the future, this trend is changing. The expectations and achievements of women in society have risen, with more women taking on previously predominantly male roles in business, government, law enforcement, construction, firefighting, truck driving, and so on. This corresponding change of demographics, unfortunately, extends to crime as well, as women involved in criminal activity has also shown increases over the past three decades.[*] Women have moved from playing an auxiliary role in gangs to having their own exclusively female gangs.[†]

Figure 35.24 Bonnie Parker. (From http://connect.in.com/bonnie-parker/photos-1-1-1-dfac837ba865ac458c610abf199e1242.html.)

---

[*] K. Heimer, "Changes in the gender gap in crime and women's economic marginalization," https://www.ncjrs.gov/criminal_justice2000/vol_1/02i.pdf.
[†] M. Carlie, "Into the abyss: A personal journey into the world of street gangs," http://people.missouristate.edu/MichaelCarlie/what_I_learned_about/GANGS/gender_composition.htm.

Figure 35.25 Kate "Ma" Barker. http://www.bing.com/search?q=images+Ma+b arker&qs=n&form=QBLH&pq=images+ma+barker&sc=0-12&sp=-1&sk=&ghc=1

Figure 35.26 Aileen Wuornos. http://www.clarkprosecutor.org/html/death/ US/wuornos805.htm

A shift in types of female crime has also advanced, from passive crimes such as shoplifting and embezzlement to active crimes like assault and murder. Women of the past generally killed with poisons, blunt instruments, and a knife or ice pick. Today's female criminals are as likely to kill with a gun as a man would. Following the trend of female violence and participation in all nature of crimes, it can be projected that the percentage of women criminals will grow exponentially.

The Future of Civil Liberties and the Law

Plea bargain—An arrangement between the prosecution and defense that allows a plea of guilty, or cooperation with law enforcement and the prosecution in exchange for a lesser sentence for the defendant.

The get-tough-on-crime mentality and the war on drugs have had a very serious consequence on the overall criminal justice system. The number of individuals arrested and incarcerated has grown so large that the court system and corrections have been become inundated with people who have been arrested for nonviolent crimes such as drug possession. This has led to courts with filled dockets and delayed trials, as well as jails and prisons that are extremely overcrowded. The Supreme Court has ruled (in *Brown v. Plata et al.*)* that prison overcrowding is a violation of the Eighth Amendment provision against cruel and unusual punishment, leading counties and states to look for alternative provisions. One primary option is an opportunity for arrested defendants to agree to a plea bargain—an arrangement between the prosecution and the defense that allows a plea of guilty (or cooperation with law enforcement and the prosecution) by the defendant for a lesser punishment, often resulting in a suspended jail sentence and probation. Plea bargaining has, and will continue to be, a very effective means of keeping court dockets at manageable levels and jails and prison populations reduced to court-sanctioned degrees. As powerful as the advantages of plea bargaining are, there are also some disadvantages that must be considered. For one, defendants may plead guilty even when innocent because of the threat of prison and other sanctions if found guilty at a trial. Another issue to consider is that many more convicted defendants will be placed on probation, resulting in the necessity of training and hiring more probation officers to supervise the probationer.

"Moral" Law and Legislative Law in Modern Society

Legislative or statutory laws are those laws enacted by elected representatives of Congress or the legislature by a will of the people. In keeping with the wishes of their constituents, legislators propose and pass laws that reflect society's conscience. For the past several decades, the public outcry has been for stricter laws and harsher penalties. Politicians have referenced this as a get-tough-on-crime policy. Legislators often propose, pass, and insist on strict enforcement of laws that enhance security for society. Does this forecast a future of surrendered civil rights for security? Our civil liberties have been continuously degraded. Is there any reason to think this will not continue? What sort or future can we anticipate?

As public awareness of terrorism, sexual offenses, and cybercrime grows, many have begun to call for more laws defining restrictions and penalties. This is the swinging pendulum of the get-tough-on-crime polices of politics. How far will the pendulum swing before the populace

---

* *Supreme Court of the United States; Brown, Governor of California, et al. v. Plata et al.* appeal from the United States District Courts for the Eastern and Northern Districts of California No. 09–1233. Argued November 30, 2010, decided May 23, 2011; http://www.supremecourt.gov/opinions/10pdf/09-1233.pdf.

realizes they have sacrificed freedom and liberty for security? Benjamin Franklin is credited with saying, "They who trade freedom for security deserve neither freedom nor liberty."* Most governments (federal, state, and local) in the United States have codified their laws. If a law has not been passed and entered into the code, the activity is not illegal. New laws and recommended punishments are published for public notification. Very few localities today rely on the English common law of custom, tradition, precedent, and common belief that was brought to English colonies from England.

Local, state, and federal governments have tried to legislate morality—for example, prohibition of alcohol, drugs, adultery, gambling, and prostitution—with mixed results. Morality refers to what is considered good behavior. It means being ethical, trustworthy, and considerate of others. It can also mean following the dictates of a "higher power" according to and interpreted by a religious leader. In the United States, following legislative law, a person can and will be punished for an immoral act only if there is a specific codified law against it. By religious law, a person can and will be punished for violation of morality laws as the religious leader dictates. In an actual example of religious law, in Iran in 1985, a mother of four was accused of adultery by her husband who wanted to marry a much younger girl. By religious law, the wife had to prove she did not commit adultery. Because she could not prove it, she was condemned to death by stoning.† These types of laws and executions are still being carried out today in various parts of some Middle Eastern countries.

Religious law is in the eye of the beholder because of the arbitrary nature of what is considered "good behavior." Good behavior, according to many interpretations, means women must cover their hair and not be seen in public with any man other than her husband or brother, and that citizens must pray daily and never indulge in alcohol, drugs, or prostitution. Religious laws are often very strict and enforced in draconian ways—often meaning death—very similar to the early religious Puritan colonies in America. These laws tend to be very discriminatory against women.

Some states have proposed laws to assure that religious law (also known as moral law or Shariah law in many cultures, especially in conservative Muslim countries) will never become part of the state's criminal justice system. However, the United States Constitution, under the First

---

* This Benjamin Franklin quotation has been used to the extent it is now a cliché. But the truthfulness of it remains as a warning for the future.
† F. Sahebjam, *La Femme Lapidée* (The Stoning of Soraya M.) (1990). Although no actual or accurate records are available about the actual number of women yearly stoned to death worldwide, stoning is an acceptable form of punishment throughout many countries of the world, especially the Middle East. For further information, see http://search.yahoo.com/search?p=numbers+of+women+stoned+to+death+each+year&ei=utf-8&fr=chr-yie9.

Amendment's separation of church and state, already prohibits enforcement of religious laws. In some countries, Shariah law is the law of the land because the church (religious leaders) is more powerful and influential than the government (political leaders), and there is no separation of church and state.

Relativism and Absolutism

Law enforcement officers have a wide range of discretion; they enforce the spirit of the law (relativism), meaning what was the intent of the legislature when the law was passed. If every law was enforced exactly according to the wording of the law (absolutism), the jails and courts would be bottlenecked and jammed. According to the Greek philosopher Aristotle, everything has a direct opposite (day–night, white–black, positive–negative, liberal–conservative, etc.). Therefore there is also a middle ground. In the spirit of the law and letter of the law question, the middle ground is the area of officer discretion.

Discretion—Sound judgment, freedom to decide.

Relativism—There is no absolute truth; individual choice; laissez faire; room for mitigating factors; tolerance; very liberal.

Absolutism—No freedom of choice; no mitigating circumstances; zero tolerance; very conservative; extreme authority.

As the criminal justice pendulum swings toward the get-tough-on-crime policy (absolutism) and away from leniency (relativism), the future bodes that enforcement of the law will slant steeper toward the letter of the law, restricting an officer's discretion. Arrests, no matter how minor the violation, will become mandatory. Under the theory of letter of the law, absolutism, and zero tolerance, especially when meting out justice, the question becomes one of asking for justice or revenge. Does society want justice, or does it demand revenge?

In criminal justice, the concepts of relativism and absolutism are in constant debate. Relativism favors enforcing the spirit of the law, in other words, the intent of the legislature at the time it was passed. Absolutism, on the other hand, favors enforcing laws exactly according to the wording of the law. In an effort to find a middle ground between these two philosophies, law enforcement officers are granted a wide range of discretion and freedom to act in a manner most appropriate to an individual situation.

Critics contend that as the criminal justice system leans increasingly on an absolutist, get-tough-on-crime policy, and away from a relativist policy of leniency, law enforcement will slant steeper toward the letter of the law and will restrict an officer's discretion. Arrests, no matter how minor the viola-tion, will become mandatory. Under the theory of letter of the law, absolut-ism, and zero tolerance, critics say that the line will become blurred between meting out justice and inflicting revenge.

In some cases, discretion has already been removed from the courts with mandatory and determinate sentencing laws. A judge must follow prescribed guidelines in pronouncing a sentence of punishment often counter to his own beliefs of justice in a case. If an offender is found guilty of a crime, the penalty is automatically assigned without provisions for mitigating circumstances or a probation report with sentencing recommendations to the judge. A 1970s television detective series called "Baretta" whose title character was played by Robert Blake, had a catch phrase "Don't do the crime if you can't do the time." In the 1980s, the motto was shortened to "Do the crime, do the time, as the wellspring of the national get-tough-on-crime policy became a prelude to a future of "rubber stamp justice"; if found guilty of a crime, the penalty is automatically assigned without provisions for mitigating circumstances or a probation report with sentencing recommendations to the judge.

Corrections

The criminal justice term *corrections* is analogous with *punishment*; paying some type of sanction for a wrongdoing. In the modern world or the world of the future, corrections may be an incorrect term to describe the intent of justice. If justice means punishment, then punishment by prison or other sanction should not be considered corrections. If correction means to change from wrong to right, perhaps a much better word is *rehabilitation*.

Rehabilitation

When the term *rehabilitation* is used in the context of meaning change from a life of crime or repentance for a crime, then a drastic change in the correc-tions system is necessary. Under the doctrine of tough on crime and with severe economic social conditions, stern punishment is the byword for con-victed criminals with rehabilitation-type programs, including education and job training, being greatly curtailed.

In George Orwell's *1984*, the Ministry of Love used the term *cured* to describe Winston Smith's corrective rehabilitation to loving Big Brother.

Lack of rehabilitation programs in prison may be a factor in recidivism. Without education and jobs, a person may turn to crime. In prison, the con-vict learns more ways to commit a crime when he gains release. With no job or other opportunities, he will continue his ways of crime. Given the opportunity to become educated or learn a trade, he may never return to prison. The economic resources saved by not providing rehabilitation programs in prison does not offset the balance of maintaining a prisoner who commits a crime because he has no education or job on his prison release and is returned to prison.

Punishment as a Deterrent

Critical Thinking: Does society want justice, or does it demand revenge/retribution?

The purpose of prison and other rigorous sentencing as punishment for commission of a crime is to serve as a deterrent for others who consider committing a crime. Fear of punishment does deter some people from committing a crime, but there are many other factors that must be considered as reasons for deterrence, such as the social stigma, legal and financial costs, and family considerations. Critics argue that deterrence is not effective because people who commit criminal acts rarely believe they will be caught. Criminals will continue to commit crime regardless of deterrence efforts.

Death Penalty

It is said that hanging was the penalty for being a pickpocket thief in eighteenth-century England. It is also said that pickpockets were in abundance and very active at their trade at the public hanging of a convicted pickpocket. The hangings were intended to serve a double purpose: to punish and to deter. However, the deterrence was ineffective. In modern-day twenty-first century, a potential death sentence is still not a deterrent. In mid-2011, the state of California had over 1,000 people on Death Row. To reemphasize a previous statement, "The person committing the crime believes he will not be caught."

Use of the death penalty is a hotly debated issue in the United States, and methods of execution are controversial as well. In the United States, the death penalty has been carried out in several different ways. They have included hanging, the electric chair, cyanide gas, and lethal injection (Figures 35.27 to 35.30). Another is by firing squad. The most notable firing squad execution was of Private Eddie Slovik on January 31, 1945, the only American soldier to be executed for cowardice since the Civil War (Figure 35.31).* The most recent use of the firing squad was of Ronnie Lee Gardner in Utah on June 18, 2010, at his own request as the method of his execution (Figure 35.32).

---

* http://www.executedtoday.com/2009/01/31/1945-private-eddie-slovik-desertion.

Figure 35.27 Gallows.

Figure 35.28 Electric chair.

Figure 35.29 Gas chamber.

Figure 35.30 Lethal injection chamber.

Figure 35.31 Private Eddie Slovik.

Figure 35.32 Ronnie Lee Gardner.

The Future of Capital Punishment

With the number of people on Death Row in California in 2011, if only one person were executed every day, it would take nearly four years to execute everyone because more people are added to death row every year. So as some are executed others arrive to take their place. Courts have ruled that methods of execution from hanging to the electric chair, to the gas chamber and last to lethal injection are all forms of "cruel and unusual punishment" forbidden by the Eighth Amendment. Scientists are researching to find ways to perform an execution that is quick and painless (more humane, if putting a person to death in the name of "the people" or the state can be considered "humane") while the numbers of people on Death Rows will continue to grow. The United States is the last of the first-world countries to maintain capital punishment as a penalty for heinous crimes. The question of whether to uphold or abolish the death penalty continues to spark debate among lawmakers. In 2012, voters in California voted to retain the death penalty instead of life in prison with no possibility of parole.

Scientists, science fiction movies,[*] and novels have explored human cryogenics as a means of carrying out a quick and painless death as the person to be executed would be instantly frozen at temperatures of approximately −197°C[†]. (Figure 35.33). Although it is possible that human cryogenics

Figure 35.33 Humans in cryogenics. (From stylefrizz.com/human-cryogenics-at-14-per-week.)

---

[*] A cryogenic execution was a feature of the movie *Demolition Man* (1993) starring Sylvester Stallone and Wesley Snipes.

[†] The term *cryogenic* applies to temperatures from approximately −100°C (−148°F) down to absolute zero (the coldest point a material could reach).

will represent the future of the death penalty in the United States, there is also a very real possibility that the death penalty may be eliminated entirely. Opponents of the death penalty argue that there is no such thing as a humane way to put someone to death and that the death penalty is not an effective deterrent for crime.

Human cryogenics—A system of preservation of the human body at temperatures of approximately –197°C (liquid nitrogen).

During the days of early exploration and colonization several countries, most notably England and France, transferred convicts to desolate penal colonies. Perhaps in the future, convicts will be transported to some distant and remote planet or satellite.

Probation and Parole in Tomorrow's World

In an absolutist world, intolerant of crime and criminals, under the strictest aspects of conservatism and letter of the law, probation is seen as coddling the criminal. "He must get what he deserves" is the cry from a public demanding revenge in lieu of justice. The same philosophy is advocated in consideration of parole. This devotion to the strict letter of the law will become even more demanding in the future as the get-tough-on-crime policy becomes the law.

Threats to Constitutional Guarantees

Every time a new law is enacted, it either prohibits or requires something. In other words, restrictions and orders are placed on the governed. As legislation and judicial review have embraced the concept of get tough on crime, laws and decisions have opened more doors to authority. By doing so, some critics worry that these laws have encroached on the commonly accepted and acknowledged freedoms and liberties of everyday citizens. As newer types of crime and threats to the security and safety of the general population increase, due to technological innovations and a growing influence of terrorist groups, a major concern has grown regarding possible endangerments to the rights and liberties guaranteed by the U.S. Constitution.

Ratified in 1787 with a special addendum of the Bill of Rights in 1791, the U.S. Constitution has been a living document, enduring as the basis of all laws for over 200 years. The Constitution has been amended only 27 times, but is constantly changing with various interpretations of constitutional challenges and issues brought before the Supreme Court. With the evolving face of crime and the advent of technology and movements toward stricter enforcement of laws, a growing debate is occurring about changing several aspects of the Constitution, most notably the Bill of Rights. Several Amendments have been challenged or have subtly changed. An analysis of the trends will rightfully conclude there is a movement toward a harsher system, even challenging the democratic way of American life, very reminiscent of science fiction dystopian stories of the future such as *1984* and *The Matrix*.

First Amendment—The right to freedom of religion is being challenged by fundamentalists who believe the United States was founded strictly on Christian beliefs and are intolerant of other religions, especially those from countries following religious law as the foundation of government. The right of freedom of speech is challenged by an order of "political correctness," that is, eliminating any words with a connotation that others will find offensive, such as words that reflect upon a person's ethnicity, racial background, or religion. The freedom of the press or news media is being restricted by journalists required to name their sources of information and prosecution of those who refuse. Freedom of assembly has been subtly changed in regard to dissident demonstrations. Demonstrations are allowed but only in designated areas, usually in areas screened from the public or away from areas that could be considered security risks to attendees to a convention, for example.

Second Amendment—This amendment, which dictates the right to bear arms and own guns, is also being challenged. As the numbers of crimes and murders involving handguns and repeating rifles (assault rifles) increase, many citizens are increasingly calling for laws to restrict ownership and possession of guns.

Fourth Amendment—Advancing technology and security demands have serious consequences about the fate of the Fourth Amendment and illegal searches. Machines that can "see" inside containers, vehicles, buildings, and the human body present serious challenges to the probable cause and searches without a warrant clauses of this amendment.

Fifth Amendment—The largest question stems from consideration of who must be advised of their rights against self-incrimination. Are terrorists who have been labeled "enemy combatants" entitled to this warning? Or perhaps a person who has not been labeled as an enemy combatant but has participated in activities that are considered terrorist acts? What about minors and young children, and when are they deemed "in custody"?

Sixth, Seventh, and Eighth Amendments: Are persons considered enemy combatants entitled to an appointed attorney, a speedy and

jury trial, and bail? Should they be tried by military tribunals under
military law?

Fourteenth Amendment—Should there be exceptions to the clauses
of due process and equal protection, especially for noncitizens,
immigrants without authorization to be in the country, and terrorists
and enemy combatants? Challenges are being posed regarding the
provision that all persons born in the United States are automatically
citizens, even if their parents are visitors or have entered the country
without legal authorization.

What Will the Future Bring?

As we move into the future, criminal justice administration must and will
change with the times. Technology and science will be leading the way to
bring about changes in protocol, procedures, evolvement, and definitions of
crimes. The protectors of society must keep pace through education, training, experience, and innovation.

Will changes in the criminal justice system result in less or more freedom
for a free democracy? The trends and indicators are pointing toward a world
society of less freedom and stricter laws and security. Databases, collection of
personal information, "all-seeing" technology, family DNA, and calls to edit
and change constitutional protections are all becoming more frequent in the
name of security. Present generations are the ones who will be making the
decisions affecting future generations and their rights and freedoms under
new challenges to criminal justice. The future belongs to those who prepare
for and make the right decisions.

Summary

Throughout this chapter, theoretical perspectives of the future of criminal
justice were introduced. Perspectives were based on an analysis of current
trends, indicators, practices, and technology.

- Maniacal serial killers to fanatical religious dictators and the entire
  subculture of killers, crooks, and "cold case" perpetrators will surely
  be caught, prosecuted, and imprisoned through technology and
  science, and the development of identifying a suspect through DNA
  analysis. There is much debate about the effectiveness of capital punishment as a deterrent, but surely justice will, in the end, prevail.
- Technology and science have provided amazing breakthroughs in
  crime detection and prosecution. Trends and indicators hint toward

a society valuing security and freedom from crime over individual liberties by the concept of get-tough-on-crime policies. As the pendulum of justice swings toward the conservative right, laws reflective of that policy are enacted through people's initiatives and politicians who pander to the call of endorsing laws like the three strikes, Jessica's, and Megan's laws.

- Police of the future (with greater participation of women) will form closer ties to and partnerships with private security, with private security patrols taking over the majority of current police patrol duties. While police departments become more militarized, they will focus more on specialized crimes such as terrorism and serious felonies like murder and major white-collar crimes. The police subculture of us versus them will continue but with the "to protect and to serve" mandate giving police greater authority and power. Law enforcement will engage tools like greater collection and analysis of intelligence, profiling, and predictive crime prevention.
- Recent U.S. Supreme Court decisions have weakened portions of Constitutional protections against unreasonable searches and redefined exigent circumstances. Only the future will reflect the consequences.

Glossary

adversarial law: A system in which two opposing sides present a case, with the prosecution attempting to prove the accused guilty beyond a reasonable doubt and the defense attempting to create reasonable doubt in the mind of the judge or jury.

copyright piracy: Illegally making, marketing, and distributing copyrighted material by computer technology without proper authorization of the copyright owner.

crisis management: Planning, response, and mitigation to an emergency situation in an effort to restore normalcy as quickly as possible and to protect life and property.

cyber financial crime: A crime of fraud or theft through the manipulation of accounts securities and other monetarily related devices by computer technology.

cyber stalking: Creating fear, intimidation, and invasion of privacy through the use of computer technology.

exigent circumstances: An exception to the Fourth Amendment requirement of a warrant for an in-home arrest; can arise when there is an immediate need to protect an officer or the public from danger or in other emergency situations.

fusion centers: Central depositories for data collection, analysis, and sharing among intelligence and law enforcement agencies.

hate crime: A crime with an enhanced penalty for commission of a crime motivated by hate, prejudice, or intolerance based on the victim's religious beliefs, racial ethnicity, or sexual orientation. Common hate crimes include assault, arson, and murder.

human cryogenics: A system of preservation of the human body at temperatures of approximately −197°C (liquid nitrogen).

inquisitorial law: A system in which the accused is assumed guilty and must prove his or her innocence.

intelligence: Information and data that have been collected and analyzed with conclusions and recommendations disseminated to users with a need to know.

moral law (Sharia law): Laws following a strict moral interpretation of religious dogma.

police authority: Power of arrest, search, and seizure allowed to a sworn officer of the law by a political jurisdiction.

police culture: The strong feeling of loyalty and solidarity with fellow officers.

predictive crime detection and prevention: Crime analysis and mapping combined with a mathematical formula to predict when, where, how, and what type of crime will be committed.

professional courtesy: Allowing fellow police officers special treatment.

profiling: Building a "picture" of a person through psychological, sociological, and human behavior patterns.

reasonable and necessary: The facts and circumstances justifying, but limiting, the use of force needed to effect an arrest or to save the life of someone.

rule of man: A nondemocratic form of government, usually a dictatorship, whose only voice is the single powerful leader or council. He is considered above the law as he dictates the law.

strategic intelligence: Intelligence gathered for long-range planning.

tactical intelligence: Intelligence gathered for immediate use.

trends and indicators: Recognizable patterns of instances, events, or occurrences over a period of time.

Index